from the
Heart of Thunder
to the Color of Grace

The story of how God transformed a convicted Murderer into a Minister!

Michael J. Decker

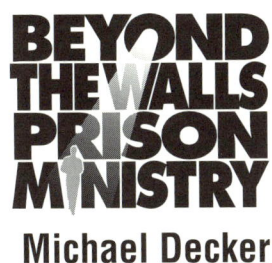

Michael Decker
Pastor
Canyon, Texas 79015

2003
Beyond The Walls Prison Ministry
PO Box 866 • Canyon, Texas 79015
Phone: 806-655-9322 • Cell: 806-674-5141
Fax: 806-655-9322 • E-Mail: decker4btw@aol.co

Copyright @2002 by Michael J. Decker
ISBN: 0-9729641-0-x

All rights reserved. No part of this book may be reproduced,
stored in a retrieval system, or transmitted, in way form or
by any means, electronic, mechanical, photocopying,
recording, or otherwise, without the written permission of
The Crossroad Publishing Company.
Printed in the United States of America

This book is dedicated to a very special lady who stood on the Word of God and remained steadfast to the promises of His scriptures. Forty-seven years of constant daily prayer was dedicated to seeing her son become a man of God, called forth into the Kingdom to preach the Good News! Betty Brown Johnson is a woman anointed by the presence of Jesus Christ, walking in the blessings of the Holy Spirit and doing the Will of God.

To the men and women of Barn Church Dream Center under the mighty leadership of Pastor Randy Bird, thank you for the launch into the ministry.

To Trinity Fellowship Church, their pastors and leaders, especially Pastors Paul Bates, Tom Lane, Garvin McCarrell, and Senior Pastor Jimmy Evans for their examples of being mighty men of God.

To Pastor Chuck Garrison and all the great people of Oakdale Fellowship, the first true Evangelist I watched and learned from.

To Bill Gruhlkey and all of the men from the Wednesday Barn Bible Study out on the farm in Wilderado, watching the manifestation of the Holy Spirit and learning how to minister, individually.

To my brothers and fellow warriors from the Divine Grind Thursday morning study group in Amarillo, the unity and love shared was witness to the purity of God's grace, mercy and love.

To Pastor Kyle Paris and the many leaders of God's Kingdom church for believing in the calling and edifying and encouraging the ministry.

Finally, I want to dedicate this work to all of the men and women behind bars. Standing there in their whites, blues or khaki's, and serving the King of Kings, they are my heartfelt brothers and sisters. I will serve my Abba Father in bringing each of you the truth and majesty of His Word.

To Sherli for putting up with my late night and early morning pecking on the typewriter and loving me!

Table of Contents

Learning to Survive 1

First Marriage and Vietnam 44

College, Football, Montana Mining Company 90

Mafia, Money, Murder and Deception 145

Trying for a Normal Life,
    Introduction to the DEA 198

One Night, One Event, My Life Changed Forever,
    October 2, 1976 279

To Prison and the White House 293

A New Love, a New Life, Almost 331

Back to the Streets, Back to Prison! 359

Off to the Virgin Islands, Prison, and
    Finally Coming to know God! 369

Beyond the Walls Prison Ministry! 396

CHAPTER 1

Learning ^{to}Survive

Canyon, Texas October 27, 1948 a new son is born to the proud parents, Hank and Betty Decker. Hank, the father stood 6'6" and 245 pounds, with brown hair and hazel eyes. He grew up in the basketball haven of Indiana and would go on to play college ball at West Texas State University. Later, he would head for the pros with New York and Chicago, then on to Europe and the "House of David." After leaving basketball, he went to Las Vegas and Lake Tahoe to run casinos and enjoy the fruits that life entails. Betty Brown Decker, the mother, was 5'8", 125 pounds, with brown hair and brown eyes, she was a very beautiful lady. Betty grew up in the southern areas of New Mexico and the panhandle of Texas. She earned her BA from West Texas, and her MA from Texas Tech. She then went to the teaching arenas of Albuquerque, New Mexico for the next twenty-five years. A sister, Susan, now age "almost two" is awaiting the arrival of her new baby brother. Of course this great anticipation would not last as little brothers wear out their welcome very quickly. Yet Susan would go on to travel the world and be a successful mother of two and very committed church member and religious leader.

Now the young boy's name is Michael John Decker, he was born with brown hair and hazel eyes. Though, in years to come there would be many alias and identities, some given by "Uncle Sam," others were taken on to cover trails and gain access to some of the most privileged places around the world. These would include both the civilian and governmental strongholds and "security safe" installations. Eventually, he would travel to every country in the world except Red China and Turkey. Visiting all island groups and spending extensive periods of time in the southern borders, such as Mexico, South America, Central America and the Caribbean.

Early survival training for Michael came as a result of having a real pioneer and outdoorsman for a grandfather. This man was fondly called "Grandee," by Michael and all the other family members of the younger generation. To the rest of the world he was Mithero Brothers Brown, better known as "M.B." He was one of those men that had provided for his family with his rifle, shotgun and fishing rod for much of his life, and knew how to survive. He knew what to use to get his quarry and utilize the natural provisions that most people just walk on by in the wilderness. Marksmanship, control, and no waste, were drilled into young Michael's brain. Along with the added instruction of Grandee's brother Harris, a trapper and guide for big-money hunters, the finer traits of a marksman and sharpshooter were attained. Additionally there came a sincere love and appreciation for the outdoors and nature. The relationship that developed between Michael and his grandfather would be a bond more than most understood or could ever hope to understand.

"Hold the target in your sights; then hold a breath, slowly release your breath and squeeze the trigger at the end of your breath," Grandee said patiently with his hand on Michael's shoulder.

"How did I do?" replied Michael, eyes wide in anticipation.

"Just fine, you'll be a good shot one day. Just keep practicing."

This scenario was replayed thousands of times over the first twelve years of life. The enthusiasm, commitment and patience were forever accompanied in the teaching and training that Michael received from his grandfather. Oneness with nature and the wilderness became an outlook, as well as a refuge for Michael in the years that violence began creeping into his life.

The life of a complete family didn't last long as infidelity struck early with Michael's dad. The family babysitter became the source and this catapulted into many affairs on the part of Hank Decker. Finally, as Michael turned age two and a half, a divorce came through.

Not long afterward, six months in fact, Michael's dad kidnapped him and took off to Florida along with a girlfriend and his buddy Briggs, a registered boxer. Each day was spent running up and down the beach without a care in the world. This scenario was not to remain for long as a Texas Sheriff and Grandee came to serve a warrant and collect Hoss. This was the name given to Michael by his grandfather. Nobody was going to take his grandson.

"Hey Hoss! Come up here and see me."

"Oh, Grandee, when did you get here?"

"Just now, came to take you home," Grandee exclaimed.

"Does Dad know?"

"He will soon enough" Grandee continued, "Run on and get your things."
"Okay, come on Briggs." Michael said as he and his dog raced back down the beach.

It was mid-afternoon the sun was blazing down and seemingly intensified as Grandee and the Sheriff walked toward Hank's cottage that was just up the short stretch of sand.
"Hank, you need to come outside," the Sheriff yelled as he pounded on the screen door.
"Don't try to pull anything, we already have Michael John in the car."
"I'm coming, I'm coming, hold your horses," Hank replied. Muttering under his breath, "Why in the hell did this have to happen."
"Okay here I am, what's up," he answered as the screen door closed behind him.
"Hank, there is no use in beating around the bush, You screwed up by taking Mike, and only by the grace of God and M.B., am I not arresting you."
"Well1!"
"Well, nothin', we're taking Mike back to Canyon and that is that."
There was a tightness, that began to grow in the pit of Hank's stomach and his big frame bristled. His thoughts turned to hatred, and his heart cried out, "Please don't take my boy." Yet, he held his tongue and remained silent, knowing that this was not the last time he would see his son, nor his last CUSTODY.

Six months later, he would again cruise through Canyon and abduct Michael. This time traveling on to Englewood, Colorado and landing a coaching job with the local high school. Because of the car payments on his new Chevrolet, Hank's trail would be discovered, the bank just had to have a return address. As a result of this information, the sheriff came once again, this time by himself. He wanted Hank to truly understand that he meant business, so Hank took a trip to jail. This would be the last time that Michael would see his Dad until almost nineteen years of age.

A scene very identical would unfold and replay itself, some twenty years later with Michael and his son Christopher. Seeds planted, seed watered, harvest reaped. The chain can only be broken if the sin is cancelled. For the next thirty years, the sin would anything but be cancelled, exemplified is closer to the reality, and darkness now begins to grow.

Ages four through six were lonely years for Michael, not only from a standpoint of no real father at home, but also the new image was one of ridicule and abuse to not only he and his sister, but to his mother as well.

Betty Decker was now Betty Thomas, marrying a friend of a friend, Lucian Thomas. Lucian was a handicapped man in a wheel chair and the loss was taken out on everyone else. The first few weeks of quiet were replaced with anger and violence, this coming in both verbal and some physical areas. It seemed to be everybody's fault that Lucian couldn't walk.

Michael was in first grade and his first full-fledged fight and assault came at this juncture in his life. Two older boys, a third and forth grader, thought it would be fun to steal the new kids bike. Wrong, one bloody nose, a black eye, a strong kick in the groin and Michael got his bike back. The anger, which had already begun to grow, was beginning to show its results. But, a quick divorce with the help of Betty's father, Michael's granddad, and this phase was history.

Moving and getting settled in Albuquerque, New Mexico would consume the next two years of their life. Susan and Michael attended Megan Elementary and Betty was teaching at Highland High School. They were living in the Girard Apartments and surviving. Just the ordinary adolescent quarrels were for the most part, the norm. All too soon, came the true beginning of violence that was about to be introduced into Michael's life.

This due to the fact that Michael's mother would meet a man named Glen Hancock during a brief summer break at Platoro. The trips to Platoro were planned since Grandee was building a summer cabin there, with his love for fishing and the flourishing lakes and streams, a vacation there was inevitable. The trout were literally everywhere and for an experienced angler like M.B. Brown, "Look Out."

The introduction to Glen and the subsequent relational times spent, allowed for Betty and all to see that he was successful, apparent from his speech and manner of dress. Additionally, he owned a resort in Colorado, property in New Mexico and was the regional general manager for School Pictures Inc. A sense of financial security was there and he "seemed" nice enough. Yet down deep in both Michael and his sister Susan, an evil darkness was felt. In fact when consulted by their mother as to what they thought of Glen Hancock, they spoke openly.
"Well, what do you all think about Glen."
"He scares me, I don't think he's a good man," Susan said quickly.
"Yeah, he's too bossy and stuff," Michael added.
"Don't you think in time that will change, when you get to know him better?"
"Nope, I don't want to know him better," Michael was already convinced.
Seeing that the opinion was unanimous and that any further conversation was useless, Betty felt that he would still be a good provider and

in time the kids would change. But the change that occurred was one that was the antithesis of what was planned.

Thus, on Friday October 8, 1957 a wedding took place and the two came back to Albuquerque to begin their lives. Michael and Susan knew that the feelings that were so evident in their hearts were about to unfold. And unfold they did, very quickly.

After purchasing a home at 8040 Snow Ave. in the Sandia subdivision of Albuquerque, N. M. life began for the Hancock household. It was an average home, with beige stucco and the typical southwest flat roof. It had a medium sized front and back yard, single car garage and carport. A house that any middle-class family would live or abide within, and abide would be a compliment for the life in this house.
"Get in this Goddamn house now!" Glen bellowed.
"What did I tell you about going outside in just your socks?"
"I'm going to beat your ass!" he continued, the veins pulsing in his neck.
"Yes sir, I'm sorry."
"I didn't mean too!"

Glen snatched Michael by the back of his neck and hurled him into the house.
"When I tell you to do something, by God, you'll do it."
"Now get to your room and bend over the bed."

The fear literally began to stop Michael's breathing, as he hadn't ever seen this kind of rage and anger. Death itself seemed a sincere possibility he could barely manage to make his legs move in the direction of the bedroom. Bending over the bed he knew it was going to be an experience he would never forget, if he survived!

Thoughts racing through his young mind and the sounds of heavy breaths and pounding feet only added to the horror coming down the hallway. Striking distance almost at hand, Michael closed his eyes and held his breath. An inner prayer saying, "oh dear God don't let this be forever. Please let Mom get home." But Mom was still at school teaching and Susan was at a friend's house playing. What remained was the inevitable and the door was opening for its entrance.
"Now you little son-of-a-bitch, you will know that I mean business."

Holding a thirty-eight inch heavy leather belt with a large silver buckle Glen began to rain down blows on the nine-year-old boy. The first swing was so strong and hitting Michael in the lower back, brought pain from somewhere the child never knew existed. Sounds, crying or otherwise, could not come forth as there was no breath possible to move his vocal chords. The onslaught continued for several minutes and by the end, the slamming of the door was barely even an audible noise.

   Shock or something very close must have been present, for it was a long period of time before Michael could begin to feel just how damaged he really was. Bruises, red welts and severe marks were present and accounted for, from knee to mid back. Within minutes the dark discolored skin was evident and the fear within this young mind was rampant.

   This event, or the "terrible" infraction that had just occurred, which had set this scene in motion was so serious. Two days before, Glen had told Michael not to go outside without shoes and socks. Michael had just arrived home from school, kicked off his shoes and was grabbing a snack in the kitchen. A ring of the doorbell brought him to the door to discover a friend and his new puppy. Wanting one so bad for himself he dashed outside to play and frolic, just at that time Glen drove up. The explosion that occurred at the sound of the booming voice was a signal to NEVER come back to Michael's house. The young friend that was visiting relayed that very message to all his classmates. This was to become a scene reenacted many times in years to come. The situation was intensified by it being a secret to most of the family, as Glen made it very clear that what took place between he and Michael would not be discussed otherwise. If it were even brought up, Michael's mom would be the object of the discipline necessary. No way was this young boy going to put his mother through what he was experiencing. He would just suck it up and be tough.

   Tough is a major understatement as to what developed from this treatment. For the tears that would normally flow from a small boy, would not return until much later in his life, Michael's that is.

   A tremendous amount of the inner struggle that was to go on inside the heart of this tormented little boy was consoled by his Nana, his mother's mother, she was full of big hugs and love. She was always in the kitchen making good things to eat and seeing to it that everyone was stuffed, beyond walking. She made the best German chocolate cake in the world. Nana and Grandee were to Michael, a refuge from the violence and misdirection that he would observe during the next few years. Trips to Canyon, Texas and the farm, were a much heralded event because it meant "No Glen."

   Summer of 1958 came and the first day after school was out, the Hancock family headed for Platoro. This too became an annual pilgrimage and the content of EVERY summer for the next seven years. What could have been a very rewarding and fruitful experience was to soon become a literal nightmare for young Michael Decker.

   Platoro, Colorado sat up in the Rocky Mountain National Forest around 9,500 feet in altitude. There were big mountains, crystal clear streams and lakes filled with Brook, Rainbow, Cutthroat and German Brown trout. There were also, Deer, Elk and multitudes of other wildlife close enough to see on a daily basis. Aspen groves by the thousands of acres and Pine and Spruce trees covered the full expanses of the valley down below. The town or village consisted of six privately owned cabin sets, anywhere from eight to forty-five units with only the Skyline Lodge being the sole stable and horse establishment. No more than one hundred fifty regulars and the rest of the summer population would bring the census to around eight hundred. Except for weekends like the forth of July, when including campers, it would rise toward 1,500 to 2,000.

Glen owned the Conejos Cabins, one of the smaller sized facilities but far and away the nicest. He had constructed the cabins and the complete layout over a ten-year period and the craftsmanship was apparent. The cabins were actually duplexes with two bedrooms in each unit. They had a full kitchen and bath with a pull out sleeper couch in the living room. All of the units were facing the Conejos River, with no more than eighty feet from the front door to the stream. The property also had one large workshop and garage, and the main cabin, which was two stories, was a two-bedroom lodge. Beautiful hardwood floors with hand peeled, oiled and varnished logs and white chinking, expansive flagstone fireplace with windows viewing not only the property, but also the entire valley and mountain range. To get to the lodge at Platoro required navigating through about fifty miles of dirt road, which wound and twisted around every crag and cranny. Michael and Susan got carsick on a very regular basis as the dust and swaying motion of that Plymouth station wagon took its toll.

That first trip was five hours of thoughts racing through Michael's head, "Oh God, what's in store for me now, here. No friends, no phones, no T.V., and Glen twenty-four hours a day."
What was hell like? In his mind it was much too vivid to think that it would be any other kind of trip other than "pure hell." Yet somewhere, deep down in the remote areas of his heart, Michael thought maybe just maybe, things would change. They did, but not in the manner that he was hoping for.

As the family wagon rounded that last turn the cabins came into view. It was kind of desolate as there had been no one on the property since the previous September, when everything was "winterized." As the vehicle pulled to a final stop and the brake was set, Michael and Susan burst out of the car. So thankful that the trip was over and relieved that the boring ride with the wonderful company was complete.

"Get the Hell back here, we have work to do. Get this damn car unloaded." Godzilla had spoken again. The next half hour was consumed with orders and directions and all the "do this and do that's." Then the question came forth that Michael was to learn later was the implication of the TOTAL control Glen was to have each and every summer for the next six years.

"Where am I going to sleep, there is only two bedrooms?"

"You'll sleep in the pump house, there is a roll away bed, that's all you'll need." Glen made this statement with a chilling tone and it bit to the very core of Michael's soul.

Dejected at first, the young boy trudged out of the main lodge towards his room. A fleeting thought came forth, "maybe I'll be able to stay away from the bastard." But this was far from the reality as the very first night would show and reveal a destiny of continual abuse.

Around four o'clock that afternoon the beer started to flow. It was a daily routine that must have gone on for several years, but now that everyone was in such close proximity, it showed blatantly. By six o'clock dinner was ready and Michael ate quickly to finish before Glen got to the table. Then he was out the door and to the river.

Finally peace, quiet and solitude, the potential for exploration endless, and things to see and do, WOW. A brisk chill was in the air and the full breaths that Michael was gulping burned a little, but felt good, "alive." He knew that this was Gods paintbrush and had colored all this scenery and built all these mountains and carved all these streams, filled all these lakes and taken the time to hold each boulder and place each one individually by His mighty hand. So many thoughts and feeling were flooding his young brain and heart, wanting to understand the depth of what was taking place in his life.

"Mike, where the hell are you!" The voice crushed the picture and brought reality flooding back.

"I'm down here by the river."

"Get your ass back to the cabin, now."

"You don't leave without asking."

"Understand!" He continued with the accusing voice.

"Yes sir, yes sir." What is going to happen now Michael replied, with a silent voice inside.

As he slowly approached the vision in front of him, his body was saying "don't get too close."

At near six foot and 185 pounds, red curly hair, reddish skin tone and standing staunch with hands on the hips and black eyes pulsing with anger, it was hard to even take one step, much less get within striking distance. Michael's motion stopped which only accelerated Glen from the porch, cuffing his right hand to the side of his head and knocking the boy to the ground.

"Get to your goddamn room."

"I'll be there shortly." He turned to go get another Coors, his daily beer brand of choice, at the very least two to three six-packs.

The fear and anguish that cascaded throughout Michael engulfed him. There was no remote spot of his body that was not trembling. Yet, it was not only in fear, but anger as well. Deep within a voice said "NO TEARS" "NO CRYING," show him that you will not give him the satisfaction of breaking you. He may break your body but NEVER your spirit. There was a satisfaction, no matter how small, that this was going to be the energy. This was the very source of strength to cope with the next seven years, almost eight.

"Now you little bastard, I'm going to show you whose boss." The words burst forth with the opening of the door and it crashed against the wall. The pump house was about one hundred and fifty feet from the main lodge, and the river noise roared in the background. Glen knew that Betty would never hear a sound, after all he had said that he was going for a "walk."

"May I go with you." She had asked quickly.

"No, not now, I'll be back shortly." He might as well have said hell no because she knew that he had no intentions of spending quality time with her.

The first action was a grab to the front of Michael's shirt, which allowed Glen to punch at will. Followed by four or five blows to the chest and stomach then spinning the child to the wall while lashing punches to the back and spine. He was always careful to strike where clothing would cover his dirty work and not betray the truth of what he was doing. Breathing was almost impossible but the inner voice said, "hold on."

When the onslaught had concluded, the grip released and Michael crashed, slumping to the floor. His body writhing with pain, a small trickle of blood seeping from his mouth, something inside had broken, but not the little mans spirit.

"Now, do you understand that you will do absolutely nothing, not go anywhere or do anything without my permission?"

"Answer me you little shit." Faintly a response came whizzing forth from Michael's lips.

"Yes sir."

Glen turned, a look of sincere satisfaction crossing his face, slammed the door and left. The echo of the assault still ringing ear to ear in the head of this young victim, "Don't give up and don't quit, someday you'll get to pay him back for all the injustice and pain."

The thoughts kept repeating themselves and the feelings kept reinforcing the thoughts. Michael drug himself to his bed and barely had the strength to roll onto the covers, sheer pain racking his chest and swollen places everywhere making any movement agony.

Sleep came but not for a long time. Yet even in his slumber, Michael's thoughts repeated the message, "NO TEARS, NO CRYING." As he awakened the next morning early, he crept down to the river and used the chilled water to revitalize and freshen his body. Hardness and strength was overcoming what had happened the night before. This was the beginning of the mind over matter, survival of the fittest, enduring all personality, which would develop inside this young man. Thereby creating a man that pain could not defeat, and it would soon became a way of life.

Heading towards the main lodge that first morning, the look on the young face and ease of movement belied what had transpired. Miraculous recovery was a gift, and in the next few years it was one of many that Michael would need to survive what would lay before him.

"Good morning Mom." Michael quoted as he walked through the door, watching for the reaction of Glen and the rest of the family. Knowing that there was no way his mother would ever know what had happened only a few hours before.

Glen looking smug as he sat there at the table having morning coffee, with a sneer that probably was only detected by Michael since it was shadowed by his mustache. "Make sure you eat quickly, we have a lot of work to finish today."

"Yes sir." A reply, which exalted the extent of words that would come forth from Michael's mouth for the next week, as far as his conversations with Glen were concerned.

Work was something that was expected of Michael from early morning until late afternoon. Working six days as week, every week from early June through late August, until it was time to go back to school. Being only ten years old made no difference whatsoever in Glen's eyes. Everyone that worked was expected to do the same amount of work regardless of size or age.

No matter how much it weighed, how big or how difficult the task, just do it. That first day, truly most of the first summer, was one of ridicule and pain. No matter how hard he tried or how good Michael performed a task, it was never good, or fast or done in the right way. A compliment was something that was never uttered from

Glen Hancock's mouth to Michael, Susan or their mother Betty.

Beatings continued almost nightly, after the required numbers of brews and the right number of sick thoughts cast through Glen's mind. Here he came to play the big man, the big bully. But after awhile, Michael just stood and took it. He would go mentally to another place and hold on to thoughts of his mother, Grandee and Nana and friends. Later in life this mind transferring developed into Mu Shin, a mental conditioning in his chosen style of Isshinryu karate. Allowing him access to mental and physical capacities most people never even dream of attaining.

By the time two full years of this way of life had been completed, some things were crystal clear. Glen wasn't going to change and the ritual of daily life was set until some sort of escape came through. Following this period of time, when young Michael had turned twelve, his grandfather gave him a brief escape.

Grandee had told "Hoss," (remember the nickname), when he was much younger that when birthday number twelve came around, a deer hunt would be arranged. Plans orchestrated through Uncle Harris, Grandee's brother, to go on a hunt in the northern mountains of New Mexico. He had been trapping and hunting this region for almost forty years and knew where all the BIG deer hung out.

"Mike, phones for you," Mom called out one Thursday afternoon.
"Hello."
"Hoss, what's going on?"

The voice of Grandee echoed joy in Michael's heart, knowing that his promise of years gone by was going to be delivered.
"Oh, just doing my homework," Michael exclaimed excitedly.
"Think you might get a bag packed by tomorrow night."
"You bet!"
"Cecil Briggs loaned me his 240 cal. rifle and I know it will be just right for bringing down your first deer."
"I'll be ready whenever you get here."
Grandee's voice smiled and this was always the case by the tone. It was a sound that lingered with you after the call was completed.

Glen was out of town at one of his many school contracts, thus no confrontation, no hassle. He wouldn't be back until six thirty Friday night and Grandee was picking Michael up, at five, funny how that time sequence was worked out.

The turquoise and white Ford F-150 with the overhead camper was loaded down. Aztec, New Mexico came and went and on to Chama where the roads got much steeper. Darkness had already settled, yet in his mind Michael could see everywhere. Knowing what awaited, the next day energized him and no nagging stick-in-the-mud to make things gloomy, like Glen Hancock.

About nine thirty the pick-up pulled off the road and roughly fifteen minutes later the glow of a campfire marked base camp for the next few days. Uncle Harris was standing there, the fire outlining him in a red-orange glow, cowboy hat tilted back and a large chew of Beech-Nut filling one side of his mouth.

This scene was not unlike many with Grandee and Michael where a campfire, hunting and fishing went hand in hand along with the chew of tobacco and a few yarns from previous hunts. Grandee was a master storyteller with all the emphasis at just the right places to make ears perk and hearts beat quickly. Interlaced with his stories were a "ditty" or two. These were little sayings and rhymes with a tune and melody, which only added to their candor and flavor.

"Peter C. Wallace and Peeannus Jones, Thomas E. Bittamus and Christopher Holmes, walking through the valley and climbing the hill. Looking for some fun, lookin' for a still."

This was one of Grandee's favorites, but only one of many.

"Uncle Harris, hay nice fire," Michael exclaimed as he jumped out of the truck and running quickly to shake his uncles hand.

"Yep, goin' to be colder than a Polar bear's butt tonight, so I made a big one."

"Mithero, how was the trip." A big spit of tobacco hit the ground as Harris asked his brother.

"Not bad, little traffic between Farmington and Aztec as usual. You know its Friday and all the Navajo's are heading for the firewater." A grin was accompanying the ending statement.

"Well, Hoss let's get ready to hit the sack, a big day awaits us tomorrow."

"You bet Grandee. And I'm going to get the first deer." Michael had just a hunch that this would come true. He was going to cross his fingers and toes all night, just to hedge the bet. Sleep would be long in coming though as excited as he was.

Morning broke early, the first crackling of the tender for the fire brought Michael blasting out of the sleeping bag.

"Brrrrrrrr."

"Goodness, its pretty chilly Grandee." Michael blurted out as he jerked his clothes over the long handles he had worn the night before. Dressing didn't take long and the first log was hitting the blaze as he stepped down from the camper. A heavy frost coated the truck and the ground was nearly white. Harris had the cowboy coffee going in the two pound coffee can and a Dutch oven with a load of biscuits, nestling in the coals of the fire. Gravy would be whipped up shortly, from renderings left over from drippings the day before, a good spread of chunk sausage and the meal would be complete. It was plenty to keep this parcel of hunters going for the bulk of the day.

Upon finishing the meal, clean up was done promptly and the fire put to rest. A few large flat stones were placed over the coals then dirt on top. This way, there was no danger of fire and the coal bed was preserved for later use. Who knows, maybe we will have a venison steak on the grill by dinnertime.

This thought roamed through Michael's mind, not realizing the hanging and aging time necessary for "good" meat.

"Let's take the Jeep, Mithero." the old military CJ-3A of Harris's would climb the hills like a mountain goat.

"Grandee, do you want me to ride in the back?"

"Yeah Hoss, get your rifle and ammo and load up."

"I think it would be best to start up near Bear Lake trail."

Harris knew the way and his judgment was never questioned up in these parts, by family, friends or anyone else. In fact he was the only guide, who was a white man that was allowed on the Jicarilla Apache Indian Reservation for many years. His ability to track, trap, and his regard and respect for the wilderness was known for miles around.

Thirty minutes later a big valley came into view as the Jeep rounded a large boulder. A salt lick had been put out several weeks before for the game, both deer and elk, and from the lick marks it had been used immensely. This was a good indicator of the amount of game in the immediate area. About half way up the valley the Jeep slowed and came to a halt.

"Hoss take a look over there by that stand of Aspen." Grandee pointed off to the left some two hundred fifty yards. A fine eight-point buck was taking in the view of the intruders to his valley and territory. Electricity etched in the quivering shoulder muscles and instant flight in the making.

"I see him." No sound of air moving from his lungs Michael whispered.

"Mithero, you and Mike get out here. I'll go on up about a half mile or so and get out there."

"You guys work your way up to the edge of the trees. I'm going to circle around up on top of the ridge and see what I can flush out." His statement held with it the wisdom and experience of a true outdoorsman and the confidence of thousands of hunts gone by.

"We'll meet up near that point of rocks there, below the big Blue

Spruce." Grandee replied taking his 270 cal. Remington from its scabbard, as he pulled the thermal hunting gloves out of his jacket pocket.

The beauty of what lay before their eyes was breathtaking. Peaks rising to 11,000 feet, snow capped and rugged. Bare limbed Aspen with their beige and white trunks and the deep green of the evergreen. A slight hint of light green still capped the tall grass, as the first big snows had not yet arrived. Curving and snaking through the outer edge of the valley lay a small stream, which along with the grass, was all the food and water it took to produce large herds.

"Hoss, you go on up in the trees about sixty yards or so. I'll stay right along the rim to watch the opening."

"I'm on my way. I'll watch close and let you know if I see a good one."

"Make sure your rifle is loaded and the safety is on."

"Yes sir, I-I-I promise!" Michael was literally floating on air as he drifted up the mountainside. He knew this was going to be a day to remember, strictly based on the company, the view and all there was to take in. No matter the outcome of the day, it would never be forgotten.

Occasionally a rifle blast would be heard in the distance as many hunters were making their bids for a nice buck. The crispness of the early morning air transported sound for many miles, the echoes off the cliffs were a built in amplifier.

Harris had parked the vehicle and trekked up to the ridge, enabling him to see the entire valley and plotting his path towards the aforementioned Blue Spruce. He started out toward the southeast stopping every hundred yards or so and rolling a rock down through the trees. This pattern of movement continued for about an hour with only a few spike bucks and does coming into view.

Meanwhile Michael was near having a heart attack with every rock as it rolled off the mountain. Hearing the crashing and feeling the movement, just knowing that a big buck was about to come jetting from around the next tree, excitement filled the air. Sure enough, when he had finally settled down a little, carrying his rifle at half mast, a thundering noise crushed the silence. This was either a big animal or Harris had caused a landslide.

The eight-pointer that had been seen earlier was flying through the trees running directly at Michael. Bringing his weapon up quickly, the first shot was a trace high. At the speed the animal was moving there would be only one more shot and the cocking of his rifle gave Michael just the right amount of time to find the correct sighting and fire.

"I GOT HIM! I GOT HIM! I GOT HIM!"

"YAHOO, I GOT HIM!" Michael was jumping up and down waving

his arms, his hearty smile beaming on his face, the exuberance of many emotions letting loose.

"Good shot Hoss. And he's a nice fat one. Bet he's been sneaking down into somebody's corn patch for the past few months."

Grandee's pride was overflowing as his grandson had gotten his first deer. The joy he could see in Hoss's face was one he loved to see. Yet so often when he got to see his grandson there was a hidden darkness, a withdrawing, that hid something else he knew had to do with Glen.

"Well, well, well would you look at that. Mithero, I think this young buck might make a hand after all. The final test will be when he starts field dressing his kill." Harris came around a stand of trees and saw the picture before him.

"Boy he's a big one isn't he Uncle Harris?" Michael continued, "I want to mount him and put him in my room back home."

"Well, why don't we just see if that can't be arranged, after all one's first deer is pretty important." Grandee always said things, which made Mi-chael proud and his heart was about to burst with joy.

The field dressing consisted of racking the deer off the ground by the antlers and cutting his paunch (stomach) open. Then take the large intestines out and be careful not to hit the scent sack or the bladder, which would taint the meat. Final dressing would be done back at the base camp, skinning etc. Michael completed his first field dressing with flying colors, although if any mistakes were made, nothing was certainly said. What a comparison to the continual harassment and scrutiny constantly back in ALBUQUERQUE.

That afternoon with a lunch of jerky and crackers and some Velveeta cheese out of the way, the hunt resumed. Grandee made an incredible shot of some four hundred and fifty yards to drop a nice ten-pointer. Harris added another eight-pointer, which was just a tad smaller than Michael's eight. Some teasing and ribbing was had between Harris and Michael, on the trip back to camp. In the end the victor was Grandee because of having the largest buck as well as the best rack of horns.

The next morning camp broke early since the limits had been filled, and the long trip home had begun for Michael. How he hoped that Grandee would just keep on going back to Texas and not stop in Albuquerque.

Arriving back in the city was no treat for the young man, but the memories of the weekend would carry him through. No matter what transpired over the next few months, or what ridicule came his way, he was a good hunter. Grandee told him so.

The summer following the deer hunt, June 1960, it was back to Platoro for the Hancock's. Turning twelve would make several differences for Michael's workload from Glen. He would now be expected to work as hard and complete equally as much, as any of the grown men working at Conejos Cabins. The depth of this requirement would unleash a new range of confrontations between Michael and Glen, resulting in beatings that would border on death.

A new addition on the cabins was being started which would bring two more units to the resort. It would be much larger and more modern with a large recreation and picnic area as well. In this new phase there would be a foot and fishing bridge added, so that the guests would have access to the west bank of the river.

New construction meant foundations had to be dug, cement had to be poured and finished and logs would need to be peeled and cleaned. Of course, since this was up in the remote mountains, all labor had to be done by hand. So pick, shovel and sledge hammer were the tools of choice. The terrain was rugged with rock more than dirt being the main obstacle. Work started at seven in the morning, there was a half hour lunch at noon, and work stopped when it began to get dark.

Michael ached after the first few days of work. His back and shoulders were so stiff it seemed like they were made of wood. He had cuts and blisters and bruises covering his hands. The pain he felt was in a very unique way soothing, for he knew that the result would be strength. With strength would come power and a better ability to withstand the force that would surly come. Thus he bent his back to the sun and worked like someone twice his age and strength, determined to out work every man in the employment of his stepfather. It didn't take long for the first confrontation to occur. Mr. Perfectionist ridiculed everyone's work but he took pleasure in constantly riding Michael.
"Didn't I tell you to dig that damn foundation footer thirty-six inches deep?"
"Yes Sir."
"Well shit, I just measured it and there are several places that are only thirty-five inches."
"I know, but those places are solid rock and I couldn't get the rock to break up anymore." Michael stubbornly commented knowing that he couldn't win no matter what.
"Get your ass back to the start of the footing and start over again. You don't stop for anything until it is finished and finished right!" He slapped Michael hard against the back of his head knocking him down, as he was turning to get the tools, and walk away.

The glare in Michael's eyes could have cut stone, hatred flooded from every part of his anatomy. He wanted to pick up the shovel and give Glen back what he was feeling. But instead he just swallowed hard and gritted his teeth, knowing that someday, somehow he would get to give Glen the pay back that he wanted to give today.

"There something you want to say?" Glen taunted and glared back.

"No sir." Michael sharply replied. The other men had stopped and were looking on at the situation, but quickly commenced their work as Glen turned to go. The look in their eyes confirmed what they thought "glad it wasn't them getting the chewing."

Michael looked at the clock as he sat on the edge of his bed. It was EIGHT THIRTY and the time stared across at him. Glen should have already been there, yet he was still drinking, and had now finished over a case of Coors. The anticipation was worse than the actual punishment because it lasted for hours while the blows would subside in three or four minutes. Stretching and clenching his fists to the point of showing white against every knuckle, the thought came to him, "Why not fight back this time? It certainly couldn't make it any worse."

Boom, the door was flung open hard, back against the wall, the devilish glare from the alcohol-reddened eyes, looked surreal in the limited lighting. Something monstrous and evil loomed within, struggling to get out of the body it had taken over.

"Your time is up you fucking little shit." His words were crisp and he moved with a stealth that belied the rage bursting and ready to explode.

The strike came as a fist to the chest followed by a sharp crack to the side of the head, ringing his brain and forcing Michael hard, into the wall. Reacting instantly he thrust his foot into Glen's groin and lashed out with his fist striking him in the chin. Even in his staggered state from the first attack, Michael was letting the inner will and pent up feelings direct him.

Surprised at the response, the fire raged inside Glen and he lost all control. Rage literally rained over Michael, being knocked across the room, the past reserve of not striking in the face was history in the making. For now it was open season and every area an open target.

By the time it was over, Michael was barely conscious, as he lay beaten and bloody on the concrete floor. The cold hardness of the surface, though rough, was somewhat soothing. He felt pain everywhere. Swelling had already begun to engulf his face and rib areas. Blood seeping from a gash over the left eye and streaming from the side of his mouth, he knew that it would be several days until the pain went away. A thought seemed to flicker through his brain, "Yeah, I hurt but Glen has some sore balls and I did get in at least one good lick in the face."

This scene in varying degrees came and went for most of the summer. All it really accomplished was that the hatred and resentment were intensified. Susan and Betty for the most part didn't have to put up with the abuse. He was too busy with Michael, for this the young boy was thankful. Protecting a woman, any female, became very important to him. After what he had watched he didn't want ever to see a woman abused or hurt, even if he had to risk his life, and that he would one day.

With only two weeks remaining in the summer an event took place that would make several differences in Michael's life. It was a twofold experience and would pattern some later in life circumstances.

One afternoon after work, as Michael stood on the back porch of the main lodge, he had taken his shirt and shoes off to go in and clean up for dinner. The sun was on its final decent behind the mountain, with the river roaring in the background. The flood gates had been opened to full run, to provide maximum water down stream and to prevent overflow on the lake's spillway. Thus the current was extremely fast and all the rocks were covered. Two young boys had gone fishing upstream, Billy and Jimmy Shattuck, age four and seven respectively.

Jimmy came running, breathless a look of sheer terror in his little eyes, with a grayish-white color, to his face. As he rounded the corner by the porch he gasped, the words springing from his lips.
"Billy fell in, Billy fell in!!! Quick he is face first!!"
"Where Jimmy, where?"
"There, right there!" Jimmy pointed for Michael to see at the red jacket bobbing up and down and this tiny figure of a child could be seen quickly moving downstream.

Instantly, with no hesitation whatsoever, Michael launched his frame towards the bridge. Taking long strides and gaining speed with every step, he coiled and sprung skyward. Launching to get as far in front of the jacketed form as possible, he landed about ten feet downstream, turning quickly with a thrust of his torso and grabbed the young boy as he came towards him. The commotion had brought many to the rivers edge and men, including Billy's father Jim were making a human chain from the bank to where Michael had landed. As the second man took hold of little Billy he let out a big cry. It was one of the most wonderful noises, or sounds Michael had ever heard. He was all right. The cold water had made him hold his breath. Other than a scare and a couple of small bruises, including one little one on his ego, he was going to be fine.
"Michael, I don't know how to ever thank you enough."
"You saved my boy's life and I will be forever grateful to you," Jim Shattuck, a sweet tenderness in his eyes exclaimed.
"Thank you Mr. Shattuck, glad that I could help."

The excitement continued for several minutes. Seeing the look on Michael's face, Betty was very proud of her son. She just glowed and hugged him in a special embrace as he came to finish getting ready for dinner.

"Mom, not in front of everybody," Michael squeaked as he tried to get through the screen door. He loved his mother so much and wished that somehow it could go back to just the three of them again, no more Glen.

Later that same week the second event came to fruition, one that Michael would never, ever forget. He had dreamed of this happening but never thought that it would really come true, a dog of his very own becoming a part of his young life, not one that just came along or one someone had given the family, but his very own.

It had been brought up that some friends of Betty's, Smokey and Vi Swanton, were breeding their German Shepherd to a sire that had just won the world championship. Yorkdom's Pak had been awarded this coveted position at the Westminster Show and was the top sire nationwide. The puppies were selling for a lot of money and some how or another a deal was cut for Michael to get one.

After working some seven hundred hours that summer, Michael was given his wages, the sum total of two hundred and fifty dollars. Guess what the cost of the puppy was? You got it, two hundred and fifty dollars. Somebody, maybe Mr. Shattuck or Michael's mom or his grandfather had made the final deal. But no matter, Chico was delivered and the joy and happiness that consumed Michael would make a mark that nothing and nobody could ever take away. They became literally inseparable and the relationship created a bond between the boy and his dog that was limitless.

Twenty-four hours a day, they were together. Michael let Chico sleep on his bed, he would bring his breakfast or whatever mealtime it was, out on the porch, so that even that time was together. After work it was off to the mountains and dashing through the forests. The release for Michael was one that came at a very critical time in his life.

Chico became the outlet for talking and sharing problems with. It was a companionship, which had no rules, no objections, no hatred or ridicule. They shared a love, totally devoted and unconditional, available everyday. Very realistically if Chico would not have come along, Michael might have gone over the edge. The situation with Glen had eaten inside the core of his soul, and the festered wound was near bursting. He needed to share what had been going on but was terrified that his mother or sister would take the brunt of what the sharing might resolve. Thus, no way did he want that burden on his shoulders.

Through the next school year things were pretty standard, in fact the next three years were a continuing saga. Michael got taller and stronger and Glen got even more violent and he griped more. The heart scarring that had been going on now for almost six years, had built a wall of stone around Michael's heart. With it came the determination and will that were evident in Michael's way of thinking, there was a hardness way beyond his years.

Alcohol became an outlet at times, by the age of twelve he had been drunk several times. Fighting and assaults became a weekly occurrence at school. The reputation of being a tough guy began to follow him. But in a special hiding place, that only a few people would ever get to see a glimpse of at this stage of life, there resided a tenderness.

When he was alone with his mother, with Nana or with Chico, smiles would flourish. Secretly, Michael and Susan would talk about what they wished would happen, because both of them truly hated Glen. The foundation bricks had been cemented together in a manner that was almost impenetrable, Michael's fortitude.

Nary a single tear had crossed his face for going on five years and none would drift across for many years to come. He had entered high school at Del Norte High in Albuquerque, New Mexico. As a sophomore he stood six feet one inch and weighed one hundred sixty-eight pounds. He was thin but strong, calloused and hard from all the work up in Platoro and had legs like steel. The runs with Chico up through the mountain trails had fortified the tendons and muscles with incredible strength and endurance. Making football tryouts a coach's dream, here was an athlete that they didn't have to worry about getting into shape. It was there already.

School year 1964-1965 was also a transition year for Michael. As the year began at Del Norte but didn't finish there, a military school would take over before long and rescue the rest of the year.

Uncle Bill and Aunt Jo, along with their three kids, Faye Ann, Barry and Linda had come for a visit. This was Betty's brother and family that had come over from Texas. The first night that they spent, a major escapade ensued. Michael and his cousin Barry had been assigned to stay in the office with sleeping bags, it being outside the main area of the house allowed for easy access to the keys and the car. Of course a drivers license was still eight months away. But the past six months Michael had been sneaking out along with two friends, Kurt Ehlert and Danny Abrams, and had been stealing cars, or at least going for a joy ride. Well on this evening Michael decided to try and impress his cousin.

"Barry, are you sleeping?"
"Nope," Short answer and with a cautious tone, cousin Barry was overly cautious.
"I stole the keys to the station wagon and I'm going to go cruising."
"Not me, Dad would kill me if we got caught."
"Caught, Huh, we aren't going to get caught. Come on it would be fun." Michael taunted and tried to break Barry's choice.
"Uh Uh! No Way! No How!" Barry replied, knowing that Michael was probably going to venture out anyway.

After getting dressed I took the keys, which had been stolen earlier. Yes, Michael and I are one and the same. I started for the window, climbing out onto the driveway and cautiously creeping toward the 1956 Chevrolet Station Wagon. A Nomad, two tone green, 283 cu. in. V-8, automatic, perfect for the cruise to see all the big kids. I pushed the car out of the driveway and let it roll down the block three houses before firing up the motor. Then it was radio on and strutting my stuff.

The strut was very short lived however as flashing red lights reflected bright in the rear view mirror. Pulling over careful and way two slow, the policeman had a very inexperienced driver, I'm sure is what he was thinking. Yet, he gave me the noose and I took it.
"May I see the registration and your license?" Calm, cool and very collected, I answered.
"What's the problem officer?"
"I wasn't speeding, was I sir?" This was not going to work, the look in the officer's eyes told me that.
"Your license?"
"Oh, I must have left it at home!" Sure, sure, sure I could tell immediately. He had only heard that excuse probably two thousand times.
"Tell you what son, hand me those car keys and I'll call your home and ask your parents to verify you left your license there." Extending his hand slowly into the window opening, his uniform starched and shining, the shadow that his six-foot plus frame made with the aid of streetlights, was very intimidating.
"I may as well tell you," pausing and taking a deep breath, "I don't really have a license," waiting for a response, and not knowing what to do but hand him the keys with the end of my answer.
"Why don't you step out of the vehicle and come sit in the patrol car with me young man."
"What's your name?"
"Michael Decker sir."
"And your address?"
"3225 Georgia N.E." We had moved from the Snow heights address

about a year earlier.

"I'm sure you know that this was very stupid for you to attempt this stunt?"

"Yes sir."

"Isn't there any way to work this out other than calling my family? You don't know what's going to happen with my stepfather."

"He is very violent and will beat the hell out of me." Maybe, just maybe there would be someway things might be okay with the policeman standing nearby. Also, with Uncle Bill and his family at home, maybe it wouldn't be as bad as I thought.

"Don't worry son, this won't be that bad." But he didn't know who and what I did.

He dialed the station and thus they connected him with home. Glen must have answered because the officer had a sudden change in tone of voice and manner of speaking.

"Damn, your step dad was really upset!"

"I told you so." The bomb was about to burst, and I could feel it. Man, that thirty minutes of waiting was more like thirty hours in one way and thirty seconds in another.

As the Plymouth came driving up to the police car the officer motioned toward the vehicle.

"Well let's get this over with."

It didn't take long for Glen to clobber me. As I rounded the squad car, he cuffed me behind the ear and took a wild swing making the air rush past my face, missing by less than an inch.

"Here now, we won't have any of that crap here!"

"Mind your own damn business, this is my business." Glen blurted out with his normal rage.

"Well, while it's here it's my business, and one more move like that and you'll spend the rest of the night downtown!" "Do you understand?"

Very reluctantly Glen answered, "Do what you need to and get this over with," with a sultry viciousness in the tone of his words. The "paperwork" didn't take nearly enough time, because of what was going to happen thereafter.

"Betty, you drive the other car and Mike will come with me," he ordered, with no hesitation whatsoever.

"Get in the goddamn car, NOW!"

Something was exchanged between the officer and Glen but glass and the traffic noise didn't avail me the opportunity to hear anything. The gestures alone were enough to signify what was being said, or at the very least the general content.

The car door jerked open, several vulgarities murmured under Glen's breath as he entered and started the car. Knowing it was coming, I mentally prepared for the hand. I knew that it was coming, just when, was the question, not if!

"You must be real proud of your self, you little fucker."

"I promise you this, you will not drive any goddamn car when you turn sixteen or for a long time thereafter."

Whack! Whack! Two blows to the side of my face, I knew it couldn't last for long.

"When we get home you will come in the house and sleep on the fucking floor. Do you understand that?"

"Yes sir." The sir that came from my lips was one word alone, that there had never been the normal respect that should have accompanied it.

"Also you will not speak to anyone unless I am present, that means absolutely no one."

"Yes sir."

You could tell that something else was up in the recesses of his mind. Only three days later the underlying thought that had been pre-planned for some time was about to unfold.

New Mexico Military Institute, in Roswell, New Mexico, founded back in 1918 had very quickly established itself as one of the premiere institutions of military science and overall excellence in education in the United States. This was to be my home for the next two, plus years. Once again it came at a time when to stay in the same house with Glen would have been a tragedy in the making. At the same time, it became an opportunity to study military strategy and technique, advanced weapon training and a physical fitness program that was second to none. It would avail me the chance to dive into many things that were interesting, and also the added immense pleasure of "NO MORE GLEN!"

January 1965 broke cold and the sky had a grayish hue to the north. Remnants of blue fringed the gray and a pencil line of pink marked the beginning of a new day. A new era of an existence, marked with turmoil and tragedy was displayed by the four story towers of the "Sally Port," which would be passed through twenty times a day for the next few months.

My next major contact was Col. Thomas, twenty-nine years with the Army Airborne and three tours with the American troops in the "big wars." Every thread of his uniform pressed perfectly, medals and ribbons displayed with pride and honor. He had earned them by risking his life many times and leading his men through countless battles. The piercing gaze that illumined from his eyes showed strength and determination.

An air of confidence flowed around him that carried with it a note of leadership and ability. This was his school, his campus, and his outfit. To be a part of it, meant one was going to do it the RIGHT way, his way.

Driving up to the institution from Albuquerque to Roswell, New Mexico took roughly three and a half hours. The immense stone structure was built to impress the viewing public and this it did, with the military precision in which it was designed.

As the car came to a stop in the circle drive of the dispatch lot, nerves begin to vibrate and thoughts raced rampant. "My new home," this is what I stated and asked of myself at the same time.
"We'll just see how tough you are now." Glen had to get something smart interjected before we had left the car.
"Oh, Glen." Mother didn't finish the thought, as it would have done no good.
"Cadet Decker."
"Yes, Sir!," extending my hand to Col. Thomas.
"Sergeant Stuart will show you where to begin your orientation and issue."
"Sergeant take Cadet Decker to the infirmary and get things rolling."
"Yes, Sir, Colonel," Sergeant Stuart replied quickly, a smile faintly crossing his face.

A very quick goodbye to Mom, and it was off to the races for my first day of training. The anticipation was great but the relief of knowing that the daily onslaught of Glen Hancock was ending, overpowered all others.
"Grab your gear, Decker, and follow me."
"Yes, Sir!"
"No, it's 'Yes, Sgt.' I'm not an officer."
"Yes, Sgt."

As I marched, or thought I was marching behind the Sgt., groups of guys about my age or older were drilling and moving about the campus. Green uniforms, Army issue, the campus was much larger than I had anticipated. Large cottonwood trees and evergreens lined each and every street and walkway. There were vast lawns and landscaping adorning all the buildings and barracks.

Our first stop was the barbershop and I thought, "Hey, I just had a haircut." Yet the haircut I had received was a light trim, compared to the peeling that was in store for me.
"Now you look like a soldier Decker, get your things and follow me to the clothing office."
"Yes, Sgt."

24

The issue of uniforms from New Mexico Military Institute was basically the initial issue from the regular Army, which consisted of two dress uniforms, one formal, three standard and four sets of fatigues. One pair of dress shoes and one pair of combat boots rounded out the wardrobe.
"Well, Sgt. Stuart, is this the new halfass from Albuquerque?"
"Yeah, he's the one that his father said was such a little shit."
"No problem, we'll take care of that attitude."

Glen had made the comment to the Col. and who knows what else he "mentioned" in the way of information. But I knew who I was and what I was made of, military and strict discipline were not going to be a problem. My mind had been made up that the punishment that Glen thought was to be so terrible would in reality be a blessing.

The term "halfass," I was to learn, was the phrase they used for guys starting at the mid semester point rather than the first of the school year.

My new home was "A" company in the east barracks of the "Quad." Shortened for the quadrangle, which was the square structure of barracks. It was three stories tall, double bunked housing, with approximately one thousand high school age cadets.
"Decker, you take 212 with Bramberg."
"He's a halfass, thus you will be matched." A hearty chuckle was issued with the statement.
"Get your gear stored, change quickly and bring me those damn 'civvies.' We want to get rid of that contraband."
"Yes, Sergeant."

I changed rapidly, ducked my gear in my locker and returned promptly to the Sergeant's quarters. His room was on the first floor. He was to be my first Sgt. for the remainder of the year. Sgt. Gregory was of Indian, Navajo, background, and had been at the institution for three years. He seemed to have a good grasp on the WAY things were to operate, and physical hazing was his specialty.

As I stood in front of his door, I banged sharply announcing my arrival. The door opened to reveal four "old cadets," cadets who had finished their "rat" years. Rat years were the first year spent in the institution a full orientation of what life was to be like in the future. They all stood around with looks on their faces reflecting events seen, felt and about to be administered.
"Decker, get your ass in here and stand at attention."
"Yes, Sergeant."
"Here's how this is going to work Decker. Everyone that starts here at NMMI gets initiated. That means you get the privilege of getting your

ass smacked with this here broom."

The oak handle had a shine to it from many turns at the bat. God only knows, how many young butts this instrument had "initiated" into the welcome wagon of NMMI, mine, being the next in line, what an honor.
"Grab your ankles, Decker."

The four of them took turns two swats each, until they felt the hazing was complete. Their faces reflected looks of satisfaction and pleasure on a job well done. What they didn't know, was that this level of physical force was so light in comparison to what I was used to, that it was hardly recognizable. Of course I didn't tell them that!
"Well look at this, no tears."
"Yeah Smitty, most of these little halfasses go away crying to the Col."
"You can't make me cry, so don't even try."
"Oh, are you a tough guy Decker?"
"I'm just me and this test or whatever the shit you want to call it, is over! You want me to do something, give me an order. You want to beat my ass, call me out and we'll see who the tough guy is."

Astonishment, literally speechless they couldn't believe, some new halfass much less, had the audacity to say something like that. With this statement, I left the room and returned to my quarters.

Shortly, very shortly, as I had begun squaring away my things, the door came flying open. Standing there was the company bully who had just heard what had taken place.

Corporal Mason was about six three and weighed in the neighborhood of two hundred fifty pounds. He was from Oklahoma, a senior, eighteen years old and he was bad. At least if you ask him he would tell you that. His size intimidated most of the other cadets but he didn't have the fire and anger that I was used to. Besides that, my Grandee said, "it's not the size of the dog in the fight. It's the size of the fight in the dog." This dog was a junk yard fighter. With six years of heavy construction under my belt, and a thousand beatings from a "real" tough guy, as well as several hundred fights, after and during school for practice, I was more than ready.
"Decker, Take your young ass down to the head, we're going to get this damn attitude and your smart mouth altered."
"No problem, I'll be right there." The blood began to pulse in my veins, adrenaline glands activating, raw cords of muscles developed during thousands of hours of hard labor twitched and flexed. Bottled anger from years of getting my feelings crammed down my throat began to rise. As I walked out the door, the stoops were lined with people the

word had spread like wildfire. "The new guy is going to fight Mason!"

Each step down the walkway gave me more strength, and the breaths came even and deep. Warmth turned to heat and heat turned to fire. The inferno had been ignited and it was ready to burn. Some seventy-five feet separated my door from the "proving grounds." Upon turning into the head (bathroom) door, the four old cadets that had welcomed me to the facility were lined up against one wall. A smug look graced their faces. You could see the delight they were anticipating.
"Okay, Decker, let's see just how good you think you are." Mason's big fat body was jiggling with assured laughter tauntingly.

Words were cheap, and none came forth from my mouth, I let my hands do the talking. Quickly moving through the door, the distance separating us was negated, and a crushing right hand into the bridge of his face, exploded the Corporal's nose, knocking him back six feet. Following with two vicious hooks to the fat belly and ribs and a thrusting kick to the groin, this confrontation was rapidly concluded. Mason lay semiconscious on the floor, blood flowing from his nose and mouth. Bruises were already beginning to form, from the force of the blow to his face.
"I'll take an order, but I won't take a beating!" This statement had reverberated throughout the compound. Many of the young men I'm sure, thought that I was showing off, but later their thoughts changed. This due to sharing the real history of just where I had come from.

David Lovelady, John Black, Harris Frangos, Bobby Wilson, Benny Smith, Marc Black, and many more too numerous to mention were a big part of the life. Life as the NMMI cadet, that is. We ruled the single "A" division during the mid- to late Sixties in almost every sport. Of course, having the training facilities of a college campus and our own private dining hall didn't hurt things. Not to mention, that with an all male campus there weren't so many distractions.

That first semester flew by, and much to my regret, it was time to go back to the "family," My grades were above average with a grade point average of 3.35, but the scores in Military Science and on the shooting range were special. Special in that they were not subjects that took on the limelight of study. Final scores in Military Science were 98.7% and my field scores bordered on the 100% accuracy table most of the time. The degree of master sharpshooter, from the NRA was in my hand by the end of this first period of study.

Summer of 1965 turned into rather a surprise, Glen had negotiated the sale of the Conejos Cabins while I had been away at school. The new owner was none other than Jim Shattuck, the man whose son I had saved three years earlier. Thus the job was waiting for me when I arrived in early June, and Glen was NOT my boss any longer.

What a difference working for Jim, "night and day" was a vast understatement of the duality of these opposites. Every chapter and verse of the way Mr. Shattuck did things was the antithesis of Glen Hancock. A compliment and a smile were reactions to my work that were foreign to the workplace before.

Gary Childress and Tommy Pelton, along with Steve Everett, all full summer guys that were in Platoro at their respective cabins, had gone on to do other things that summer. My sister, Susan was now out of high school and had taken a summer job in Montreal, Canada, so most of the regular crew had deserted the frontier. Somewhere deep within my heart, I felt that this would be the last time my feet would walk these known terrains. Things turned out, just in that manner.

There were a few run-ins with the likes of Glen, but he wasn't near as ready to get rowdy these days. I had grown another two inches and put on twenty-eight more pounds of muscle. Knocking on the door of two hundred pounds, and my first four and a half months of martial arts training from a friend at NMMI, had changed the confidence that accompanied me. Also, every night after work I would strap the weights around my ankles and head up the mountain with Chico for a run and work out. I just couldn't get enough physical exercise and was consuming vast amounts of food.

There were some great moments of solitude enjoyed on the weekends, that summer. Unlike Glen, Mr. Shattuck didn't work every single day. So off to the upper meadows and streams, Chico and I would venture. Enjoying some of the best trout streams ever placed in the Rockies. The fly fishing was at its peak come mid-July to early September, and the big browns and cutthroats were rolling the mayflies. Chico and I would sometimes leave the cabins at daylight and travel twenty five to thirty miles in a day. The upper meadows above Platoro Lake had no roads back then, only horse trails.

Flash, that was the feeling of how fast that summer flew by. The lack of hassles with Glen made an incredible difference. NMMI was a sound in the back of my mind that brought with it visions of pleasure and MORE training.

Most of the guys from the football team had really worked out that summer, and Coach Black was truly impressed with the outcome of the season, undefeated and the state championship, including a win over El Paso Belair, the Texas five "A" champions with a score of 32-7. NMMI, the Colts, rolled over everybody that year by four, to as many as nine touchdown favorites.

Physically I put on another ten pounds, and the martial arts training I was pursuing was pushing me towards my brown belt by the end of the school year. Studying in this first phase of my training in the Korean style of Tae Kwon Do, I was obsessed with the new found art, and by mid-semester was just completing my seventeenth birthday. Christmas break was very different. I really didn't want to go home, but for my mother's sake, home I went.

Grandee and Nana came over for the holidays, so Glen was on somewhat good behavior. I almost regret that he didn't try to confront me. I was getting to the point that I felt I could finally hold my own with him.

Thankfully the break went quickly and back to NMMI. By February or March of that year, 1966, Grandee had offered me a position down in Canyon, Texas for the summer. The plans were finalized and off to Texas I was bound, as soon as my classes were complete. Upon arriving in the little town of Canyon, the welcome mat had already been laid out for me.

"Hoss, I've been thinking about it and you would be a lot better off staying in town this summer. I have checked into a boarding house situation and I feel that it will work out really well. That way you can get up early and head north of town, since your working the John Campbell place for now. What do you think?" Grandee explained.

"Sounds great to me, but what about transportation? How will I get out there each day?" I asked.

About this time one of his friends came driving up in a blue, 1954 Ford Fairlane, it was a two-door, three-speed with a six banger. Of course, I didn't see all these things when it first arrived, this was later to be discovered.

"Well Mikkus, (an every now and then nickname), how bout' this little Ford for your travels?"

"Gosh, really, do you really mean it?"

"You just do a good job and mind your Ps and Qs and the car is yours for the summer."

My heart would not stop pounding. I felt like it wanted to literally jump from my body. There had never been someone who did the things in the manner that Grandee could. He had a way of giving that you knew that it came from his heart.

The boarding house was a sleeping room with breakfast and dinner served by the landlady. She really knew how to spread a table though, as most of the women from this part of the country could muster, so good eats and a warm, dry bed was had for fifty dollars a week. This came to one fourth of my pay, but it was well worth it.

Steve "Skeeter" Downing and I became the best of friends and along with another friend Steve Evrett, the three of us roamed the streets of Canyon and the shores of Buffalo Lake for the summer. The local public pool was a hangout on occasion where Skeeter would demonstrate the acrobatic dive the "horny spider" to the delight of all the gang. Especially the guys, but the girls snickered almost as much.
"Come on Skeeter, give us a good one."
"Yeah dude, Betty Graham is watching real close."

The following stares would accompany him to the board and the long slow climb to the top of the high board. Three full strides and a gathering of the coiled torso, then flying through the air. Arms and legs spreadeagled and undulating and humping the air, writhing and twisting with that ecstatic look on his face, boom and into the pool, another quality performance of the "horny spider."

Most nights after work the three of us would jump into either the Ford or Steve's new little red Mustang, cruise to the D.Q. or the Tastee Freeze and hang out for the girls who might be out running around. Then we would all make a dash up to the Buffalo Chip, a mid-county beer house, grab a couple of twelve packs of Lone Star or Pearl and out to the lake.

Needless to say my first experience at sex had taken place in Platoro, but the likes of this full fledged fling of the single life was my real initiation. Julie Puckett taught me things that I am not real sure I had even dreamed about, much less thought of in any real way. I didn't know that they even existed. Wow, what a summer to write home about, but no letter was ever penned, wonder why?

That summer was one for the record books as far as I was concerned. To leave all the fun and frolic was truly a let down. Yet the taste of the freedom was enjoyed for many months to come. I turned the little blue Ford back over to Grandee and said goodbye. He already had it sold, so the transition was easy. The new owner was a sixteen-year old girl and I'm sure that the memories kept on being made.
"Hey Bamberg, how was the summer?" I asked, shortly after returning to NMMI, he was the first one to come in contact with.
"Decker, hey what's going on? I had a great summer but it was over way to fast!"
"No kidding, I was major tempted not to come back, but here we are, seeing that it's our senior year and all."
"Have you seen many of the guys yet?" Mark Bamberg knew that I hadn't because we were the first ones there every year. But he had to

carry on some sort of conversation, because I knew what his great summer consisted of. Sitting behind the desk at his father's office and getting two thousand a month for doing simple office work. Also, his "fun" was probably doing a math problem or balancing the checkbook.

As always, the first few days back were just busy, as regular classes didn't begin for two more weeks. Only the football players were back for the high school as well as the junior college. Huge meals were served three times a day along with two big snacks. We had morning workouts from eight to eleven, then afternoon workouts from three to six. It was plenty of exercise and lots of fuel to keep the fires burning.

There was such a radical difference between the regular school programs and the institution's. As an example, our high school lineman averaged 6'2" and 245 pounds, the backfield 6'1" and 210 pounds Marc Black, our All-American halfback averaged 235 yards a game and ran the 40 yard dash in 4.61 seconds.

The first few games of the season went as expected, we were 6-0 and the state championship was already in the bag. After the Friday night game that October night, six of the "boys" decided to sneak out of the barracks. There was a big party going on over at some local kid's house. There were no parents and plenty of things to drink. About thirty-five people showed up for the event and the fun started rolling and the music got loud.

"Decker, check the unit on that little fine thing in the yellow dress!"
"No kidding Wilson, she is prime and fine. What's her name?" Donnie Wilson being from Roswell knew all the locals and kept his close friends hooked up.
"Sarah Fredricks, her Dad is a doctor and they are megabucks around here."
"Well damn, don't just stand there, make the intro, Bubba!"
"Sarah, this is my friend Michael Decker, but we just call him the Mojo man!"
"Give me a break, Bobby. Sarah, it's a pleasure to meet you."
"Thank you, Michael. Sounds like the Colts are the team to beat this year."
"Yep, we should kick butt all the way to the state finals. At least that is our plan."
"Have you seen any of our games yet?"
"Yes, in fact I was at the game last night. Nice touchdown!"
"Well thanks, I really got lucky." I really thought that I had done great, but not too much flash so early.
"Lucky, huh, you and Marc Black are always making all the touch-

downs and the big plays. I think it's neat how they write about the two of you in the paper. "Black & Decker power their way for another NMMI win!"

"Yeah, it is sort of unique. I just wish that Black & Decker would send some of that big money our way. But I guess that's a dream."

Sarah had the most astonishing eyes, almost a brilliant green shade that had deep pools of reflection. She had long blonde hair, below the shoulders and about five foot six. Very well built, from head to toe, or as we say, in Texas, BODACIOUS!

The beer had flowed freely for about five hours now and all but one of the guys had started back to the campus. Time was pushing the clock past midnight and everyone knew that the tactical officer would be making his rounds soon. Of course, everyone else in the group that had snuck off lived on the first floor of the quadrangle. Michael, me, myself and I lived on the fourth floor above regimental headquarters. "Just one more beer and I'll head back, no problem." All the others were safe in their rooms before I even started to negotiate the obstacle course of climbing unnoticed up four flights of stairs.

"One flight, aaah, two flights, it looks like I'm going to make it." I thought to myself. Suddenly the exercise and additional blood flow had also pushed the last several ounces of alcohol into the blood stream.

"Damn these stairs seem to be moving," I said to my self.

"Be quiet Decker, the tactical officer is down in "C" barracks." My roomy Bamberg had been waiting for me to get back for over two hours.

"Okay, okay."

Rounding the stairway railing, the wind started to make a low howling as it passed through the limbs of the trees. The stench of stale beer was everywhere. As the last few that I had consumed had dribbled and spilled. But on I plowed towards the apex of the barracks, bound to get to the final resting space and crash.

"Halt! Who's going there on the regimental stoop?"

"Freeze, and maybe, just maybe, he'll forget I'm here. After all it's dark and he doesn't know who it is yet." I thought.

"I said STOP and identify yourself cadet!" Lt. Col. Graden knew damn well that it could only be one of two people, because no one else lived above regimental headquarters but Bamberg and Decker. The flashlight suddenly flooded my face and the upper doorway where Bamberg stood. Along with the Sally Port floodlight the entire area was brighter than a noonday sun.

"Damn Decker, what in the hell are you doing out here?"

The stench of the beer answered that as Graden came strolling up, to the stairwell. Busted and no excuse was going to get me out of this situation with just idle chatter.

"Sorry Col. Graden, I really messed up tonight. Can't you give me a break, just this once? You know for the team and all?"

"Decker, being out of your room is one thing, but you're filthy drunk. I could lose my position and possibly my commission for not reporting an offense like this." The tone of his voice was enough of a sober slap that ten cups of coffee couldn't have done more. Waves of nausea flooded not only my stomach, but also every other part of my body.

"Oh shit." Bamberg muttered to himself, knowing well what the outcome of this was going to be in the end.

"Come on Col. Graden. The only ones that know about this are you, Bamberg and I. It will never go beyond us, I promise." Every ounce of my heart was in those words, coming from the innermost recesses of my soul.

"Bamberg, give Decker a hand and get him to bed. We will finish dealing with this situation in the morning."

The plea had been totally discounted and the matter of fact way that his closing statement had been spoken, closed the issue in its entirety. There was no use in trying to further the conversation because Graden was on his way to the duty office. Pure anguish creased Bamberg's face as he reached for a grip to aid me in making those final few steps to the room. Riveted to what had just taken place, no way was sleep in any form going to visit this body tonight. Hours drifted in unison with no real time passing, thoughts making it useless to try and concentrate. A wrenching was going on inside that threatened to tear my guts out. "Why the hell didn't I leave with everyone else, dammit. No Decker, you had to stay and play the big man and see, you lost." Statements kept revolving through my brain, regardless facts were facts. Damage had been done, that was in no way going to be changed. The breaking of the sunrise was to bring another major phase of change to my life. At the same time, one of the most tender and close acts of bonding that I had ever witnessed was about to unfold.

A light drizzle had coated the entire quadrangle in a soft mist that Saturday morning. Overcast skies mirrored the mood already spreading with the news of the previous night's event. Less than a half hour and the entire compound was aware of the circumstances. Over the loudspeaker came the order:

"Decker, Michael J., report to the commandant's office." Thunder couldn't have announced what was about to take place any louder. It was the longest walk I had ever experienced as I finished that last flight of steps. Four command officers and the commandant himself were waiting in the office as I opened the door.

"Cadet Decker, front and center."

"Yes sir commandant." My dress uniform was perfect to the smallest detail. Countless hours of spit shining had put a wet gloss like glass on my boots. The firmness of the attention stance was one of statue like form with every medal and piece of brass polished to sheer brilliance on the lapels of my starched collar.

"Cadet Decker, I have just finished going over the report from Lt. Col Graden and to say that I am disappointed isn't even close. You had such a strong career ahead of you here with scholarship offers from several colleges already. Not to mention, the military and the corporate world beckoning with open arms and wallets. How could you take a dumb chance like that?"

"No excuse sir." The reply was quick, but the "HAD" in the commandant's statement told my heart what decision was on the table before me.

"That's right Cadet Decker there isn't one damn excuse that could possibly change the immense stupidity on your behalf."

As he continued to lecture me the weight of lost pride, spirit and purpose began land sliding upon me. Knowing what was about to be stated, the reality of having to go back and live with Glen made me wretched, but it was my own damn fault. Nothing more said could have brought me down any farther. In fact several minutes passed in conversation that were inaudible as my thoughts began to anticipate what the final outcome of going home was to bring.

"So in closing Cadet Decker, let me say that the decision of this panel is to expel you from the institution effective at 0900 hours this morning. You will pack your trunk and be off campus by that time. Arrangements have been made for bus tickets back to Albuquerque where you will rendezvous with your family. Is that clear, Cadet Decker?"

"Yes, sir, Commandant Saunders."

"Then you are dismissed."

A salute was my final act as a cadet that morning in October, I turned aboutface and marched out of the office. Stepping down to the pavement on the Sally Port, my eyes were full of tears, of pain, and frustration. The bugle calling company's to muster and form ranks for breakfast was blowing at a high pitch. Roughly one thousand cadets, new ones running and old cadets walking quickly to their respective company areas, marking off and coming to parade rest, in their stance. Company commanders and first sergeants yelling orders of "dress right...dress" "parade rest" finally "Attention."

Leaving this position of the barracks gave me the entire field of view of all company's, a view that had bred pride and determination for the past two years. We were one hell of a group of men, the group had just one less member in their ranks that early morning.

As I stood there taking in all of this one last time, an announcement came over the loud speaker.

"Cadets attention." The entire group came to attention at the sound of the command and there was no doubt from the voice who it was.

"This morning Cadet Michael John Decker was expelled from the ranks of this fine institution. The offense was for drinking alcoholic beverages and being out of quarters. Cadet Decker has been one of the finest cadets both athletically and in military academics this institution has ever produced. His dismissal is a tragedy both to himself and NMMI. The message needed to be understood and lived by every cadet at this institution, that this type of behavior WILL NOT BE TOLERATED in any form. As of this announcement Cadet Decker is a civilian and will be treated as such. Company commanders take charge of your respective units."

The whirl of comments uttered under peoples breath was heard everywhere, eyes of all the teammates from the football team were on me standing there at the end of the quadrangle. The first to break ranks was Bill Mattox, our big offensive tackle from Midland, Texas. Within seconds my buddies were leaving ranks from throughout the field, heading straight toward me.

Company commanders started to object at first and then seeing the futility of the act gave in. It was an experience not only to and for me, but the entire institution. By the time most of the guys were getting to me, men from the junior college barracks were coming as well.

After some initial goodbyes my closest friends from the team made the climb to the room, here was about twenty guys crying and giving me hugs. I knew that I would miss these dudes more than life, very quickly. It was a fraternity I didn't want to leave. Most of them were closer than family, this was the type of closeness the New Mexico Military Institute bred in young men.

Packing didn't take long and the cab awaited me upon reaching the Sally Port and the circle drive beyond. This was the same circle drive that mom and Glen had let me off at two years earlier. Arriving at the bus station gave me many reflecting moments to sort out. Like whether or not I might get some other ticket and maybe just take off. It was very tempting but the result was something that I didn't want to deal with later. So two hours later, I was sitting on the northbound Greyhound and heading back to where hell began. "Oh God, what is it going to be like this time?" The words came out echoing from my mouth.

Albuquerque hadn't changed in the two odd years since I had lived there. The Sandia mountains, and the Rio Grande valley beyond still stretched endlessly to the north and south, cottonwoods lining the river for miles beyond where the eye could see. Martineztown and Bernalillo, along with Belen were just as dirty and dusty as before. Neon lights and their flood lamp backups still glowed bright from the upper stories of the First National Bank building. Sandia and Kirkland Air Force Base were still overshadowing the Sunport, Albuquerque's version of an International Airport. First through Fifth Street downtown had the usual wino and streetwalker on duty, and the Greyhound bus terminal kept all facilities moving twenty-four hours a day.

As the big rig came pulling into the station it was 7:34 pm, and a long ride for just two hundred miles. Of course with that distance came twenty-three stops at every trading post and hamlet. With an average stop of fifteen to twenty minutes, thank God it wasn't two thousand miles.

Mom was waiting there as I came down the aisle of the bus, dressed in slacks and a warm fur trimmed coat, to keep her neck warm. As always a look of love on her face, though somewhat reserved, but still that warmth of a true mother showed through. There was a slight furrow to her brow, worry of what lies beyond I'm sure. The biggest surprise was that Glen was not there.

"Where's Glen?" I just knew he was waiting around the corner in the car.

"He's out of town for a week or two taking care of the Farmington and Aztec schools."

How could I be so lucky? What a relief to not have to put up with his guff for few days.

"I'm sorry, Mom, really sorry."

That was all it took. The tears started to flow with a tremble from her lower lip. Pain, which I had caused, was searing her heart and leaving another scar.

"Why, Mike, why would you take such a chance?"

"I know, Mom, it just happened, I didn't mean for it to."

"I know you didn't mean for it to happen, but you can't be doing this kind of thing. Glen is going to hit the roof. When he called today I just couldn't tell him. It's me that gets the harsh words and punishment, not just you."

The words cut deep as they were thrust through my heart. Once again I was the cause of something unsettling in the household. Not just unsettling but the brunt of this situation was going to reverberate for months to come. Glen never just dealt with it one time. It would be brought and thrown back in my face a hundred times.

"I called Del Norte today and they will let you start on Monday. Coach McGinnis and Coach Nesbitt were excited about you coming back. They have been keeping up with your statistics while you were down at NMMI."

We had been in the car for about ten minutes when she made this statement, knowing that it would break the icy chill and heavy tension in the air. She always wanted to be the peacekeeper.

"Thanks Mom, you didn't have to do that, but I really appreciate it. It will be good to see a lot of my old friends from public school. I'm sure that a lot of them are still in this school district."

"Yes, and I also called Glenn Von Dreele to let him know you would be returning to Del Norte."

Glenn and I had been friends since fourth grade in Mrs. Hixenbaugh's class at Inez Elementary School. A little sunshine, just a small ray of hope glimmered through the darkness. Maybe, just maybe, it wasn't going to be so terrible after all.

"Thank you for not telling Glen, yet."

"Well I will wait until you are back in the swing of things at school before I do. But let me tell you there will be absolutely no extracurricular activities except for football for some time to come. Is that clear?"

"Yes, mother, I know."

"You had better really knuckle down in your studies as well."

"Mom, I have been doing real good in every subject at NMMI."

"I realize that but this is not the study like environment or setting of the institution."

She was right, because good grades and high performance were not only expected, but also demanded at the institution. This included a two-hour study period every night.

Driving up in the carport brought with it a relief. Finally, a good night's rest and tomorrow is a new day, things would be okay in a few days. The white stucco was gleaming from the reflection of the street lamp. The turquoise trim freshly painted added a nice highlight around the windows and doors. A familiar bark came from the backyard. My friend, my bud, was smelling me and just enjoying knowing that I was home.

"Chico, hey guy, what's going on? Did you miss me?"

Jumping all over me with his tail thrashing everywhere, and everything around him, his big wet tongue slurping my face as I knelt, low enough or tried to kneel beside him. For as soon as I got low enough, he bowled me over and gave me an attack welcome.

His coat was so thick and had a luster from brushing and constant care. I knew that my mom had done this for me. She had two little Poodles named Mimi and BoBo, they absolutely loved Chico and would play endlessly with him out in the backyard. Chico was so patient and gentle with the smaller dogs. I knew in my heart that he would be a source of strength and comfort for me in days and months to come.
"Good night Mom, thank you for kind of understanding."
"Good night Mike, please say your prayers tonight. God will help you get through this."

I gave her a good bear hug and it was off to bed. After no rest for almost forty-eight hours my body was beginning to slow down. After saying my prayers, or having a little talk with whoever God really was, I drifted off to sleep.

Monday morning was here and showing itself early. I had awakened around five o'clock. The morning sun was just breaking over the crest of the Sandia's. A slight frost coated the lawn and the trees outside, with a silver hue. Brilliant clear blue skies, cloudless and pristine framed the view from my bedroom window. Chico's hot breath had caused a small ice patch on the sliding glass door at the back of the house. He had almost a grin on his face as I walked through the living room and on to the kitchen.

Mom had gotten up early, and the smell of fresh blueberry pancakes filled the air. She was standing there in her favorite apron with the big flowers on it, one that Nana, her mother, had given her years before. There were a few spots of flour on the edge where it had touched the batter ever so slightly, and she had on fuzzy pink house shoes to keep her feet all snug and warm.
"Oh, mom, you didn't have to go to any trouble, I could have just had cereal. But thank you very much." The words came as I walked up beside her and placed my arm around her shoulders.

For some reason she seemed shorter than I remembered. Gosh, I must have grown some more.

The pancakes were like normal, incredible, cooked nice and light with butter, a load of syrup, and a jumbo glass of milk, about a quart. She had kept my monster glass, my favorite because of its size. It was accompanied by a large glass of orange juice and I was set for the first day of classes.

It was three and a half miles to the campus, the walk was always a great way to get everything working and the blood pumping. I left an extra thirty minutes early, just so I could have some time to catch a few of my old friends before the day got into full swing. Only six cars were in the parking lot by the time my steps were carrying me across Montgomery Blvd., the main east-west corridor in the heights. All but one of the cars was in the teacher's lot, but the next thirty minutes would bring them in by the hundreds.

That first week came and went with no real dramatic events. Which was just as well, as the public school system was so major different from the orderly run system of NMMI, I had truly forgotten how noisy and chaotic it was. Most of the same teachers were still at Del Norte and the entire coaching staff was there. The Knights, as the team was so named, had a fair team. Even though they were four "A" and had a student body of over three thousand, the comparison of this unit and the one I had left was enormous. It wasn't nearly as physical or tough.

Wednesday of the following week Glen returned from his trip to northern New Mexico. Oddly enough, he didn't say or do much of anything. Almost too quiet was the mood around the house, like maybe he was planning something to get back at me, I really didn't know.

What took place the following weekend struck me like a lightning bolt. Saturday morning I awoke to find Chico staggering and listless in the backyard. He had thrown up several times and had several bowel movements, his eyes were glazed and a hot nose told me that getting him to the vet was the only thing to do. By midday Chico had collapsed and was being fed by I.V. We had found out that eleven other dogs in the neighborhood had been poisoned. All but Chico was found dead and lifeless. He was so strong and his size had given him a chance. It was like I was lying there dying with him. Chico "knew" things I had never told anybody else, and had witnessed events never discussed outside my room. No one could ever know how he had been the one that had saved me from so many "shut downs."

The concrete floor of the clinic was cold and the medicinal smell permeated my nose. The clanging of cages and barking animals filled the air. Gasping for air, Chico lay on his left side with eyes only partially open.

"Oh God please don't let him die. He has been so good to me and everybody." Tears fell from my face at the sight of him laying there suffering.

" Why did this have to happen?"

"It's just not fair."

Chico had me as a companion every day for almost three weeks, after school. On weekends I spent the whole day with him. He sure as hell would have done the same for me, he already had. But on November 16, 1966 he went to the big mountain ranch in the sky. The vet told me that he did not know how he lingered as long as he had, with the level of toxic chemicals in his blood.

The return home that day was one of emptiness, a void hung in the air and throughout the house. I was mad and sad and just wanted to be alone. As I walked through the house mom was sitting in the living room reading, her moist eyes told me what she felt. Her love for Chico was second only to mine, she realized what an important part of my life he was and the loss was going to leave a hole. Glen never said a damn thing but that was no big surprise, he was a bastard anyway.

It just gave me one more reason to hate him. His not caring was the standard act for anything that meant something special to any of the rest of the family.

Just before Christmas that year, 1966, a letter came from NMMI. It stated that the board of directors had reviewed my expulsion and made a new directive on my case. They stated," Michael Decker will have the option and opportunity to return to the institute for the spring semester. Upon doing so his cadet status will be reinstated and have the chance to graduate with his class of 1967." To say the least I was shocked at the invitation, how they had made the decision was a mystery to me. Normally when a decision had been made, it was final with no rescision possible. God had been looking out for me in a way that I not only didn't recognize, but also discounted.

Mom was excited, Glen was indifferent and I couldn't make my mind up. The weighing factor was the new flame in my life, Patty Hunt. She was five foot seven, with blonde hair and blue eyes and the most beautiful girl (to date) that I had ever been with. Her stepfather was William Rockefeller and came from the "money" way of life. She had been the homecoming queen and her reputation was that she only dated college and older guys. This was a challenge that I took and never looked back. The weekend following the receipt of the letter I decided not to return to NMMI, though in years to come there would be times that I questioned the depth of my decision. The spring semester at Del Norte did little to further any part of my life other than the social area.

January through May was spent getting by in school and having the occasional runin with Glen. I hardly saw him the entire semester as I was up and gone before he would awake. He would be out in his office when I came home from practice and I went to bed before he came into the house for the evening.

Patty and I fell in love during this time, and we spent a lot of time together. The prom was okay but left no indelible mark on either of us. We were ready to graduate and get on with our lives.

The one promise, I can ever remember Glen keeping was that he would buy me a car at graduation time. Shortly before senior week was to begin, my social studies teacher had advertised his Mopar. A 1964 Belvedere Plymouth, four-speed, with a 426 Hemi, pearl white with blue leather interior, totally set up for the drag strip and only 12,000 miles. What a boss car, and Glen and my mother had no idea what a racecar they were buying for me. It turned in the mid tens at the drag strip. Thus senior week was a blast and thank God I didn't kill anybody or demolish myself during those seven days.

Shortly after graduation I moved into an apartment with one of my friend's older brother. I had been working at Montgomery Ward's in the Winrock shopping center for a couple of months. Patty had been sneaking out on a pretty regular basis and spending a good deal of time at my place.

On one Friday night in particular she had come over and we were hot and heavy in the bedroom when a loud pounding started on the front door.
"Open this damn door. Michael, I know Patty is in there."

It was her folks in a rage outside. I peaked through the curtains of the bedroom window to verify the source.
"God, Patty what are we going to do." Both of us buck naked, we began to jerk clothes on, red faced and sweating from the sexual pleasures being enjoyed for the past hour.
"Oh shit, maybe we can just be quiet and they will leave."

As the words were stuttered from Patty's lips a reply was being delivered from the door beyond.
"If you don't open this door in two seconds we are calling for the police to come and open it for us." Her mother Charlotte was the mother from hell, and I knew that she was dead serious. That was referring to dead serious over my bones.

Heading for the door I said to Patty, "Babe, it's better to face this right now and get it over with."

Fear and the unknowing gripped her face and was causing my throat to tighten as I reached for the door.
"It's about damn time! Just what in the hell do you think you're doing here, young lady? This crap is over and done with FOREVER. Get your things, Patty, we are going home now." The look on her mother's face accompanied the words and stopped any reply that Patty even remotely thought of making.
"This is my fault. I know you said that you didn't want us being here

alone. Please blame me not, Patty."

"Michael this is not the first time. We both know that so don't try and make it out to be. There is no excuse for this behavior, and our daughter will not be a part of it!" Her father was laying down the law with no exceptions.

"Patty, I'll call you later." I was going to at least get two cents in.

"Don't bother, she will not be talking to you anymore and that's final!" Cutting through to the core, her mother meant it for real. With tears flowing down her cheeks, Patti ran to the car, embarrassed, ashamed and hurt beyond words. At first I was sad, but anger flowed even greater within me. Sitting there and drinking a beer, it began to boil inside of me. I have to do something, I can't just let this go like this. Statements of reasoning kept coming to my mind until I knew what the action necessary would be. Go and talk to her parents, face to face. No matter what it would take, I would work it out and make it better for Patty.

Grabbing the key to the Mopar, I jerked on a T-shirt and my shoes. Thunder roared from that big hemi, as the engine caught. Five hundred and ninety horsepower of pure speed was about to launch into orbit. Smoke billowed from the Goodyear racing slicks as I pulled from the parking lot. Patty I'm on my way, drifted across my mind as the white stallion sped to the rescue.

Ding-ding-dong, the vibrations could be felt outside as the chimes played their tune, announcing my arrival. Waiting and wondering what to say, I shifted weight from one side to the other. The door suddenly opened and Patty's Dad stepped out to confront me.

"You have not one bit of reason to be anywhere near here, NOW LEAVE!"

"Please, Mr. Rockefeller, just give me two minutes to talk to you and your wife. Just two minutes, and I will go if you insist." Pleading for a chance, I stood waiting for an answer. Knowing all too well how easy it would be for him to throw the door closed in my face. Please, please just one chance I said to myself. He just stood there, the silence so loud I could hardly stand it. Mrs. Rockefeller hearing the commotion peaked around the doorway.

"Oh God what now? Don't you ever give up?"

"No, not when it comes to Patty. Please, just give me a couple of minutes to talk to you and I will leave."

"Okay, two minutes and my watch will be ticking."

Two hours later I left holding Patty's hand, as she walked me to the door. The ultimatum given me was harsh, but fair as well.

First off I had to leave the apartment and move back home. To accomplish this, I had to also sell my car. This was a choice directed by my parents as a condition for moving. Additionally, I had to join the service and get some education behind me. This was not a problem, as the draft was in full force and several of my friends had already enlisted. Any dating done between Patty and I would be on a very, selected basis and with both parents approval.

Finally, one mess up and it was final curtains for Patty and me forever. I agreed to each and every term of the agreement, and carried out the requirements to the fullest extent possible.

My enlistment date was for the twenty-third of August 1967. This meant that I had only two weeks left to spend with Patty and say any goodbyes. U.S. Navy here I come!

CHAPTER 2

first Marriage and Vietnam

San Diego, California August 1967, was a turbulent time. Far across the oceans, some sixteen thousand miles away, America's youth were dying. They were dying for a cause, which at best was questioned by both politician and civilian alike. "Are we the world's peacekeeper," everyone was asking. Demonstrations and rallies were taking place nation wide. Lyndon Johnson was trying to run the country from his pocket book, and the crooks that surrounded his cabinet and "his war."

Me, I'm headed for boot camp and the wild blue yonder. For the next four plus years the U.S. Navy will consume everything that has anything to do with my life. Stepping down from the Navy bus shuttle Chief Edwards greets the new recruits with warmth.

"Get your panzy asses off the fucking bus and stand at attention, on one of those white spots. God what a sorry bunch of seaman! You bastards will wish that your mommy's had kept you home. Do you understand?"

Only six people of the group of thirty-five made a sound. My voice boomed above the rest, this wasn't the first muster I had attended.
"Yes, Sir."
"Don't you pussy's know how to talk?"
"Yes, Sir." Finally most of the guys were getting the picture. Chief Edwards was painting the piece with large colors and wanted it to be noticed.
"These next sixteen weeks are mine, you're mine. Whatever and wherever you little shits came from, I don't care. From this second forward the world you exist in is my world, mine and the U.S. Navy. Any fucking thing you need to know, I'll tell ya. If I didn't tell ya, it didn't need to be told. Now grab your cocks and your socks and make a double column. It's time to get all that damn fur cut off. Company 626, Forrrrward March!"

The ragtag struggling company of the 626 started their military existence. The sun was glaring down at noontime force, at ninety-one degrees, the wind was not enough to wiggle a gnats wings. The blacktop was soft from that big heater in the sky, radiating with a heat index of 125 degrees.
"I said march, not stroll. Listen to the count. Left-left-left-right-left, left-left-left-right-left. Stop looking around or I'll break your damn neck, sailor! All you need to see is the neck fuzz in front of you!"
"Company, halt." You can only imagine the stopping precision.
"Dammit, that means stop!" Chief Edwards was going to have his hands full. Only one other man, other than myself, had any background in marching and formation movement. Thank God for NMMI.
"Before you pencil necks get trimmed, is there any one of you buttheads that knows how to march?"
"Yes, sir, Chief. I've had two years military school and Army R.O.T.C."
"What's your name, mister?"
"Decker, Michael J. B725026, sir, from Texas." I said with a little extra zeal and pride.
"Texas, I heard there are only steers and queers in Texas, Decker. Which are you?" From the sarcastic tone and the smart-ass grin on his face, I knew he was loving this.
"I guess a steer, Chief, because I'm sure not a damn queer."
Well, well, so you think you can run these seaman as the Recruit Chief Petty Officer? Are your balls big enough?"
"Yes, sir."
"Well then 626, this is your new RCPO. Any comments or complaints that you have will come through him. Decker, you are now in charge of this company, anytime I'm not around. Is that understood?"
"Yes, sir."
   Damn, in the Navy fifteen minutes and already got a promotion. At this rate I'll be an admiral by Christmas. I had to pride myself with a few pats on the back. With that out of the way, Chief showed us the door of the barbershop. It was a concrete building, gray with black trim with two doors on the street side of the building. We lined up in single file and filled the three chairs. Thus the three barbers went to town, very closely looking like they were shearing sheep back on the ranch. I was last in the line and so I got to see the first few as they left the exit door. They were bald as cue balls. The remaining men were gasping and stifling laughter, striving to stay in formation.
   As I took my turn, I turned to the barber and said, "Just take a little off the top."

He nodded and took the clippers one swipe across the top and handed me the result.

"About this much?" He chided in.

With that statement, he proceeded to skin me just like the rest of 626. The entire process took less than ten minutes, no wasted time or motion.

"Fall in, fall in. That means for you cue balls to get in formation, just like you did coming off the bus."

Quickly, though somewhat disorganized still, we got into place. I took my position at point right, and noticing that Chief Edwards was standing silently with a stare, waiting. I shouted,

"Company, forward march!" My first official duty had been carried out, and the blazing sun felt much hotter on all of our lily white scalps. Thank God, the next stop was clothing issue and a hat.

That entire day was spent getting all the gear and I.D. cards, stowing everything away. Our barracks were on the south corner of the compound area, so it was somewhat isolated from the entire facility. With twenty-two hundred men, seaman apprentices in rank, in boot camp and somewhere around 12,000 active and civilian workers on the base, it was a very busy installation.

Finally, catching the chow hall at five thirty, that first blast of Navy food wasn't bad, not quite as good as NMMI, but in the same ballpark. Moving the men back to the barracks, per Chief Edwards' previously given order, after completion of the meal, the entire evening was to be spent learning how to wash, dry, fold and perfectly arrange all of the clothing issued in the small lockers. It was scrub brush and cleanser, with mountains of elbow grease and a sixty-foot long stainless steel trough, with thirty water faucets. Standing there in our skivvies and scrubbing the Jesus out of our brand new clothing, we were learning very quickly the difference between regular white and "Navy White." Remarkably enough there is a noticeable difference, and anything less was totally unacceptable. Chief Edwards made this redundantly clear and thorough. Locker storage was next. Not just throw it in, but each and every single, individual piece, smoothed, press folded to exactly the same width and stacked uniformly and straight. Underwear, socks, t-shirts, and whites, all arranged so that when the locker door is opened it looked like a neatly stored display. For some of the guys this meant folding and refolding and restacking, over and over until it was a perfected act. This was routine and basic for me because NMMI had already predicated this skill and habit. Finally the 626 got it right as a group and Chief Edwards made the announcement.

"All right, you peckerwoods, you've got thirty seconds to get it ready because lights are falling." There was a scramble to the pisser and head, grabbing a toothbrush or any other necessary implement and quick. The sight was quite amusing, black-white-brown-yellow bodies running here and there, boxer shorts flying around the barracks completing last minute tasks. It was ten o'clock and seemed much later, but the adrenalin was pumping through these men and no one knew they were tired, yet.

"Okay, 626, we've got five seconds," my reminder to the company that wasting time, was "burning daylight," as we say back home in Texas.

On the dot of thirty seconds from command, Chief switched the darkness on. The sound to be heard, was rustling sheets and squeaking bunks, used by countless thousands, maybe ten thousands, fart here, cough there, chuckle multiple places.

"Damn Loeding, nice fart," Smitty whispered, a grin crossing his face, "sounds like everything is working okay."

"All right, you shit heads, no noise and get to sleep. You will wish for every single second of rest tomorrow. I'm going to work off those little monkey butts of yours."

With that, Edwards slammed the door and headed for the NCO club. At least, that was what I assumed was the destination. That big beer belly was not grown overnight, but looked to have been well fed on a nightly basis.

Within seconds of the departing Chief and his footsteps fading, the chatter began to flow.

"Decker, do you think we will all make it?" Peterson from South Carolina asked, the twang deep and drawled to the slowest possible point, skinny as a rail post and hair almost white. His Dad still made a living in the area around Placerville, making moonshine. He had let many of us know that at night chow.

"Hell, yes. There won't be a better company than the 626 anywhere on the compound in a few weeks." I was going to give it my best and pass on everything that I learned at the Institute.

"Shit, Decker did you really go to military school?" Smitty, the cocky dude from California asked. He was a surfer, but pretty cool with all that beach lingo that many of us had never heard, before. His family supposedly had the big bucks.

"Damn right I did and it was great training, it will pay off here in boot camp and beyond."

Conversation flowed for a few minutes, and then died out as sleep took over the barracks. For many of us the day had begun some twenty hours before, from across the nation we had come to embark on a military commitment.

Down deep in my heart I knew that some, a few, would not cut the mustard. Whether it was the physical push or the mental strain, some would falter, taking what they would think at the time to be the easier route. Lessons played out here though would realistically become life scripts for the most of us.

I lay awake for several hours planning the following days blueprint. Sleep hadn't been important to me for many years, and I began to think about the program. Chief Edwards was going to be tough, he was a salty old boatswain's mate who had been on "sea duty" for most of his military career. He knew only one way, "his," I would have to stay very alert and read him closely. The efficiency I showed would give me more responsibility. Truly I wanted the 626 to be the best. Second place, was last in my way of thinking, we would be physically strong, mentally tough and prepared.

Finally in the early hours of the morning I fell asleep, yet even in the dreams I was still preparing for what may lie ahead of me. Along comes the ticking of the clock, 4:45a.m.

"All right, you lazy shits. Rise your butts out of those fart sacks and hit the deck." The boom of Edwards' voice was added to a nightstick banging a trashcan lid. Hit the deck is what several of the guys did, they were so startled that they flew butt first to the deck.

Eyes looking wild, pee hards (erections) thrusting from many pairs of boxers, scrambling for position at the end of the bunk line and snapping to what many "thought" was attention.

"All right, sailors. Attention! Maybe someday, a fuckin' sailor. Stand up tall; suck those guts in tight. Chin up and eyes straight ahead. The only thing that you should see in front of you is that ugly bastard," pointing to the man across the rack from one side to the other.

"You have got five minutes to dress and make your racks. Store your gear and square everything away. Decker, get your company mustered outside in five minutes."

"Yes sir Chief. All right, guys, let's move it."

Chief walked slowly out the door. Stopping to pick up a huge coffee cup, that he had put down before waking us. The redness of his eyes showed me that I was right about his destination of choice, after leaving the night before.

Sheets flapping and pants getting legs thrust through them, t-shirts being yanked down over heads, arms pushing quickly in the sleeves. Brogans being tied and hats straightened and creased.

"All right, 626, let's hit the compound and get into formation."

Racing for the doorway, the first full day of Navy life was about to unfold and present itself. That moist sea smell flooded our nostrils and gave a slight sting to those not used to the salty air. A light cloud cover was moving through and the sun was breaking the horizon with golden, orange shafts of light. Seagulls were squawking as they watched the men coming from the chow hall in the compound, many tidbits tossed over countless days and groups of men. Two other recruit companies came marching by, from the precision displayed it showed that they had been here for some time.

"Fall in men, Chambers front right, dress-right-dress."

"Attention. Chief Edwards, ready to march to chow."

"Well then take them to chow and back here in twenty minutes."

"Company 626, right face, forward march, left-left, left-right-left." The sound of marching brought back vivid memories of NMMI, but these guys had a world to learn before coming close.

After chow the balance of the day was consumed with drilling and making the shot line, vaccinations for everything known to man. The air guns that the corpsman used were nasty. They would always turn up the pressure before the first man was shot. Shooting a "test shot" in the air, it would fly twenty feet or more through the air. Eyes were bulging with anticipation, lips pursed and tight jawed, readying themselves for the blast.

When the serum hit the skin it would puff up and look like a wound for a few minutes. Like the line outside the barbershop, the first few guys in made grimaces and acted like it was terrible. Just to give the men in the line fits, while they waited there "patiently."

The thermostat climbed back up in the nineties by midday so the tarmac was steaming for the afternoon drilling. Men who had done no exercise in months or in some cases years, paid the price. Blisters were given out to almost everyone by the new brogans. Some twenty companies had started together with the 626. Thus the compound was adorned with whites from side to side, commands being given and language used that needs no repeating to visualize.

Day in and day out for the next three weeks was the way the schedule continued. There was some improvement in the quality of marching, but not enough for Chief Edwards or myself.

Back in the barracks one of the following nights, after the Chief had made his exit, I had decided to have private drill session. There was no other way to get the 626 to the point of precision necessary to be the best.

"626. Fall in around the bunk area. We need to have a talk."

"What the fuck is this all about? This is supposed to be free time." Smitty thought he would push the limit of just how much authority I felt I could show. I didn't have any problem showing any level necessary to complete the task at hand.

" Smitty, we have got a lot of work to do and some things we can accomplish here will save a lot of grief out on the compound. So just shut your mouth and learn something."

The glare came but nothing to back it up. Seeing this, the rest of the men fell in and we started going over the basics with a little extra thrown in. It was amazing what transpired in such a short amount of time. Within three days the 626 was a totally different company in drill. The sessions had built with them a comradeship that began to work as a unit. This unity was the integral part missing in the previous weeks and the link necessary for advancement and perfection.

Chief Edwards was amazed, the look on his face showed it. Of course, no comment was made, who would expect a compliment? By the fourth week of training, we began seeing the films about the various ratings and jobs that were available to us, and which schools we could qualify for and also possible career choices. At this same time they showed a film about the U.D.T. that stands for the Underwater Demolition Teams, with a short section on the Navy's elite men the S.E.A.L.S. Instantly I knew that the training and this kind of elite force was where I wanted to be. The stories of the S.E.A.L.S. were legends from all branches of the service. Everyone knew who the best was and I wanted no other.

During these first four weeks the letters from Patty kept up at a rate of four to five per week. We had a chance only once to talk on the phone, she sounded in good spirits and was missing my company. Busy with work and school, she was keeping herself occupied.

After viewing the films, it was very evident that I was going to have to be in the best physical condition of my young life. So, every chance I got, no matter how short the time period, I was making my body stronger. Each night after lights out I had been practicing my katas and stretching. Yet more was necessary to attain the level of excellence necessary to make the cut for UDT, my body was at a stage being nineteen, of rapid development. All the countless hours in the weight room and the sport programs at NMMI had built a base. This, with the early punishment of the Platoro schedule, had left a very strong body. Quick reactions and flexibility from the years of martial arts dedication was an immense benefit.

During the eighth weeks of training the notice came about a physical fitness test as a prelim to qualifying for the UDT group. It was to be the following Thursday afternoon. After the first day of the showing of the "bad boys in black," my nickname for the UDT film, I was in the chow hall and another recruit named Jim Loeding said he was really interested in the teams. This resulted in an immediate friendship developing between us.
    Jim was from the northern part of Utah, and had been in R.O.T.C. before. He was very well built, 6', 200 pounds, with sandy brown hair and wide set piercing eyes. His eyes had this darkness in them that held you with their deep "knowing" gleam. He had been training with his father for almost seven years in the art of Akido. His father was a second degree, blackbelt and had been studying for over twenty years.
"Well, Loeding, are you ready for tomorrow?"
"Damn straight. Let's do it to them, with a vengeance."
"Me too. I'm ready to kick some major butt. Probably be hotter than hell tomorrow." We both had the streamers bursting in air inside. Tomorrow was D-Day.
    The test was given to about sixty men, from several different companies and levels of completion at the recruit facility. Three men, who were members of the UDT/SEAL base out at Coronado-North Island had come down to NTC San Diego to administer the test.
    The physical condition of these three guys was very easily observed. "Muscles in their shit," was a common comment. They had laid out a test that would encompass many arena of fitness, running, exercising and swimming, to show all strengths as well as weaknesses. "All right, men, this is the test for today. You will run a mile run, to begin with, followed by three hundred situps and two hundred fifty pushups. Then to the pool for a one thousand yard swim. Only the breaststroke or the crawl can be used in the swim, finally an eight hundred yard sprint on the track and fifty pullups. We will be counting and timing each and every event and section of the evaluation. Do your best. Because if you don't finish one section, this doesn't mean that you have failed the entire test, so do your best."
"Any questions before we begin?"
"Yeah, how many guys are the UDT looking for?" It came from a tall skinny guy in the back of the group. Several of us chuckled when they turned and saw his stature and build. It was Peterson from the "moonshine" country and the "group" was going to be in for a surprise. This guy was an absolute gazelle when he ran, he was tireless and had run cross country in high school. Also, he had been on the swim team as well, so I was sure that he probably swam like a barracuda.

"No certain number, just quality men, for the test here today and the sixteen week basic UDT course with 'HELL WEEK' thrown in cuts the number of completions to a minimum."
"Let's get started."

As expected the long legs of Peterson were soon burning everyone's butt in the mile run. His stride was graceful and the arm movement fluid and in unison. His blonde hair had grown out to about one half inch since the buzz, and glowed with the bright West Coast sunshine.

Loeding and I were in the front ten or so and competing with each other, as well as the group. We crossed the finish line with him in third and me in fifth, as the finish line was crossed the three leaders were yelling:
"All right, give me the 300 situps and the 250 pushups. Buddy up and count each other. If you cheat, you are cheating yourself and UDT. We don't take cheaters."

The words were understood, let there be no mistake. A shortfall in number here was one thing, one in the jungles under fire was quite another. We understood and believed, in what was said that day.
"Get your ass crunching, Loeding. Push it, Bubba."

Loeding and I had buddied up and were pushing one another. The sweat faucet had been turned on to full pour. Both of us were soaked and driving to the completion of the two exercise groups. Smoking through both sets, we had caught up with Peterson and were racing for the pool area.
"All right, Moonshine, I'm going to smoke your butt in the Pool."
"Yeah, Loeding, in your dreams." Petersons long stride gliding him to the door of the pool area.
"Strip down to your trunks and hit the water. You will be doing fifty yard laps, so give me twenty laps."

I popped my shoes off with the toes of the opposite shoes, pulling my socks off and heading for the edge of the water, Jim was right on my heals.
"All right, Decker, let's see how well you learned to swim in that damned horse tank you told me about."

My grandfather had taught me how to swim at about eighteen months by grabbing me by the seat of the pants and throwing me head first in the horse tank. Of course, nearly scaring the life out of my mother, that is until she observed my little head coming to the surface.
"Okay, anchor ass, watch and see."

The water felt great, exhilarating, after the run and exercise. I stretched out long and cupping my hands got the maximum thrust from each kick and stroke of my arms. As the remaining recruits finished the run they would come rushing through the door and hit the water. One guy came through and was so excited he dove in and still had his tennis shoes and socks on.

"Hey, dude, you will probably swim a little better if you take those off." One of the instructors exclaimed, grinning.

"Yeah, right," feeling like the dumb butt of the day.

Only about forty guys finished the swim in the required amount of time. So, it was the final run and pullups that would show what you had to finish. Loeding was about twenty yards ahead of me when I hit the track, with two ahead of him. Yeah, Peterson was one of them. The muscles in the back of my legs had tightened during the swim, so the running felt good and the heat off the track warmed the tendons and ligaments as I ran.

I caught Loeding by the first turn and could tell by the tightness in his neck that he was beginning to push the barrier. I began a rhythm in my stride, not for speed, but for a cadence to keep up and flow with the group ahead. They were about thirty yards in front of me. By the six hundred yard marker I was dead even with the guy in second, and the position at that point was also the finishing order.

Tom Sanders, the guy next to me, from Florida, I would find was a hell of a competitor, now on to the pullups. By this stage of the test muscles were fatigued and the strength was ebbing, especially in the guys who had not been in any serious training.

"Come on, Loeding, run, dude."

Gasping he replied, "Damn where did the oxygen go? Don't feel like I'm getting any."

"We'll make it, let's head for the pullups."

My goal was to do three sets at this point, fifteen twice and twenty once, for the total of fifty. The first twenty flew and the next two sets went to three, fifteen, ten and five for the final set.

Peterson was fine and in front until the pullups, but they became his mountain. Even though I had so much more body weight, the muscles developed from years of punching and lifting weights and peeling logs and running a wheelbarrow, paid off.

"Come on, Peterson, pull your little skinny ass up there."

Loeding and I were not going to let him not finish. Sanders joined in the cheering and helped. As Peterson made the final chin, we busted loose with hoots and hollers. I think it was more of a release, than a celebration.

Overall I had finished first, with Loeding, Sanders and a guy from

Arizona, Bill Paxton rounding out the top four. Peterson finished fifth and there was no doubt that with some upper body workouts he was going to be a terror. His heart was already one of the biggest I had ever seen.

"Well we made it, Bubba, what do you think about that?"

"Yeah, Decker, we made it and I'm tired as shit."

We all had a grin, large in size, and were proud of the accomplishment of the afternoon. Knowing that the chance was before us, to go on and train to become the finest fighting men in the world. This was my opinion as it was that of many others, as well.

By the twelfth week of training, the balance and ability of the 626 was very evident. Marching was becoming automatic, and the step had a life to it now. There was no better unit on the compound and only one in fact that even came close. Their RCPO was from military school back east, so they had the extra training and a few "secrets" of their own.

Each day after chow I would march the 626 in some flash moves doing double obliques and full reverses. Regularly as we passed the west fence some of the local kids, civvies, would be driving by and yell something smart. On this particular day, I saw it coming and prepared the company.

"Company Halt. Right Face. Present Fingers."

The entire company flipped the bird in unison and it was truly funny. Looks on the receiving parties faces were in complete disbelief of what had just taken place. It seemed very appropriate action from where I stood.

As the holiday season was closing in for Christmas, the recruits had the option of going on leave for the holidays or waiting until the end of boot camp. There was a fifty percent split that decided to go home, and the balance of the companies combined, made up the units. These units had anywhere from four or five to twenty, from varying companies. Any remaining RCPO, like me, stayed in charge as far as the recruit chain of command was concerned. My group, "A" company, just like at NMMI was housed in the same section of barracks as I was previously assigned, making the transition much easier.

The first week of these temporary companies went fairly smooth. By the end of the week though, the guys who really wanted to go home but couldn't or didn't, were getting on edge. One such individual was assigned to me, what a shit head he turned out to be.

His name was Terry Miller, from somewhere around St. Louis or at least close. He came from some well-to-do family and rumor had it, he was a pretty tough guy back home. One Thursday night, just about midway through the holiday break he decided to test my water. After lights out, there was to be no jacking around, especially for the first hour or so. The Officer of the day, the OOD, checked fairly regularly. Anyone caught up or doing anything was going to get busted and the RCPO was going to get the same punishment. No way was I going to get in trouble for this asshole.

Sure enough, within fifteen minutes after lights out, Miller flames a cigarette right there in his bunk. This was a major infraction, and one that meant a write-up, which would be carried in your permanent file. At least I thought that it was a cigarette. It turned out to be a joint of marijuana, the telltale smell filling the air as I went to confront Miller.
"Miller, put that damn thing out, NOW!"
"Fuck you, Decker."
"What did you say, you fat little shit? I said to put that damn thing out now." I knew from the tone of my voice and my body language he could tell I was not playing games.
"Don't tell me what to do, I'll smoke when and where I want, understand?"
"The only thing I understand, you had better understand. That's to put that fucking butt out before I put you out."

The blood and adrenaline began to pulsate and the muscles in my hands began to contract automatically. My shoulders began to flex and my legs started to tighten and release.
"Oh, is that right, you think I'm scared?"
"I could really care less if you're scared Miller. This is my last statement." This son of a bitch was going to push the envelope too far, I could tell. Trying to play the "man' in front of all the other guys, he had no idea who or what he was about to take on. By this time the entire company was more than aware of the confrontation. Necks were craning and people were sitting up or standing to get a better view.
"Okay, Miller, we'll just settle this thing, once and for all. Meet me in the head." Being open with a terra cotta floor and approximately twenty by twenty foot, the head gave ample room to take care of the trouble at hand. Miller followed me to the head and the entourage followed him.
"Loeding, watch out for the Officer, Peterson, you man the door. I want you as a witness."

Peterson had at least ten extra helpers vying for good seats at the doorway. Loeding took the upper bunk by the far wall so that he could see the walkways from two other directions.

The swagger in Miller's steps showed that he thought it was a done deal with me. Standing about five ten and weighing near two fifty, he was thick. Yet, this only showed me a larger target to connect with.

"Miller, you won't know and understand what I am about to tell you, for some two or three minutes. But the lesson you are going to learn will stay with you for a long, long time."

"Talk's cheap, Decker."

With that statement he took a bounding stride and launched his husky frame at me. Swinging in big arcs with both hands, slipping first left and then right I allowed him to miss and rush past on the first charge. Spinning quickly, as he swept the air with both fists and didn't connect, Miller tried to kick my shins. A shunt kick blocked the kick and a back fist to the face quickly broke his nose. His hands shot to his face covering and clutching the damaged area. I followed with a back kick to the chest, which slammed him six feet back into the wall, with the wind leaving him and choking feelings grasping his lungs. A rapid cross step, snap kick to the groin and three reverse hammer fists to the face. The tree was falling, for the roots had been cut and the foundation gone.

"Quick, the Officer is coming around the corner."

Breathless, Loeding came running up to the doorway and peered around Peterson's shoulders. His face carried the same expression as the rest of the guys in the door.

"Damn," Peterson asked in a strange voice," Where did you learn to fight like that?"

"Christ, Decker is he alive?" Loeding added quickly.

With the announcement that the OOD was on his way, people began to sprint for their bunks and out of the line of fire.

The noise of people yelling and the fight itself had brought the Officer. Yet, I personally didn't hear anything, my thoughts were elsewhere. Blood was pouring from Miller's nose and above both eyes. He was breathing but very labored and a wheezing could be heard with each breath taken. The walls, floor, sinks and mirrors were sprayed and spotted, a small pool was forming next to Miller's face on the terra cotta tile. Red exit lights, being the only lighting on in the head, made a strange grayness to the normal red color. I stayed there with Miller and to the approach of the Officer on Duty. There was no reason to avoid the inevitable.

"What in the hell is going on here?"

"Jesus, Stevens get me a corpsman and alert the hospital." The first statement came in response to the initial picture, second on the radio to the headquarters office and infirmary.

"Who's responsible for this assault?"
"I am, sir. Decker, B725026 out of A company."
"What the hell happened here tonight?"

I told the story about the preceding thirty minutes in the barracks, trying to hit every detail and leave nothing to the imagination. Hoping to let the Officer know what had happened in a complete manner. No holds barred.

"You're lucky this happened with Miller and not someone else, Decker."

"Pardon me, sir?" I said not fully understanding his statement.

"This is the third fight Miller has been in since he has been in boot camp, a real troublemaker so far. But he won't be one anymore. From the looks of him, he won't want to fight anyone for a long time."

Over the time period of the evening and the next morning the fight was covered up, for several reasons everyone wanted the event just to fade into the sunset. The officer thought Miller had it coming, and no real permanent damage was done. A broken nose and jaw, cracked Sternum and three cracked ribs, accompanied two major raccoon eyes.

I was lucky, because it could have been far different in the outcome and charges could have easily been filed. The remainder of the holiday break was quiet, and returning to the regular company units was anticipated and awaited by all of us.

The New Year 1968 was to bring with it many startling changes and events. Not only in the Navy but also back in Albuquerque, where a lot was going on that I, at the time, had no idea whatsoever. Patty had been very distant for about a month and at times would not communicate with me at all. I knew, down deep that something had to be going on behind my back, someone else in the picture was a very definite possibility. The freedom, from her letters and the referrals in her phone calls began to heighten my senses. It would be only a matter of weeks until the truth and all its gory details would flood across my heart and my life.

Upon returning to the Company 626 barracks and all the furlough men back from the holidays, things seemed to move back into the regular routine. At least for the first week, they had that sort of flavor, marching, drilling, learning about ships and equipment used by the fleet. There was plenty to keep a body and mind busy and dead tired at night. Our first weekend back from the break in regular routine was to offer a definite change.

It was a Friday night in early January 1968 there was a cold chill in the air that set the temperature for the air of the evening. 18,000 miles away the men in 'Nam were getting their asses shot off, from the largest offensive ever witnessed in the Vietnam conflict. The TET offensive had begun this same night and all hell was breaking loose for the troops stationed in both the south and northern sectors.

Troops concentrations and weapon influx was at a level not realized by anyone prior to this event. 1963 thru 1967 were tough in their own way, and we lost men. Compared to the elevated assaults which were seen, countrywide, the war had now expanded.

Casualty levels never before seen, were now headlines nationwide, L.A. to New York. The insurgence of the special warfare groups came to an all time high. Navy SEALS would play a very important role in the completion of these teams. Operation Phoenix, the CIA undercover, and covert actions would grow to its largest function in the war, to date.

This night back in San Diego, in the barracks of company 626, an event began to unfold quickly, dangerously, and possibly deadly.

"All right, you motherfuckers, get in front of your bunks. It's inspection time." As the words from Chief Edwards boomed across the floors and walls of the unit, the tone carried with it one of impending threats. The wild, red-eyed stare that followed from the salt weathered face, had a gleam of evil to it. Something or someone had crossed Edwards' path, and the rage that resulted was about to be bestowed upon the 626.

"Thomas, you sorry black bastard, I said to stand at attention."

"Yes sir, Chief." Seaman Thomas was scared to death as he trembled from head to toe. A cracking flowed in the words of his answer. Fear tightened every muscle in his body to a statue like rigidity.

"I've been to easy on you sons-a-bitches, and now it's going to change. I think I need to just kick some ass around here and get this company in shape."

"Decker, front and center."

"Yes, sir!" Running to the spot directly in front of the chief, knowing full well that literally anything might be about to transpire. My awareness factor was on full alert, reaction time on instant, if need be.

"Give me that fucking piece." Chief Edwards pointing to the M-14 stacked against the bulkhead (wall).

I hesitated to fulfill the command, but fulfilled my duty as ordered. Handing him the M-14 with great reservation and reluctance, having no idea at all what was next on the Chief's agenda. As the stock touched his hands he took it forcefully, and stood there in a threatening stance.

Seaman Thomas was about to pass out from not breathing, and the fear showing was the same for every member of the company.

"Chief Edwards, why don't you let me carry the weapon for you?" I knew that this was not going to make him budge but I had to try and defuse the situation as the air crackled with the exclamation of this fact. "Mind your own business, Decker, I am fully capable of taking care of this weapons, any way I see fit."

The plural on the weapons, accompanied with the slur, and my first whiff of the Chief's breath wrote the scenario. He had been to the NCO Club for several of the preceding hours, doing his normal power drinking, plus the addition of nearly ten shots of Tequila. This came from later reports, which would be confirmed.

A looming darkness began to settle over the Chief, his focus going to first one recruit then the other. Someone was going to get hit soon. The only question was who was to be the intended victim?

The whirling motion as Chief Edwards moved past Seaman Patterson answered the question for all of us. The M-14 caught Patterson on the side of the face, opening a three-inch gash across the cheekbone and knocking him unconscious to the floor. He never moved or twitched, just fell seemingly lifeless to the flat, cold tile.

"Jim, go get the Officer of the Day and the MP."

As the words came forth, I was launching myself toward the Chief, grabbing the weapon and twisting the stock from the grip of his hands. "Help me get the Chief." Everyone was frozen until they heard these words. Then six men were on the chief and pinning him to the floor.

Struggling, he gasped, "Get the hell off of me or I will see each and every one of you court martialed."

"Fuck you, Edwards, and shut your mouth." The words came from Thomas for the fear had left the two hundred fifty pound former defensive tackle. His tone said with it, "One more word and I'll beat your butt."

The OOD and the MPs on duty came rushing in the unit and took control of the situation very quickly. They were trained and well counseled on dealing with this type of situation. Thankfully so, because the men of the 626 and I were ready for some peace and quiet.

Twenty plus years of service kept the Chief from being court martialed, but part of the agreement was to resign earlier than he had originally wanted. Many of the men of 626 wanted more but for the most part everyone was satisfied. Only two weeks left until the end of boot camp, just finishing was the most important factor to us all. With a new "temporary Chief," our company completed training and headed in some forty different directions. My directive was for just across the pond, so to speak. A little island named Coronado, or North Island as it is more commonly referred to.

Monday following the graduation and commencement exercises, all of the men of company 626 had mustered near Headquarters. A bulletin board there contained the final reviews and assignments of all the new recruits. We had just been promoted to E-3, or a full Seaman, making now the incredible sum of $147.00 per month.

Excitement and reservation both cast their lot on the eager eyes awaiting "orders." Some were going to various schools and others had orders to report to units aboard ships for sea duty. Some had been chosen, because of their high test scores, to go to the elite electronics and nuclear power schools. Since I had passed the test and filled all the requirements for UDT/SEALS, there was no doubt, until I made my way to the front of the group.

Casting my vision on the paper that held everyone's future, I saw Decker, Michael J. B725026, report to Memphis A/T school electronics/avionics, Memphis, Tennessee, 0630 February 4, 1968.

"Can't be! My eyes must be playing a trick on me." This was a statement, which was repeated over and over again.

"Excuse me, Lt. George, Seaman Decker here requesting some information on the transfer sheet?"

"Yes, Decker. What can I help you with?"

"Sir, I had completed all the tests and physicals for the UDT/SEALS and my name says that I have been assigned to the Avionics school in Memphis, Tennessee. There must be some sort of mistake!"

"No, Seaman, there is no mistake. Your test scores were so high in math and science that the base Commander personally asked that you be assigned there for AT school. You see, he is a former Navy aviator and he felt that you would make an excellent avionics tech."

"I appreciate the compliment Sir, but I would make a much better Special Forces member. I am a blackbelt in karate and have put myself in excellent physical shape."

"Orders are orders, Seaman. Your only possible chance, to get back to the UDT/SEAL units are to get the base commander in Memphis to grant you a possible review. In so doing also ask for another evaluation and if awarded the chance, get back here and make a go of the Teams." The look, that look, in his eye told me that he felt that the Teams were "it" in the service.

My heart crumbled with the news that I was going to have to start over in Memphis trying to get to San Diego. But one thing for sure, I wasn't going to quit until the TEAMS and I were one and the same.

The trip from San Diego back to Albuquerque had one layover in Phoenix. Just another forty-five minutes to hash over the orders and decide how best to follow up on the assignment I wanted. There were only thirty-seven passengers on this leg of the flight, so the quiet was nice. Visions of Patty began to dance through my thoughts, not only the visions, but also the memories of so many weeks without a letter. Down deep a rumbling stir sent a stream of choked anger across my chest. Whatever the hell had been transpiring while I was gone was going to come to light. She and I were not going to sleep until the "truth" was out and dealt with.

With only a one day layover in Albuquerque on the way to Memphis, Patty and I had very little time to smooth the rough edges out from the past few months. She was distant in a strange way, my family noticed it right off as well, especially my sister Susan. She and Patty had been discussing living together for some time and the final details were being worked out. This was fine with me, as it would give me an "in" for knowing what was going on when I was away.

The goodbyes were short and not very sweet, the truth was going to have to come out before I lay my heart out for a trampling. My mother was sad about my going away again, she wanted a little more time with her son. Glen couldn't wait to get me out of the house. The little boy that had left, had grown, substantially. He was now 6'3" and weighed in around 228, rock hard and ready for whatever may come along.
"Well, Lady, maybe you could find some time to write me now." A statement, but from my tone and the raised eyebrows she knew what I was inferring.
"I know, I know, I will, I promise. It's just hard sometimes to write. I'd rather talk on the phone."
"Yes, it's easier and one heck of a lot more expensive."

Her eyes cast toward the floor with that little turn of her face and right foot. It always worked and made me mad for letting it charm me. She was so damn pretty, my weakness. One big hug and a medium sized kiss was the sendoff for the wild blue skies toward Memphis, Tennessee and beyond. Dressed in my dress blues, winter dress uniform, white hat gleaming in the New Mexico sunshine, I waved all a hearty so long.

Continental Airlines and its golden tail were whisking me to a town that I had little, at best, knowledge of. The naval installation there was only for the electronics school and little else in Memphis concerned the Navy in any way, shape or form. Near 8000 men were assigned here and the bulk of them were students from San Diego and the Great Lakes recruit training facilities. Men from coast to coast were trying to get the start on their Navy commitments. Most having enlisted for four years, this was their first duty station.

School was exactly that, Ohms and volts and tables and tons to memorize. Learning about currents and amps and why electricity and electronics were a cohabiting team. Nerds running rampant through this school, and I wasn't a nerd. Just because I had scored high on a test, the chosen field for me was now delayed.

Chow and barracks were basically the same as in San Diego except for the colors, no navy gray and black on the inside of the classrooms. All the instructors were first class and chief petty officers, with from eight to twenty-five years of active service behind them. Most were married and their families were enjoying one of very few assignments, for their spouses that they could accompany their husbands. As most of the duty stations for the Navy included overseas and SEA Duty which did not allow for families to be with them, this was a luxury of some sort.

Liberty, time off on the weekends, was rather limited for most of the base personnel. There had been several major assaults in the previous year so many places were off limits. One of the main areas off-limits to all service personnel was all the clubs down on Beale street. This being mainly a black neighborhood, Beale itself was definitely a "NO WHITE BOY" arena. Of course there came a challenge with this, that a group of well-lubricated sailors would find enticing.

Four weeks into the routine of Memphis brought with it a Friday night from Hell itself. Two thirty a.m. someone is shaking my arm and yelling in my ear.
"Decker, Decker. Get your butt up and come to the OOD office."
"What is going on? What happened?" Words pushed out with haste as my brain kick starts into gear. There were several grunts from nearby sailors, trying to sleep as the noise and conversation ensue.
The Fire Watch continued, "You have some sort of emergency phone call."
"I'll be there in a minute." Launching from the top bunk to the floor I grabbed my pants and jerked them on as I was descending, with a shirt, socks and shoes following quickly. Two shoves with extended fingers smoothed the hair adequately. Grabbing my cover I was out the door.

Only about three hundred yards separated the barracks and the OOD office. Just over thirty seconds and I was giving the required three knocks before entering.

"Seaman Decker, B725026, reporting as ordered, Sir." Saluting quickly.

"At ease Decker. I'll get your party on the line."

"Yes, sir!" I thought for sure it must be a sickness or death in the family. But who or what, I didn't have the vaguest idea.

As the OOD was dialing I noticed that he was doing so with an El Paso, Texas area code. There was another number written on the message slip, it looked to be my sister Susan's number. What is going on here, I began to question.

"Okay, Decker. I have the party on the line."

"Hello, this is Michael Decker." My heart raced in anticipation of what I was about to hear. A brief silence, static filled, was soon interrupted by a faint-frail and familiar voice.

"Michael, this is Patty," Her voice quivering she continued," I am down in Mexico. I need your help." The tone and the urgency had my nerves on edge, something very wrong and extremely hazardous, was taking place, maybe even life threatening.

"What's wrong, Baby? What has happened?"

"Jenny, a friend of mine drove me down to Juarez. She was supposed to wait outside the clinic for me."

"What clinic, Patty? And for what?" The curiosity was killing me.

"I might as well tell you, I-I I'm pregnant. Or I was pregnant."

The final word of the sentence brought forth the overflow from the dam of emotions of Patty's heart. Tears and sobs so heavy that I wanted to jump through the phone line, and hold her and tell her it was going to be okay.

"I was three months pregnant and came here for an abortion."

As the words, their sound echoing redundantly empty, emitted from the receiver, with them the real truth of what had been going on behind my back for the past few months, followed. Patty had been seeing someone else, and not only seeing, dating. God, how could I have been so ignorant?

"Who's baby is it, Patty?" Cutting, icy, shivering with the gut wrenching tone that following them, the words ebbed deep thru the phone.

"His name is Jon Reynolds, I only saw him for a little while before Christmas. It is long over. I can only imagine how you must feel. I'm so sorry Michael, because I really do love you." Tears with the words choked out continuously, in complete emotional honesty. I didn't and did, want to know all the sordid details. Yet the most important thing was to find out where she was, exactly, and where her "friend" had gone. No matter what, I loved this lady and LOVE means being there through it all. Good, bad, and the ugly.

"Where are you right now, Patty? I mean exactly. What has happened to your friend?"

"She left, she got scared. I'm bleeding and I don't know where I am exactly." Fear began to make the sound of her voice change an octave. The desperation of what was facing Patty was very, very serious. She had gone to one of the many "clinics" which offered quick abortions in Juarez. They were notorious for inadequate and sloppy facilities and procedures. She could very realistically be hemorrhaging to death, at this very minute.

"Is the phone in the clinic?" Praying that this was the case.

"No, it's down the street. One sign says Sanchez Calle."

"Patty, that means Sanchez Street. Please try to be brave. I know you're scared but I will be there in just a couple of hours. Try not to move and please, as careful as you can, be still. It will keep you from bleeding so bad. Remember that I love you, and we will make this better, I promise."

"Okay. Just please, hurry. I've never been so scared."

"I know, baby, I'm leaving now."

"Decker, I could tell from the call what the situation was. Here are your emergency leave papers and a three hundred dollar advance pay slip."

"Lieutenant, I owe you one and more. Thank you, sir."

Hustling back to the barracks I grabbed my duffle bag and was out the door to the airport. The cab driver set a record getting me to the gate. Arriving there, I was about to see a face, which I would never forget, nor the event, which was only hours away from devastating not only a culture, but also a nation for years to come.

Standing there in the terminal gate, the plane, which was to deliver me to El Paso and Patty, was beginning to unload passengers. Midway through the process, Dr. Martin Luther King and his accompanying group, were departing the plane. What a shock to see him face to face. The depth of knowledge, air of faith and sincere heart caring pride of serving his God flowed from every pore of his being. A peace and power accompanied him that I had never before witnessed in any man. Our shoulders touched, brushed, as he left the area. Only a few steps later, both of us turned and took one last fleeting glance, mine in astonishment, his in an unspoken prayer.

Even though the flight to El Paso arrived in only one hour and forty-five minutes, it seemed forever. Somebody was truly at my aid though, because a driver was waiting for me as I left the gate. Lt. Simmons had prearranged the service before I had even left Memphis. Now I owed him two. From the airport, I was in Juarez in fifteen minutes, tops. I quickly grabbed a local cab and started looking for Patty on Sanchez Street. Growing up in New Mexico had given me at the very least, fundamental skills in Spanish. Along with the cabbie's broken English we sped to the area which should have Patty.

Juarez, Mexico was to the eye nothing but filth and garbage everywhere. Adobe, cardboard and scrap wood shacks and huts, were the norm. Most of the buildings had been around for years. Tattered paint, faded from countless years of neglect and fierce burning rays from the sun occasionally flavored some resemblance of color. There were signs on some of the buildings, but for the most part, the buildings along the streets, were known for the service or product they provided. If you were not from Juarez, you could never have found even the street, much less the individual shop or store.

Eyes trying to pierce the early morning lights first rays, small streaks of orange and gold filtered the rising dust with a ghost like haze. Lazy, scavenging street dogs roaming for their first possible meal of trash or discarded tidbit, in abundance. I was hoping that I would find Patty coming from the shadows, somewhere. I silently prayed "please, soon." I began to pound on the dashboard of the Chevy compact, with frustration beginning to still the patience so far existing, but leaving promptly. The jarring thud of my fist startled the driver to speak.

"Que paso, amigo, mi comprende muy importante."

"Yeah, it is very important, and you had better have me in the right area."

" Si, si este calle es Sanchez." The glare from my look was no reassurance from his reply. Anxiously, he hoped we would find Patty as well. At, 5'4" and 135 pounds my towering frame was somewhat intimidating, "Gringo es muy grande," was on his mind.

"Oh, God, it's her!" Yelling the words I shouted, "Stop the damn car!" grabbing the wheel and turning sharp to the curb.

"Patty, it's me, baby, it's Michael."

My heart was pounding and a swelling lump moving to my throat as her curled, frail silhouette loomed before me. Kneeling quickly I gently took her in my arms, there were patches of blood staining her pants, I knew she had already lost a lot of blood.

As my warmth and comfort enveloped her, she cried out, releasing the pent up emotions from the withheld fear and isolated abandonment.

"Oh, God, Michael, I was so scared," She sobbed and convulsed with each word.

"Please .... please .... get me home and away from here."
"You're safe now, Patty, I won't let anything hurt you. We will be home soon."

Slowly, using great care, I lifted her in my arms and carried her to the car, placing her in the back seat and laying her head on my lap.
"Get to the airport, and quick!" It was more of a command than a statement or request. The driver exited the area and quickly had us on the way back to the plane.

During the hours which had elapsed over the past half day, much had been happening back in Albuquerque. My dear faithful sister felt it her duty to inform everyone what had been going on over the past twenty-four hours. This included Patty's mother, father and younger sister, and my mother had to be shocked as well, with the news. The bickering and arguments were erupting everywhere, laying the stage for an explosion upon Patty and I returning to Albuquerque. Truly I was hoping for a quiet, safe, relaxing evening, this was nothing near what awaited our return. Meanwhile on the plane, Patty had fallen fast asleep on my chest and shoulder. My long jacket serving not only as a covering of warmth, but also to hide her bloodstained clothing. If only I could have reached down inside her body and heart and taken all the pain and suffering.

"Patty .... Baby ... We're almost there. Time to start waking up." I whispered into her ear as I stroked her hair and caressed the side of her beautiful cheek. I was wishing that peaceful look on her face would remain until she had regained her strength. She began to awaken, with little moans and barely parting her lips with a deep breath. A sudden gasp, I knew that some of the pain from the injury had suddenly reminded her of the recent event.

"Michael, I am so sore. It really hurts bad," Wincing and a small frown coming to her brow with the words.

"It won't be long, honey, you'll have a nice bath, and clean clothes to put on. I'll cook some dinner and all you have to do is rest, I promise you." Not knowing the war party standing at the gate, these words of assured peace were given. As the wheels of the big jet smoothly creased the runway and began to taxi to the arrival gate, we gathered our things.

Coming to a stop at the entrance tunnel I looked through the window to the waiting area beyond. What filled the landscape was far from what either one of us wanted to be waiting there. Both of our families in their entirety were assembled.

I knew what was going to transpire as if a recording had already been made. Her mother would try to run and boss everyone, taking her usual place of "wearing the pants." Patty would completely lose it, breaking into total hysteria, complete pandemonium resulting everywhere. All the participants would do their share of adding to the overall confusion.

As we exited the turnstile area, I quickly cut off what was about to happen. I really didn't care to have any more anguish put on Patty. Her mother Charlotte began to say," Patty you just come with me. And…" I interjected and in a thunder all my own said:
"I'm going to say this once and only once. Patty and I are leaving here together. There is no room for discussion. You can all say your two cents later and if you don't like this situation, you can go to hell!"

A truck could have been driven through the jaw and open mouth of astonishment on her mother's face. Literally shocked and probably flabbergasted at my abrupt rude statement, I really didn't care one damn bit, if they liked it or not. The air surrounding me and the look on my face, said that in no way was I kidding.

Picking Patty up in my arms I directly left the group and proceeded to the taxi area and left. One inaudible note came from Patty's mother, but what word it was I'll never know. The father of a friend of mine was a pharmacist and it was there I went before continuing to the apartment. Quickly letting him know what had taken place over the past day and asking what I might need to take care of Patty. He told me to go on home and he would prepare all the necessary things I might need, then I was to return in about a half hour. Quickly getting back to the car we continued on to the apartment and quiet, I hoped.

Another surprise was something not in the plan of things. If anyone coming to visit was anyone other than she and I, there was going to be some trouble. This was a situation, which I had taken over and was going to see through, no matter what. Arriving at the house, quickly paying the driver, I carried Patty to the door and inside.

The apartment was the one Patty and my sister Susan had co-leased about three months earlier. Moderate sized two-bedroom, which was nicely furnished. Tonight it looked as if a tornado had recently swept its destructive path through the halls and living room. There were clothes thrown here and yonder, dirty dishes in the sink of the kitchen. Knowing both of the women living here, and their tidy living habits, it was easy to see that a lot of strain and stress had developed here.

My first concern was to get Patty comfortable and lying down, with her feet and knees supported on pillows. She was really weak and needed some nourishment quickly. Laying her down on the couch with the pillows and a comforter, I stated. "Honey, you just lie here while I get something for you to eat. As soon as that is taken care of I will give you a bath and let you sleep while I run to the pharmacy."

"How about if you give me a sponge bath first? I can't stand these clothes any more, they're filthy." Her voice was weak, and accompanied by a yearning that could not be overlooked. A small tear gathered in her beautiful blue eyes. Softly I took my size 15 ring finger and dabbed it from her cheek.

"Sure, baby, we'll do the bath first."

I left the room and prepared the warm, sudsy water with solution of Phisoderm soap and peroxide/water. Gathering a washcloth and large soft towel with the pan, returned to the living room.

"Okay, lady, here's what you wanted."

Trying to be very careful with moving her, I got Patty undressed and began to tenderly sponge her with the warm fluid. Trying not to be shocked by the amount of dried blood and hideous way that the dressing had been applied in Mexico, I completed the bathing.

I began to feel anger boil inside at what had happened in the "clinic." Thoughts of making a trip to Juarez with some friends and doing some remodeling while there, demolition, raced avidly. Soaking the worst areas first and then cleansing them, I could tell that it really was soothing for Patty. Not just a physical, but emotional cleaning was taking place as well. She kept looking at me, and her eyes were saying all the things she was feeling from her heart. The pain, anguish, guilt, all was there as well as the question, "please forgive me."

"Patty, this will be over and done with very soon. Don't worry about anything, we are fine, I love you the same as before, maybe more, let's just try to forget all of the past few months, okay?"

"Okay." The words barely a whisper, tears flowing freely down her face, dripping on my hand, which was stroking her tenderly.

Finishing the bath and getting her dressed in a soft nightshirt, I cleaned up quickly and began to prepare something to eat. A quick Spanish omelet and some fresh orange juice truly hit the spot. I was amazed at how much and how fast Patty gulped down the food. With the last bite I could see the heaviness of her eyes and sleep was quickly approaching. Tucking her in and slowly leaning down for a kiss on her forehead, I was ready to go get the supplies.

"Don't think you are leaving with only one of those kinds of kisses!" She had such a spirit about her, reaching her left hand up behind my neck and pulling my lips back to hers.

Their soft, moist fullness were a savoring dessert. We both loved to play kissy face, anyway.
"Okay, sweet one, enough already. Now you get some rest. I'll be back very soon. Make sure you just stay in bed. Okay?"
"All right, I promise." She said with a feathered smile crossing her lips. My heart took an extra beat, what a beautiful lady. No matter the facts surrounding what had transpired, I loved her so much.

Grabbing the keys to her car, I quietly left for the supplies and wanted to get back as soon as possible. Hoping that Patty would not be disturbed while I was away, I had taken the phone off the hook and double locked the door. Dead bolt included for safety sake. It was only a short drive to the store, and the breath of fresh air necessary to exhale some of the stress built up, over the past twenty-four hours. Pulling sharply into the parking lot I saw that the pharmacy was basically deserted, thankfully. Walking through the automatic door, I waved and started to the rear of the store.
"Mr. Jurgenson, I can't begin to tell you how much I appreciate all that you have done tonight. You are a life saver."
"No problem, Michael. You need to watch Patty very closely for the next twelve hours, especially. Any abnormal bleeding or high fever and there is no choice, directly to the emergency room."

The concern was not only in the words, but the look on his face. He really cared for Patty, as he had known her family for years. Also the history of some of the personal tragedy she had dealt with as a small girl.
"Yes, sir, I will stay with her for as long as necessary. I have ten days emergency leave and I will use all of it if necessary."
"Additionally, Michael, I am going to have a friend of mine call you in about an hour. He is an intern and if there are any complications going on you can discuss them with him."
"Gosh, Mr. J, thank you so much." Extending my hand over the counter, I grasped his hand heartily and smiled.

Paying for the medicine and everything in the bag, I left the store. There was no way that all of the contents of the bag was $0.95, the medicine alone was probably ninty dollars. Mr. J was like that, though, always willing to go the extra mile.
"Please let everything be okay when I get there," I said to myself on the way home. There had been enough confusion and chaos for a long time. Yet the "situation" had only amplified while I was away. Turning into the parking lot I saw my sister's car parked there, and she was standing with her arms crossed on her chest and a look of terror on

her face. Slamming the car into the space marker for #112, I launched from the car and rushed to where she was standing.

"What the hell are you doing here?" The look in my eyes made Susan step back before she could answer. Glaring I stood there awaiting her answer.

"Dammit, answer me!"

"I just came by to check on how things were…and…Patty and I started to talk…and…"

"And what the hell happened?"

With this statement I was continuing towards the door of the apartment. Fearing what my eyes were about to see.

"Patty's not there!" A chill went up my spine, whirling around to face Susan and reply.

With a seething and angry viciousness to the tone I asked, "Where the hell is Patty and what the shit happened here? Tell me NOW! "

"We had an argument and she left the apartment."

"How in the fuck did you think that you had any damn right to come over here after all the shit that has gone on, and have the audacity to say anything to Patty?"

She didn't answer me, just stood there. There was no doubt in the least, having known me all her life, just how upset I was. Any level of communicating with Susan was a complete impossibility. She could go to hell and stay there.

"Get your ass out of here now and stay away. I don't want or need your help. I want all of you fucking people to keep the hell away from here. Understand?"

She shook her head in acknowledgement, remaining speechless.

"NOW LEAVE!"

Dropping the package of medicine on the couch, I ran to find where Patty had gone. I prayed that nothing had caused her to start hemorrhaging and…God, please no. I circled the parking lot completely and then on to the street beyond. She was nowhere that I looked. I kept calling her name and continuing to run through every nook and cranny, every bush and around each house.

"Patty, Patty, please answer me." No answer for now almost fifteen minutes. I thought possibly of returning to the apartment and calling the police to find her with their help. Praying that I could find her, without the fiasco that would ensue, if that were necessary. Continuing to run down the block I stopped and yelled with a thunder from my soul, crying out.

"Patty, this is Michael, where are you?"

A faint sound from the shadows of a house to my right came drifting ever so lightly to my ears.

"Michael, please, Michael." It was more of a cry, than a spoken word.

"I'm coming, baby." A gun couldn't have fired me there any faster. As I rounded the corner of the house, I saw her there propped against the stucco wall. The large stain of blood on the front of the nightshirt struck fear into my heart. Kneeling and lifting her in my arms, I pulled her body close to my chest, to quickly get her home.

"It's going to be okay, Patty, don't worry."

"Why, why don't people just leave us alone?" With the question came the river of emotion convulsing her in spasms against my body. Holding firmly, I quickened my pace to the apartment and once inside quickly laid her shaking body on the couch.

"Oh, Patty, are you hurting, baby?" No words seemed adequate for the pain and anguish that must be riddling her body and mind. Trying to comfort her and settle the quivering going on inside, I picked up the remote phone and called Mr.Jurgenson and asked that the intern friend of his could come as soon as possible and meet me at the apartment.

I guess the good Lord had been looking out for us, because it turned out that the intern, Dr. Stevens, lived minutes from the apartment and was on his way. Taking one of the large gauze compression bandages, from the pile of things from the pharmacy, I lifted the comforter and asked Patty to hold it firmly against her.

With an elapsing of time of mere minutes the doorbell rang, and Dr. Stevens stood there at the threshold. I quickly swung open the door.

"Dr. Stevens, Michael Decker, please come in." I know that the expression on my face, told him much of how I was feeling.

"Nice to meet you Michael, where's Patty?" He was very professional, and with a true concern that any patient would want to feel, he stepped into the room.

Dr. Stevens was thirty years old and from the northern part of Colorado. He had graduated from the University of Colorado Medical School. Standing six foot tall, slender build, blonde hair and green eyes, he had a soft seriousness to his demeanor, and dressed comfortably in slacks and a light sweater. He carried a small black attaché bag with his medical supplies and equipment.

"She's right here on the couch," pointing as I turned from the door and walking with him to the couch. He knelt and reached out to touch Patty's forehead for temperature, at the same time putting his other hand on her hand to comfort her with his presence.

"Patty, I'm Dr. Stevens. I want you to tell me where or if you have pain."

She hazily looked at his face and the confidence and warmth her eyes beheld, immediately softened the situation. He spent a few moments examining her and checking things, like pulse, blood pressure, and temperature. I stepped back behind the couch on the end, where Patty's head was resting on a pillow. Holding her face and stroking her hair to help calm the nerves frazzled and consumed in the episode with Susan.

I would deal with her later, I thought, that is, I ever spoke to her for the next century. Dr. Stevens was very thorough, and discovered no hemorrhages or major abnormalities. He assessed that the abortion had been done and the main problem was the fact of very little effort placed with sterile conditioning.

Thus he very acutely took great lengths to make sure that no infection would cause a problem. He cleansed the surgery area and gave Patty two shots for pain and an antibiotic. His "bedside manner" truly made a world of difference for Patty. And the professionalism and encouraging words helped her to relax, and begin to get the much needed rest her body was crying out for.

The whole process with Dr. Stevens took about forty-five minutes. He finished with Patty and as he was getting his things in order, as he gave me instructions on her care. Most of all he stressed that any further care, in the event of an emergency, could only be done at the hospital. So relieved, my lungs took their first full inhalation of air, in over an hour.

"Dr. Stevens, I don't know how to thank you enough for all you have done here tonight. Please let me do something, in some way to pay you." I didn't want to insult him, but I felt so obligated to do something. "Take care of your lady and that will suffice my payment. You will have to stand by her, Michael. She is very delicate with all that has gone on. The mental position I see clearly denotes some very suicidal tendencies. She feels that everyone is against her. Give her a reason to live."
"Yes, sir, I'll do all of that and more."

Shaking his hand firmly, I escorted him to the door.
"Thanks once again, Doctor."
"William, Michael, my first name is William." A grin on his face gave me the familiarity to call him by his first name.
"Thanks, William, and good night."
"Good night."

Closing the door and locking it, I turned to come back to Patty. She was still barely awake and I sat down on the couch next to her. Taking her hand in mine, I massaged her fingers and palm gently.

"Patty, I love you, baby." I wanted to take my big heart out of my chest and wrap it around her to warm and protect her.

"I love you too, Michael. But I'm no good for you or for anyone. It would probably be better if I just left this world and went away."

A glazed fear radiated from the moist surface of her eyes. Bringing with them a tone in Patty's voice that held all of what the doctor had spoke of and more. She had been through pure hell for many weeks. The guilt of what had happened originally, the trauma of Mexico and the desertion of her friend. Finally, there was the airport and climaxing with the onslaught from Susan. God, enough was enough.

"Patty, don't say those things. I am here, I love you and it will all work out. No matter what it takes to make everything better and get this situation finished. Don't forget it, and most of all that I love you." I was trying to say the right things and be honest with her, as well. I meant everything that I had said.

"But, Michael, what do you possibly want with someone like me?"

"That's just it, Patty, I want you, for you."

"You would be better off without me, much better off."

"That's not your decision, young lady, I am here because I want to be and how I feel hasn't changed, nor will it."

"But where do we go from here?"

"How about after you get some rest we make some plans on where and when to get married. What do you think about that, baby?"

Of all the things that she thought I might respond with, I am positive that this was the furthest from her mind. Yet it seemed like a perfect solution to me with all that had transpired over the past few days. It would take care of all the problems and the separation at the same time. Patty started to respond, but quickly I said, "SHHHHH," and snuggled the comforter up around her neck and chin. Smiling at me as I touched her lips with my word, she closed her eyes and drifted off to "never never land."

As I sat there looking at this lady whom I had loved now for almost a year, my thoughts drifted to what it might be like to really be married. One thing was sure, I would have to get a night and weekend job. As one hundred and forty dollars a month, wasn't going to provide all the necessary things we would need. Also, what would happen if I got orders for 'Nam? I sure couldn't work a second job over there! Choosing not to dwell on all of these facts, I instead just enjoyed the solace of being close and quiet with Patty.

Her rest was a deep and exhausted body kind of sleep. Very thankfully it lasted for almost nine hours. The shot had done the trick and totally relaxed Patty's body. I, on the other hand, had been up for thirty-six hours straight. But my body never had needed much rest to survive, anyway. As her body moved and eyes fluttered open, well almost open position, she pursed her lips saying,

"Have you been awake all this time, young man?" She reached for my hand as her statement was declared.

"Yep, didn't want to miss all those funny faces you make while you're asleep, and the neat way you drool out the side of your mouth." I didn't want to miss any opportunity to tease her. I was certainly wanting to lighten the load of all that was weighing on her shoulders. From the very evident smirk on my face and the laughter in my eyes, she smiled.

"Come here, you big tease, but be gentle, and give me a kiss."

With a fake astonished look and raised brow I leaned across her breasts and deftly parted her lips with my tongue. Tasting her softly with light pressure and enjoying the feel of Patty's body next to me. It had been a long time, too long. Regretfully we both knew that it could not go much farther. So we snuggled carefully and took every ounce of pleasure possible.

"How are you feeling?"

"So much better. The rest made all the difference in the world. I'm even hungry." She said with a hopeful wink, coming from that cute pair of blue eyes.

"What would you like, as if I didn't know," Mornings like this we both loved to have BLTs on toast with tortilla chips and hot picante salsa. Of course it had to be Pace brand, not something made in New York City.

"Give me five minutes, my love," bowing courtly and waving my hand in front of me as a servant. The kitchen was about to be invaded, not only to cook in, but also to get cleaned up as well.

Patty went to the bathroom with my help in getting there and freshened up a little while I got things ready. She was such a perfectionist with her make up and hair. Many years of modeling and doing photo shoots had made this fact a habit.

We ate and by the end of the meal a noticeable difference in her level of strength was beginning to take place. Now that Patty had something in her stomach, I gave her the antibiotic and pain medicine from the night before. It gave me a real sense of satisfaction to see the change and near return of the beautiful lady Patty really was. The incident with the other guy would fade from the memory banks very quickly once we were "together" again.

Later that afternoon Patty talked on the phone to her mother and several of her friends. A commanded short nap was in order, during the marathon on the phone, which was directed by none other than "Miguel." Rested, she continued to improve and get stronger by the hour.

By the next day she was up and walking for short spurts, per the doctor's recommendation. That next afternoon she asked how I felt about her mom coming for a chat. I said that whatever she felt up to was fine with me.

Also over the course of the day passing, we had talked several times about the possibility of getting married. We were even going on to the planning stages, remarkably enough her mother even agreed with the thought and helped to work out the details.

While they were talking I took the opportunity to call my mother and tell her that Patty was better. Also to drop the bomb, that was what it seemed to her, about getting married. Her opinion was that it was going to be a big mistake. She refused to give either her permission or blessing. So after saying that it was not really up to her, since I was over eighteen, the talk concluded with hurt feelings.

Years later it would amaze me how much smarter she was than I was willing to admit at the time. Bordering on brilliant was much closer to the actual truth, not only in maturing but in the fact she was one of the most intelligent people I would ever meet.

Two days more and Patty was almost back to normal. Her color and energy level had steadily increased. It had been almost a week since I had read a paper or watched any news on the T.V. So that morning, I decided to turn on the world news and see what all had been going on.

Headlines across the screen, "Martin Luther King assassinated in Memphis, Tennessee," I couldn't believe what my eyes and ears were receiving. It couldn't have happened. I had just seen Dr. King alive a few days earlier. Yet it was true, it had taken place, just like the "never to be forgotten" event with President Kennedy when I was in eighth grade at Cleveland Junior High School.

Dallas, Texas and the library repository building had etched their picture along with the grisly scene of the President going forward then back as the bullets tore through his skull. I had seen that film so many times.

"Patty, come and see this. You will not believe what has happened out in Memphis." Relating to her what had transpired at the airport during the departure, only days before.

"I can't believe it." She was just as shocked as I was.

"What is this world coming to? I bet there will be riots and all kinds of problems reverberating from this incident."

"No kidding. It's terrible."

What a week it had been for the nation, for the two of us, and our respective families.

That afternoon I called the base and told them that I would be returning the following day and ready to get back to my training schedule. The OOD was courteous, but short in saying that I had to be back by 1800 hours.

Patty and I spent the night together, and made final plans about getting married. Allowing the closeness to be a partial healing of the distance that had somehow brought us back together, the tears flowed once again as I left the airport gate the following day. My heart told me that all had been settled and it was time to go on to the next chapter and station of my life.

I was amazed at the number of security personnel covering the airport terminal when I arrived back in Memphis. Both Federal and State officials, including FBI, ATF, and the U.S. Marshall Service, were in very evident maximum alert. The murder of Dr. King basically turned this facility, Memphis, and the entire area into a police arena. An investigation of this size and scope would go on for months. Thankfully being in uniform, with orders, allowed me to circumvent some of the red tape and delay that many could not avoid.

A thirty-minute taxi ride to the base took me away from the chaos, controlled to some extent by my departure from the area. Double sentry guards were posted at the base gate, and instead of the normal wave-through, military I.D. and destination were logged for one and all.

I immediately reported to the OOD desk and got my leave orders signed and certified. Back on post, back on duty and easily before my 1800 hours reporting time. As luck would have it, I had been assigned fire watch for the barracks that first night back. My shift was the 0200 to 0600 watch, which was the quietest and easiest one to do.

I hit the chow hall for a little gourmet food, and made contact with a few of the recent friends I had made. A little brief chat and I was off to the bunk for a few winks before watch.

The internal alarm clock went off at 0100 hours. Quick shower and I went ahead and relieved the early duty watch by 0130. I was up and ready so why not let him catch a few extra minutes rest? Not that I was being a good guy, I was just way too restless to sleep much anyway.

There was a pay phone at the end of the first floor wing. From this position I could see all the way to the other end of the unit. Double bunks stretched fifty in a row, one hundred men to a floor. The floors were so heavily waxed and buffed, to such brilliance that from the end of the hall, with only the exit lights, it looked to be a long pool of water, with the bunks floating motionless therein. An occasional grunt, snore or fart was the only telling that any life existed there. Yet three hours earlier or from now, the noise level would blast your eardrums.

Around 0230 I decided to make a quick call to Patty, and make sure she was tucked in and okay.

"Hello, (yawn)," a sleepy voice said, barely audible.
"Hey, little one, this is your sailor man."
"Oh Michael, it's so late."
"I know but I just wanted to say hello and make sure you were safe."
"I'm fine and I haven't had any problems at all."
"You are taking all the medicine, right?"
"I promise that I have not missed any at all."
"Good, go ahead and go back to sleep, baby, I'll talk to you on the weekend."
"I love you, Michael."
"I love you too, lady." Continuing, "Bye, pretty one."
"Goodbye, Michael."

Knowing that she was safe and doing fine was a relief to my spirit. She needed all the rest that she could find and I didn't think that there would be any more problems with anyone in the families. The next three and a half hours were quiet and uneventful. I finished the shift and went with all the other men to chow at 0600. Being a normal day the base was alive and buzzing, men running and getting to work, school, duty stations.

"Damn, Decker, how did you swing the transfer?" One of the guys I had met, Ted Thurman asked. He was from Nashville so not really far from home. His family had a lot to do with the music and entertainment business there.

"What do you mean, 'transfer'?" I inquired eagerly, as my heart began to energize.

"Haven't you seen the order roster and transfer call out? Well that's a dumb question since you have been gone for almost a week."

"Hell, Dude, you have been transferred to the Special Warfare School in Little Creek, Virginia. Shit man, that means UDT/ SEALS and all that Kung-Fu crap you're always doing." The same grin was on several faces of the guys at the tables. They gave me the dickens all the time for the stretching and strange breathing noises, along with the hours of katas (fighting forms) I did in practice.

"Thurman, if your pulling my leg I'm going to kick your monkey ass all the way to Nashville."

"No, I am serious, man, the sheet was posted the other day and none of us could figure out how the hell you could get a transfer when school was not over yet."

"Is it posted over at the OOD or at the Administration Building?"

"It is over at the Admin, and the word is that some Commander from North Island requested your transfer." Maybe he wasn't kidding after all, the look on his face was darn serious.

"I'm out of here. You guys can have my breakfast!"

Food, hell no, not when the one thing that I had dreamed about from the very first week in the Navy was possibly sitting there, waiting for me to grab. Like a bolt of lightning striking across the prairie, I was sprinting towards the office.

"Hey, sailor!"

Turning promptly I suddenly realized that I had flown past an officer without saluting.

"Sorry, Lieutenant, I was in a major hurry, Sir," saluting sharply with an extra crisp pop.

"Okay, sailor, as you were."

"Thank you, Sir. By your leave." Dropping the salute I picked up the pace once again.

Man, could this really have happened after the week just passed, could a dream like this come true? Along with the hope was an equal amount of doubt. How often do big dreams come true in your life? The wait of knowing was about to be rectified as the steps to the Administration building were suddenly before me. Taking five or six at a time I launched into the passageway.

"Pardon me, young lady, I need to find out about some orders to Little Creek, Virginia? My name is Decker, Michael J."

Dressed in her whites, brunette hair done up in a bun, the personnel man third class turned to reveal a absolutely beautiful face and body. The name tag saying Caswell, everything else saying "OOOOhh, La La!" The smile on my face and the look of appreciation in my eyes made her blush.

"Yes, Decker, what is it that you need?"

Finally by the end of the sentence she allowed her gaze to meet mine. The smile she gave was slight, ever so slight, taking great strides to maintain proper composure and professionalism.

"Yes, Ms. Caswell, I am looking for any and all information concerning a transfer to the Special Warfare School in Little Creek."

"Just a moment and I will pull your file and the transfer order log. When was this transfer to be taking place?"

"As soon as possible if it's up to me!" The excitement could in no way be kept down or covered with any disguise whatsoever.

"We are ready to leave yesterday it seems?" Her eyebrows raised and a smiling look passed with the phrase.

"You have no idea how much this chance means to me. I was hoping to get the chance to do this training right from boot camp. But for some reason I didn't get the right orders."

Opening the log and pulling the order sheet for my last name, she turned to the section of immediate order for transfer.

"Let's see here, Decker, Michael John, B725026, hometown of Canyon, Texas. Birth date 10-27-48…brown hair…hazel eyes…"

"Caswell, you are killing me with all the information that you and I both know. What the heck do the orders say?"

She knew full well what she was doing to me, by making me wait for the final answer and she was enjoying the manipulation immensely. She had the power of the information.

"The orders seem to say that you are going to get to take a break from Avionics school, destination Little Creek, Virginia. To report by 0700 hours next Sunday."

"Wahoo, YES, YES!"

"I take it you are pleased with the news?"

Her smile was almost as big as the grin stretching across my face from ear to ear.

"You have no idea how pleased. Thank you very much for the help. I mean that, thank you." Reaching for her hand to shake, I grasped Ms. Caswell's delicate little hand and gave it a courteous squeeze.

"Your welcome, Michael, very welcome. Do you mind if I call you Michael?" A small tone of flirt accompanied the words.

"My first name is Cynthia."

Reaching for her hand once again I replied, "Very nice to have met you Cynthia Caswell. You just made my day!"

"It was a pleasure, my pleasure. What will you do for the next few days till you are to leave for Little Creek? Any plans?"

No doubt about the forward message now in the least. She was interested in this here Texas sailor. The answer she received was the last thing she probably wanted to hear.

"Probably try to get back to Albuquerque and take a day or two to see my girlfriend. Maybe even get married."

The disappointment was evident not only in her face, but the words and emphasis on her reply.

"I see! Well good luck with your plans." It was so monotone and without feeling that I felt a twinge of pain from breaking her small bubble. Yet with over a thousand men on the base, she had a lot more to choose from.

"Thanks again." I restated my appreciation as I left the office and proceeded on back to the barracks.

Whew, it had really come true. The orders to Special Warfare Group had really come through. It was my chance to be a part of the most elite fighting group in the world. This was not just my opinion, but also the judgment of any branch of service member worldwide. These men were the best trained, finest physically conditioned and mentally strengthened military force ever put together. Serving together in small teams they accomplished goals and completed missions not thought of by normal military units. Nor even in the slightest way considered to complete the tasks they took as the normal everyday work at hand.

This body had been beat and pushed and worked for the past ten years just for the chance at hand, to be a member of the Special Warfare/SEAL commandos. I knew that all the anger and rage from the abuse Glen had put out for the past ten years was going to have an outlet.

It would be a constructive outlet, which would allow the aggression to be channeled into areas which would allow it to function. This in fighting for a cause, braving the enemy and letting him take the brunt, the force and try to deal with it. Just to think of this opportunity pumped me up and made my heart pound.

The next step was to call Patty and tell her what had happened. I wanted her to know the great news and also to work out a quick resolution to getting married. I felt she would be happy with the news as well, knowing what joy it was giving me.

"Patty, are you there?" I shouted through the answering machine when no one picked up the line.

"Hello...anybody home?"

"Hey, Michael, I'm here...just sleeping."

"I know it's early for you, Lady, but I've got some great news. The orders for Little Creek, Virginia and Special Warfare School came through while I was in Albuquerque. Isn't that super?"

"Yeah, sure if that's want you want."

"What I want! Shoot, it's everything I've dreamed of for months!"

"I'm happy for you then." There was no real excitement in her voice, but I thought that it must be that she just hadn't fully been awake. At least I hoped that was what it was.

"I'm going to try and get leave for a couple of days and come home to get married. How does that sound? Think you can be ready in time?" With a little teasing tone to my voice and trying to get a rise.

"No problem, I'll be ready and waiting." Now the excitement began to flow. After all this was something for her to be a part of. Where the Little Creek transfer really didn't concern her, down deep, she still needed to be happy about the news.

"Well, I am going to get started on finding out what they will allow me for leave. I'll let you know something as soon as they give me the word. Take care and I'll call soon."

"All right, Michael, get here soon. 'Bye, now."

"'Bye, lover."

There were only about four thousand different thoughts traveling in my brain, all the possibilities, all the opportunities, which now lay so close before me. I knew that these next few months would cram years of training into themselves. All the prep I had done from NMMI, Karate, and physical conditioning was going to be put to the ultimate test. I felt the test would be not only a challenge, but also a chance to perform at the absolute peak of my ability. Utilizing every part and function of the mental and physical prowess processes, all systems would be pushed to the maximum levels of efficiency.

Making the leave orders was no real challenge. I had not taken much of the available days due to me, so the OOD readily approved the two days to Albuquerque. His only hesitation was whether or not I was really ready to get married. Explaining what a big step it was going to be. I simply said that I was ready, and that I didn't need to think any further about the decision.

I called my mother to tell her that we had decided to get married. She was greatly disappointed, in fact said that she would not be a part of this fiasco. Of course it was the antithesis of that reaction for Patty's parents. They were more than willing to get this thing over with, almost to the point of pushing us through the door. This would later become evident as they pulled back much of the normal support that Patty would ask for in months to come.

The wedding was a little "Justice of the Peace" affair, no frills in the least bit. A friend of Patty's was her maid of honor. A witness was a closer point of reference. The entire deal took less than fifteen minutes. Out the door to the awaiting motel and a little personal time together, then for me up early and back to the base for checking and prepare for transfer.

I realized that the luster of romance was void, but we would have a "real" wedding later and invite all the friends and family. Take a real honeymoon to some exotic place, letting ourselves be pampered and spoiled. Right now, there was business to attend to, important business.

The trip back to Memphis brought with it a realization of just how little time Patty and I would get to spend together in the next few months. With training and assignments, the chances for us even seeing each other's face was doubtful. I hoped that she would not only understand, but also be all right with that fact.

I had only four more days till I would take off for the Amphibious base at Little Creek. Knowing this I took the short prep time to get a good run in each morning and evening. Spent nearly six hours a day in the gym and tried to squeeze at least two sessions a day in the swimming pool. Eating almost everything that was placed before me, I didn't want to lose any weight, as the heat and training schedule there would carve every ounce of non-muscle fiber and sinew to rock hard steel. I wanted as much energy stored up as possible.

"Decker, Michael J., B725026, reporting for transfer, sir." The day had finally come to start on my quest. Walking in the administration building and announcing my intentions was the first of many proud moments that day.

"Yes, Decker, you are the one that was taken out of Avionics, and is being sent down to Little Creek, right?"

"Yes, sir. Damn proud of that fact, Commander."

"Yes, it appears so. You would have made an excellent technician, though. If you had stayed and finished the school, that is."

"Thank you sir, but this is absolutely what I want to do."

"Well, the Special Warfare training is the some of the toughest physical conditioning in the world. You will be pushed beyond anything you have ever experienced to date."

"Yes, sir." Hoping that the grin on my face would not leave any scars from stretching my face so wide.

"Well, all the paperwork is in order so just sign here and be on your way. The transport to the airport is outside."

"Thank you, sir." Saluting after I signed the papers, I turned to leave.

"Good luck, Seaman Decker." Ms. Caswell waved from her desk.

"Good bye, Cynthia, thank you."

If there hadn't been a Patty in my life, I would have stayed in touch with Caswell. She was not only very pretty, but sharp and full of energy. She seemed to love life and probably would have been a lot of fun to spend time with. Yet I never took the time to even recall her after that morning, instead, it was Little Creek, here I come!

I had made an assumption that the ride down to the base was to be on the airplane. But in reality after boarding the transport van, and reading my orders carefully, it was the bus. Back here in this part of the U.S., there are towns, little tiny towns, every thirty to fifty miles. Thus, after what seemed like three hundred and fifty stops, and twenty-three days of rolling along, the Greyhound bus pulled into the station. Cramped up from the minimal leg room and uncomfortable seats, it felt fabulous to just get out and move around.

Little Creek, Virginia, U.S. Naval Amphibious Warfare and Atlantic Communications Facility was the ticket for several of the top teams trained and utilized. These Special Warfare units were the advance support for all of the operations, critical in nature, in the Atlantic and Mediterranean. They were constantly called upon to facilitate special assaults, intelligence gathering and placement/extraction of "beyond the known zone," troops.

Many men had and would cross under these portals, giving their all for a chance to be one of the chosen few. Yet of every one hundred who had qualified to get the opportunity, only ten percent would get to first base. Thus eliminating the multitudes that came, which just in coming was a true honor.

The sun had burnt away any trace of cloud cover. Azure blue skies, with that big golden globe beaming down, lit the grounds with crystal clear detail. Every lawn, ever shrub and tree was perfectly groomed and landscaped. Brass rails and door handles polished to the highest sheen possible. Dress whites starched and crisp on all whom passed before me. The sound of efficiency and look of order was present with every maneuver and turn. Salutes popping with excelled pride and honor, these men and women of the U.S. Navy demonstrated their military discipline.

I was about to be part of all of this, grabbing my duffle bag and hoisting it to my shoulder, I advanced to the command office center.
"Sir, Decker, Michael J., B725026, reporting for duty sir."

The Lieutenant at the duty desk raised his head from the duty roster that was holding his attention. A fan oscillated from its position being mounted on the wall, whirring steadily to cool the room. Two yeoman typed steadily at the rear of the office, never breaking their steady rhythm. The command duty officer was barely visible behind a glass window in a side office.
"Where are you reporting in from, Decker?"
"From the Memphis Avionics School, sir."
"Avionics, hell, sailor, we don't fly planes here, we are frogmen not pilots."

"Yes, sir, I'm aware of that fact. I…"

"At ease, Sailor, I'm just giving you a hard time," cutting me off in midsentence as he replied. "Yes, sir."

"Your orders say that you are to report to duty for the Special Warfare Group training." A pause long, enough to give me a heart attack before he continued. "You will be housed in barracks Alpha Two, Bravo section. Take your gear and get over to the barracks, there will be an on-duty Petty Officer there. It should be…let's see…Williams, 1st Class."

"Yes, sir, I'm on my way. Thank you, sir." Saluting, I turned an about face after coming to attention, leaving the command office.

As I walked through the ground areas, my heart pounded with the cadence of my steps. I think maybe at a double beat at times. Hell, I was really here. No more wishing that I were, this was the real enchilada, jalapeños and all.

A first class petty officer, three chevrons with the eagle on top, walked into the foyer of the barracks just as I stepped through the hatch. Standing about six foot tall, short crew cut, and his XL shirt stretching to stay together at the short sleeve wrapped around a nearly eighteen-inch arm. His arms along with his massive neck and shoulders revealed countless hours in the gym and in the water. Had to be Williams.

"Are you Decker?"

"Yes, Michael Decker from Texas." Extending my hand with my name, knowing it was going to be a firm shake.

"Williams, Thomas, Charlotte, North Carolina. Born and bred."

I liked the air and heart of this man instantly. His eyes looked directly at me and there was no bullshit in the least. His tone of voice and directness was solid, just like he was in the field when the chips were down, I'd stake my life on this fact. This man was part of the fraternity that had developed the level of excellence which had been demonstrated the world over.

"My pleasure ,Williams, I am mighty proud to be here."

"Well, see how proud you are to be here after tomorrow. The first day you will have a few surprises, maybe more than a few."

The expression on his face said, "beware the monster stirs," or something to that general terminology. A hearty chuckle came after the statement as well. With that he turned and motioned for me to follow him back to the main living quarters. Sparse and a "working" area only, it was very basic with double gray colored rack bunks, ten to a side and footlockers at the base of each rack.

The floors shined liquid like, nothing, and I repeat nothing out of its place. Full ten man showers and heads (toilets). It had a high ceiling with open beam construction, approximately twelve feet.

"You have got locker 22, so get your stuff stowed and report back to me. I'll take you to the equipment issue and get the rest of your gear issued to you."

Moving rapidly to get finished I replied, "Be right there." Taking less than a minute to stow my duffle bag in the footlocker, I rejoined Williams in the foyer entrance.

"This way; let's go." I joined in behind him as we left the barracks. Then to his side when we cleared the doorway. He walked just as I suspected he might, striding with powerful steps moving us ahead at a fast clip.

"Enjoy the slow transport today, for tomorrow you will run everywhere you're going for the next sixteen weeks." His glance to me also stated this "if you're still here by then."

"I'll still be here, Williams," Being very direct but not trying to toot my own horn.

"The fire inside this dog has been burning for a long time and dying to get out."

"Let it burn then, Decker, let it burn. We can put any size flame to the test. Believe me I have seen every size and shape try and cover this course of training. It doesn't just consist of the physically strong, but the mentally tough and hardened. The brain tells the body to quit long before it truly has to shut down. When you build the two to work as a combined unit the result is far greater than most people can even imagine. I've seen guys finish exercises and then realize the "small" pain that they were experiencing was a broken arm or leg or worse. But they completed their mission with that being the most important part of every exercise at hand."

"Sounds great to me, I'm ready."

"Well, here is the issue office, let's get your gear and get back to the barracks. Most of the other men in your training unit will be in during the next hour or two." Jungle boots, black shorts/red T-shirts, hiking brogans and sweats rounded out with a helmet and bedding, the issue, Williams said that the "rest" of the issue would come in a few days. Yahoo!

While I was carrying my gear back to the barracks, Williams had headed out while I was packing everything to view several teams that were moving around the base. Running in cadence, chanting various calls and sayings. I thought some of the ones down at NMMI were rank, huh! Williams was right, they were moving along at a clip, everywhere their leaders were directing them.

Sweat pouring from their foreheads, shorts and shirts drenched from the intense perspiration. In the three units that came by during the walk back, two were definitely advanced and one only a few weeks into the program. Very possibly two were working teams and only one a trainer. I looked forward to meeting up with the rest of the guys that following evening. Where all they came from and what had made them choose to go this route of military service. All were things that I was interested in finding out.

Many had told me that within each team there was a level of understanding that was beyond knowing. Each man knew, by almost gut instinct, what one another was about to do or how they would react to every situation. This is one of the many reasons that they could accomplish so much with such few men.

Looking up I saw that two other men were just arriving to the barracks as I came on to the main street. Damn, they were earlier than Williams had predicted. Accelerating my stride, I reached the passageway and entered to meet the new men, my fellow brothers.

Passing through as Williams was giving them a short break down, I decided that I would catch up with them when he brought them to the main living unit. In this way I would go ahead and stow all new and existing gear, and organize everything neatly.

Over the next four hours a total of forty-eight men filled the barracks, forty, which would consist of men from all over the U.S., Puerto Rico, Guam and the Philippines. The other eight were the staff instructors and "hell week helpers." It wouldn't be long before hell week and help was an understatement as to the pleas voiced. Most of them would burn your ears, probably even this paper. Everywhere you turned someone was folding this, storing that, trying on boots, shoes, shorts, literally every piece of gear issued. It had to fit, especially the footwear, or the price paid would be "ring the bell." This was a sound, which would become familiar over the next few weeks, yet one that nobody wanted to hear or much less be part of.

"Ringing the bell" stood as the final drop from the program and the teams. Great care was taken not to have bad feet. The level of physical requirement was absolutely all you could give, 100% was just getting by, for it took at least 150% or more.

0400 hours, Boom-Boom-Boom-Boom, the short bat on the trash can lid thundered, from three positions in the barracks passageway.

"Let's go, pop to, you lazy shits. Time to take a morning walk." The announcement came not only from big voices, but a hand held microphone also.

Bodies launching from the racks, grabbing shorts, socks and anything else hanging out. Red eyes squinting from the intense overhead lights blaring down. It was mass turmoil, that first morning.
"You men have got two minutes to get it together and fall in formation. Now, gentlemen! Move your ass!"

Williams was right there, as expected by everyone, his engine revving and ready to roll. The rest of the staff were in a similar aggressive posture. Two minutes later formation was mustered and dressed, at full attention. Four abreast and ten deep, the command came instantly.
"Forward at the double time. Marrrrrrch!" Forty-eight men took to the runway of a path of no known destination. No known length or course, it was just follow the leader. A light dew, coated the street and all of the vegetation, giving everything a salty moist smell and a texture to the air.

Each breath was hot to the lung and caused a fire to begin to ember and grow from down in the cauldron of the soul. This was the first of the first, to see if we had what it took to be the best of the best. "No frills, just drills," as some would say. The mile long stretch to the beachfront was the warmup, and then the sand and "shortsurf" would give the resistance and weight to the legs to make the fire grow stronger. Five miles later they would have a fire of their own. Lungs taking short, deep gasps, creating a rhythm of breaths. In-In-Out and another twenty or more combinations, this one was mine.

The turn around point was the logs, five 16" logs twenty-five feet long. Later that day on the second visit, we would find out what the logs were all about, for now it was turn and head for home. There were chants and calls echoing from the enthusiasm bursting from all of us. It was the beginning of an adventure unparalleled for any of us.

One mile from the start of the beach run a severe cramp hit Goodman, guy from Colorado, hamstring pulled and knotted like two fists. He hit the ground. Larry Guadarama, my bunkie from Arizona, looked at Goodman at the same time that I did. No hesitation, we all had to make the grade. Each grabbing an arm we ducked down letting Goodman's arms drape over our shoulders, grabbing each other's forearms and wrists. From this improvised human platform we continued, trying to make up the lost distance.

Five hundred yards or so, two more men fell back and we leap-frogged teams of men until we hit the street areas. By then the bulk of the cramp had eased and in a hop-along manner, Goodman finished the morning stroll.

Lungs burning, throat parched, legs with a rubbery tensile to them, we hit the rest area in the front of the barracks. Time for a quick break, fifteen minutes for chow, fifteen for clean up the barracks and take a fast testimonial "dump." Then back in formation, as the warmup for the day was over. It was time for some real exercise.

This included a three mile swim, and five lift and stride to the ocean with the logs on our shoulders. Grab from a kneeling position, hoist, taking the log from the ground to the shoulder; then jog, making sure you were in sync and don't dare drop your position. God, DON'T DROP YOUR POSITION! Only one drop in the first week, it would never happen again. From the strength gained while working the logs we moved on to the boats, hitting the surf and rowing our butts off.

Weapons training of every make and description, night forced marches, preliminary diving and underwater skills, equipment checkouts and testing, combat fighting techniques, explosives and demolition, we were up and running at 0400 in the morning until near the midnight hour, seven days a week. Many nights it wasn't near midnight, but it sure as hell felt like it.

Ten weeks later the bell had rung twelve times. The first bell had rung the fourth day. By week fifteen, it had tolled nineteen times; the group was much smaller but also much tighter. No gaps anywhere, every aspect of each other's life was becoming second nature. Now we all understood, why they said the "TEAMS." No other terminology could describe their function any better,

Sunday night 0200 hours, this wakeup call would be the last for the next seven days. A few short buddy up rests and collapses, but other than that no real rest or sleep. Hell week had begun and the non-stop push of physical and mental onslaught would be to break down even the slightest imperfection of a man's being.

Driving and pushing him to levels not before thought humanly possible. From the boat, PBR, high speed pick ups to the buddy scuba mission offshore on a timed interval, to the "showers" brigade in the running in place exercises, if a breakdown was possible, this would bring it on.

By the sixth night, the bones ached, muscles cramped. A chill had set in so deep within the core of the body that a deep freeze could not have made the cold any more brutal. Eyes red, raw, salt and water and sand strained. Staff kicking and cajoling and laying it on heavy, "more give us more," they cried out.

Then suddenly a sound in the distance, no it's closer than that, hell, it's coming nearer and nearer. A familiar sound, maybe a tune, a song from somewhere in the past, but what, what is it, what is it?

What is going on? Why is everything suddenly slowing down? Or is it just me?

My God, it's the National Anthem; yep that's it! The sound brings with it the stop, the halt, the finish, the conclusion of hell week. "It's over, really over, damn, I made it."

"Shit, Larry, it's over, we made it."

"You sorry shit, how did we do it? Is it really over?" Tears and sweat and dirt and grime and both of us had the astonished, bewildered looks of the century.

No more words were possible, gazing around the group it was, I'm sure, as if we were looking into a mirror as the rest of the faces came into view. The hoops and hollers, along with the laughter and continuing tears of relief and joy continued for some time.

This first part was over, completed, accomplished and conquered together as a team. It was a sense of great pride and would be worn with such, for a lifetime to come. Nobody could ever take away from us the joy associated with this feat. It would be a source of commentary and camaraderie between men of the armed forces forevermore.

It took two full days to begin to feel somewhat normal after the outlay of energy during hell week. But this was to be a start of the "real reason" the training was so important to the Navy, and Armed Forces in general. Immediate orders were issued because of the outbreak of opposing forces in the Delta and Northern Province regions of Southeast Asia. Vietman looms ever closer to you and the perils of war, to some men, to us was the opportunity to go and kick some "gook butt." For it would not take long in the field, to feel this way toward the enemy and much worse, not to mention more sadistic.

Immediate transfer to Da Nang, assemble for departure at 0700 hours, San Francisco, California. Board C-141 military transport. Team to be on alert standby until that time. Duration of duty assignment…Unknown. Code Line Charlie 14 Romeo.

The message brought an air of "knowing" to those of us standing there at HQ command. No more trials, no more tests, this was the real thing, for keeps. I called Patty and my parents and let them know that I would be coming through for a single night's stay on my way to California. The rest of the message I would fill in later.

CHAPTER 3

college, Football, Montana mining company

By the time I arrived in Albuquerque, it was already 2000 hours, 8:00 p.m. My mother picked me up at the airport and on the drive home I told her where I was going. Of course the reaction was not to be unexpected. Her son was going off to war, and the tears flowed.

Many emotions were flowing through my heart, one of the main ones was, how Patty was going to take the news. "Were the emotional scars and wounds of the preceding trauma of the abortion still too recent? Had there been sufficient time for healing, and just how long would I tell her I would be away?" All of this and more was tossed back and forth with no real definite answer to the question at hand. I knew that she would be sad, the main question was how sad. I had promised her that I would take care of her. Leaving was sure as heck not taking care of her, but the commitment that I had made to the Navy was one that I had made before the one to her. I was not using this as a cop out, but a reality. Somehow, someway it would be okay – I hoped, anyway!

Patty had been out of town on a photo shoot, one of the modeling assignments she had been doing for the past three months. This being one of her pursuits, to get out of the city and let the new surroundings and people bring refreshment, and resolve to her life. My being gone so much already, this allowed her some companionship and company. As she was very talented, and the natural beauty she possessed truly exploded on the camera. It was therapeutic during the sessions, giving her an outlet to vent some of the frustrations and pain.

Because of her not having arrived back to Albuquerque and not due back until the early hours of the morning, I had gone on back to the house at 3225 Georgia with my mother. Pulling the long green Plymouth station wagon up the drive and on into the carport was like going back in a time machine. It had been so long since this residence had been my home, if ever. There were so many memories of the abuse and lack of family life. My mother struggled for so many years, trying to keep the unity and bonds together. How she survived the onslaught of so many years not being, really loved and cared for, I don't know.

She, being such a beautiful woman not only in stature, had such a loving and giving heart. She had compassion beyond the call of duty, consistently with a vibrant and fun personality. These qualities coupled with her intellect and educational excellence made her such a prize and wonderful choice. I frankly believe she endured the pain and suffering to assure a home and family setting for my sister Susan and I, certainly not for the life she gave up to keep it.

Knowing the devotion and love, bonded so deep and warm from her mother and father, my Nana and Grandee, had to be a major factor in her patient struggle. As I turned the key off to the ignition in the car, the quiet was almost too quiet as the engine came to a halt. Glen's light in the garage office was still on. He would be finishing his second or third six-pack by now. Sitting there contemplating some business deal or how best to upset the evening, it being my last on the United States soil for many months to come.

I grabbed my duffle bag and throwing it over my shoulder, held the door for my mother and in we went. The house smelled of leg-of-lamb, one of my favorites, a Boston Cherry cream pie sat on the counter by the stove. She had gone all out for her boy, for this and German Chocolate cake were the absolute most wonderful desserts ever thought of by mankind.

"Well, goodness, trying to get me fat for the last night I'm here, huh?" I reached out and gave her a hug as I said it. Not realizing the statement and reference of "last night" didn't need to be said. For the tear I caught in her eye slowly building was answer enough.

"Mom, it is going to be okay, don't worry about me going. I promise you that I'll be safe." Trying to console her in some way that would lighten the mood.

"I know, I know. It's just that you will be so far away."

The words came from so deep within her heart, a longing and urgency in her voice. Something else was coming out, I could tell.

"Mom, what is going on here? Has Glen done something?"

Waiting for her reply, the blood began to thrust through my veins. If he had done something, anything, I would take him apart in a thousand pieces. The little boy he had last seen had changed from the person he had beaten and thrown around for so many years. Now near two hundred and thirty pounds, rawboned and tuned to a tight bow, he would have more than he ever bargained for.

"No, no, it's only you going," she replied, trying to calm what she knew I intuitively was feeling. I let it go for now and for her sake.

We, she and I, sat and talked while we ate and enjoyed the great spread of food. Remembering so many things, mainly about the three of us, Glen certainly not included. Finishing off the meal and near a third of the dessert, now totally stuffed, we took a few minutes to tidy up the kitchen and retire to the living room. There we continued to talk for maybe another half-hour.

"Well, mother, my dear, I think I'll go lay down for a while, and wait for Patty to call. It will be late I'm sure."

"Go right ahead, I'll see you when you get up."

Giving her a hug and a kiss on the cheek, I went on back to the room I had grown up in as a boy. Stripping down to my skivvies and stretching out on the bed, the quiet allowing for my mind to flow in many directions of thought. It wouldn't be long before the quiet was broken. Echoes of so many hundreds of nights of the past were reverberating through my brain and my soul. This would be the last straw. NO MORE.

Like so many other evenings in this damn house, Glen had now finished nearly a case of beer. He came through the back door, through the den area, up three steps and on to the level with the dining room and kitchen. My mother was waiting for him and keeping dinner ready, sometimes for hours and hours. The demanding threats, the vulgarity, an onslaught which would continually fill many nights of every week came very quickly.

"Well where is the 'guest' of the evening?" His tone so sarcastic it was sickening.

"Michael went to lay down for a while and is waiting for Patty to call."

"Oh, his little prize of a wife."

"Glen, please, not tonight. It's Mike's last night here."

"I don't give a damn whose night it is, this is my goddamn house. Understand?" The elevation of the conversation had begun.

"Yes, Glen, it's your house and I understand." Even from my room I could see the facial expression of my mother, the pain and anguish riddling her heart. It was one that I had witnessed a thousand times.

"Then if you understand, give me my damn dinner, now"

Lying there in my bed, the conversation had lit the fire already. I was trying to stay away from the situation, the best that I could. But, if it kept up, I was going to end the conversation, my way, in his house. The sorry bastard wasn't going to talk to my mother like that anymore. I would tear his head off first and then shit in his neck.

"I guess you gave the best cuts of meat to that damn son of yours."

"Glen, I merely carved the meat and served it. That's all and nothing more. I'm sorry if you are not happy with dinner."

The weight and monotone of her words was breaking my heart. Why couldn't he just leave it alone, just for once?

"LOOK AT ME WHEN YOU TALK TO ME!" He screamed and grabbed her arm. Jerking her to the table where he sat.

"Glen, stop! Now!" Before the words finished from Glen I was already flying down the hallway, my mother's reply coming as I rounded the corner of the kitchen.

The look of total shock on both their faces with my mother in fear of what might happen, Glen glaring at the person running to the aid of his mother. This person had no resemblance whatsoever to the youngster his memory banks were still conjuring up as to who and what I was. The inches and pounds had been honed, sharpened, trained and skilled to protect, defend or destroy. Whatever level of efficiency and force was necessary to take care of the task.

Grabbing Glen's right wrist and twisting the bones and nerves together with unyielding force I snapped his hold on my mother.

"Get your filthy fucking hands off of her." Voice low pitched, slowly delivered and accompanying the movement of my right arm.

The nerve maneuver shot a deep dulling pain to Glen's senses, the torque applied just to the point of snapping the bones in his forearm. The air crackled with the energy delivered, as his body came lifting out of the chair to ease the pressure I slammed him to the refrigerator, heel shunting his chest with a force great enough to take the breath away and cause near blackout from the blow to the heart. Yet, only close. There was no way I wanted him to miss what I was about to say.

"Now, you listen to me, you sorry bastard. Understand? This is it, this is it for you ever touching her again. Understand? If in the smallest most infinite way you ever even consider breathing offensively to her again, I will kill you. That is not some small threat. It's a promise that I will carry out with a force that your little skinny ass will not be able to do anything about. If I have to go AWOL from the service I will. I will see you in hell. Understand?"

The volume, the intensity, the force of the statement came from fibers of hate that had been intertwined and woven to a thickness beyond knowing. It took every ounce of control ever trained and taught through the years of discipline to keep from taking his life. Then, there and now! The veins, hyper-extended from my neck, eyes turned a golden hue of rage and the trembling from the tightened and cocked hands and feet had nothing to do with fear. He felt, more than heard, what I had said. I had left no room for misunderstanding, no way.

It ended almost as soon as it started. His spirit broke, the rage and hatred he saw in my eyes and body had collapsed the once before "boss" of the house. His authority had been taken away, his wall of bullshit crumbled. The laws he had so ruthlessly enforced over the past decade and more were cancelled and void.

That night, that minute and situation, was the last confrontation of physical force ever delivered to my mother. She would never have to deal with the abuse and the mistreatment again. Glen BELIEVED- what I had said, though never responding verbally to the statement I had made. His eyes couldn't hide the transfer of feelings. Suddenly the fear that he had instilled in us for so long came back to haunt and reside inside his soul. The result would be a divorce, finally, in the not too far distant future.

Thankfully for the family, the threat I had made never had to be carried out. Yet at times, I almost wished it had been.

Glen left the kitchen that night like he was carrying a hundred pounds of weight on his back, never uttering a single sound. Within seconds of releasing his arm the dark blue bruise was forming on the wrist from the extreme pressure exerted. His chest looked similar, I'm sure.

"Mother! Come here please. It will be all right." Taking her in my arms and trying to comfort the tears and agony of the night. She buried her head in my chest and just let out so much of what she had privately carried. Shuddering tremors accompanied the tears and little breaths of air.

"I'm sorry, I'm so sorry you had to have this happen tonight." Her heart always tried to carry the burden for so many, even now, she was trying to apologize for what Glen had done.

"No, no, hush now. It was bound to happen some time. I'm glad it happened tonight. Now I can leave and not worry about you being safe here," Taking her face in my big hands, I looked into her eyes and finished. "You are going to be okay, Mom. He won't ever do this again. I love you and don't ever forget that. Also, God will take care of me. I'll be home before you know it. Promise, I really do!"

"You had better." Just a faint little turn of her lip, told me that she was over the worst part. For me it was time to go to Patty's, and wait on her arrival. Quickly dressing and grabbing my gear; a taxi on the way, I gave her my final hugs, and so longs.

Many moons would come and go before I would see her smiling face; at least I hoped that I would one day come home. Vietnam loomed in the recesses of my mind, the warfare already beginning to formulate.

The yellow cab was right on time in coming to pick me up. A short ride and he pulled to the curb, shutting the meter off and turning to say. "That will be $7.55, wait a minute, are you heading out to overseas? You know, my son is in Vietnam right now."

"Yes, sir, my flight leaves tomorrow for that foreign land."

"Then you take this ride as my farewell and please be careful." He smiled warmly and thoughtfully, extending his hand in the greeting.

"Well, thank you, sir. Thank you very much. That's real friendly of you."

"You just go on now and like I said, come back safe."

"Yes, sir, I'll do just that." Waving to him as he slowly left the lot and turned south back toward the downtown area for another fare.

Taking a seat on the porch of the apartment entrance, the night air was still and with a fragrance of the evergreen next to the sidewalk I gazed at the stars above my head. So many miles away they were, just like my thoughts. So much had transpired over these past several months, both for me personally and for so many members of my family. In the months that would follow, more would continue to change and reconstruct their lives and the way they lived.

A pair of headlights turned on the corner and headed in my direction. Looking carefully for anything familiar, I waited to see if this was the passenger I had awaited. Sure enough, it was.

"Oh, Michael, I'm so sorry I was so late in getting here." She exclaimed as she flew into my arms, with a passionate embrace. Taking her motion and body weight, I caught up the embrace and lifted Patty to my lips. Her feet dangling in the air below as our passion took the opportunity and the moment to ravish one another for a brief, hungry few seconds.

"God, I'm glad you finally got here. My time is very short, so let's please get inside." Taking all the luggage and my things she unlocked the door and we went inside. I quickly placed the bags on the floor and kicked the door closed with my foot. Her purse barely had time to drop to the carpet as I said,

"Come here to Poppa, sexy lady!" Her look was all the encouragement necessary, for the two of us to take the next two hours and fall into a dreamland, where no one else was allowed. The climactic ecstasy taking us to heights of urgency, and thresholds of passion we both had desired for so long. So little time for so much feeling and love to be passed on to one another, our bodies becoming the palette of a large painting, the oils becoming the colors and our hands the brushes creating the masterpiece. With each stroke, each touch, another scene portrayed, another dimension enhanced. The final stroke, a caress of depth and warmth flooded the heart of the portrait, the frame encased, the painting completed, now to just lie back and bask in the afterglow of the created work.

Two hearts, two minds, two souls, communicating through love, no words necessary, each and every sentence perfectly formed, delivered and understood. The hours quickly passed, the depth of feeling and closeness attained, one that we would miss from one another in the months to follow.

"I know you don't want to hear this, baby, but I have to start getting ready to go." It was almost like a shattering of the glass walls, which had been our refuge for the past hours. Shutting out and away all of the world and its problems and concerns, yet reality was at hand, coming to stay and not leave.

"No, Michael, just a little longer. Please just a little." It broke my heart to hear the yearning voice of the lady I loved. Knowing that the reply I must make was going to seem hard, but had to be said. The time had run out for, a little more.

"Honey, I have waited all the time I can. My flight leaves in one hour and fifteen minutes. That and it is a thirty minute drive to the airport."

"All right." Aquaducts had no more control over the water and the flow began to come, unchecked. No matter what I might think or do, it would not ease the situation at hand. I was going to war, now, and whether or not I returned or what exactly was to be my destiny was up to God, and no one else. I couldn't stop the feelings or the fact that I must leave.

"Patty, I love you more than life, lady, but the time has come for me to go. I have already called for a cab. Before you hit the ceiling, I felt it would be best. It is hard enough as it is, that I have to go. We would only have a few minutes, at best to be together if you took me to the airport. By the time you had found a parking space they would be calling for the flight. I will write you as soon as I can. Please know that I will send my love through the stars and the sunshine with every night and day that passes. I love you." She embraced me with a strength I didn't know that she possessed. I tried to put the feeling inside, to somehow sustain me, with her affection for the time to come. No verbal goodbye was ever said, only with her eyes, one which I would never, ever forget. The door closed softly with her face slowly retracting back inside the apartment, a last look, for who knows how long to come.

San Francisco, here comes all I've got to give. Vietnam, the refuge of so many lost and maimed, death had walked their last steps, their names would some day be etched on a long black marble wall in D.C. After countless tries to resurrect what had really gone on over there for almost fifteen years, now it was time to add the few small verses that would have my history recorded.

Mounting the plane from Albuquerque, I left all the things and people behind and the future took its first step with me aboard.

San Francisco, California, June 1968, the height of the "Peace" movement, had reared its head and deposited thousands along the coastline, San Diego to San Francisco. It was a vast sea of long hair, long beards, two fingered peace salutes and LSD, Purple Haze, Credence Clearwater Revival, Jimmy Hendrix, Iron Butterfly, Moby Grape, Country Joe and the Fish. The ebbed beginning of a band which would symbolize a following lasting three decades would emerge, the Grateful Dead. Jerry Garcia would become an icon in the minds of many.

The Beach Boys, Jan and Dean, would head the "surfing scene." Motown would be promoting The Drifters, Four Tops, Otis Redding and many more great groups like the fabulous Supremes. Haight-Ashbury was flourishing with a culture and way of living which would grow into large "communes" and cult groups across the broad reaches of the United States. A multitude of defectors and draft dodgers would be on the pipeline to Canada. Many were looking for a sweet deferrment which would cancel their obligation to go and fight, or at least do some sort of military obligation.

Yet I, along with the half million plus others would take the oath and the responsibility to go and do our time. More than fifty thousand would give even more, their life. This was the absolute ultimate, for everyone else, even the ones who had run away. Navy, Marine, Army, Air Force, Coast Guard, Reserves, both stateside and serving the world over in different situations. All these men and women would be represented as I stepped on the airlift to Da Nang.

The C-141 had long since been loaded and prepped with all the equipment and supplies. All this time we thought that we would be on the flight with the equipment. Yet quickly we found out they had chartered a Flying Tiger airlines aircraft to shuttle all of not only my group, but also the Charlie Company 1st MPs of the U.S. Marine Corps. A group of guys who would come into play and focus many months later during an assault on the perimeters of Da Nang, Vietnam.

Many of the forward position landing craft, of course, was already in service throughout the DMZ (Demilitarized Zone). The Nineteenth Parallel, above which we would never be sent to complete a mission, at least not on the books of public knowledge. PBR, river patrol boats and the Hueys would be our main assault positioning deploy vehicles.

Names like Phu Bai, Chu Lai, Arizona Territry, Operation Meade River, Rock Pile, and finally Operation Phoenix would be locked into our memory banks and our consciousness, never to be removed. Etched, scored, tattooed, and burnt into the deepest cells and structures the brain could experience.

Nineteen hours later the diaries would begin to fill, the headlines start to be written, the records began to be broken. Left behind would be hearts and families, children and memories that would fade as time passed. Clouded by the onslaught of mutilation, piercing cries in the darkness and isolation never before known possible, death was an everyday occurrence. The enemy would be one that no other American force had ever experienced before, until now. For their uniform and faces would change daily as well. Their age would be six to sixty, male-female, children with a lost innocence, just as deadly as those in their twenties.

In short, as the plane touched down for the landing, the words could have been painted on a flown banner. "Welcome to Vietnam," the stack of black zippered body bags over a hundred in number, greeting our first vision as we left the aircraft and caught a glimpse of what was to become our home for the tour. "Just what we had all been looking forward to." I truly don't think anyone could have planned, or foreseen the picture that greeted our eyes. It was to be a war that would ravage the bodies and minds of hundreds of thousands till their death and beyond. Just because they came back did not mean that the war had ended. The fighting in many instances had only just begun.

Jail, prison, alcoholism, drug addiction, the numbers would stagger the statisticians when compiling the records in years to come. But for now, the war raged on, "Tet" was in full swing and the level of confrontation was at its highest. June, 1968, temperature 116 degrees, humidity 94%, two Huey copters set down that morning, Monkey mountain-hill 337 the backdrop to the scene. There were local peasants and farmers working their crops in the dikes and rice paddies, there was also an occasional water buffalo. The lush green trees and jungle growth, was so thick from the air, that it was hard to believe that a man could move through that dense of forests.

There were coned, hand-woven hats on most of those below, a few children scattered and dispersed in the scenes as they came into view. I knew, that along with the men beside me that a level of drama orchestrated into hearts that would belie the chance of trying to live a "normal" life, later on. All this and more would be learned in the struggles, which would ensue over a man's individual conquest, while in this foreign land.

As it had been since the beginning of time and men in conflict, weeks became months, months in time became years, young innocent men and women aged more than mere birthdays. For they witnessed a war fought from too far away. People sitting behind desks in their large stuffed leather chairs making policy and deciding what and how it should be fought, most never truly understanding why we were really there. Hands tied behind the backs of many who could easily have had the war over in months. They had to sit and watch the chaos roll on, waiting for the approval of Congress or the Senate.

Meanwhile the black market became a beacon of greed, with the under the table and over the counter selling of military and PX goods, supplies and equipment. As well as the millions and millions of dollars paid to various "officials and politicians" some masked as farmers for their land and holdings, which the military needed for their bases and installations. Literally billions of dollars wasted from the mismanagement and lack of control on the quantities of food and supplies. But the war went forward into battle.

Meanwhile the death toll continued its toll, the wounded numbers reaching towards a half million men and women. So many of us wanting the chance to go out and turn it loose, really let us take all the power available and finish this thing once and for all.

A curious chain of events was taking place over these months of my service in the Asian theatre. One of the most singular was the fact that my sister Susan had met a military man, Robert Meredith, on leave in Albuquerque, and awaiting transfer to Vietnam. They had three weeks to get acquainted and on the night before taking the long flight overseas, he asked her to marry him. Six months later, when he qualified for an R&R, Susan, accompanied by my mother, flew to Hawaii to meet him and they got married. While awaiting his flight and the R&R to the islands, he and I met on the airstrip in Da Nang

The letters from Patty had begun to fade by the time I was out of the country only four months. Then by eight months they had stopped for all intents and purposes. It was my time for an R&R, so quick plans were made to meet there in Hawaii with Patty for the six days, five nights. She had put on almost fifty pounds since I had last seen her and changed so much. Realistically though, the major change had come in me. Another birthday had passed for me, but I had aged five years, possibly more in my heart.

The time spent together was a disaster, because of her weight she didn't want to go to the beach, she just wanted to stay in the room and sleep and eat. I finally had all I could take of the confinement and rented a motorcycle and took off on a tour of the island alone. Almost unbelievably looking forward to getting back to my unit and team, our goodbyes were very distant. I wondered what, if anything, would remain after the tour was completed.

Returning to "The 'Nam" was so different than the first flight in country. The schedule and the terrain and everyday life had become a pattern, a habit. A change was in the air one that I had not counted on, nor figured would ever come to pass. Yet it did.

April 30, 1969, 2120 hours, Da Nang, enemy infiltration to perimeter, Charlie Company 1st MP of the Marine Corps, a great group of guys are getting a large concentration of fire from the northeast sector. We had just come back from a long day and were resupplying and reenergizing, then it came, a full call out of all hands to aid in the defense. Enemy sappers, trying to blow the two hundred, fifty thousand gallons jet fuel storage tanks. As well they were trying to detonate the bomb and rocket dump facility. This storage area contained all of the aircraft ordinance, which was quite an array of explosive devices. Concentrations of 250,500 and even 1000-pound bombs, as well as the big 5000-pound Blockbusters, which were used for clearing instant chopper pads. Navy and Marine Corps F-4 Phantoms were flying major air support just north of us with ground strikes. A-6 Intruders showering the enemy with "willy peter" (white-phosphorus) and napalm.

Some of the aircraft were coming into Da Nang for hot fuels, never shutting down with bombs fully loaded and armed. There were men scrambling everywhere as the planes came rolling in, grabbing tow-bars, tractors and fuel vehicles. The whomp, whomp sounds of rocket explosions in the distance clearly told the trained ear that they were "walking them in." Each explosion was coming closer and closer to the airbase and the ammo dump.

"Decker, you and Guaderama head up to the perimeter emplacement and help out there. Take the SKS," Thomas yelled as we began to split up and facilitate our expertise.

"Larry, bring the M-79 along with you, we may need to lob a few pinecones and soften a few concentrations. I said to my buddies, "Piece in hand, my man, piece in hand."

Reaching the forward observation post, we promptly set up and began to survey the situation for enemy infiltration. Very quickly we saw five gooks moving along the razor wire at the outer defense point. They were working their way to the fuel storage.

"Yeah, they're moving down that channel of ground to take a chance at heaving a satchel charge. Let's wait and let them get closer and I will let the little M-79 do the lob-n-strike. It'll take the whole group at once."

Sure as he had said, they moved within range and boom, they were gone. The siege lasted for about four hours, not too bad. The rocket fire was somewhat intermittent. Securing our area, Larry and I headed back to the compound, as it was time to finally get some rest.

About two clicks from the main compound we heard a rocket go overhead and suddenly burn out. It was falling, from the glowing embers of the traced tail towards the ammo dump.

"Shit man, hit the cover." The words came out of my mouth as the flash and resulting thunder, a wave of incredible force swept across the ground. The first fireball was at least one hundred fifty feet high and three hundred feet long. It was a direct hit, to the dead center of the ammo dump, the secondary and subsequent explosions continued to "cook off" the big units. The concussion so great that it felt like the times we were up north and the B-52s would start laying it down. Making you feel the earth pound underneath your body as if it had a heartbeat of its own.

"Hell. Decker, you okay?" Larry looked and watched for some movement after the dust had somewhat cleared.

"No problem, man, hell, what a fireball."

"Shit, it was like the sun had probably just come out."

"Quite a show indeed," I replied to the comment.

Continuing our trek on back to the compound, the bombs and ammo continued to ignite, laying waste to the countryside. On approaching the flight line area where so much of the activity had been going on as we left, things were still cooking. Planes moving in and out like ants in their beds. Men scurried to and fro.

As luck would have it, our arrival would also bring the arrival of a very unwelcome guest. Especially with the company of close relatives in such close proximity. WHOMP, WHAM, WHAM!!! The explosion of the rocket round hit one of the barrier walls, and a fire immediately erupted. Not fifty feet from a F-4 being hot fueled, six 250-pound bombs, armed and hanging under the wing. Everyone came to a standstill, but hell, we had to get those bombs off that damn plane and quick. Pointing Larry to the bomb racks I ran to the plane and started directing traffic and men to facilitate getting the situation under control. Five bombs quickly dropped and we headed for safety out of the reach of the fire. Many other men were fighting the blaze itself.

One more bomb, just one more to move and the immediate threat would be taken care of. Reaching through to unlock the release pen from the far side to save time, I pulled the safety release and prepared to drop the unit.

WHOMP, another explosion hit and rocked the aircraft, just twisting the plane and causing enough torque to dislodge the pin. My arm was thrusting out of the way but not fast enough, a hot pain flooded my right leg sending fire to the very bone.

The right hand and forearm had made it through the gauntlet but the little finger had gotten smaller. Roughly two inches of the finger was stripped of all tissue, the final inch no longer there at all. That pain in my leg was from being blown up and ripped apart. A piece of steel matting that had dislodged, became shrapnel, and hit me in the right outer knee. It tore a three-inch-wide and two-inch-deep hole, it felt like my leg had come off.

Bracing myself against the place, hitting the down switch on the portable bomb carrier to lower the 250, I sank to the ground with the carrier, waiting cautiously for another blast. One of the guys from the fire group, seeing what had happened, ran to my assistance and pulled me a safe distance from the area.

"How bad are you hit, man?" There was a chilling look in his eyes.

"My right leg and hand, other than that I am fine. Decker, Michael Decker is the name," thanking him quickly. "Chris Roberts," he yelled above the noise of all the activity. That name would become a very big part of the rest of my life, he would become a close, close friend. But the next two days were spent on the tarmac of the runway waiting for a medical airlift to take me and about one hundred men to the U.S. Naval Hospital in Guam. I lay there out in the open and watching the bombs and aerial display of explosions, as the dump continued to burn off and detonate everything within. There was absolutely no way for anyone to get there and put it out. Consequently the airbase was pretty well shut down for the chance of something blowing up and damaging one of the aircraft.

My fellow team members would pay a constant vigil as the time passed, making sure that I had all I needed or wanted. Finishing the tour with them was not even a possibility as they had an immediate deployment up north. At the same time, I was scheduled for several surgeries to put the pieces back together.

Finally cleared for take off on May 3, 1969, the big bird lifted off for the island beyond the Tonkin Gulf. My stay there was approximately seven weeks, then on to the U.S. Navy Hospital in Corpus Christi, Texas, for some therapy on my hand and my leg. This duty station was really cake duty, here's why:

"Decker, says here that you have been serving duty in Vietnam for the past several months." Commander Gesling commented, as he read my chart, "wounded in action."

"Yes, sir, Commander." His stare caught my attention.

"I think you should have at least four weeks of therapy on that leg of yours. Monday and Tuesday mornings I want you at the clinic here, rest of the time I want you to take the liberty bus down to Padre Island and spend that time on the beach and in the ocean, it should be great therapy."

The look on his face told the real story, he was giving me a month of free passes to go down to one of the most crowded beaches on the Texas coast and cruise.

"Thank you, sir."

With that "okay," this was what made up my every week for the next month. The leg and my overall condition flourished in the warm, ocean water. The salt and swirling current, along with the good food, accompanied with an abundance of exercise and I was feeling great and in top form.

Multiple duty stations would come and go before me and during the continuation of my enlistment. Jacksonville, Florida, Barbados, Sigonella, Cicily, Rota, Spain and a few more.

Patty and I, after all this time had drifted farther and farther apart. Thankfully, to me, I had kept my promise to myself and never once cheated on her while the many months in Vietnam had come and gone. Yet one more, short affair, had taken its toll on the bonds which had been given many years before. We gave it one last shot by trying a three month stay in Rota, Spain, while I was assigned there. But this turned into a disaster of its own. So it was back to Jacksonville and preparation for my mustering out of the Navy. My dear sweet grandmother, "Nana," died soon after my return from Spain, ironically enough on Patty's twenty-first birthday.

A close friend, who had been trying to call "Nana" on the phone drove to the farm and found her collapsed on the kitchen floor. There was flour on her apron and hands from making pies all day. She had a soft peaceful look on her face. Grandee, my grandfather, had been down near Turkey, Texas hunting quail, as he loved to do. She would be missed by us all, especially by my grandfather. They had so many wonderful years together. The day of the funeral, a time to say goodbye for all of the family, was a very sad day. I took four days emergency leave to attend and then had to return back to my duty station.

Taking part of the proceeds of my savings, I purchased a new 1971 Buick Grand Sport Skylark, it was gold metallic with white leather to make the trip across the continent. I towed the little blue VW back with me, as it was to be part of the settlement to Patty. She was back in Phoenix by now staying with friends. A divorce had already been filed. My delivery of the car and then signature would complete the entire process. A free man indeed, I would be. Being separated so much, and all the problems, had long since taken away the bond of our hearts. Yet I would always have a special place for Patty in my heart.

I worked a job down in Ajo, Arizona for the Phelps Dodge copper mines building houses for the miners for about three weeks, before heading on to my final destination, Albuquerque, New Mexico. Earlier I had decided to give the college life a try, and maybe play a little football.

The divorce from Patty had been finalized, and the trip back to Albuquerque was a quick one. That Buick Gran Sport, with its 455 cubic inch motor rolled right on down the highway. Lucky for me the highway patrol seemingly had taken the day off or at the very least happened to be having coffee or lunch as I passed rapidly through their quadrant. Albuquerque itself was growing at an amazing pace. It was 1971 and technology breakthroughs had elevated research and testing in nuclear, space, and early computer hardware. Sandia Laboratories and many other national firms were moving to the southwest. Xerox, and many like sized companies had made this city, home. Levi Strauss and other manufacturing companies followed close behind in these shifts of industrialization. The University of New Mexico had grown to an enrollment of near forty thousand students, along with the dotting of seventeen high schools around the metropolitan area. This campus was about to be my new home of residence. Some education was on my list and a lot of football. This would be just the ticket for a 22-year-old freshman.

The added age and maturity would be a real advantage on the field, and of course with the ladies as well. Now that single was part of my life, it had cast its shadow around my feet. Finding a place to live was relatively easy as many of the friends that I had graduated from high school with were seniors and living in the Pi Kappa Alpha fraternity house. All of which just happened to be located only four doors down from seven of the largest sororities at the school. I am sure that this had a lot to do with the fact that the cumulative grade point average of the entire fraternity was 1.18.

Quickly settled into the third floor of the "house," I went down to the athletic department to talk to the football staff.

"Coach Dickson, my name is Michael Decker and I'm interested in playing ball for the Lobos." Putting my hand and a large smile out with the statement.

"Decker huh, are you any relation to the Decker that played ball down at NMMI several years back?" There was a knowing speck of familiarization in his tone.

"Well, yes, sir, I am the one that played down at NMMI under coach Brown. How did you know that, if I may ask?" I was curious and awaiting an answer.

"Coach Brown and I are old friends and back in '66-'67 he had told me about you and Marc Black and recommended you both for a scholarship. Then some kind of incident happened and you were expelled. Went on to finish out the season with Coach McGinnis here at Del Norte; that's right isn't it?"

"Yes, sir, that just about covers the whole deal." I couldn't believe that he knew so much about me and I was coming to tell him my story. The part of being expelled from NMMI was not in the report that I had planned either. There must have been a knowing look of shame on my face, as his reply indicated.

"Michael, what happened five years ago doesn't have anything to do with the here and now. If you came to play football, I'll give you a shot. You will be a "walk-on" and if you're good enough, we will discuss some of the options as far as tuition and meals, etc. Is that fair enough?"

"Yes, sir, that is more than fair. I promise you I am in great shape." Boasting with some pride and it was a fact of my conditioning.

"Yes, from the looks of you I would say you're lean and hungry." He smiled with a look of approval of having a freshman with the growth maturity and development I offered.

"Coach, I appreciate your time and the chance. When does spring ball start?"

"It will begin in three weeks."

"I'll see you then." Shaking his hand once again I left the field office and proceeded back to the Pike fraternity house.

The semester had just begun, January 1972, and the cold winds blew the mountain chill off the Sandia Crest and the snow covering its peaks. Traffic on the university, ran north and south and the east to west main drags of Lomas and Central, was heavy each and every day. Many of the students were commuting from the heights and valley schools.

On campus during these chilly mornings, the fraternity house with its three-story frame structure was a favorite hangout of nearly fifty in the living room alone. I had skipped most of the normal hazing and initiation processes associated with pledges. My age and the fact that all of the officers were fellow buddies of mine from many years back, shuffled some paperwork, so to say.

One of my fraternity brothers, Jim Maloof, was well connected with the local Coors beer distributor. Joe G. Maloof and Co. was Jim's father and he had consented to let us keep a keg tapper down in the basement. Free beer, sorority girls and a big house to party in, Yahoo! It truly was a free-for-all during the day and maximum overload at night.

My interest in the football program lasted about three months, it was cut short. That is, being a student and allowed on campus lasted only about three months. One of the first things I did after moving in the house was find out about a job offer working at the Silver Slipper nightclub. I was to work as a bouncer and doorman at one of the "HOT" clubs that many of the students attended. I checked IDs and maintained order and threw the drunks out and controlled the fighting. Getting paid three hundred a week, working only four nights, and along with the five hundred a month from the G.I. Bill program, I had plenty of spending money.

But being around so much drinking and partying began to take its toll. Downing a couple of beers before work at the house, two or three through the evening and a nightcap or two, it was a downhill spiral. The fights were becoming very commonplace, and my participation was brutal. Not only to stop the fight, I finished the fight on a regular basis.

Of course I was "in the right" as far as the law and the management was concerned. They loved the control I employed and the smooth running of their club. It was packed every night, and one of the reasons was that I allowed many of the sorority babes in that were not yet 21. It made my love life full, but also set up an altercation that got way out of hand.

April 30, 1972, a normal evening by all local standards. It was just another night to go to the Slipper and bang a few heads and flirt with a few girls. Finishing my shower, after a good workout and stretching routine, I put on a nice pair of slacks. A black silk shirt and pair of Ostrich boots rounded out my ensemble. Waving and saying good night to several of my frat brothers, I headed on down to the parking lot.

Awaiting me there was the new, to me, 440/Magnum R/T Dodge, red with a white vinyl top. Leather interior and the motor had been "played" with in the form of a full blueprint, pumping out near four hundred horsepower. The tuned Hedman headers and duel exhausts had a nice throaty, low growl to them. Turning the key allowed the beast to come alive.

Enjoying the looks as the car passed out of the parking lot onto the University, I turned left and again on Central. Waiting at the light for the turn signal my foot pulsed on the accelerator, revving the motor. Power of any form was entertaining to me. As the light changed I hit the pedal and allowed the big motor and the Torque-flite transmission to flow through the gears.

I headed east on Central, all the lights of the night lit the sidewalks with a neon rainbow of color. I left the windows down and was enjoying the cool breeze of the mid spring air. The trip to the club only took about fifteen minutes, and I rolled into my assigned parking place around 7:00 P.M.

Setting up the cash registers and getting the money from the safe, turning the pumps on and flooding the club with lights was the first tasks at hand. Completed in quick abandon, the other employees began to arrive around 7:15. The night began as usual with a crowd for the 7:30 to 9:00 power hour. It was ninety minutes of "two for the price of one" drinks and snacks. Most of the regulars were here, near a hundred people by the eight o'clock turn of the clock. Jimmy and Kathleen, two very efficient bartenders, were serving all the normal pours, interjecting the occasional "Screaming Orgasm or Sex on the Beach" personals.

As the crowd continued to grow, closing in on three hundred, the liquor flowed steadily in abundance. Adding the deep bass of the driving music and the stage was set for another blistering night of college party mania.

Michael Mercer, Tom Walker, Rodney Wallace, and several of the football squad were in attendance, along with many of my frat brothers. Hazy clouds of smoke gathering among many of the small clicks of students and young adults, chatter rising in volume with the amount of liquor consumed. The conversation was centered around who, what and where of all the many facets of campus and fun times. Many of the guys were making their ploy for a babe early, laying some groundwork to call upon later. The ladies were doing their thing in looking good and strutting their stuff.

Some of the more forward women were taking the challenge of trying for the company of a favorite "jock" or frat guy. All the games of courtship and "body shopping" were in full swing by 9:30P.M. Another two hours of continual drinking and the ambiance of the mood setting and many of the guys, primarily were well on their way to "beyond control."

With this event, a nightly event I might add, came the need to remove or at the least, reprimand some of the offenders. This usually was accomplished with words and limited physical contact. Yet now and then someone would want to get "froggy," resulting in his friends carrying their unconscious associate home. When they went that far, ten years of very devoted martial arts training came into being.

Most of the crowd had witnessed the outcome of this type of confrontation and wanted things calmed quietly. But in every group there would come, at least one, who wanted to test the bouncer and show how tough he was, a large mistake indeed.

As the bewitching hour of midnight struck soundly, along with it came six guys from the SAE fraternity to make their play for the evening. Having previously done near ten shots of Tequila, which I would later find out, and a case of beer on the drive down. Their power hour had gone far beyond the limit of control.

Steve Chamberlain, Barry Goldman, and Tom Summers, I knew, the other three were new to town and the club as well. They were all "rich kids," their daddies money providing the good life even before they had earned it. New cars, private apartments, fancy clothes and all the spending money that their spoiled asses could burn up.

Chamberlain was their frat president, really cocky, 6'4," about 245 pounds, thought he was God's gift to women and a real stud. He also thought his boxing skills made him a "bad boy," yet all of the fights I had heard of were with guys drunk off their butts, or much smaller dudes. Rumors had been flying around for months about his boasting that he could kick any bodies butt. Wrong.

On this eventful night he made many mistakes, the first being that he slapped a lady in my bar. She was not only a lady, but also one of the Pikettes. Who just happened to be our little sisters of the Pi Kappa Alpha Fraternity.

"Michael, Steve Chamberlain just slapped Julie and she's bleeding." Kathy, one of the cocktail waitresses, came running to tell me, a look of fear in her eyes.

"Where is he now?" My eyes were flashing and taking in a full span of the club. His boasting hand was pointing toward someone and he had a smile on his face. This is what I instantly saw, that smile was to disappear, just as instantly.

"Chamberlain, you made a big mistake." The words cut through the noise of the crowd, their cold, slowly spoken directness piercing the room. The words stopped conversations, turned eyes and heads as they focused on what was happening across the bar and the impending disaster.

"What's wrong, Decker, one of your little sisters crying?" The sarcasm was sickening as his glance was directed toward his comrades for their complete entertainment and approval.

"Yeah, she's crying and bleeding, you punk piece of shit. Just exactly what you are going to be doing, shortly." My gaze was one of rage, true born, bred and developed rage. Too damn many years of watching Glen Hancock abuse my sister and mother. It was a button, one that when pushed had no recall, only forward into battle.

"Oh, is ...." the last part being "that right," never finished crossing his lips.

A flashing right back fist broke his nose, a snap kick to the groin buckled him over. The axe kick chopping down to the back of Chamberlain's neck and the base of his skull dropped his face and body crashing to the floor, OUT COLD.

"Now the rest of you go get your fucking pal here out of my club and don't ever come back. Understand." Two heads shook in agreement, the rest stood there in partial shock. Their big bad friend was bleeding profusely from the nose and mouth. Tears streaming down his lily white skin and cheeks.

"Huh, yeah, you're a real tough guy," I said as they carried their friend from the bar.

Checking quickly on Julie, I found her in the office with Kathy, she had an ice pack on her cheek. There was a small red spot of blood seeping from the left corner of her mouth. Julie was about 5'3", and a hundred fifteen pounds soaking wet. Beautiful raven black hair/green sultry eyes and the face and figure to make a man dream, yet I was her big brother at heart, and that fact would never change.

"Hey there, little one, how's the cheek?" Reaching down to comfort her with a gentle touch to the shoulder and a soothing tone to my voice.

"I'll .... be fine. He is such a butt." An anguished blurt of an answer, her frustration was showing through completely.

"I know, I know. But he will never cross through that front again. Never! I promise you that for a fact." Assuring her that the situation was well under control and over with.

"Good," she answered.

"Kathy, I really appreciate your help tonight and the way you took care of Julie." Continuing, "I owe you big time."

"Well dinner would be okay to thank me with." A smile that went way beyond the mere aspect of accepting a thank you, shone across her face. Her near six foot frame so well put together and almost violet colored eyes, soooo sensual, she had grown up on the coast and the California girl still carried some of her Valley girl accent.

"I will be more than happy to reward you with dinner, and more. Maybe I'll even be the chef and offer dessert specials!"

"Served with a smile and maybe my boots on as well, if you are lucky that is." Teasing her just a little to lighten the mood "Whew, you in just your boots and a napkin or towel draped over your…"

"Goodness, Kathy!" Shocked and pleased at her forward suggestion in front of Julie.

"Hey, guys, remember…I'm here too, the one in pain." Julie jumped into the middle of the flirting.

"Yes, yes, I know, I'm sorry for carrying on." Quickly apologizing for shunning her during some flirting for a worthy cause, I moved the conversation forward.

Returning to the club floor, it was with many accolades for the act of, some thought heroism. Steve had pissed many people off over the course of his University experience. It was now near 1:00 and closing hour. Most of the bars stayed open until 2:00am, but our crowd was always too far gone to give them another hour of drinking and partying. As I was giving last call, a page for a telephone call came from the bar.

"Michael, you've got a call on line two." Jimmy said handing me the phone.

"This is Michael Decker, may I help you?"

"Yeah, mother fucker, you sure as hell can. Meet me at the SAE house in one hour and we'll see just how tough you are, PUNK!"

It was Steve Chamberlain, at his best, mouthing off and insulting me with a challenge. His hanging up the phone before I replied, told me a lot. First, that he had gone back to the frat house and drank himself into courage, along with his brothers, pumping and adding to the problem. I could just hear him saying that I had hit him from behind and all kinds of feeble excuses. This came as bottle after bottle of "tough guy" was poured down his throat. Okay, if you want to settle this, man to man, I'll bite. Julie walking through the bar as the call came, with her face beginning to swell and discolor, sealed the deal.

I made a quick call to Michael Mercer, he, Tom Walker and Rodney Wallace had gone to the house, right after I had busted up Chamberlain. I informed them that a fight was "on" and I would be by in thirty minutes to pick them up.

"Jimmy I want you and Kathleen to lock up tonight! I'm going to head out a little early, just drop the deposit in the upper box of the safe and I'll take care of it tomorrow."

"Sure, Michael, no problem. Is everything all right?" There was a frowned look on his face that accompanied the question.

"Yeah, fine, just fine. I need to take care of something personal in nature. No big thing."

"You got it, Bossman."

I waved to everyone as I left the door, and left them to close down. Jimmy had been with the owner for many years and knew the routine for closing probably better than I did. The Magnum fired and the Dodge was making tracks for the Pike house and a change of clothes. I knew that Mercer and the boys would be ready for all and everything. Their asses had been fried by the action earlier in the evening as well. SAE's wanted a fight, they'd better pack a lunch and call the national guard. We're coming and we'll deliver. Better than Pizza Hut. (Domino's wasn't around yet!) Comment to the editor only!!

"Deck, what's up man? Can you believe this guy's bullshit?" Mercer, five foot seven, 230 and about as kin to a fire hydrant as possible. Countless hours on the weight pile had double pumped his frame. Walker was to his left, and looking eager, at six foot and tipping the scales near 255. He was the right guard for the Lobos, and then there was Big Rodney. Funny how he got that nickname, 6'7" at 285, defensive tackle for the World Champion Dallas Cowboys. Down for a visit with some of his ex-Lobos, he had graduated from UNM two years earlier.

All three were primed and refined for the action.

"No I can't, but if he wants a more complete version written for him, I'll just have to dot his eyes and cross his teeth."

"Decker, you and your damn words." Walker chuckled.

Looking for something loose and comfortable I chose an old pair of GI fatigue bottoms and a cut off sweatshirt, with a Pitbull on the front, just for a little effect.

"Well troops let's make a move." Motioning to the rest of the team I made my way to the door. Goodness what a scene if the "boys" had been with me. Calm the rising storm. Yet the storm had begun to build long before now.

The clouds had begun to form with the striking of the first blow, earlier in the evening. They had thickened and darkened, and grown in height and width. By now the thunder began to rumble and shake its beginning. Lightning charging and readying for an explosive strike and deliverance of the power it contained.

We jumped into the car. Mercer was in the back with Walker. Big Rodney was in the bucket seat next to me. Once again the fire breathing dragon hissed his fire and the big Mopar launched from the starting gate. SAE house, here we come, as called, the thought circling the air.

Strange as it may seem the fraternity house was almost totally dark as I drove up and parked across the street. The four of us exited the vehicle and stood there for a moment surveying the outlay and the surrounding perimeter. Two large four feet tall concrete lions on their pedestals, painted gold, lined the entryway to the front door.

Something was strange, maybe they had chickened out, got smart by some miracle. Or just maybe this was some sort of trick, or dumb stunt. Sucking down a quick 12 ounces of Coors, enjoying all that Rocky Mountain spring water, I advanced to the enemies' turf. Everyone else was following close, Rodney at a very leisurely pace. He had a big contract, so being careful, he was mainly an observer.

"Michael, what do you think?" Mercer asked.

"Let's just see who the hell is home."

Jumping the four steps of the front staircase with one stride, I slammed my fist twice on the entry door. Announcing my arrival, and a few words to boot.

"All right, you chicken pieces of shit. Are you going to come out and finish this or do we have to bring it to you?" Shouting at a level which carried ten houses in either direction on the block.

"Especially, that punk sissy Chamberlain, damn hell of a president, SAEs."

No reply, but movement from within the house and a faint whispering as voices tried to communicate silently. Turning to Mercer and Walker I said.

"Fuck these guys, let's have a party." Jumping down to the concrete pedestal one of the two lions was perched on, I ripped it off the stand. Taking the two hundred pound beast and started for the door. Letting it fly as I yelled, "Now it's time; now it's time."

The force of the mass splintered the frame and crushed the door into the main hallway, driving the door nearly eight feet back inside the house. Two loud yells and the twenty some guys inside were caught in total surprise. Closest to me was about six feet and the crossed step and flanking maneuver, accompanied by a driving back kick to the solar plexus and he was down for the count. One down, and many more to go. Mercer came right in behind me and had knocked some paper-assed freshman into na na land as I turned, there were two down and out. Within three or four minutes, fourteen dudes would be pummeled. Four required hospitalization and ten a visit to the clinic for stitches and the like. Chamberlain was nowhere in sight, by this time I figured him to have run for cover.

Mercer and I had worked our way through the house and up to the second floor. The sounds of the battle, so one sided it was pathetic, were coming from throughout the house. Whimpers, moans and the frantic statements of pain and impending doom coming from those who were trying to help their fallen comrades. The strike of the lightning had been delivered, but not in the force and to whom it was still awaiting.

"Hell man, these pussies can't fight worth a shit. Let's get the fuck out of here." I said to Mercer as we turned to start down the stairway.

"Yeah, we should have sent the Pikettes for the revenge! He was attempting to rub the salt into the wounds of all the guys scattered throughout the encampment. Their shame and complete humiliation was the icing on the cake, indeed.

"Decker, look out!" the shout came from Rodney out on the front porch. He was looking in and just in time to see Chamberlain come out of a closet carrying a baseball bat. As I stepped down off the last step and turned the corner he let the bat swing. Full force, flying towards my head and face, it came.

Quickly shunt blocking with a high hand deflection move, the bat slammed into the edge of the outer corner of the staircase. Wood and drywall were splintering and came crumbling to the floor. An eighteen-inch span of the corner trim crushed and the 2x4 corner brace dented one and a half inches deep.

The look of terror on his face was one of utter panic. Steve had screwed up. His coward heart and shame of hiding was to be suddenly rectified by the blast to my face and his conquering of the foe, which was me. But the turn of events, not only now, the entire evening had been the biggest disaster of his young life. The ridicule and result was to be a loss of pride, honor and very quickly, the worst ass whipping he had ever experienced.

Grabbing the bat by the handle, I took it from his hands and broke it with my shin. It was a trick that a ROK Marine (Republic of Korea) Special Forces commander had shown me back in Vietnam. A truly powerful kick, it can snap a man's leg, like a twig of wood. The fear further heightened in Chamberlain's heart and mind.

"Well, the real punk finally showed his pussy face, huh." Looking directly into his eyes with a stare from the depths of a dragon's lair, the flames leaping from my eyes and tone of my voice, I watched as the fear began to mount.

"Anything you want to say before I kick your ass?" Knowing he was not going to say a damn thing, yet I waited. With a scream of terror, adrenaline aided and caused, he launched a wild punch toward my face. Side-stepping the blow, I reverse punched him square on the jaw, allowing his full body-weight and size to be moving forward before throwing the strike.

It was delivered with the torque thrust of my thighs, hips and coiled back and shoulder muscles. The strike had driven through not only to its target, but also beyond into deep flesh, bone and inner tissue. The center, large calloused knuckle, hardened from years of training on a Maki Wari board, and breaking demonstrations of bricks and concrete blocks, scored its mark.

The blow stopped his forward body motion and drove his face, then his body reeling backwards. Crunching bone and flesh as the shockwave continued through his jawbone. Hard bone turned to soft mush, as the knuckle drove deep into the jaw cavity. His form lay crumpled on the floor, the war was over, victory was ours. That is if there was any real victory to be had.

"Let's go get a beer, guys." I waved to the men-at-arms, we left and mounted our steeds, Gallant knights and dragon slayers.

By early Monday morning, the campus was alive with the rumors of the preceding weekend. Of course the story had grown in size and dimension, if not devastating enough on its own. Most of all, the staff had gotten wind of the altercation, including the athletic staff. The investigation rapidly came into focus and a counsel hearing set for the following Friday afternoon.

As quick as the investigation started it ended, case closed and verdict issued. Seems that one of the "victims" father was on the board of regents of the university, he saw to it that the decision was rendered with no mercy or consideration of the facts leading up to the fight. The SUB, student union building, had a posting of the final decree: "All three of the students involved in the assault at the SAE fraternity house, Michael Decker, Michael Mercer and Tom Walker are to be expelled from studies for a period of one year."

Of course this also meant that my G.I. Bill benefits would stop and the football scholarships, yes, I had been given one, were null and void as well. In addition to all of the fallout at the campus, the following Monday a civil lawsuit, was filed on the three of us for "malicious assault and battery." We, as a group, decided to just bypass all the legal mumbo jumbo and settle out of court. This finished up by taking nearly six thousand dollars from each of our pockets. That night had cost our education, sports and finances, to a degree, that left us broke and searching.

Thankfully for myself, at least, I still had a job, and I could stay at the fraternity house until the end of the semester. Also, I had met some guys who were trying to put together a restaurant deal down on San Mateo and Central Avenue at the First National Bank in the old vault located down in the basement of the building. They were having a few challenges with the construction, so I thought I would go check it out.

Montana Mining Company, what a name for a restaurant. Just how did they ever come up with a name like that? The corporation started down in El Paso, Texas back in 1971. With a money man, William Crombie, three guys with some guts-energy-smarts and talent, they dove in and gave it a go.

Montana Street was the first location, utilizing an old Lum's building, the quick food joint where they cooked the hotdogs in boiled beer flavoring. No wonder they went out of business. Gutting the building the group went to the old Santa Fe Railroad roundhouse that the city was tearing down. Making a deal for all the big timbers, solid oak, they began to design and build the interior to the theme of an old silver/gold mine.

There were individual dining alcoves, lots of wood and antique mining artifacts. Handmade oak parquet tables and bar, adorned the entire facility. Little miners' lanterns on each table, and a buffet salad bar made from three ore carts from a closed mine up in Colorado. This filled with ceramic pots and crushed ice for a beautiful display of color when the veggie's were added along with the homemade dressings.

Next they located a source for a big thick robust steak. Served it with a baked potato, corn-on-the-cob, glazed mushrooms or an artichoke. Toss in a big loaf of sourdough bread, 13oz. mug of beer or a 2oz. call mixed drink. Add a smiling face and a firm handshake, open the doors and give the people some "real" service = $$$$$$$$$$$$, it worked. Number 2, that is Montana Mining Company #2, came

along four months later. All the intangibles of the successful restaurant had been seen, created, organized, changed and delivered to the public at large. "Them" being the following list:
1. Great Location
2. Great Atmosphere
3. Tasty food and drink
4. Fabulous "personalized and courteous" service

All of this coupled with timing for the market and the road to the bank was worn with the trips to it. The cash rolled in at an alarming pace. Average net income per store, $34,000 each month, and growing as the popularity grew.

By the end of the first year, reason number one was not as important as when they first started. The reputation became such that people would drive for miles and stand in line or wait for up to three hours on a weekend night, just to get what Montana offered. It sure as heck didn't take long for me to find out all the particulars and want to join the team. There was something about being on a team that appealed to me, no matter what the category or group.

"Excuse me, my name is Michael Decker and I am interested in talking to the owner or manager about a job." Seeing someone who might know what was going on as I walked into the "Mine."

"You need to talk to either Rich Moe or Doug Smith. Mr. Moe is the large guy, about 6'8" over there at the salad bar. Doug Smith is the short guy with the mustache talking to the blonde at the end of the bar." Friendly enough fellow, he later turned out to be Bill, but went by the nickname Bullet.

"Thank you for the information. I'll see what they have to say."

I shook his hand and then headed toward the salad bar and waited for Mr. Rich Moe to finish his conversation. As I reached his immediate vicinity it was easily noticed that he was truly big, not just tall, but large framed and huge hands. Just had to have played some ball somewhere, no doubt.

"Mr. Moe, my name is Michael Decker and I am very interested in going to work here at Montana Mining Co. Are you doing any hiring?"

He turned slowly and took a short pause to answer while sizing up the voice that had asked the question. He looked to be around twenty-seven or so with sandy brown hair and brown eyes, a small scar to the side of his nose. It was very similar to the one that's given by a football helmet being jammed into a face during a head on tackle.

"Michael, Rich Moe, my pleasure. What kind of experience do you have in restaurants?"

"None, as far as work."

"But I sure as heck have eaten in enough of them. I love being around people and giving good service. I have been running a night club here in Albuquerque for the past few months and making a real good profit." He listened and smiled when I mentioned the fact that a good profit had been realized.

"What type of position were you going to try for, Michael?"

"Well, what do you have available, at this time?"

"About all that I could possibly use at this time, is someone to work as a waiter." Watching my eyes for a reaction he continued, "Would you be interested in that position?"

"If it's the ticket to get in the door of this company, yes, very definitely I am interested. After you see what I can do for you, then we can possibly talk about another job or direction."

I left it open-ended on purpose and the reverse look to see his reaction returned with favor and interest.

"Michael Decker, you've got a job. Be here at 3:30 this afternoon for some training and I will talk to you further at that time. We will discuss pay and work schedule and line out your first week here. Also the name is Rich, my dad is Mr. Moe." A pleasant smile followed the words and a firm grip said our goodbyes.

Charged and full of energy I took the stairway three steps at a time for the climb back to the ground level. Yes, I had lost almost everything as far as school and the campus life, but a good shot at a possible career had come to me as well. This was one chance that was going to get my full attention. Closing the door of the car, and cranking the engine, I turned on the radio to KQEO and let the Moody Blues and "Tuesday Afternoon," take me down the highway. Maybe things weren't quite as bad as I had originally thought. Let the past just filter away and allow the new beginning to be just that, a new start. Driving the R/T always made me feel better as well, with that powerful motor, and it was totally perfect, all the time. Washed at least once a week, most often twice, and waxed and detailed once a month. I took a great deal of pride in all the vehicles in my life and this one was certainly no exception. I also enjoyed the smiles and appreciation of others, both walking and driving past, as they gave their approval. The lines of the Dodge were sleek and had a class all their own. This car was one of the fastest on the street, not only said, but proven over and over in drags. Sunday afternoons at the Albuquerque Raceway was a confirmation of that fact. This added a little spending money to my pockets. One Sunday was ride along weekend and my mother took a chance and tried the thrill of coming out of the "hole" when the lights turned green. She was a fan at many things I enjoyed.

During my first few months back in Albuquerque, the final chapters of my mother finally getting her freedom were being written. She had already moved to an apartment and set up living by herself. Done the first motions of filing and started the property division stages with Glen. Of course he was being a real turkey's butt about the whole thing and making it as difficult as possible to get anything finished and agreed upon. One thing that had come down the pike, so to speak, was that the last night I had seen him, was the last touch or physical abuse she had ever experienced. From that night before heading to Vietnam my mother had told me that not even in the most remote way had he touched her. For her sake this fact was very important to me, for the resulting consequence would have been ...devastating to glen. Notice the small "g." Why?

The entire process of the final decree came six months from the file date. Betty, my mother, was finally free to come and go as a liberated free lady, a beautiful one at that. She went back to teaching, which was a godsend for the students who were fortunate enough to have her talents and expertise. They, as her students, would succeed in college and further studies because of the care and patience she continually gave with the highest standards of excellence. Her tenure and long history of success in the classroom, allowed for an easy transition back to the educational halls. She began to do things with her friends and her inner self, which had been stifled for so long, blossomed and unfurled its elegance for all to see and enjoy.

All of this was happening and I was trying to be as comforting and supportive as possible. Yet a plan was in the making as well. The two month period from my stay and exit from Arizona, to the start of classes at the University of New Mexico, took a small detour. I took off, to the mountains of the Sierra Nevada's and the gambling of Lake Tahoe. This was due to the fact that my father Hank Decker was working for the Sahara Tahoe in the Casino. He had run casinos and worked around the gambling business for now almost twenty years. It was an easy stride from the world of professional basketball to the halls of chance. Angel Nevus and others had been close associates with the money business for years.

I decided to go for the chance at possibly making some sort of relationship with him on the mend. To set a base and let time work from there.

After the long drive from Albuquerque, the lights of the upper stories of the larger hotels loomed on the horizon. Upper Donner Pass gave a complete panorama of the valley and the riches below. The two tallest towers were like beacons wooing the travelers to their web. Saying, "Come to the Sahara Tahoe, come to the Harrah's Casino, deposit your money here." My eyes took the sight as finally reaching my destination.

The air had a crisp, clean aroma and a purity that had been nonexistent to my nostrils for many years, since Platoro, as a young man, decades before. Towering blue spruce and pine trees added their "pine fresh" evergreen flavor and the reflection of the massive waters of the lake was a silver table beckoning all who dared. Breaking from the forests edge and nearing the town itself the commercialization of the businesses had created the "Strip" and all it had to offer. Twenty-four hours a day, just like Vegas, but with a slightly slower and much more friendly pace.

It seemed that most of the illusion was the fact that they took an approach of saying "welcome" and "thank you" more readily. The money all the same, would remain in their hands and out of your pockets, as you drove away from the visit. Kind of like the southern mentality of "Well welcome pardner, ya'll come back now, hear!" People just seemed not to mind losing as much by the tranquil lake and mountains, rather than the hustle and bustle of the asphalt/light jungle down at the foot of the mountains and spreading across the desert. Turning into the Sahara entrance, a red jacketed valet ran to greet and take the car.

"Sir, welcome to the Sahara. Here is your valet pass for the duration of your stay. Please enjoy and the best of luck to you." He had repeated that phrase probably ten thousand times, at least. Smiling with a seemingly genuine joy, as best he could, he was giving the warmth to get the tip. Taking the receipt I walked toward the entrance of the giant room. Not getting the name from only its size alone, it was absolutely huge, but the grandeur flowed with a regality, style and elegance. Wave after wave of kelly green felt bordered with maroon leather padded arm rests, their smartly dressed dealers all starched and wrinkle free. White and black their colors of choice, business colors for sure. Stacks of chips in a rainbow of colors, piled high for the taking or, losing. Pit bosses, shift managers, eyeing the tables and their players and then overhead, there were hundreds of cameras recording every detail and deal, experts scrutinizing every aspect and turn of the card, or roll of the dice.

A sea of people were sitting on stools, standing and moving

through the masses and different arenas. Cocktails were flowing, and the beautiful serving staff was watching for the big winners. With every holler of a winner, the waitresses hurrying to the customers side, in the hopes of that "big tip." This was the money business and their only reason for being there. It was a little less flagrant than Vegas, as previously mentioned, but all the same angles still within their scope of profit and the take.

"Excuse me, could you tell me where Mr. Hank Decker might be located?" I was smiling at the fine waitress, a flirting tone accompanying the question, P.J. were the initials stamped on the employee tag pinned to her breast pocket. Easily I noticed how full the pocket was that held the badge, her brunette hair lying softly down her shoulders framing of her face. She was a very attractive lady indeed.

"Are you Michael?" She asked in a coy and smiling, knowing way.

"Excuse me?" I said shocked how in the world she could have asked such a question. Hell, I had not introduced myself or made any announcement.

"Your father is a friend, acquaintance, well really my boss. He said that you were coming and gave a brief description for several of the cocktail waitresses to be on the lookout for."

"I see. No surprise possible in this joint, right?"

"Not with Hank, he knows everything about everything. Believe me all of us working the floor realize that." Her expression showed a look of total agreement with the fullness of her facts.

"Which direction would be my best chance of finding him?"

"Try over by the "No Limit Craps," there are some Saudis here and playing some major hot games right now. Because of the betting level, he has been keeping a close watch on the proceeds, understandably!"

"Thank you for your time, P.J., I'll head that direction and see if he's still close. Hope to be seeing more of you while I'm here."

Moving through the ocean of hopefuls, I took a left turn towards the craps area. A hearty yell told me I was going the right direction, someone had hit it big. Really big! Approaching the table, "the tower" of the casino could be seen from a distance. The nickname many called my dad, being 6'6" and with the boots, 6'8", he cut a wide swath as he moved from section to section of the casino. Tipping the scales near 270, he had a large frame and always dressed immaculate.

From the rear, as I approached, the gold silk blazer seemed a yard wide, and was complimented by black pressed wool trousers, and a belt closed with a gold nugget buckle. His shirt was a light pearl and out of fine linen, with a beautiful Italian silk tie. The only two pieces of jewelry were a diamond face, President Rolex and a size 19, gold, sand cast, ruby ring with the initial "H" on it.

"Excuse me Mr. Decker, I would like to bet a million on the hard eight." I was giving him a little buzz statement as I came to his side. One of his stories from days gone by was a man who had done just that and won, many years before. Whew!

"Hey, Mikkus, how are you?" Something he called me occasionally, thank God.

"Hello, Dad, how are the tables turning tonight?"

"Christ these damn Arabs keep driving me crazy. They have so damn much money that they bet on the craziest things and sure as hell some of the bastards are winning." There was a frustration in his voice, but he was fully in control of all around him, consistently.

"Maybe they need a chauffeur or something! What do you think?"

"Hell, these guys couldn't surprise me with whatever they might request. They're always wanting some off-the-wall thing, or food, from the most remote part of the world. Pain in the ass sometimes, but they pay for it in the end."

"You just wish that it would end a little sooner, right."

"That I do, my son, that I do. Have you had any dinner yet?"

"No, I just drove into town and headed straight to the hotel. There is plenty of spare room to eat maybe a cow or two."

"Let's go up to the private room and have a bite then and catch up on everything. Chuck, take over here while I go up and spend some time with my son." He called to the shift manager as he motioned which way to go by placing that large right hand on my shoulder. Several of the dealers and waitresses turned to see just who Mr. Decker's son was, as we left.

After a meal fit for feeding about ten rather than two, I could hardly move. Steak, lobster, and so many side dishes I couldn't even name all of them. Stuffed beyond, way beyond the call of duty. He said that he was going on back to the casino. So I parted company and took to the house. It was time to settle in and relax. More than anything else I wanted to call back to Albuquerque and check out what was going on and how everyone was doing, especially Lisa.

While I was back in the city a friend of my mother's, Darlene Carlson, was dating an engineer from the Sandia Labs named Carl Cianciabella. He had a daughter named Lisa Christine, and she was someone that Darlene was just dying to introduce me to. Once the intro was accomplished the rest was fate.

She was five-foot four, dark wonderful tanned skin, long beautiful hair, and the exotic eyes of her Cicilian heritage, with the fire and sensuality of the Latin. Her father being the first and her mother the second. Soft sultry voice, without even trying, fabulous figure and a heart so giving and warm, we had an immediate chemistry and the history was in the making.

Hoss, the big crossbreed was waiting for me as I drove up to the house. A large, more like huge Mackensie Husky. A special crossbreed with the Akita and the Blue tipped Malamute bred and the offspring then bred with a Timberwolf. Big, bad and he absolutely loved the water. If you didn't know him or vice versa, don't even think of coming near the house! He was "always hungry."

After a fast roll and wrestle with the wolf dog, now coated with hair and slobber, I brushed off the main coating and headed for the door. Barely getting in the door with all my things and keeping "Fido" out. Throwing everything on the couch, I turned to the phone and dialed the "505" area code and hoped she was home.

"Hello!" That voice of honey and gold stroked the lines between the states and floated to my heart.

"Hey, baby, what's going on in big ABQ?"

"Michael, oh it's so good to hear your voice. I miss you so much already. I love you." Instantly I wanted to turn and head for the car and drive back to New Mexico.

"I know, Lisa, god it already seems like forever since we were together. I love you too, so much."

"Guess what I already have a surprise for you! Listen!" The sound of "our" song began playing in the background. Turning it louder so I could hear better she returned to the phone.

"Can you hear it?" Her voice was so excited and trying to please.

"Goodness, yes I can hear it. And believe me I r-e-a-l-l-y do remember the firsts of everything with you, lover."

Roberta Flack's "First Time Ever" continued to bring back the memories, flooding my heart and mind with the close, intimate joy and special ness of days and weeks gone by, Sharing and holding one another, and being close ... so close. Almost dreaming.

"Me too, Michael, me too."

Cooing and verbally loving one another for nearly an hour, we finally cut it off, but not by choice. Her dad had to use the phone. So giving our goodbyes, regretfully the line disconnected.

Shortly after getting to the Tahoe, much more commonly called than Lake Tahoe, I began dropping the seeds and planting not so subtle suggestions. A lifelong dream had been for my father and mother to get back together. For years and years I had thought about the possibility. Now, with her divorce final, I began to earnestly pursue this conquest, both with her and my dad as well.

After several conversations on the phone, and a few roses sent along with some letters and so forth the stage was set. It was time for me to get back to Albuquerque and allow prodded fate to bring the lovebirds of twenty years ago, back together again. I had stuck my nose into it as far as possible, in reality, too far. Shortly after getting back home, Betty and Hank spent a weekend together in Tahoe. Accompanied and chaperoned by none other than Ms. Matchmaker herself, Darlene Carlson.

It went well and soon thereafter Mr. and Mrs. Decker had become a reality. Instant joy for me, but it was a joy that would fade quickly into darkness. For what I had tried to orchestrate and attained, had not been anything close to what should have happened. God had not blessed this union and because of it, it fell to waste. My efforts to create new happiness to the mother I loved so much, had in reality created sadness, pain and remorse.

A note on the dining table, three months after the ceremony, was the last word or sight of Hank Decker for many years to come. All he had been, in the dreams when I was a child, and the reconciliation I had made come about, caused more pain than I could have ever imagined. The lies told and the deceit exhibited, accompanied by the spineless non-verbalization, broke my mother's heart. For me I hated this situation, my involvement, and the man who had once again betrayed the kindest and most wonderful woman to have ever lived.

She shed many tears in private, but very few with us as her family. A shield quickly came up, to cover the frailty of her heart, for God in His all knowing care and protective healing way, sheltered His child. She was one that had and would serve and honor Him, every single day of her blessed life. Of all the wrongful men that had woven into her life, thankfully a saint would grace her heart before it was too late. A man that would love and pamper and caress her soul, a union anointed by the Heavenly Father. Time would pass before this took place, healing and mending time.

I could never forgive myself for the mistake and the blunder I had caused, me totally. I not only couldn't forgive myself, but the man who had amplified my grief. He could go straight to Hell, all the way straight to Hell.

First day, Montana Mining Company, I was ready for all the tests, trials, or whatever may lay before me. As I pulled the enormous brass handle, with the logo of the four miners carved and cast into the faceplate, the heavy metal door swung to allow my entrance. Dark, short weave, heavy commercial grade, wine red carpet led the way through the simulated shaft. Paintings and antiques from the "Gold and Silver Rush" era adorning the walls. The indirect and spot lighting showed the antiques thereby setting the mood for the patrons as they proceeded to the waiting and bar area. A large center circular fireplace, allowed for multiple seating in the lounge. During the long winters it was a welcome relief from the walk across the large parking area to escape the chill. As well as a wonderful place to gather and converse during the wait for a chosen booth and table.

A long single curved bar, with full mirrors and a back mantle taken from some old mansion of centuries past, adorned and promoted its look. It was solid oak with massive side pillars to hold the intricate shelving and mirrors. Custom millwork down the sides and across the bottom and top, scrolled beautiful patterns and decorative grooves to the fine sanded and finished grains of the wood. All this added to the ambiance and charm of the layout. Leather and walnut chairs and matching stools placed throughout to allow for ample seating as well as space to move about.

Directly off the main lounge the open buffet salad bar and expanded grill rose from the floor. This half walled area allowed the waiting customer, while making their own custom salad, to view the hearty steaks and lobster tails while the chiefs created their masterpiece. Because of the size of the salad plates, and good appetites, whetted by the extended waits for seating, monstrous creations were seen regularly.

This made for great tidings in the way of leftovers, many of which were not spoken for in the manner of a "doggie" bag to be carried back for later. The staff called these delectable treats "grunts," which were collected, trimmed and savored after a shift. Many times made into a mammoth sandwich, created by using a full loaf of sourdough bread, the meat with lettuce/tomato and other trimmings and a coating of homemade thousand island or blue cheese dressing. I would learn all of this and other tricks of the trade, quickly, very quickly.

Dining was done in individual dining alcoves, which consisted of four to five tables that were separated by divider walls. Solid to the halfway point, then alternate spaced 4x4 posts continuing to a height of near seven feet. All the wood in the restaurant stained to a dark hue and left raw and of course sawed for the rugged and more authentic aura.

A splash of bright color was placed in a panorama of vivid patterns of Mexican tile on the counter surface of the salad bar and the entire backsplash of the open grills. This brought the entire package to its completion and the theme was repeated over and over again across New Mexico, Texas and Oklahoma. They were just some old country boys trying to make a living, so to say.

"Rich, where do you want me to start? "Seeing him standing near the bar, I asked for my first orders as an employee.

"Michael, nice to see you. This is Doug Smith the new manager of this store. He will be the one directly in charge of all the operation on a weekly basis. "

"My pleasure to meet you, Mr. Smith."

"This must be the one that had mistaken you, for your dad, Rich" He was breaking the ice with a statement about my calling everyone "Sir" when I had first come to see Rich Moe. Evidently they had done some cussing and discussing about it earlier.

"Michael, its Doug and probably something else under your breath by the end of the night." I would soon learn that Doug Smith was always letting his dry and sometimes wet humor get interspersed within his normal conversations.

"Well Doug ... what first?"

"You might as well go see Janie and get all your paperwork out of the way. She is the cute little blonde in the office there and will show you all you need to know, or might want to!"

Taking the cue I headed for the office, it was a small area in back of the waiter's station where all of the tickets were processed along with the guest checks, cash and credit charges. I introduced myself and she took a few moments to show me all that needed to be done, then Janie continued to prepare for the nights business.

The first night was very easily accomplished, and a full week had passed before I even knew it. It was a great place to work and everyone chipped in, helping and making the work a source of joy rather than the normal pain. Friendly and warm and everyone doing their part, it was a group trained well and pleased with being in the people business. Tips the first week of $560.00 made quite an impression on my pocket book, which had been hit so hard with the university civil suit. Recovery from that incident was to be fast in the making. In fact two months later and the coffers were once again beginning to fill.

Lisa had come down to the restaurant on my first night off and by the time our meal was over she had a job there as well.

"Well if that isn't a fine how do you do! Take my lady to dinner and she woo's the boss into a job." Acclaiming all she had accomplished this evening. The smile on her face was a beaming light of both pride and embarrassment. Her beauty was so pure and natural.

"Michael, I was just inquiring about the "possibility" not anything definite. Mr. Smith just offered."

"Yeah, he offered, all right. He knew that your personality, charm and good looks would aid him in making money. Of course, in his strolls around the restaurant, catching a glimpse of your figure could have had something to do with it." She was glowing by now and I knew that the slap on the shoulder was coming. Whack!! I knew it.

"I can't believe you said that." She had her hands on her hips with just a hint of a pout. A slight uplifting of the right corner of Lisa's mouth brought forth the stifled chuckle about to escape!

"If you hold that too long it will jump out of you." She burst out with laughter, which came from right below her navel. I had seen it quiver when she laughed before, as we lay naked, playing on the bed. The memory of those times came casting their pleasures as I sat there and watched this wonderful young woman.

Finishing dinner we left the dining room and headed for the front entrance. Passing through the lounge area, Doug called out across the bar. "Okay, you two, thanks for coming in and we'll be seeing you tomorrow. Lisa, about 5:30 p.m. will be fine."

Waving to all of them we took the cues and walked on to the car. Lisa had to be in by midnight, it was 11:35 so there was no time left for anything but making a beeline to her house.

A quick, deep kiss was all we had a chance to work in. Wanting more, but also wanting to keep what little bit of a relationship that had been established with her father, we called it a night. He was not at all in favor of his youngest daughter seeing a man with my experience. The age difference was only six years, but the fact that I had already been married really bothered him.

Lisa and I snuck in as much time as possible to be intimate, and enjoy all the pleasures of the fiery chemistry that remained between us. But we wanted more and as the months flew by, our patience dwindled and the only solution was to make the next step.

Things with Montana had gone so well that they had put me in their managers' training program. This meant that every possible job there was in the restaurant had to be mastered. I cooked, bartended, waited tables, washed dishes, bussed tables, cleared, even did hosting and was the cashier. No matter what might take place in the restaurant, they wanted me to know each detail and procedure. Little did I know that the owners; William Crombie, Rich Moe, Bill MacMorran and Hector Martinez, were planning on making me an offer of considerable status and a big raise.

Lisa and I were married in April and decided to take a quick trip to El Paso for the honeymoon. Of course this was where the main offices of Montana Mining Company were. Rich Moe, in wishing us a happy marriage, asked if we could take a quick minute and stop by the office while in town. Not to take any large amount of our precious time together, just a few things to discuss.

The ceremony was small, fast and simple, what we both wanted. It took place at St. John's Methodist Church, with only the immediate family in attendance. Once the minister said, "I now pronounce you husband and wife," it was a kiss and "hasta luego," see you later. We were out the door and heading down the highway.

"Well, sweet lady, I'm proud to have you for my bride. I will love you forever." I reached over the console and took Lisa's hand. Taking small glances to her pretty face and eyes as we motored down the highway to El Paso, I was realizing what a lucky man I was.

"I love you too, my sweet man. Finally we can be together whenever we want." An expectant look of passion and desire was flowing from those sensual Latin eyes. The long eyelashes waved a message as they closed in a wave of whispers. My heart was racing with what I saw, the heat building in my loins. I knew in my mind, that there was no way in the world, we could make it all the way to El Paso. Another fifty miles, maybe, but then a detour down a side road, promptly would give us both what we wanted.

Sure enough it was only ten miles further and we made the first of three stops on the way to El Paso. The fire just wouldn't stop burning, it was raging between us.

"Well Mrs. Decker." I said, with a smirk of pride and a grin of satisfaction on my lips. "You keep this up and I will be old before my time."

"No you keep it up and I'll just enjoy it!" Her eyes opened wide and expressed the implied metaphor. The smell of passion was lingering from the lovemaking in the car. A sweet perspiration, mixed with excitement overflowing into lust. Chuckling to her comment I replied. "How about if we go by the office as we come through town and then we can take care of the visit, first. That will leave all the rest of our time for each other. What do you think?"

"That's fine by me. No problem."

With the agreement sealed, we took the exit to the office as soon as we entered the border town of El Paso. The sign signaled that Crombie, Moe & Assoc., Montana Mining Company was just around the bend. Seeing it up ahead I veered over in the right lane to make the turn into the parking space.

Rich Moe and Bill MacMorran were in the lobby as Lisa and I opened the door. The interior had a direct flavor of the old West, one of Mr. Crombie's hobbies was collecting memorabilia in the way of paintings, bronzes and artifacts.

"Well it's the two new lovebirds and newlyweds. Congratulations! Come here little lady and let me give you a hug." Rich reached for Lisa as I shook Bill's hand with a smile.

"Yeah Lisa, save one for me too please. Rich always tried to get all the good ones." Bill added with a false frown. They, along with all the managerial staff and owners, loved Lisa. Her personality was such a pleasure to be around and her charm was infectious. I had been diagnosed as terminal!!

After finishing all the formalities we got down to why they had wanted to have me stop by. Lisa and I both sat there in great anticipation, waiting. Rich began the meeting." Michael, the reason I, well all of the corporate staff, wanted you to come by is to give you an option of moving up with the firm. Not in direct management as in your own restaurant to manage. Yet you would be an outstanding manager, many of us have made that statement already. We here at the Mine have done some investigation into the construction background and ability you have in meeting deadlines. From all we have found out we are impressed. Due to this fact, I, as the President of this corporation, in full and complete of all the officers would like to offer this to you and your new bride. Michael, we want you to be our new Superintendent of Construction and Development Supervisor for our new restaurants. Also in conjunction with that position, Lisa we would like you to be on the staff as a field trainer for all the new stores, that Michael builds. As part of the package of benefits you would be put on salary, with a bonus and override program, full medical and dental insurance and a retirement program. Of course this would mean that you are a junior executive with Montana and would work directly with all of us here at corporate headquarters. In conjunction with your acceptance of this position, you and Lisa would be traveling to Tulsa, Oklahoma and building the next Montana Mining Company. This is to take place, the move, during the next three weeks. From there, you'll go on to Dallas, Texas for two more restaurants in the Northpark and Promenade Shopping Centers. From there the potential is truly unlimited. From your performance we expect a limited partnership by the end of your first year. What do you think?"

Goodness, what a dissertation. We both sat there almost speechless. The "meeting" was much more than I think either of us could have ever dreamed of. We were young and loved to travel and see new places. No anchors or holds on our lives to tie us down. Goodness, it was perfect, absolutely perfect. Looking to Lisa for the confirmation that I felt sure would be there, I met her eyes and spoke.
"No time is necessary to think this over Rich. You have just hired Montana Mining Company a new construction manager, as well as the best trainer for the new stores in Lisa, right baby?"
"Gosh YES!!" She was so full of joy it was running over.

Bill went to the back room and brought out a bottle of champagne, Dom, as a gift from the new marriage and jobs. We hugged and shook hands once again, then floated on out to the car. The realism of all that had been offered at the meeting would take the remainder of the afternoon to sink in and be savored.

The rest of the weekend was spent in total jubilation and complete celebration of all the many wonderful things that had taken place over the course of the day. Little cafe's out of the way and off the beaten path, became our preference, nothing fancy. Shopping for little gifts to take back to friends and family, the "horse trading" with the locals across the border, was enjoyed by both of us.

One rapid, fleeting recollection of the night I had come for Patty ran through my mind. As Lisa and I came through the general area, this was the only thought having anything to do with anything else. There was far too much happiness for any trauma to be interjected. The two of us loved one another, and sharing this love was the happiest I could ever remember being. Lisa had a spirit that encouraged me and caused energy to build and build. I knew that this was the start of something wonderful. It was a dream that had finally come true.

Getting back to Albuquerque was exciting with the news that we could share with both of our families. Allowing the excitement to be enjoyed by all, they gave they're blessing and well wishes. Most of the next three weeks were spent getting things in order to leave for Tulsa, Oklahoma. I had things to order and blueprints to begin doing take offs with, studying the outlay of the shopping center and the general location of the proposed site as well. 47th and Sheridan was a busy intersection, our chosen site, and I wanted to be very familiar with the vicinity. I needed to know what other businesses were in the center as new neighbors, and where all the best supply houses were located. In so doing I would have everything down pat to utilize all the time more efficiently and have a thorough game plan in mind.

Lisa shopped and spent a lot of time with her three sisters and some close friends. She was excited all the while, because of the new home and job offer.

"Can you believe we are really on the way?" I asked Lisa as we headed down 1-40 westbound for Amarillo and on to Tulsa. It was sunny and clear, the first week of May and the car was packed to overflow capacity.

"Yes, yes I can believe it and I am so excited Michael. I have never been to Oklahoma before. It will be such an adventure finding a new apartment and watching you build the new Montana Mining Company." Her effervescent smile confirmed each word of her answer. It made me happy to know that she wanted this to happen as much as I did.

Tulsa, Oklahoma was still in the main basin of the Baptist Bible Belt. Thus unlike a normal establishment that served, or wanted to serve liquor, it had to be done with a license issued as a private club. This application was the first thing on my list to get working when I began my check offs of things to accomplish.

Next on the agenda was the building permit and paying all the necessary deposits for the power, phone, water and refuse pickup. This building had been several other types of stores in the past. So there were ample things to remove before the real construction could begin. My days were full as I left the apartment at 5:30a.m. every morning and did not get home until seven or eight in the evening.

There was never a complaint from my new bride. In fact she would bring me lunch each day to save the time of going out. Several of the first days were spent tearing out the old layout, and Lisa jumped right in to help. She was truly my "soul mate" and fulfilling every expectation I had dreamed of in a wife, even more.

This first restaurant was built with my bare hands, so to say. To save overhead costs and due to this being a very small facility in comparison to all the other stores, I did it all. Hiring two laborers and working those hours allowed for the final inspection to be done in only eight and a half weeks.

Carpentry, plumbing, electrical, carpet, paint and furniture all completed and ready for customers. The decor was just a scaled down version of the bigger stores. This was due to, mainly testing the market before building a larger facility. Marketing strategy had shown a great potential, in this location and all the demographics. Yet the teller of the tale was when the doors opened for the first taste to the residents of Tulsa.

Our manner of advertising was to open for the first three nights by invitation only. Utilizing guest list from country clubs and other business sources, we compiled people who would spread the word of our arrival. This was accomplished by giving all of them a tasting tour of the restaurant. First night, all you could eat and drink on the house. Believe you me they took advantage of the "Texas" hospitality and gorged themselves.

All of the corporate staff had come up for the gala occasion, bringing their respective wives as well. Lisa had gone and bought a new dress and looked absolutely beautiful. The accolades, for the overall performance and the quality of work, was truly over whelming. Lisa and I both were pleased beyond words.

Praise in the community followed and when the first official night to the general public came to pass, success followed in its wake. From the first night and beyond, Montana Tulsa was a moneymaker and Lisa and I had been a major part of their success package.

Mr. Crombie insisted to Rich and Bill that a pay raise was necessary to retain my talents, so no one else would steal me away, he stated. They were in full agreement with his wishes and I certainly did nothing to deter that agreement as well. My momma didn't raise no fool.

Several of the people that the corporation had chosen as trainers, the top people from throughout the chain in their individual areas of expertise, had come to Tulsa. Four of them in fact, were from the team that Lisa and I had met, back in Albuquerque. Two of these guys were Charlie Vanstory and Monte Hough. A destiny with these men would be formulated which would last for many years to come. There will be more details later concerning the exploits of the three musketeers, sometimes four or more. Lisa had been such a large part of the success of this first store. Several nights a week she would pamper me with a massage and having everything I needed done long before my day had finished. She was a prize of rare, if even possible equal.

Packing was taken care of by hiring it done, this time, which was one of the other perks Mr. William Crombie had insisted upon. And who was I to argue? Dallas bound was on our agenda and the trip took place five days after the Tulsa opening. The weekend was for travel and the following Monday morning was to be opening day for work on the Northpark store. It was one of the largest shopping centers not only in Dallas but the United States. Neiman Marcus, Lord & Taylor, Saks, Titches, all of the luxury and upper crust stores were here. Accompanied by some three hundred filler stores. Raymond D. Nasher had developed this project over the past ten years and it was expanding to include business towers and an abundance of lease space.

This was going to be a challenge, to build the restaurant in the spot where the lease was made. It being the old garage and service center with the hydraulic lifts and all the equipment associated with the running of that type of operation.

A complete new design had to be facilitated and blueprints drawn up. This project would justify many subcontractors and craftsman as well. By the beginning of the full start, there would be roughly forty men at work. It was going to be a showpiece, with the potential to become a major cash producer. Not only that but it was a great opportunity for me to get in on the design production and make some of the ideas I had for a layout, come to fruition.

Eight days after landing ourselves in the metro area, Lisa and I had set up housekeeping, opened new bank accounts, and were ready for the kick off of Montana Dallas' project.

As the first tactor/trailer rig backed up to the front of the service area, it was "GO" for the count, that is countdown to completion. The new manager and assistant manager came that first week as well. I had talked it over with the corporate staff and discussed this possibility.

"Mr. Crombie, I have been considering something that I think will be very beneficial to both the individual and chain wide operation of Montana Mining Company. After looking at some of the overhead maintenance costs, on the data sheets from accounting, I think there is a way to cut costs. Most of the basic maintenance associated with the operating of a Mine, is really just that, basic. Adjusting this, tightening that, replacing a fuse-bulb-screw etc. with all of these tasks facilitated by the local managers. Training and the "know how" of the workings of the facility and the equipment is the key. By allowing for a basic understanding of these overall functions and operations, it could mean a reduction in this area of overhead by some thirty to forty percent.

When the dollar signs began to light the room, all of a sudden the limited attention became very acute. For now it was net profit, a difference in year end bonuses that was being discussed.

"Go ahead Michael, go ahead." Mr Crombie, being a moneyman himself was definitely interested. Moe, MacMorran and Martinez as well leaned forward in their seats.

"A restaurant is constructed in a certain way. Wiring and plumbing and equipment are installed and hardware like hinges and closers purchased and utilized. If the incoming new manager and Assistant manager could be a part of this ground floor installation, and visualization of the process of putting it together, a lot of the maintenance could be avoided. Allow the new men to be part of 'the actual construction team itself. Say during the final four to six weeks. Grab a hammer, screwdriver, paint brush, get dirty and take part in the actual building of their store. Let them see first hand what it takes to make everything work and how it is put together. A lot of the maintenance, we are currently having to hire done, is due to no preventative maintenance being performed. This can be accomplished by the managerial staff assigning these tasks to employees they have personally trained and overseen. They individually will have the knowledge necessary to accomplish this feat. The individual tradesman and I can take the added time to allow their observance of each step. I also think there will be a certain pride instilled to this team for sweating their stores to completion."

"Hell of an idea Michael, hell of an idea. I like it a lot. Gentlemen what do you think?" A full approval came from all of the corporate members, it was a unanimous decision. Thus it was instilled in the new opening bylaws that very day.

Pursuant to the new decision, Richard Selke and his new assistant came to the construction site and became a part of the actual labor force. I truly don't think he had ever done any physical work in his life. His creamy white, soft hands were so blistered and red after that first day, I knew he would never forget it. This was exactly what I had hoped to accomplish with the implementation of the work along program.

"Well Richard how do you like doing manual labor?"

"Damn, I know why I went to college and looked for a managers job. I couldn't do this everyday, no way in hell." His words were from his heart. There would be some character building done with this man in the next few weeks.

"Just hang in there Dude, you will profit and make many things easier for you and the store by learning how it's put together."

A few words of encouragement were given to feed the starving ego, or at least his self esteem.

Driving home that night I stopped off at the florist for a dozen roses. Lisa deserved something special and I thought that the flowers and a bottle of wine would say the thank you that I wanted to deliver.

"Hey pretty one, surprise!" Holding the flowers and the wine, I opened the door. The apartment was absolutely immaculate, just like she kept it every day. She was coming around from the kitchen as I stepped inside. She was doing her domestic "stuff," her long hair slightly drifting across her dark tanned cheeks. The halter top showing the rest of the almost black tan, as well as the full crown of her lovely breasts, what a sight. Her smile was growing as she rushed across the living room and pressed them against me. A flood of tingles shimmering up my spine with her body's warmth bonded to me. Our mouths met in enveloped eagerness, caressing one another's lips as if eating passion fruit.

The strength, the tenderness, the satisfaction of making love to one another stirred something so deep, so pure within the core of our being. A knowing without words, poetry and verse, musical lyrics of notes not remembered, but symphonies created ... enjoyed. Time passing as if there was no time, like the trail of a shooting star suddenly appearing and then fading into the night, yet it had been preparing for entry into the heavenly spaces for eons. It was a casting of the ultimate brilliance of its journey for a vibrant journey, bursting with such purpose and then slowly ebbing in the glow of the ended ride. This was a tranquility that caused all parts of the original mass to find peace, and final rest.

Hours later Lisa and I awoke to shower and sip the fruit of the vine. I had brought this home earlier with such good intentions of a quiet and restful night. It had worked, but the evening probably would not have been different even if I had not brought it home. That was just the way our love was, wonderful.

One month later the work was in the completion phase and the Dallas Montana was a thing of beauty. Walking through the eight by eight foot dual bronze door with the logo cast brass handles, brought you into a foyer with a twenty-foot high ceiling. Surrounded and supported by six of the solid oak timbers which had been left over from the original Mine in El Paso. Saved just for such a building, they were breathtaking. Turning right out of the foyer, brought the massive open circular hearth fireplace and waiting lounge into view. A large steel connecting collar suspended from the upper roof joists, at fourteen feet allowed six 8"x16" beams to be attached. They were twenty feet long and gave the room a cathedral span of big oak timbers. Two large ore buckets with their original turn buckles were shadowboxed above the beams and done with soft indirect lighting for a realistic effect. From this main floor area, which had a seating capacity of near eighty, and with the oak parquet table and leather chairs, then two six step stairways took you up to the main bar area to your left.

To the right was the passageway to seven individual dining alcoves, which held from twenty-five to thirty people each. While straight ahead was a dual access waiter station and triple cook station. All of this was done with the buffet salad bar made from four ore carts.

Each of which had been hand mounted to their original tracks. It had a beautiful antique copper canopy covering it with some of the most exquisite Mexican porcelain tile that I had ever seen. The dark walnut stained wood was rich with warmth and character, and was accented by the deep burgundy carpet. Indirect floor lighting on the corners and staircases reflected a polished luster to the brass hand rails and foot rails of the bar. Miners pan, picks, shovels and even and old slush box made the authenticity come to life. It was full of the matches with the logo on them, which were a collection piece themselves.

The kitchen was done in double thick white Marlite sheeting. The floors were covered and sealed on quarry, brick colored stone tile. The stainless steel tables and racks and equipment gleamed and said, "Look how clean I am and how efficient everything is stored." The Bailey coolers and freezers, were 12'x16', and held all the condiments and meats for the menu supreme. Wide work areas and hot water rinse stations for the six, brass floor drains allowed for quick, sterile cleaning. A health inspectors dream after all the traps he inspected each day.

All of the ideas, which I had given to the firm had been implemented and utilized; it was a joy to see them almost finished. Yet the largest part of my satisfaction was about to take place. My mother had flown down to meet an old friend from college and they were coming to inspect the results of my labors.

"Well, good afternoon ladies." I was waiting for them outside the front entrance. Watching my mother and Evelyn walk from the car, I knew that they would be impressed.

"Welcome to the Montana Mining Company, come right in and see the sights.

"Michael it's so big, and so beautiful. Gosh Betty I didn't realize that it was going to be so large. And my word, look at those doors." Evelyn was impressed and she hadn't seen anything yet.

"Oh son, this is just wonderful, please let's see the inside."

Almost like a little girl, her enthusiasm was overflowing as she stepped to the opening of the giant doors.

"Come right in ladies. Come right in."

They absolutely loved every aspect of the work and the design. My mother was so impressed that she could not believe her son really knew how to build all these things. After taking them on the full tour, I met Lisa at a local restaurant and entertained them completely.

Charlie Vanstory and Monte Hough came the next morning for the final set up, stocking and training of the new employees. From the first days in Albuquerque until now, each meeting had further bonded our friendship. We were definitely three peas from the same pod, with a fourth pea of the pod, Gary Smith very near.

It was a gala first three nights for the Northpark opening. As all of the "who's who in big "D" were there. So much advertising was accomplished by "word of mouth" during those three days that not once in the first two years of operation was there a night under four hundred dinners served. Many weekend nights hit the six hundred fifty mark. A record was seven hundred thirty four. At an average billing of $45.00 per person, it really was a gold mine.

Luckily for Lisa and me, we did not have to move for the building of the next store. It was just eight miles north on Coit Road in the Promenade Center, 2nd floor to the left of the escalator. It was six thousand square feet of blank space and looked huge when we first walked in that Monday morning. I had taken a week off after the store opening and traveled back to Albuquerque with Lisa, a visit as well as looking at another possible heights location at the intersection of Wyoming and Menual.

We said hello to all our friends and family and then quickly returned for the start of Dallas area number two, in Richardson. The work was definitely keeping me busy and left no idle time, but there was still a void in my life. An emptiness that neither Lisa nor my work or anything else was filling. Strange at times, being in such a full, seemingly so, lifestyle. There was a beckoning which I continually swallowed, a searching for drama, almost to the point of addiction.

A challenge was issued at the start of the Richardson facility by the Building Permit Department. While waiting for the permit to be typed, in a brief chat with the head building inspector, he asked how long it would be before I would open. Casually I threw out the figure "sixty-five days" from issue of permit to service of steaks.

"Are you trying to kid me? There is no way in hell you can open a restaurant of that size, built to code, in sixty five days."

"Mr. Peters, I'll take that bet and when you lose your loss will be that you have to take the entire staff of the building office out to dinner. That being on the first night we are open to the public. If I lose, I have to treat you all to the same meal out of my pocket, not the company."

"You have got a deal." Everyone in the office had overheard the bet and either way they were going to win. With knowing pride, I took the permit and left to have a very serious talk with the workers back at the center. This was one bet that there was no way I was going to lose.

"Okay, guys, this is the deal."

In very clear and plain orders, not English, I laid out what was going to transpire over the next two months. Making it redundantly precise that they would be expected to work, as they would observe me working and keep the same pace. If they couldn't keep the pace then get the hell out of the kitchen, my kitchen. My words were law and I expected them to be carried out to the fullest and most precise point possible. I knew that I could do this, make it happen, or I would die trying.

That next morning I started the pace I expected to be utilized. Strapping my tool belt on and taking that 32oz. Vaughn framing hammer and jacking it in its holder, I was ready to build. Seven days a week, twelve hours a day minimum was the expected output for the next two months, overtime paid on all time exceeding forty hours in a week. Huge paychecks were going to be possible if they stayed with the program. I kept this pace plus came an hour early to get everything ready, and stayed two to three hours later for prepping for the next days work.

It was back breaking work as every piece of lumber had to be hand carried to the 2nd floor. This included the beams as well, which was a major undertaking. Also there was no way to rig a hoist to stand and raise the beams in place so sheer muscle had to be used. I lifted things at times, which were in the four to six hundred pound category it had to be done.
"Damn Decker you are as strong as an ox. How in the bloody hell can you lift all that weight?" Charlie asked.
"Its all in the nut sack brother." There was a grin with the words, he knew that I was kidding.
"Nut sack hell. You keep lifting like that and you won't have a nut sack bubba!" Monte came chiding in with his two cents.
"I've been lifting things like this since I was knee high to a cactus." Glen had worked me like this for years when I was a little boy. I guess it just came natural.

They both stayed late that night and we clocked sixteen hours by the time our tools laid to rest for the day. We had started at five in the morning and it was now nine thirty.
"Hell of a day men."
"How about a few cold ones to wash down some of the dust and grime?"
"Count me in for a six pack."
"How about you Gary?" Charlie asked.
Gary Johnson was becoming one of the "Boys" as well. About five foot five or six and solid built for a short stocky guy. A little thin

on the hairline. He had a nickname of gopher, and was reputed to be in kinship with a horse, so the girls said.

Monte Hough was near my size and shape, his last name pronounced as if it was spelled Huff. From just north of Tyler, his father and mine, Grandee, would become friends in years to come.

Charlie Vanstory was from El Paso, cut from the mold of the old cowboy. Rough sawn and a heart of gold and I think a little brimstone as well. He was very intellectual and had a fine business mind. But a wild child when the beer flowed and the times got crazy. He wouldn't have backed down if the foe was a grizzly bear. He was definitely a bubba as they all were.

Killing the case, a six pack each, we called it a day and started out to the escalator and down to the sidewalk below.
"Hey mother fucker, get the hell off my car!" Gary yelled as we came around the corner. Six college guys were leaned up against and were actually sitting on his Chevrolet. A few beer cans strewn on the hood and thrown on the asphalt in the area.
"Are you talking to me you little sawed off piece of shit!" One of them flung back a comment. Blonde hair, about six three, 230 and near twenty or so, his big mouth was about to get shut.
"Yeah, I'm talking to your ass." Gary was clenching his fist and getting ready to go to fist city. I turned and looked at Charlie and Monte and smiled, this just might get interesting.
"If this starts let me have a couple of minutes before you jump in." They gave me a funny look at the request.

Walking straight up to the one with the big mouth, Gary got within arms reach. The group had formed a small semicircle around their, it seemed, leader of the pack.
"Just what in the hell do you think your doing lounging your shit all over my car, punk?" Gary was fit to be tied, and with the statement slipped his glasses off and gave them to Charlie.
"Oh is this a car? I thought it was a pile of junk!" WHAM! Gary buried his fist in the big guys guts. Catching him completely by surprise, and doubled him to a bent over stance. A full swing upper cut hook with the right and the blood spurted from the broken nose.

I was just to Gary's left and as he was making his second strike, two of the other members of the party tried to jump him from the sides. A spinning reverse back kick and the first to his left caught my foot thundering to his face. Planting quickly and changing my balance, a snap kick to the groin and double reverse punches to the throat and heart of the other and the fight was well over. The other three were a hundred yards away by this time and letting no grass grow under them as they left.

"Just where in the hell did you learn to fight like that Decker?" Charlie exclaimed.

"My sister showed me how to fight."

"Well don't ever sic your sister on me unless she's cute!" Monte chuckled as he got in a rib or two.

Driving home that night I realized how relaxed I was after working out at the fight that night. Was this part of what I had been missing in my everyday routine? Could this be it? The next day I made an appointment at the Texas Karate School for after work that night. For the next month, every night after work, I made arrangements to go and begin the practice of katas and strikes of years gone by. Part of the peace I had been yearning began to come back. A link in the chain of my completeness was hammered back together and made whole. Yet something, yes something was not there. For the life of me, I could not figure out what the remaining void could be.

The discipline was a large part of the tranquility returning. When a body and a mind are trained to do certain things in a patterned manner, a change from this routine causes an imbalance. Balance being the central driving force in Mu Shin, (no mindedness). In this discipline the mind goes to a state of total oneness with the breathing and rhythms of physical function. Blood flow and pressure regulation, heartbeat, lung expansion, mental processing, all these factors become one entity in Mu Shin. From this state comes the transfer to San Chin, which is preparing the warrior. San Chin releases the warrior in SeuChin, by allowing the explosive force to be unleashed with its fury. The inner core, almost from the nucleus of the atom, is the origination of this level of power.

It was an ever burning ember at the ready, ignitable on demand, in the instant of need. Turned on and off with the concentrated forces so perfectly honed and developed, a literal microswitch of the brain.

Fifty-nine days elapsed, six more to go until the wager is covered between the city official and myself. The building was proceeding at a furious pace. Night and day for the past eight weeks and strange as it may seem, all but two of the starters were still on board. The men had done a hell of a job and hung in there when the chips were down. Quality work and with the speed to boot, I was proud, damn proud.

Morning meeting, final push for the deadline, all the subcontractors and workers were assembled for this session. The concrete floor swept clean of all debris the night before. One of my pet peeves was a full clean out each night which made for the next day being so much more productive, no tripping and stumbling around, also much safer. Tool belts still slung over their shoulders and many with that last cup of coffee. A few of the men had a coke, part of their kickstart of the heart and go system. Not a cigarette amongst the group, as I did not allow any smoking on my job sites.

"Good morning men." There were a few grumbles from the crowd.

"We are here this morning to talk about the schedule for the next partial week. It is the final week of the job. I repeat, the FINAL WEEK of the job. You guys have done one heck of a job to date and I expect the same for the duration of this project. Normally with the completion of any of our restaurants, when the job is over we say so long and that's that. I am making a change of condition for this project, effective today. Each man that finishes this job with the same integrity it was started, and does so on time will get a bonus. The bonus will be a personal invitation to the grand opening. Any of the three all you can stuff nights, as I have talked about before, you pick one and that's your night. Bring a date, a spouse or a friend. Enjoy and have the best steak or lobster, or both that you ever tasted."

"In addition to the meal you will get a $100.00 gift certificate, which can be redeemed here at the restaurant. Or if you are closer to the Dallas location, it or any of the stores can be utilized for this treat. It's my way, and the company's way of saying thank you for the outstanding job you have done to date. Also for this week only, the company will spring for lunch. It will be brought in each day, so that we can take a quick break and continue working. It will not be necessary for you to leave the job site, thus giving us the added time for final completion. Are there any questions?"

"Yeah, what's for lunch?" Charlie asked.

"It's a surprise, you will just have to wait and see." He didn't really want to know. He was just being Charlie.

"If there are no more questions then let's hit the floor."

The hive of workers began the unfurling of the days ahead. There was no startup time each day. All of the power tools and extension cords were out and ready to go. Lumber and all other materials had been placed at the individual stations for the productivity to be kept at the highest level possible.

"Building office." The receptionist said when the line was picked up.

"Yes, is Mr. Peters there please?"

"Yes he is. Is this Mr. Decker from Montana Mining?"

"Yes, this is Michael."

"Just a moment and I will get him for you!" The excitement was very evident in her voice. She, and I bet all the department had been discussing the dinner I'm sure, for a bet was a bet.

"This is Mr. Peters, may I help you?"

"Mr. Peters, this is Michael Decker from Montana Mining Company. I was wondering if you could arrange for the final inspection and issue of the certificate of occupancy.......TODAY?"

There was a very noticeable silence on the line before he came back with a reply.

"You have got to be kidding me. There is no way for you to be ready to open."

"Mr. Peters, why don't you make it about 11:30 this morning and I will throw a couple of steaks on the grill for us to eat for lunch. You can have the C.O. already typed and bring it with you. That way we can do the inspection and have lunch as well, to celebrate."

"Darn, you are serious aren't you? You did it, you got finished in sixty-five days. I can't wait to see it. 11:30 will be fine as well, I'll see you then."

"Yes sir Mr. Peters, and I thank you for the prompt service. I will be looking forward to seeing you."

"Yeah, I just bet you are!"

He knew that the bet would be settled and that I would never have asked for the certificate of occupancy if things weren't totally finished.

The final three days had been absolutely a storm of activity at the Richardson store. With the workers flying, materials being delivered and a transition unfolding everything from the rough to the finished stage. It was almost like when you watch a movie on fast forward.

I had not been home for three days, a twenty-four hour vigil each day to oversee and coordinate all of the last minute details. Lisa had been a saint, as usual, bringing me a change of clothes and anything else I might need. This to include delivering some very special home cooked lasagna dinners and the like, for me. She made the best Italian dishes I had ever tasted. What a lady indeed.

"Mr. Peters, it is so nice to see you."

"Welcome to the new Montana Mining Company."

"Uh huh, I hear that tone of victory in your voice. You did this to get over on me didn't you?"

"Now Mr. Peters, would you think that I would possibly do such a thing?"

He could tell and so could I that this jostling was all in good humor and down deep he was just as proud as I was, that the facility was completed and done with grade A workmanship and skill. He had called the building office in Dallas a few times to check up on how the store had been handled and what level of expertise or work showed. Quickly he had been informed that not one red tag was issued for the entire project.

"Well maybe not. But you sure as heck won the bet didn't you."

"Yes, but in fact we both ended up winning!" A look of wonder crossed his face as I continued, with a little anticipation thrown in.

"Due to the fact that the restaurant was finished so far ahead of schedule, the company has authorized me to invite the entire building and inspection department, along with a guest with each of you, to the opening tonight. All of which is picked up by the Corporation."

His smile broadened as he spoke, "that is very nice of you Michael, and the entire staff will appreciate it. They have been waiting for this to happen for weeks now. My pocketbook is glad as well. But let me assure you that my wife and I will be regular customers and will recommend it to all our friends."

"That would be most appreciated sir, truly."

The walk through took a few minutes, as all the final tags were very much in order and evident. Throwing the two big rib eyes on the grill, they were history very rapidly.

It was a blowout, for the three opening nights of the "free" express. Not to be outdone by the Dallas store, the guest list included some of the local stars of the business and social community as well as four of the cast from "Dallas." The fanfare included a lot of press coverage and radio/television spots, also the newspapers kept up with the Jones's as well.

"Lisa can you believe that three new stores are already open? It's been only a year and look at all we've accomplished."

"WE?"

"It has been because you have worked like a possessed lunatic. Michael you can't keep this pace up. If you do I will be an under thirty widow, really!" There was a sadness to what she said. The many nights alone and seven day weeks had taken a toll on her as well.

"I know I have been pushing Lisa, but look how much money I have made this first year. You have all new furniture and clothes, and we have taken several nice trips, as well." Trying to overshadow all the time I had been away from her.

"Yes! All the trips A L O N E!"

"Honey, I know it has not been easy, but the big push for the expansion has eased now. We will go back now and build only one or two a year. At that pace I'll be home too much!"

"Too much. You just try and stay home too much and I'll wear you out." She was pouting in a whimsical manner and curling her mouth in that special kind of way.

"Is that a threat or a promise? Don't answer that! Instead let's go take a walk on the patio ledge." I led her out of the restaurant and onto the front veranda of the restaurant. It was the final night of opening and the guests had already left for home. All the employees were finishing up and some having their complimentary cocktails.

I had told several that knew Lisa with the likes of Charlie, Monte and Gary, who were already out on the ledge wall, to come. This wall looked down on the parking lot below. Lisa had seen a car in the showroom several weeks earlier, a new Datsun 280Z, light sapphire blue with the real wire wheels and customized exhaust. Silver leather interior and an upgrade pioneer stereo with Bose speakers.

I had made a deal with the dealer down in El Paso, he was a big fan of great steaks, ours! One of the trainers from El Paso had driven it down and got it broken in, while making the trip. It was polished and gleaming as it sat there under the large mercury lamp.

"Like I was saying earlier Lisa, I've been working hard but it does have its rewards. That is yours baby!" Pointing over the cap of the ledge to the car below, I watched as the excitement grew.

"Mine! That is mine!"

"Yours and only yours lover, in fact here are the keys. This key chain says Lisa, and that's your name." Smiling as I observed all the emotion and excitement coming from the lady that I love. A cheer went up from everyone else as they had been in on the surprise for over a week to insure silence.

"Oh my God!" grabbing the keys and flying down the escalator, she didn't need any more instruction for what she had seen.

With an enthusiasm, which was all hers, she drove me home that night. It took forever to get home though because for some unknown reason she kept thinking of places she "had" to go before finally we pulled to a stop. She thanked me in earnest for a long, long time that night, thankfully.

For roughly three months there had been rumors of the possibility that a major change might be in the making for Montana Mining Company. Several offers of a buyout had filtered through the proverbial grapevine. Most of the talk considered conjecture and little credence given to the rumors, by me anyway. Pepsi Cola, Coke, and many other large conglomerates were in the process of buying out chains from as small as ours to ones the size of Burger King, Taco Bell and Kentucky Fried Chicken.

These big corporations were so cash fat that they needed to diversify their holdings in order to continue their market coverage and percentage of hold, profit. After the Richardson store was finished a general meeting of the officers was held out in San Diego. This location was chosen because the corporation had purchased a 60-foot Bertram Sportfisher and had it moored there. Additionally they had just had a custom, built hot air balloon made, with our logo on the side.

Two perks for the staff and an occasional manager who had done a record setting month. While in San Diego we ate and drank and enjoyed the new toys, as well as had several down to earth sessions. Some of them got heated and one thing for sure, there was definitely some differing of opinions. One main decision was to not build anymore restaurants for at least one year and allow all the coffers to fill with the ongoing net returns. In so doing the corporation would be much more saleable, allowing for a selling price of near triple of what it could go for today.

My big stock option was not due for another year so this sounded like the thing to do. A catch was also in the plan for me, one that I didn't like the sound of. Since there would be no more expansion for at least one year, they asked me to step down from my position and go back to an individual store. In so doing, I would take about a thirty percent pay cut, but only for a year.

I had just bought a new car and all kinds of other new things and then I'm told to take a pay cut. My only other alternative was to find another position with another company. But what would I do?

CHAPTER 4

Mafia, Money, murder, and Deception

The answer was waiting for me a week later. Or should we say a bone was tossed to a possible hungry dog. A temptation beyond any that I had ever even dreamed of.

Three days back from the trip to San Diego, a phone call came from a person who had been around for almost seven years. It was a voice from the days of NMMI.

"Hello, may I help you?" A sound of light static signified a long distance call for sure. I wondered where it had come from.

"Yes, I am trying to get hold of Michael Decker."

The voice was familiar, but where in the world from? The service? School?

"This is Michael Decker." Curiously awaiting the response, listening very attentively so not to miss the tell tale accent or phrase.

"Decker .... this is Brian Dennard from NMMI. Hey guy it's been years, right?"

"Dennard, what in the hell are you calling me about. Shit I have not heard a single word from you in years."

"Yeah I know but I have been busy doing some things out here in California. Making great money and having some crazy times."

He hadn't changed a bit, sounded like the same guy I used to know back in high school. Still it was very odd for him to be calling me. There had not been any real friendship at all back in school and other than a casual acquaintance, nothing. Something here was strange.

"What kind of crazy things have you been up to?"

"That's why I'm calling you. What are you doing right now?"

"Well I am a Construction Superintendent for a growing restaurant chain and about to get my first stock option, making real decent money."

"And you just had a corporate meeting out here in California with a possible phase out of your position and for sure a pay reduction, right?"
"Excuse me! Where in the hell did you hear that?" Damn, I know for sure this bastard had not been at my private company meeting. Those meetings were closed and supposedly confidential.
"Where and how doesn't make any difference," Brian chided in confidence.
"The fact is I know for sure that this all went on, down here last week. I also know that the chances are more than good for this to take effect in the next two weeks. Your first payment on that new 280Z is due in two weeks as well."
"Brian, where in the fuck are you getting this information. None of what you are saying is in the least bit your business, true or not. I think it best if you just hang the damn phone up and get back to your beaches and sun before you piss me off and I fly out there and beat your fucking ass, understand?"

It was the reaction he had wanted. But he also had seen some of my handiwork first hand and knew I was definitely not beyond doing exactly what I had threatened. Personally!
"Whoa, just a minute I didn't mean to offend or pry into what is none of my business. It is just a fact that I work for someone that has access to whatever level of information he wants, any level, all the way to the Whitehouse. He is looking for someone to handle some of his business affairs for him. I took the liberty of referring you and your skills to him. Afterwards he said to call and invite you to his house for a chat and business offer. Before you say no, listen to the offer." "How would you like to make $1,000,000.00 dollars in the next six months or so, for real?"

This former schoolmate had lost it for sure. He was talking out of his butt and obviously must be on some kind of drug or something.
"Dennard you are just as full of shit as I remember. You can take all of this bullshit and cram it up your ass. Goodbye."

Before he could say anything I slammed the phone down and stood up to get some air. The audacity of that son-of-a-bitch to call and say what he said. A million dollars in six months, SURE.
"What was that call all about Michael? You seemed all mad?"
"Just some guy I used to know from a long time ago. It was about just a lot of nothing. How about if you and me go for that walk?"
"Sure, it's a date. Let me get my tennies on and I'll meet you at the door." She was always willing to please and go the extra mile if necessary. How in the world was I ever so lucky to have such a wife. Lucky, lucky, lucky, I was indeed.

After getting back from the walk we decided to catch a movie down at the cinema. "The Exorcist" had just begun and many had said it was one you would not forget. No kidding, it scared the hell out of both of us. That Satanic crap always gave me the willies anyway, kind of like the voodoo and black magic. I guess that anything that one does not fully understand, the unknown causes a keen suspense and chill.

When we had returned from the movie and were walking to the door, I noticed a package propped against the entrance.

"Lisa hold it right here for a minute please, just a minute." Putting my hand out in front of her to stop, she stopped instantly. I knelt in front of the package and checked for any wires or attachments. I was also checking for any presence of noise or a thickness that might indicate something other than just plain mail.

"Michael, what is it?" In a whisper she asked.

Raising my hand to signal, "patience," I said, "Just a minute Lisa, I just want to be careful that nothing funny is going on here. Please do me a favor and go get that pair of scissors out of the toolbox in my truck. Quickly! After you get them just lay them down here and go back and stand by the curb." Her eyes showed a dislike, of what was happening, also a very curious spirit. Having just seen the "The Exorcist" did not help in the least.

"Whatever you are doing is making me very nervous, Michael. So please be careful, okay?"

"Yes, honey, just lay the scissors down and wait for just a minute and everything will be fine, I promise."

The jungles of Vietnam were back and the caution necessary to keep from getting your ass blown away was there. The smells and feel were almost there as well. I must get this safe for Lisa.

Slowly opening the upper side of the package, and taking extreme care to neither jar, nor move the position of it, was painstaking but necessary. I had witnessed too many careless people overseas and had seen the grisly results, if there were any results left that is.

Making sure that a flow tube of mercury or any type of static relay or switch was not there I inspected the contents. One American Airlines ticket first class to San Diego. $1,000.00 cash in hundred dollar bills and a note that a limo would be there to pick me up if I was on the plane. If not, then this would be the last contact and to enjoy the money. Signed "Brian!"

"It's fine, babe, it is just a plane ticket and things. Let's go inside." Upon entering the apartment I sat down and we went into the full details of the phone call and now the package.

If this guy, who ever the hell he was had so easily got the information that was given from Brian, and had made this delivery take place, it was time to make this meeting happen. I was going to put an immediate stop to this foolishness, once and for all. Nobody but nobody, was going to be snooping around my family and business, not while I was still alive and kicking.

Lisa and I agreed that I would go out the next day and see what all the spy crap was all about, and who this spy guy might be?

American Airlines has a major terminal at the DFW Airport. Stretching for almost two thirds of a mile, forty-eight domestic and eight international gates to serve in the neighborhood of twenty thousand passengers a day. It's a forty-five minute drive to the beginning of the mammoth structure and parking can be a literal nightmare. Miss the right exit and spend an additional twenty minutes just getting back to the starting point.

Thankfully on this sunny day, I hit the exit on the first try and did not have to do the world tour. Flight 514 was to depart gate 16 at 11:15 am and I was getting out of the car near 9:45 for some ample lead time. During the drive I had gone over several scenarios of the day at hand. All of which I knew would be hashed and rehashed a dozen times, during the flight.

There had been a great deal of anticipation and worry on Lisa's behalf before I was out the door. All the secrecy with the package made her very uncomfortable about what all this would mean for us. Yet in her standard way she gave the support from her heart that I needed, to feel comfortable in going. It took assurances of multiple callbacks to keep her updated and current for a little of the security she felt with my presence, to remain.

I had packed light with an extra pair of Wranglers and two shirts, tossing in a light jacket as well. A shaving kit and a couple of magazines and my list was complete. My Tony Lama Ostrich boots had a double coat of polish on them. Just in case they got scuffed I could buff them with a brush and they would appear polished once again.

Not only was it a sunny day but also the sky was as clear blue as pure water from a mountain stream. This should be a smooth and relaxing flight. Terminal number four was busy that morning with all the business travelers trying to get to Chicago, Denver, New York and L.A. The suits and briefcases were rushing here and there, a mother and stroller with her infant daughter passing in front of me, probably going off to Mom's house to show off the new addition. In fact the little girl was absolutely precious in the frilly white lace outfit, all snuggled in the cozy knit blanket. Totally unaware of anything but Mom's face and the Teddy Bear cuddled under her tiny arm.

Taking a seat in the immediate gate area, I waited for the flight to be called by flipping through one of the magazines that I brought to pass the time. I was reading some of the articles of interest and also watching the parade as it marched and at times, ran by.

"Flight 514 is now ready for boarding at gate 16. Please have your ticket and boarding pass handy. Thank you for choosing American this morning and enjoy your flight."

With the announcement came the normal rush of passengers trying to be towards the front of the line. Since I had picked a seat near the boarding area, by standing I was already in line. My carryon, was all the luggage needed for the trip so the overhead fulfilled all the space necessary for storage. It would also allow for a quick exit when landing in the San Diego terminal. I wanted to be off the plane promptly and have a look around at just who would have been sent for the ride to the hotel. There was no telling just how in depth this meeting was to be, or the people possibly involved.

Two hours and fifteen minutes after leaving the DFW airport we were touching the ground on the California coast. Coming in over La Jolla and the area around Point Loma, NTC San Diego and all those white uniforms walking around like toy sailors to our left.

Phoenix had been the shuttle change for some of the California passengers. It was here that the split of San Diego, L.A. and San Francisco took place. For me and flight 514, it was to stay on the plane for thirty minutes ground time, then straight on to downtown Diego. The weather had held for the entire journey, very few bumps and jolts. The service had been exemplary, not only because it was in first class, but the flight attendants themselves had done an above average personal job. This is always a key factor in good service, attitude. Banking now across Mission Bay, Sea World looming almost directly beneath our glide path, the roar of the landing gear being deployed filled the cabin until it locked. With a light shudder and smoke coming from the tires, the big airliner made its touchdown and rolled on to the arrival gate.

I had a feeling like the touchdown in Vietnam, very similar, and began to find its way through my veins. Was this somehow related? Today was April 29, 1973, it was on April 30, 1969 that I had been wounded in the battle outside Da Nang. Some correlation possibly? A heightened awareness calling on the patterned responses so thoroughly hardened and developed, came alive. No mistakes were going to be made in this, so called offer of employment. This was business and nothing more, serious business.

Gathering my things, I dropped the lever of the overhead compartment and lifted out the small bag, then turning to make my exit from the aircraft through the mobile walkway to the terminal complex. Being in first class I was second in line and at 6'5" with my boots on I had a wide view in covering the entire receiving area. Scanning the area I watched for a familiar face or one that might seem out of place. Equally important as well!

As I left the gate area and proceeded down the corridor to the baggage and ticket counter main lobby, nothing out of the ordinary came into focus. Seeing a phone bank in this outer lobby I stopped for a quick call or two.

"Hey sweet one, I'm here and everything's fine."

"Oh Michael, I have been on pins and needles ever since you left." The elevated pitch to Lisa's voice said as much.

"Honey it's just great out here. The weather is beautiful and please don't worry because I'm in good hands, mine."

"Oh you!"

"I have to go now so take care and I'll see you tomorrow. Don't forget, I love you."

"Michael, I love you too, BYE."

Hanging up and redialing I continued.

"Hello."

"Larry or should I say Mr. Guad?"

"The Decker man, hey what the hell are you doing?"

Just to cover a few bases and possibly my ass, I was making a base contact with one of my former special warfare buddies. He would have all the equipment and personnel on hand if either was needed in an emergency.

"I am out here in Diego for two days checking out a possible offer. It has a certain flavor to it that might require some cleaning so I thought you might have plenty of soap!" He knew damn well what I was saying with this statement.

"Hey, I've just been to the store and the shelves are full. Also depending on how many loads you need to do I can find extra help."

"Thanks brother, we'll chat tomorrow."

"The Guad man, out!"

Clean, clear and precise just as in the old days, everything was ready no matter what might be needed. Throw down or shut down.

Outside the span of glass, which divided the terminal lobby and the street unloading and pickup area, the view encompassed the full length of the street. No vehicle could approach or depart without them coming into my sight. Scanning carefully, three limousines sat waiting for their prospective clients, guests or owners, whichever the case might be. A standard stretch Lincoln, Luxury Golden Eagle Cadillac and a custom Rolls Royce Limousine, black-black and Burgundy.

From the colors of the three, I choose burgundy, from the look of wealth the same. From the drivers standing by their coaches, only the Rolls and the Lincoln seemed to be carrying a piece. This told me all I needed to know for now. Turning towards the men's room I went for a short break.

Two men at the sink washing up and combing they're hair, both with that look of "the wife will be waiting," on their faces. Looking for feet under the stalls it was clear for the entire bathroom. White ceramic tile caused the room to reflect the fluorescent light to a heightened intensity. Stainless steel doors of the stalls gave it an almost hospital look. Slipping into the stall at the far end of the room I turned and shut and latched the door.

As I sat on the toilet lid I pulled down my Wranglers so that from the outside, anyone would think that all's well inside. Pulling the small carrying bag to my lap, I unsnapped and unzipped the top. From seven different small compartments I pulled several pieces of the Walther and began to assemble the weapon. .380 caliber, clip fed and just enough for emergency close in use. I had not mentioned it to Lisa, but there was no way in hell I was going anywhere without a piece. The carryon bag had been made for me by a friend, back when I was in the service. It was made with special material and could easily hide a light firearm if it had been disassembled.

Now I was ready to go to my chariot, having put some of the reins in my corner. Upon walking through the main doors and stepping to the sidewalk and curb, a sign went up from the driver of the Rolls. My instincts were exactly where they need to be. Crossing the street I approached the car, feeling the Walther snuggled up to my boot inside. The driver was a Mexican national, approximately mid-thirties, about five eight and near 200 pounds
"Senor Deeker?" Partial question and almost got the last name correct.
"Yes, Michael Decker."
"Please Senor." Opening the right side rear door for me to step in, I saw a set of shoes and trousers to the knee from the outside of the car. Leaning slowly I peered in and inside was Brian Dennard, a little heavier and a little older than I had remembered. He had blonde hair, long to the bottom of his neck. Five foot ten, 220 pounds and it wasn't from the gym it was from the table. His silk shirt so gaudy it almost

hurt my eyes. His deepset eyes were looking almost in a void, many years of drugs had found their way through this body and this system, damaging so much, their waste evident in the skin tone and color.

"Decker! Long time, dude." God he had been in California for way to long.

"Yeah, a real long time." Probably not long enough, I said after seeing his face.

"This will be a hell of a visit I promise you. You are going to be flat amazed at all I have to show and tell you."

The driver had returned to his station and was pulling from the curb into the flow of traffic. Exiting the airport around by the Sheraton and headed for the main freeway going north to L.A. and south to Chula Vista and on to Tiajuana.

As the driver pulled the Rolls in the southbound ramp we climbed to the upper level and swung into the oncoming masses. Looping just to the east of the downtown area, several new highrise buildings, both hotels and offices showed their new configurations gleaming mirrored windows and panels.

The interior on the Rolls was totally custom done, leather and real walnut, thick and rich with no veneer, chrome and crystal with the full bar stocked and waiting. Heavier panels and bulletproof glass showed that whomever this vehicle had been designed and built for was possibly expecting trouble. Or at the very least prepared for whatever might come along.

"Decker, do you want something to drink?"

"No I am fine." Watching the driver regularly checking his rear view mirror for signs, possibly of trouble, wary in his stare, I reached for the partition button and switched it to push the privacy curtain up and cancel his view.

"Now Dennard, how about you cut all the bullshit chatter and tell me just what in the hell this crap is all about. I am warning you in advance to not try and feed me some fantasy tale. If I pick that up from you, the first thing is I will beat your ass and second this fucking car will be heading quickly back to the airport."

"Christ, okay, settle down I was not trying to offend you."

"Then don't."

Cutting him off in mid sentence, his eyes and hands twitching with the nervousness brought on by the direct words I had spoken.

"What this is all about, and my boss will fill you in much more than me, is money. I mean more money than you have ever seen or dreamed of. He runs a distribution network, which covers Mexico, South America, much of the United States and even into Europe and Asia.

Thousands of people work for him and within his organization. They are moving products and taking in money daily. Like I mean millions and millions of dollars, cash money. My boss is Alberto Sicilia-Falcon and he is one of the most powerful and influential men anywhere in this hemisphere. What he is looking for is someone to take over, all his security and train a militia force for himself and several of his partners."

"Yes, and why me? Why after so many years does some guy I haven't heard from call me?" His body language was shifting once again.

"Because Falcon saw the file on you and you're who he wants to take the position."

"What file?"

"I don't know all the details, except that he told me your file impressed him and he wanted to meet you personally and discuss this offer. I'm just a delivery person for him and was told to bring you to the hotel and await further orders. That's all, I swear."

"Then let's call this conversation over until you get your further orders." Leaning back in the seat I followed the view from the window and could see that we were fast approaching the border crossing into Tijuana, Mexico. Curious just who this Falcon might be, I mean for real and not the story I had heard from Dennard. Soon enough, it wouldn't be long now.

Shortly after passing the border towers the limo took a left then two rights and another left pulling up in front of the Royal Hotel. Not exactly your Marriot or Hilton or Ritz-Carlton but adequate for the length of stay at hand. As the car came to a stop, two porters dressed in their sharply creased Royal blue uniforms, scurried to help with doors, luggage and any assistance necessary. They were both in their late teens and were probably working to help support many brothers and sisters. A gringo, Americano, was a source of tips much larger than the ones their fellow Mexicans gave, so the service was ever ready.

There was no checkin process necessary, we proceeded straight to a private elevator, and only one button was on the panel inside. It said Penthouse. A Penthouse in a standard hotel in Tijuana, Mexico, different but not completely out of the question. No eye contact from Brian Dennard, the driver or the two attendants. All were somehow lost in their own world of thought, but for some reason, I felt that world might have touching borders.

Slowly the elevator came to a stop, the mirrored walls reflecting anxious faces and small beads of perspiration on all the foreheads. It must be someone or somewhere that they all knew, something that carried with it...power. As the double doors slid to the left and right opening to the corridor beyond, everyone seemed to launch from their confined quarters, seemingly glad to have some room. The driver shifting his upper torso from the waist and squeezing his right arm against his side, all the while maneuvering the hidden weapon underneath. So obvious to the trained eye, there was a readiness locking then relaxing my hands for immediate use if needed. Then ...nothing.

It was nothing more than a huge suite, elaborate and expensively furnished in heavy wood and leather furniture. Large, very costly oil paintings adorned the walls. The view from across the room showing the vista all the way toward Ensenada and an area called a name I had never heard, Chapultapec Heights. Several large estates built into the hillside for some of the elite of the city.

Two passageways led off this large room to a master suite and also to an enormous bath and walkin closet the size of another room. The sunken tub large enough for six and the double shower a fit for two, bench included. Everything was professionally done for sure.

Easily within ones view was the ultimate care given to every detail in putting this place together. A circular bar stocked with the finest liquors and wines, there were also several cases of Crystal and Pierre Jouet Rose' champagne, as well. Six feet of the wall contained a customized sound and video viewing area for the guests' pleasure. All this had cost the owner a lot of money; it was two thousand square feet of Penthouse, extraordinary in each design. All but Dennard did their individual task of placing things and turning on lights and the like, then left immediately.

"This will be suitable I presume?" He said with an air of aloof aristocracy. "It is personally owned by my boss and only a chosen few are permitted to stay here. Anything you want, and I emphasize ANYTHING that you want, just pick up that phone and dial 40. It will connect you with a private concierge that has been fully instructed to accommodate you in every area. Drink, eat, entertainment or whatever you might come up with."

"And when will this meeting begin with your boss?" Not impressed with all the fanfare and show at all. I had come here for business and business it would be.

"You will get a phone call very soon. Falcon is assembling everything as we speak. The driver called him while we were in route to the hotel. So for now I hope the meeting goes well."

No comment necessary, no comment given as he turned and left the room. Stopping suddenly he said, "Oh I almost forgot, here is the key to the elevator. It is the only way to use it and the only other key is in the hands of the concierge. He will be the only one to come to the room from now forward. Falcon's orders." Leaving the key on the end table, he finally left the suite, and the hotel as well. I watched from the small patio off the master suite as he got into the Rolls with the driver and left.

Close to seven hours had elapsed since the departure of Dennard, and still no word, not even a call. Now 9:45 pm, I had ordered a nice filet and Ceasar salad at seven. Took my time eating and enjoying the fabulous view of the sunset over the ocean. It seems to explode in a red fireball when viewed from twenty stories up, as the sun sinks slowly in the western horizon. Then relaxed with a little music and the evening news, passing the hours away.

This situation was going to change very quickly or Michael J. Decker would be east bound and gone from this location within the hour. Walking back from the patio for one more scan of the horizon, the night bringing to life much of the downtown few blocks of Tijuana, a ring from the phone.

"Hello!" Very abrupt and stern I answered.

"Senor Decker, this is Ramon the concierge. I have just been in contact with Senor Falcon and he would like to know if tomorrow morning would be agreeable for your meeting? Around 7:30 OK? He apologizes for all the delay but something very important has delayed his jet from coming in to see you."

"Why didn't he call himself if he is so damn sorry?"

"Oh, Senor Decker, I could not say, permiso El Senor es muy importante y mucho fuerte!" His speech was suddenly full of fear.

"I really don't give a damn how important and powerful he is or thinks he is. I didn't come here to wait all damn day."

"Uno momento por favor, Senor Decker, uno momento."

One moment my butt, this was a joke as far as I could tell and the folly was about to be terminated. My patience had run its course with these yahoos. This could have been a nice evening with my beautiful wife, rather than jacking around here in bean town.

"Senor Decker, please hold the line for a third party."

"Michael this is Dennard and ......"

"Listen shithead I am getting sick and tired of the run around the flagpole routine of you and your so called boss. If you can't facilitate this meeting then I will cancel it with pleasure and go on back to Dallas. You can find some other "soldier of fortune" to carry out whatever."

"Michael, I'm sorry but something very big has come up. You are going to be compensated for the time that has been wasted. And I might add, compensated in a very generous way. Mr. Falcon has already made arrangements for a delivery to you and it will be arriving within fifteen to twenty minutes. If you will give me only a half hour I'll call you back and confirm its arrival and also your full satisfaction."

"You have one half hour to make something happen or I am on my way back to Texas. If that is the case, do not try to get in contact with me ever again. I say this fact with no meaning other than your fucking health would be in serious jeopardy if you ever cross me. You and any other sonof-a-bitch from the "organization" or whatever it is called. You have no fucking idea what kind of power and force I can make happen."

"I fully concede with what you have said Michael. Let me assure you that I do know what you are capable of, from what all I have read and heard. I also value my health and don't want any so called "accidents occurring unexpectedly. Seriously give me thirty minutes."

"Thirty minutes, it's now 10:05 and at 10:35 I'm gone if nothing happens." A click on both lines told me that the sneaking little concierge had been listening to all that had been said. Ramon was getting ready to step in something he might regret, for sure.

Ten minutes later the doorbell rang. Reaching for the Walther, I stepped to the privacy viewer to see who had come. Unlike the standard peephole of a normal door, this was a closed circuit system that availed a view from the end of the corridor, all the way to the elevator. On zoom it could almost pick up the single strands of someone's hair. Now it was quite evident that it was none other than Ramon. His little chicken ass and I were going to have a chat. Seeing that he was standing directly in front of the door, I raised the PPK and upon yanking the door open, jerked his collar with sufficient force to bring him airborne into the room.

The package dislodged from his hands as he cruised through the air. His landing was flat on his back as I twisted him in mid air and forced him to the carpet. With the barrel of the gun shoved firmly against his temple, we began our chat.

"Ramon, the next time I have a phone call or anything else that is mine you will not be a part of it. Understand? Because if there is any misunderstanding I'll let the ride from the balcony of the patio be your wake up call for thinking. Understand?"

"Oh yes, Senor Decker. Yes Senor Decker, I'm so sorry. I was just remaining on the line in case you or Senor Dennard needed anything further." He had wet his pants, the dark patch on the front of his trousers told the story. I would need no further conversations to emphasize my point. He continued with near breathless speech.

"Please Senor Decker do not tell Senor Falcon of this. He might hurt me or my family Senor."

Nodding to him, there would be no further talk between him and me, and nothing else needed to be said to anybody. Case Closed.

As the door closed behind Ramon, I laid the weapon on the table and retrieved the package that had dropped from Ramon's grip. It was a small package 2" x 6" wrapped in a dark brown cover like oil paper and had a thick rubber band securing its contents inside.

Removing the band first, knowing that the fling of the package across the room would have dislodged any trigger device, I peaked inside. In which was a stack of crisp fifty-dollar bills. Removing the entire contents and counting them revealed fifty in number, two thousand five hundred dollars. This made the total I had been paid for the first twenty-four hours of possible employment, $3,500.00. Not bad for an old carpenter from Texas. Maybe, just maybe this was going to be something to stay put for one more day and consider. The time was now 10:29 and just as I looked at the clock, the phone rang..
"Yes!"
"Are you satisfied with the delivery?" Dennard inquired.
"It will work for now."
"Will it be enough for you to stay until tomorrow?"
"I will stay, until tomorrow morning. The meeting will be at 7:30a.m. sharp and I expect it to be on time. Late and I am on my way."
"Thank you for staying Decker, and I promise that the meeting will be on time for sure. The car will come for you by 7:15 at the latest and I will be in the lobby to meet you then."
"Then that is, that."
Hanging up so as not to give Dennard any chance to say anything further, I made another call.
"Guad man, what's shaking? Are things clear?" A few moments of silence went by while Larry hooked the equipment up to sweep the line for any type of listening or recording device.
"All's quiet on the Western Front."

I took the next few minutes to outline what was to happen the next day and what I needed from him. Also I asked him to look into the Sicilia-Falcon organization and let me know what's up first thing in the morning. There would not be a problem with either request. He was still a team member and a brother. Everyone knew that was a fact, till death us do part. In blood it was sealed.

The remainder of the night was spent with talking an hour and a half on the phone with Lisa. Assuring her that all was well and not to worry. She had gone to the Dallas store and met two of her friends for drinks and dinner. Since I had the Q/A account as a corporate member all she had to do was sign and enjoy. Making all of her outings there when I couldn't be along, easy to entertain. She, as in everything else, never abused the privilege and always told me when she had made a charge. Our communication concerning money had always been completely above board and out in the open. By the end of the talk she felt better and said she would get a restful nights sleep. Hanging up the phone I knew that this fact for me was far from the reality of what the night would bring. If two hours of concentrated rest were obtained I would have all I needed and wanted. A series of breathing exercises were my preparation for sleep and in so doing, I would rest, but have full recall instantly if necessary. An old trick learned from the Montanyard tribes back in the Nam. It worked unbelievably well.

April 30, 1974 broke into existence with a red sunrise burning its way through the darkness. That big dimmer switch in the sky was about to crank all the way to level ten, Hot. The coastline revealed several sportfishermen and charter sails out early with their days' tourists on board. From the patio deck of the suite a navy destroyer moved ghostlike toward the inter-coastal waterway.

Bicycle and foot traffic abundant on the streets below, trying to get the early start before the automobiles broke their slumber and began reckless careening the streets. Like most of the border towns in Mexico, life began early and went on till way into the night. Trying to stretch an extra hour and push the twenty-four hour, barrier to twenty-five.

I'd been up and exercised, showered and dressed by 4:30a.m., having taken my required rest near 2:00a.m. All of the planning that had taken place through the night had readied the territory for the events that would unfold during the next six to ten hours. Each integral part had gone to standby alert, thirty minutes ago. Now time to check and verify all points of contact.

"Two Four Seven!"

"Seven Four Two!"

"Clear both sides brother man, what shakes in the valley below?"

"The mountaintop contains no rumbles and I want it to stay that way. What did you find out about the bird Larry?"

"Well Decker, you have touched the edge of the Big League. And I mean the majors, definitely. Falcon is a very large player in the Mexico/South American cartels. He personally controls a vast empire of hotels, trucking firms, and a distribution network, which is reputed to be one of the largest in the world. The organization must do somewhere in the area of ten million gross, monthly. There is some kind of connection here to a guy by the name Gaston Santos, and this guy's father is a former General of the Army of Mexico."

"Sounds like the files were running all night long. Anything else that is important for this morning? Anything critical?"

"Run silent, run deep brother. You and I both know that these situations can become loose and break the hell out of control. I walk with you and your lead is my follow."

"Just like the "Rockpile," set all flanking maneuvers to a shielding pattern and watch for smoke. We'll talk at 1300 hours if not before."

No goodbyes needed, we did not say farewell when going to war, or taking on a critical situation where danger might lurk. It was a routine between all of us on the team. The "Rockpile" was an old operation in the northern quadrant of the NAM. Very near the 19th parallel in a sector named Arizona Territory. A large operation had taken place there called Meade River. It was a devastating defeat to the enemy and took a body count of near two thousand by the end of the operation. One prime area of conflict was a small artillery outpost called the Rockpile named for the crags and natural formations of stone.

Towards the end of the mission a small group of men were pinned down on this post and the fighting became so fierce that no more ammunition/food or supplies could be interjected and the opposing force had near three companys on the outer perimeter. Things were becoming very critical for a possible overrun of the fences. SEAL teams infiltrated the compound during the night and carried in as much ammo as possible. They made a total of three trips in and out totally undetected by the opposing force. They set up a literal "V" shaped gun emplacement pattern, the reverse of normal warfare techniques. The point of the "V" being inward, rather than the normal outward, was to allow the enemy to cross the fence and seemingly overrun a portion of the compound before opening fire. From the inner point to the other side of the compound there were silo tunnels dug which would allow the troops to flow across the compound undetected by the oncoming force. Here, then the scenario and winning combination was built. Allow the enemy to think that this weak point was the only way to enter the compound. Pull all the main forces to the opposite side and fire fiercely from these positions. Yet in total camouflage there were several automatic weapons, M-60's and 30cal. machine guns that had been strategically placed to form the outer edges of the "V" form.

Once the entire force had formed to make their charge into the inner compound, the opposite outer wall would collapse undetected. All of these men would rush to their secret positions and with the balance made of the team members that the enemy did not know had come to reinforce, the firepower would be immense. Once it started it was like shredding firewood with cannons. The enemy was cut to ribbons and who had really been running out of ammo, was them. By mid way into the battle they were charging with no bullets, just bayonets and knives. Raging fierce for several hours and then the enemy began to run out of men.

In the final stages many of the men of the compound and team, seeing that the fight had turned to hand to hand, threw down their rifles and weapons and charged the enemy as in days of old. Letting the adrenaline charged hearts and minds release the rage and anger, that had been bottled for so long from the deaths of their comrades. The level of aggression and commitment to slaughter the enemy would have made the knights and men of the round table envious and proud.

For those that were there, it would never be forgotten. As the smoke drifted across the piles of bodies, in some areas stacked five high, the smell and sight of death was pungent to the senses and dulling to the mind. An indelible scar of something they call triumph, most called HELL. Reports of this battle would only be told and not written in the annuals of the war books. Many such conflicts had taken place where the reverse had happened. It was our brothers, husbands, fathers and sons that were slaughtered. All because of some damn politicians idea or some civilian strategists opinion. Here, years later, men still reeked of the havoc and flashbacks of days gone by. The military saying to society here, take these one million men and women that fought this stupid war. We screwed their thinking and their bodies up, maimed their limbs, destroyed many of their lives; now you civilians deal with it, we are through with them.

Then they came back to touch the precious soil of the country which was loved and missed so much. The result was some long-haired punk with a tie/dyed t-shirt and a reefer in his hand, spit on the ground we thought sacred and burnt our American flag. Yet the turmoil then had to make another ugly national scar. Kent State University, four dead in OHIO, by the "stray" bullets of a national guard troop. Stray my ass, they were shot dead by the same idiotic thinking that Johnson was parlaying with the rest of his underhanded crap to the Congress and Senate of the United States. This was after having lost a man in the Whitehouse who had the insight and the courage to step out of the main street of political reticent normality and "do something."

The mind flows to so many different thoughts when reflecting on the past and how it affects the present and the future. What had happened at the Rockpile was being recreated today as a precaution to keep the upper hand once again. All of what was about to take place would have my signature on it no matter what the outcome.

Key in hand, weapon neatly stored in my boot, body stretched and coiled, I was ready to meet Alberto Sicilia-Falcon.

0715 hours, the elevator descended to the lobby below. Men stationed along the route, unknown by Dennard and his people. Mirrored walls of the cabin reflecting a man in ready stature and confident of how this day will flow. A slight creak from the breaking wheel of the elevator cable, hydraulics pushing the inner and outer doors apart to reveal Dennard and one other in the lobby.

Other than the desk attendant, and "Larry's plant" sitting there supposedly reading the paper, no more onlookers were present.
"Michael, good morning."
"Yeah, it's morning!" Very nonchalant to Dennard, no warmth felt, none shown. His companion was nervous about my presence.
"Everything is all set, so let's get going."

Following close enough behind and yet with the distance necessary to react with freedom of movement. The Rolls, the same car and same chauffeur as the preceding day, were waiting at the curbside with the door open.
"Senor Decker, Buenos Dios!"

Nodding to the driver, I started to lean forward in the car. First noticing that the gray Chevrolet was parked up the street to my right, as planned. Entering the car, Dennard followed, his companion moving to the front seat beside the driver, still no introduction or comment who this might be.
"The meeting is all prearranged and Albert is waiting for you now so that there will be no delays as promised."
"It should have been that way yesterday!" Out of sight, had not gone out of mind and I wanted Dennard to know that.
"I know and again I apologize, but he will explain that situation as well. I think you will understand all of it when he fills in the blanks."

Again I pushed the button for the privacy partition to rise between the two compartments. I was sure that the driver did not like the fact, but that was just tough. We headed down the hill a short way from the hotel and then turned left up by the Agua Caliente Race Track to the hills of Chapultepec. The estates began to come into view, one by one their winding driveways and custom designs revealed their owners tastes. Almost all of these homes were owned by Mexican nationals, that were from somewhere other than Tijuana.

Slowly rounding the next curve the car swung to the right and crossed into the driveway beyond. Two large, thick, wood and steel doors opened by two men, weapons at their sides. As the car moved through the pillars holding the doors, the men closed them quickly. A large, steel bracing shaft slid firmly into the dual braces to secure the penetration point.

The driveway continued for about seventy-five feet inside the enclosure of the gates, ending in a large flagstone wall. It was some thirty-five feet from the base up to the eve of the structure above. To the left was an entryway door and a staircase to its left that wound it's way to the upper level and beyond. The outside of the estate, all that I had seen so far, was the same flagstone as the front wall. Exiting the car Dennard and I went to the entryway door being held by the small man who had accompanied him in the lobby before. Stepping inside the custom layout began to unfold.

An underground firing range was the first thing to see upon entering the home. Four stations and mobile and stationary target racks and cables visible. Sand bags were stacked against the far wall to absorb the projectiles, and there were three rows of indirect lighting to illumine the targets. To the right of this area was a staircase, which lead to the next level and this way we continued.

The interior finish of the firing range walls and ceiling was a sandcolored plaster and this finish continued to the next floor. A heavy steel railing rimmed the stairs providing ample strength and security for all that passed. Entering through an archway at the top of the stairs, the next room was an open area some twelve by twenty-four feet with a large, thick solid steel door leading to another room. It had three deadbolts, commercial #1 grade showing from the outside, and a heavy brass pill the only hardware remaining. It was painted a dark gold. It had to be the money room, or a valuable storage and safe.

From here Dennard continued to another staircase at the far end of this room. Furniture in the room was limited to two large tables with six chairs each and two large eight foot long leather couches. The wall finish was paneling, a deep pecan stain with satin coating, the ceiling in white acoustic. From the entryway downstairs, both outside and in, continuing through each room a security video system revealed all traffic to someone above. Just to the left of the second stairs there was another solid wood door. It looked to be another bedroom of some type, the entire inner house had been closed off well in advance of my arrival, wonder why?

Finally to the top of the stairway, this is where the "real" home began. A great room, thirty-five by seventy feet sprawled out from the archway of entering this vast chamber. The left side solid glass floor to ceiling, twenty panels three feet wide and ten feet tall in a semicircular shape. All of the city below in its vista, a large patio deck wrapping this area for another sixteen feet. From three different directions you could see whatever traffic was coming or going. Two armed guards patrolled outside the windows, cautiously keeping their vigil.

To my immediate left was an enormous pit setting of four, eight-foot leather couches, eggshell tan. Set in a "C" arrangement with one then two in the middle, end to end and the fourth on the opposite side or end. A beautiful center designer table over twelve feet long with scrolled silver and gold legs and the carved and etched top a true work of beauty and art. The sea came alive in the reverse cuts of dolphins and creatures from the oceans floor shadow carved into the glass. It was like a magnificent ice carving sculpted by Neptune himself.

To the right of the archway, there was a setting for twelve, at the dining room table of black cherry, rubbed and finished to a glass like sheen. The chairs and table legs were done with lion's claw feet, and were massive to the eye. A centerpiece of fresh cut flowers in a deep silver bowl goblet were added touches of elegance. A Crystal chandelier hung in three tiers from the gold turn cap at the ceiling. The ceiling vaulted over this area with exposed beams and masonry plaster done in spiral swirls, colored in a light offwhite.

Further in the room was an entertainment and sound system that dwarfed the custom design at the suite of the night before. Three more matching couches and hand carved tables and lamps adorned this area, looking as if the same tree had been used with the perfect matching of the grains of wood. Heavy ornate framed masterpieces hung on every open wall.

The floor was solid marble in the dining room and the rest of the expanse was covered in cashmere grade carpet, the hundred and fifty dollar a yard variety. If the furnishings were supposed to impress, the designer or decorator had accomplished their goal. From this main room, there were four bedrooms and three baths on the south side of the estate. The master suite was to the north, and it was totally separate.

Just outside the deck, which wrapped the great room, clear around the master suite and for another hundred feet, a complete forest had been designed with a large swimming pool and small stream at its center. Most of this area, where the two Dobermans and the largest Great Dane that I had ever seen roamed, was well guarded. The Dane was of the Harlequin variety and stood 48" at the shoulders, all three dogs were attack and protection trained I would later find out.

There was also a two story guest and servants quarters on the estate as well, to the right of the pool area.

Yes it was big, it was exquisitely furnished, someone had money, lots of it. Now it was time to see just who the hell Alberto Sicilia Falcon, really was.

"Michael if you would take a seat here on this couch I will go and get my boss." Leaving through the corridor that led to the master suite, a section of the house that few, very few ever dared enter, Brian made his way to the inner chamber. This tidbit would also be passed down in time to come.

The area I had been asked to wait in was the second section, with two couches. As I walked to the room I noticed what looked like a military file folder on the table. Department of the Armed Forces seal was on the outer cover, double red binder with a clasp denoting a file that contained "Secret /Top Secret" material. Another folder contained pictures one had slid partially out of its container.

As I sat down I noticed the Military Service Number on the outer jacket tab, B725026, I drew a quick breath, deep. B725026 was my service number and this was a copy or original of the file from Military Headquarters. How in the hell had this been taken out of a place so supposedly secure? Well I knew how, but I had the "need to know" as we said in the service. Before I pondered that thought any longer, the company was entering the room.

Alberto Sicilia-Falcon, thirty-four years old, there about, five foot nine inches tall, black hair/dark eyes, and clean shaven. He had an air of elegance, and was confident, and well spoken in three languages, a ruler in his own right, so to speak. Dressed casually in linen trousers, light tan in color with matching Gucci shoes and belt, a silk shirt of light blue with gold highlights. Platinum Rolex, full jeweled, meaning band face and bezel, with rubies and diamonds. The type they make for the over $250,000 price tag, and beyond. One ring on the left hand, large yellow diamond set in yellow gold. Chiseled face with high cheek bones, Cuban/Puerto Rico area of background.

"Michael Decker, we finally meet. My pleasure."

"Yes, finally we do." Holding back and keeping reserves intact, I began to read his eyes and watch the two guards that had come into the room with him. They were standing so close together, both could be taken out by one gunman. Falcon, not knowing me, had not had me searched and the Walther, clip fed, could easily have taken the group out before I was even fired upon. Sloppy, border mentality, was my observation, Pancho Villa style.

"I am sorry that the plans for the evening changed, but such is the character of this business. I know that I can be blunt with you because you are not here to have some song sung to you. And I am not here to hire anything or anyone but the best Hit man and personal bodyguard I can buy. My business has grown to the point where I need professional security, not the quality that you must have already witnessed as to being only semi-adequate at best."

I nodded as he continued to elaborate on his speech, it was partially rehearsed, I could tell.

"As you have seen, I'm sure, I have read and studied your military records and also the school transcripts from NMMI and UNM. I, and several of my associates have talked to various people who have seen you fight and also I've demonstrations. Your weapons and explosives knowledge are exactly what I have been looking for in every regard. Now let's first talk money, then what I expect.

I am offering you a salary of one hundred thousand dollars cash a month. For that, I expect to not only stay alive but have any and all special projects and contracts carried out to their fullest details. Whatever it takes to complete one of these jobs is my expense, no limits on the money, but don't try and fuck me. You try and fuck me and I will do everything in my power to kill you.

"Let's get one thing clear......at the very first ......part......of.... this ... chat. Don't ever threaten me, or anyone in my family, now or ever. Not in conversation, not in jest, never. I won't fuck you and you won't ever let words like "kill you" enter even in discussion, come forth toward me, or my family. That is no fucking threat it is an absolute guarantee. I don't play that game, and NO ONE will play it or say it with me. Is that understood?" The air sizzled and static sparks could almost be seen and heard with the energy and force of the words and their meaning. No one in this house had ever heard anyone talk to this man that way.

"Yes, I do understand. This will never be an issue from this day forward, I give you my word." He was serious but his word was that of a smuggler and   someone I would not trust past this room. If I decided to take the job I would take the utmost care to maintain total isolation of my family from this entire dimension and its existence in my life.

"Agreed." I answered flatly.

"How long do you need to think about your decision?"
"Give me a number to call and I will give you an answer in 72 hours!" His two guards, across the room, were still doing the nervous jitters from the heat of the conversation. Anguish streaking their faces and tightening the facial muscles and widening their eyes .
"I'll have Dennard call you with the number in the morning for the contact. Now just to help you with your decision I am going to pay you through the next three days. If that is agreeable to you to be handled this way. No obligation for the money, it is just to aid you in the decision making process. Also to further thank you for coming and to additionally emphasize my apology for the extra time you have spent."
"I agree with that." Shaking my head and taking grip to his extended offer to seal what he had just said. Squeezed to the point not to crush but to the point of mild discomfort, I made my point of earlier spoken, sealed as well.

Signaling to one of the staff back toward the kitchen area, a bottle of Crystal, prechilled, and glasses came delivered to the table.
"How about a quenching of the throat?"
"Half glass only, thank you!"

The champagne was poured, and this phase of the meeting was concluded for the day. Not lingering, I said my departure greetings and left the compound for the hotel. All aspects of the operation basically reversing itself in letting the car leave and reseal the fortress.

As I had entered the limo, Dennard was waiting inside the car, and without hesitation said, "What do you think of the job offer?"
"I'll let Alberto know something in three days."
"All right, then, here is the money he promised you for the days spent and the time in consideration." Handing me another package, wrapped exactly the same as the ones before. The room I had thought to be the money place, must be.

After reaching the hotel I told Dennard to take the limo back and that I would leave the elevator key with Ramon when I was ready to leave. My voice delivered the message in such a way that he merely turned to the car and left. I wanted to handle everything from this point on. First thing to call the "Guad man" and collect the drops, already in progress, I was sure of this.
"Larry's Bar and Grill!" He would never change, no matter what.
"Yeah, two burgers and a bucket of fries!"
"Hey, I had a feeling that this might be you. Well you know that is probably true since you have been back for an entire five minutes."
"Been keeping up with your home work lately haven't you?"

"Yes and the blackboard is clean of chalk." He always was on the lookout for any restricted accesses. Made talking to him all the more pleasurable. Especially from this phone because his scrambling equipment would cause any tracking equipment to read out a thousand different numbers and none of them would be the right one.
"I am getting ready to head for the airport Larry. Have the gray Chevy follow me to the airport and you meet me there in say, thirty minutes."
"Correctamundo, will do over and out." Click and the Guad man was on his way.

My things had not been disturbed, the thread I had laid on the zipper of the bag was still there and the small tape on the bottom of the main entry door was there as well. I opened the sheath of the package and as expected it contained ten thousand dollars. Five of which I took out and prepared to give to the Guad man. He had supplied four men, five hundred each, one thousand if any action had ensued. The going rate for a mercenary, $500 a day no firing, $1,000 a day when the flames were flashing. This would leave $3,000 in green for the man with the plan to have a great weekend.

We met as planned and did our normal routine, shocks the hell out of people. I'll tell you about it later. Then I was on the plane and back home to my baby. I had given her a quick call from the gate to announce my time of arrival. It was seventy-two hours and counting.

Mission Bay was exactly what I wanted to see as I turned on the exit marked Sea World, knowing that Riviera Shores drive was only minutes away. Having already stopped by the mailbox and picked up my parcel, the twenty-five thousand dollars lay next to me. Now it was time to spend a few days with Lisa and see all that she had completed with the moving and new abode. Calling the hotel earlier, the front desk had informed me that she had checked in the night before. Evidently, she had done the marathon, shopping and coordinating deliveries. A message had come in to the hotel that her request for an early morning slot had been approved for delivery of all of the items shipped from Texas. There were also several from local merchants, confirming orders. Maybe it was a good thing that I had picked up some more cash, I might need it by the end of the day.

Turning quickly to the left on Riviera Shores Drive, the long line of units, buildings and towers, lined the bay side of the street. Single family dwellings on the opposite, mature trees and landscaping, giving it a nice touch. Looking for the sign and the number 3916, I found it about half way up the block, Riviera Shores. Heavy cut stone, painted brilliant white fortified the exterior in a somewhat castle like effect. Large bronze glass windows allowed the occupants to view many directions. Parking across the street, I strolled up to the main entrance, noticing the security parking gate to my lower right. A double entry system allowed the tenant or guest to first enter from the outside and then pushing the appropriate number would activate the intercom system from the unit beyond the locked door.

As I looked to the registry of names on my left I saw, Decker #201, and buzzed the occupant.
"Yes, may I help you?"
"Mrs, Decker,?" Changing my voice as best I could, I began the game.
"Yes!"
"I have a special delivery for your home." The accent nearly failing because I am about to bust out laughing and spoil the routine.
"I'll buzz you through!" She didn't have a clue who I was or what might be delivered to her door.
As the latch pulled back from the lock I pulled the door open and stepped inside. Looking at the numbers I followed them in reverse up to number 201 and knocked.
"Hey good looking." She shrieked with delight as I jumped right in to my new casa, oops our new casa. After all her work, Lisa deservedly would get all the praise.
"Michael John Decker, one of these days I am going to get you good." Grabbing my hand and pulling me toward the interior of the unit.
"Come here and see this wonderful place."
Just inside the door to the left was the kitchen, stylish French slatted cabinets, brass/enamel pulls and solid white appliances. Plenty of counterspace and an eight foot bar area. The floor was done in stone tile, light blue, and the inserts in the pulls the matching color and shade.

Light tan/beige carpet from this point begin to flow through the rest of the house. Front door to patio beyond, the "great" room unfolded in splendid furnishings. Oak and glass dining room set and six chairs to the left after the kitchen with twelve feet of smoked mirror to enlarge the effect. Two new couches, dark brown and matching coffee and end tables, with inlaid hardwood lamps, several large paintings already hung from the walls. She had done some shopping. A 100 gallon saltwater aquarium finished off this room with a beautiful gold layered rain lamp which cascaded hot oil down filament strands to look like raindrops. A marble statue in the center of the lamp was a Greek warrior.

The only thing new in the bedrooms were bedspreads and the one Lisa had chosen in the master suite was incredible. It was an ornate velvet cloth, patchwork design done in gold, maroon and royal blue with black piping.

"Baby, this is stunning."

"Yes it is beautiful but it also cost over six hundred dollars. I hope that you don't mind the extra money spent on it?"

"Mind! Heck, it is absolutely great Lisa. I love everything you did and don't worry about the money. There will be plenty of cash for anything you might want."

"That's good because they will be delivering ALL the rest of the things I bought this afternoon." Her face was beaming with delight and joy at my satisfaction. It only made sense to celebrate the moment. Like it made a difference, we never needed any reason at all for celebrating. Making love with this lady was truly, a dream come true.

"We had better try that new bedspread out, right?" She could tell from the tone and my expression, exactly what was in store next.

We did our very best at amplifying the phrase, "afternoon delight," barely getting our clothes on before the next delivery. The technicians hooked up and installed all the televisions and stereo equipment. With their leaving I felt it only right to celebrate once again by loving one another and trying the new "bass drivers." Feelings these bass notes easily as the notes resonated off of our bodies on the floor, completing the need for each other and satisfying our need in full. The resulting nap felt wonderful as we lay embraced in one another's arms. These encounters were precious because of the inner knowing that I might be called away in a moments notice.

Always, there was so much money, we spent it abundantly. A habit easy to acquire and get caught up in, it was the very nature of the beast.

After two days with Lisa, well a day and a half, my next project was ready to initiate action. Thankfully she had decided to go home for a visit to Albuquerque, New Mexico. For me, this one would take me down into the jungles of Central America. Guatemala City, Guatemala being the take off point to locate two people that had stolen a large amount of drugs and cash from a protected warehouse in Mexico, repayment was coming in a different form this time.

Both of them had worked for Falcon for several years and had seen the warehouse job as an easy mark. Killing three of the guards hired to watch over the stash until the transport trucks could get there. Two tons of marijuana, one hundred kilos of cocaine, two hundred thousand dollars in cash, the temptation was a trap waiting for the prey. The reason it was so convenient, one of the guards was the brother of Juan Carlos, allowing an inside diversion and assassination.

Juan Carlos, his girlfriend Patricia Gomez in agreement, felt they could make enough off the drugs, along with the cash already there, to escape somewhere in the world and never have to surface again. Living like king and queen in a foreign land was their plan of action.

One major problem they did not count on, a team of jungle warfare, counter insurgency and special tactics trained men coming to hunt them down. Their trail was cold at the beginning, not amazing though, it heated up quickly after being heated by greed and lust for wealth. This by the pressure of the men in my team, and the cash I had access to, being spread around. Every piece of equipment needed for a major warfare assault, had been previously delivered and a base compound and camp fortified. When it comes to recovering this amount of commodity and cash, the noose begins to tighten very quickly. Drawing the culprits towards their eventual destiny and final termination would be Nam relived in many of the sweeps and actions which my men would utilize to destroy and conquer the forces at bay.

Juan Carlos Romero, thirty, five foot eight, 170 pounds, fought his way up in the distribution game, form a simple mule to one of the wholesalers. His downfall was sampling to much of the product, this fact so prevalent in the market. His decision making was becoming irrational, a feeling of "do no wrong." The false confidence beyond ones means and abilities, stealing from someone with the resources of Sicilia-Falcon, this would not be tolerated. All this was a certain death sentence for Romero, which had now been declared final with a specific sentence.

Patricia Gomez, twenty-six, beautiful woman, five foot two, 114 pounds, came into the organization as a money courier. She had danced with some of the major players, using her talents in the bedroom to move through the ranks. Patricia had turned her last and final trick. Taking the drug altered thinking of a standin player, not the position and power he had so readily convinced her of, was a lethal one.

My orders were to not harm either one of them in any way before Sicilia-Falcon himself arrived, after their capture. His employing me and the services I had to offer would build his organization. This particular recovery, the drugs and the cash, and the termination of the perpetrators, would send out a fierce message across the land.

Alberto had grown so fast that his security forces and enforcement especially could not keep up with the level of product and the multitude of people it would require to move the tons, thousands of them. At present some 14,000 pounds a week were crossing the border into six distribution warehouses, then satellite spiraling throughout the nation. This was only through one border crossing, Tijuana, Add to this, Mexicali-Nogales-Juarez and Laredo, the figures climbed enormously. The cash flow was so heavy, in sheer weight, that it was a major transportation item in just moving the bills themselves. Tens of millions each week, which would be distributed worldwide to couriers and banks. A trail of quick sales, small amounts, opened the door to the location of Romero and Gomez.

The word had spread much quicker than they had anticipated. They were not realizing that any large sale from a "new" face might be Falcon's dope, you buy it and you buy the farm with it. The two of them had found a small secluded fortress near the ruins of Chichicastinango, in Guatamala. Trying desperately to peddle the drugs and get their cash reserves to the point of being able to elude the doom that was coming in the dark of night.

My plan was simple enough once we had paved the way with our recon in knowing exactly where they were. The need for the quick sale set it up. Surveillance drew forth the blueprint of the operation, listing all the sentries time tables, number of people, amount of firepower and position. They had now grown to a force of fourteen, basic M-16 and handguns, two Uzi full automatic weapons, a few old fragmentation grenades.

Guad man and I had assembled a seven man team of operatives. This could have been handled with the two of us if necessary. Killing each of the enemy during the course of one evening/night and pulling the chosen pair from their sleep to face the MAN himself, this was the command from my boss. The resources of unlimited cash made having the additional men easy, for money brought the very best of their trade. The preparations made this a rapid deployment force capable of accomplishing any mission. Within seconds of the actual activation and delivery, all opposition would be destroyed, eliminated.

One main trail was being utilized for all movement into and out of their compound. Four main night perimeter guards stationed on the corners with near thirty to forty yards separating each other were the first targets. From a single sniper position, Starlite scope equipped 7mm w/silencer, the front two sentries would be history. Two men would stealth crawl silently through the jungle and with a knife between the fourth and fifth rib, free hand clasp over the mouth, cause silence to remain while death is availed. Four remaining, this force would cave in rapidly for we had already infiltrated the compound. On a predetermined signal, after the four sentries had been taken out, death would be dealt to the remaining troops.

Close in body to body, this type of warfare was home to Guad man and Jim Loeding one of the others who had done three tours in the Nam and had over a hundred confirmed individual kills, hand kills. The remaining men had performed in the upper echelon, highly decorated combat veterans. We had come prepared to take on a force up to four times this size, their mistake, our victory.

D-day, 0130 hours, no moon, cloud cover light and still, black still in the jungle beneath the ruins of the ancient ones. Blood had soaked this soil for thousands of years, a feeding to Mother Earth was about to begin. Positions fortified and manned, full camouflage clothing, grease, weapons, synchronized time on all members. Scope pointed to first sentry, starlight activated, cross hairs vectored, one down. Second sentry hearing slight rustling of leaves turns, two down. Simultaneously both of the rear guards are killed, perfect execution, proceed to next objective.

Climbing down from my sniper position, I placed my weapon on the ground and began to enter the compound area. Giving a twenty minute turn around for advancement, yet if enemy engaged early, silent termination, then proceed to final destination. Passing the first of the dead, his body never feeling the pain or knowing what had taken his last breath, I advanced to the inner sanctum. Freezing instantly, another of their force had suddenly risen from his bedroll and began to relieve himself. Urine splashing on the leaves, less than three feet away, he leaned his head back in satisfied pleasure, opportunity given and taken. The knife blade sliced deep and long, carving through the main arteries, muscles and veins, the grim Reaper collected a soul. Within five minutes from this point, all of the twelve men were deactivated, no heart beat found, Mother Earth quenched and fed.

Gomez and Romero, lying together in blissful slumber, had no idea whatsoever that anything other than another normal night was in progress. All seven of us had circled the pair, weapons moved from their reach, seven micro MegaLamps flooded them with a light that erased all of the darkness. Leaping to their feet, gasping for a breath that didn't seem to come, they stood there shaking and trembling. Knowing all too well in their hearts and minds what this moment contained and the message it delivered. Securing them together, we bound them both ankles and wrists, posting a sentry of our own.

"Cragger! You and Sullivan take that hut to your right. I want it examined completely, dismantle the damn thing if necessary. All of the product that had not been sold, money, anything and everything must be recovered.

"Loeding, get the radio fired up and make contact with Sierra 4. Pass on the coordinates and tell him to reach all the way home, rendezvous will be at 0730, have Charlie Five on ready status by 0700 with heat."
"Done!" Loeding, an expert in coded field communications, would send the messages to one of my relay points. Sicilia-Falcon, his private Fanjet on standby, would be in Guatemala City by 0715. Bill Parsons, one of the best Huey "Chopper" pilots to have ever flown in Vietnam would then shuttle him to the compound site. Four of the men of my team would meet the plane in Guatemala, then accompany and escort safely to this location. I wanted this entire scenario to be orchestrated and resolved in one area. Too many chances of witnesses when people are moved, the viewing, the rumors and stories would take place when finalization had occurred.
"Decker, we've located a stash and the storage!" Cragger shouted from the northern side of the area, everything was coming into the completion mode and readying the mission's climax.

As I approached the two men standing by a small three by four foot pit, there appeared to have been a cover fashioned from limbs, leaves and natural vegetation. Shining my light in the opening, ninety-five kilos of cocaine met my view. This was what we had been looking for, now only one thing remained, the money. It was time for a session of persuasion to whatever level might be necessary to make Gomez and Romero talk. With the money they had stolen, sale of the five kilos of cocaine, added to the five hundred pounds of marijuana that was sold. Enough to cause some major interrogation, from many sessions in Vietnam during the Phoenix program, making people talk was a specialty of my brothers-in-arms.
"Guad man, bring Romero over to that stump." Reaching in my pocket as I spoke to my associate, a small knife retrieved and opening the slim two inch blade, I readied the object that would open the mouth and spill the truth.
"Romero, the time has come for you to tell me where the money is. I am not going to play any games and I will only ask you once. You don't talk, I act. It is as simple as that. Guad loop his arms over the stump."

Romero, his hands tied behind his back, ankles bound together and then bent at the knees, were joined to the wrists. While I grabbed one side, Guad man on the other, we lifted him and slid the trunk of the tree up through the narrow chamber from his back to the tethered limbs. His no response meant that the action must begin. Taking him by the right wrist, I turned the wrist with a half turn to the outside, pulling the index finger out and up. Moving it almost to the breaking point, tendons and ligaments beginning to separate, the pain was intense. Next, hearing the groans from the pain inflicted, the small slim blade of the knife began to puncture just under the nail. The hook shaped end of the blade, surgical sharp drove deeper and deeper into the sensitive flesh. One eighth of an inch past the base of the nail the nerve cord is found and with the movement begins to be torn away from the stem. With the increased dimension of pain came a deep outcry from the core of Romero's being.

"Noooooooooooooo.......Ahhhhhhhhhhhhhhhhhhhhhhhhh! The sudden fire like intensity began to rip the nerves, one by one.

"Wait, wait, I'll tell you where it is. Please stop or he will die!" Gomez, gasping for breath, tears streaming down her face, began begging for his life. Five minutes later the money, four hundred eighty-seven thousand dollars is in my possession. The location of the other three thousand five hundred pounds of marijuana also given to avoid any further reprisal or pain, they thought.

"Great work men. This was a victory and there will be heavy bonus money when we get back to the home base. Delta Team, head for your rendezvous with Sierra 4, Charlie Five will be hot and ready." Four men were on their way to provide the necessary security for Falcon to arrive, it was nearing completion.

    The mission had taken in almost a half million cash, 2.7 million in drugs, a three million plus day. My bonus would be near a quarter million, this I would break down to five thousand each for the five men, twenty-five thousand for Guad man, the balance for me. This seemed fair and equitable in every way.

    Two hours later the noise of the chopper began to announce its arrival. The LZ rechecked only fifteen minutes ago and all was safe and secure. Orange smoke from the canister which had been thrown was signaling Charlie Five to proceed and begin its decent into the jungle floor.

"Alberto this is the way to the trail." Waving to him, my hand signal broke the men into a protective semicircle around Falcon. One of the Delta Team stayed on the chopper with a BAR (Browning Automatic Rifle) to circle and give air support, recon for anything approaching.

    Breaking into the clearing of the compound, kilos of cocaine were stacked neatly, with the money beside it, Gomez and Romero were not ten feet away, the air began to fill with darkness. The two of them, seeing us approach, held their breath, eyes hyper wide with fear. The jungle seemed to silence its own noise, bird, animal, wind. The waiting spirits of the ruins gathered as the jury, Falcon the Judge, with a sentence about to be declared and administered.

For several moments, a breath, a sigh, clothing rustling as a position was changed, was the only sound. Almost to a deafening crescendo, the silence exploded in the senses of the two, sitting there, awaiting their fate, destiny.

"Juan Carlos, how ever could you have thought that a peon like you had the ability, the strength, to try and steal from me? Knowing the power, wealth, ability, intelligence and contacts of a ruler like me, Alberto Sicilia-Falcon. How many times in the passing years have you witnessed the deaths of those that would steal or dishonor my leading of this great family? Only a fool, a tiny bug of a man, filth and vermin of the country he was born. You have dishonored all. You deserve what you are about to see. Wallow in the misery of what is about to take place."

As Falcon spoke the last word, he drew the chrome/nickel .45 cal. with the carved ivory handles. Romero, still tethered around the stump, as if kneeling against it, Gomez sitting between his bent legs with her back to his waist. Slowly the weapon rose, a shaft of sunlight catching the polished barrel and a light spectrum flashing in the air, it roared and the authority of death came to pass. Gomez, with her face frozen in fear, snapped back against Romero, throat torn open by the bullet. A fountain of blood, from the severed artery, pulsed up and began to cover Romero's chest and shoulders.

Romero, caught by some surprise with the choice, began to turn gray/blue, the flight of the bullet piercing his groin as it exited Gomez from the back of her neck. It would be a slow, mortal wound, causing great agony and death that would not relieve the sight of Gomez or the pain for over an hour. He would be sentenced to this misery for his offense, the revenge of La Familia de Sicilia-Falcon complete.

In a matter of days the notoriety of this scene, the grisly sight of the bodies left to advertise, would send a message of power and rule throughout Mexico, Central and South America. There would be no police investigation, no reprisal, only order for some time to come within the organization. Profits, cash flow and productivity suddenly boomed.

Some of the taking for granted, instantly changed, but eventually someone, the cash and power so attractive, would try again. I, my team, would be waiting, in darkness.

After getting Falcon back to the chopper and off to his awaiting jet, we mopped up here at the kill zone. Weapons confiscated and stored, main LZ and compound dismantled and packed, transport plane for the delivery of the product and the equipment back to a ranch near

Guadalajara. From there the product would be trucked back to a warehouse in Mexicali, a large lumberyard with an underground storage area capable of holding near a million kilos of marijuana.

The cash came with me back to Chapultapec, then on to San Diego for distribution, first to be formally counted and packaged. From the proceeds I would pay out all the sums, including bonuses to my team members. Instantly Falcon had trusted me, I could have taken millions, with the access I had to the vaults, shipments and moving of the hordes of money.

Having rented a small office, three rooms, just before leaving for Guatemala, Sun Conglomerates was semiofficial. The phone line was scrambled when necessary, courtesy of the Guad man, and a large safe had been installed. Here I kept many of the items and paper work, identification, which I did not want to carry home. Not to hide it from Lisa, but to protect and shield her from any undue worry or concern.

Although I had been back in San Diego for two days now, no contact had been established with anyone, not even Lisa. I wanted all of the business from the last operation to be over, no stone left unturned for something or someone to crawl out from under. There was near three hundred thousand dollars in the safe at the office, almost twenty still left at the condominium. Lisa had bought furniture, clothes and jewelry, had all the spending money she could hope for and even sent money home for her family.

As I drove back to the condominium that afternoon, I passed one of the boat dealers, show lots. The twenty-foot Sanger flat bottom, with a 454 cu. inch blown/injected Chevrolet Corvette motor, chromed and polished and customized by Phaff & Simmons, lay there on its trailer purring, it was saying "take me home," at least I think it was saying that. Bright lacquered Canary Yellow with Sapphire Blue metal flake detailing, matching diamond tufted seats and upholstery, twin buckets, definitely only a two-seater. It had been built for some rich guy and run at the Inter-coastal Canal Boat Drags, turning a new world record of 115.73 mph in its class of sprint racing. It was parked in the underground lot of the condominium by the next morning. This was a showpiece indeed. From the spoils came the spoiled, it seemed to work for me. Sitting there on the large leather recliner, (Lisa had finally convinced me to throw the old one away), I began to reflect on the past month or so and to project just what the future might bring. So easy to see that in time there would be many toys adorning my holdings and possessions, power so necessary to so many people. I could not imagine the situation changing, thus no investments, savings, or looking out for the eventual time when physically I could not do this level of performance and provide these services. Just how much longevity could accompany this line of work, and profession? Time would tell, how soon, was the real question at hand.

By early evening, sitting and watching the sun slowly make its plunge deep into the oceans cresting waves, I decided to go and do some shopping for myself. Ten thousand dollars later I had several things to fill the expansive walkin closet, shirts, slacks, sport jackets and a beautiful Pierre Cardin suit. A pair of Horn Back Lizard boots, peanut brittle color, at nine hundred dollars, they felt like gloves on my feet. Also I had some off white linen slacks, a matching lizard belt, and a Polo shirt by Ralph Lauren, medium soft yellow. My dark tan was a nice contrast, the freshness after a long shower and shave, Stetson cologne giving me a little shot of Texas. On the way home from shopping I had stopped off and had a marvelous massage, four handed for an hour and a half. Two hundred dollars of pampering, this would become a regular part of my weekly routine.

A great steak seemed to fit the bill for dinner. Carl's place down on Ventura Drive would be the location for a quiet dinner in seclusion. I had already been there twice. Making this trip made me a regular, just as it had been back at Montana. Carl Chambers, the owner, reminded me of Doug Smith from the Montana Mining Company days, and did a fine job. He greeted me heartily as I came through the door.

"Well Mr. Decker, it's so nice to have you back again so soon."

"Carl you keep serving me those good steaks and I'll be here almost daily. After being in the business and eating every single day in Montana Mining Company, I am very spoiled."

"I have several business associates that travel extensively and some have told of the wonderful time they had eating there. The one in Dallas, Austin and in Albuquerque especially have been spoken of." His words were stated in appreciation of a job well done. Knowing all to well what it took to make it all come together, day after day.

"That's great to hear. Have you thought about expanding into multiple outlets?" Curious as to what he had proposed. Maybe I could sell him a few pointers.

"I have thought about it several times, but with the family, I decided to stay and do the best I could with just the one restaurant."

"Maybe a smart move, you certainly have a great operation going for you, with a good location, and please, call me Michael from now on."

"Thank you Michael, I appreciate that coming from a fellow restaurateur. We have about a thirty minute wait, would you care to take a seat in the lounge until your table is ready?" The personal service and pleasant attitude was a big draw for his business.

"Sure, that would be fine."

"Jenny, please take Michael to the bar and find him a good place." His right hand swept in that direction in a circular motion.

Seventeen, going on twenty-one, Jenny allowed me to follow her cute little figure to the lounge. Nearly fifty people were having cocktails while waiting their turn at dining. Mostly couples, but a few tables of two and four, all women or men. Of the ten seats at the bar, seven were taken. There were two Polynesian looking women seated on this end, by me. A stool was free next to the nearest lady so I took the one next to her.

"Jenny, this will be fine, thank you." Dismissing her to return back to the hostess station with a smile and pat on the shoulder, I leaned back on a barstool. The name tag with James, this must be James, as the bartender came to serve my libation.

"James, give me a cold Coors Light and what ever these ladies are having." Glancing over to my neighbors on the right with a smile, a tip of the hat so to speak and waiting on a response.

The bartender looking at me like "how did this guy know me already, not thinking about the I.D. on his chest.

"Thank you very much, but you didn't have to do that." Her smile, as she spoke was revealing perfect white teeth and full lips. She had long black hair hanging to mid back, the tight dress showing a tan with no lines from its backless cut.

"Truly my pleasure ma'am, to you both, my name is Michael, from Amarillo, Texas." Reaching to shake the delicate hands, one at a time and making sure to keep eye contact, I replied.

"Very nice to make your acquaintance, I am Kaehla and this is my friend Moneeka. We are from Hawaii, Molokai to be exact." Her accent flowing with the words like a tropical breeze, drifting across a secluded beach, and cooling ones face. I should not have heard her answer that way, but I did.

"I have been to Hawaii but not to the island of Molokai. Must be a very lovely place." Almost staring too much, at the beautiful almond shape of her eyes, makeup very refined and classy.

"You should go there sometime, it would be a wonderful trip for you." Her eyes were roving the full length of my body, a look of approval coming in the gaze.

"Are you here for dinner or just for a cocktail?" For some reason hoping it was for dinner.

"Oh! Dinner for sure always, we love this place. Whenever Moneeka's husband has to work, and we have the night off, we try and come here to start the evening." She didn't say anything about her husband.
"Start the evening?" I quickly replied.
"Oh yes, we love to go dancing and having fun, it is a break from watching everyone else having fun. I work at the Polynesian Room as a dancer, Moneeka's husband does the fire dance."
"Must be quite a show, not to be too forward. But you must look fabulous in a grass skirt and a tiny little top!" What in the world did I say that for, I asked myself. The answer was obvious and she had an air that intrigued me. Blushing she smiled and said." I think that was a compliment, wasn't it." There was a shyness, innocence flowing with the answer.
"Absolutely Kaehla, that was very much a compliment."

Five drinks later, we were having a good time, laughing and teasing one another. Moneeka joined in but the jest of the conversation coming from Kaehla and myself. She had touched me on the arm twice while we talked in expressing what she was saying, once on the thigh as she broke into a big laugh, from a story I had told. We had skipped our table call twice and asked to be put farther down on the list. Now it was time to get something to eat.

They had been there before me, so I wasn't sure of the count for them, but with their smaller bodies, the level of alcohol must be taking major effects by now.
"Well ladies, how about if I go and see if Carl can seat us for some dinner?"
Looking to the two faces, aglow with the buzz of the evenings pour and mix, they answered quickly.
"Fabulous, that would be simply fabulous!" She said with a sultry emphasis like someone from the movies, like Mae West.

Rising from my stool, I walked to the front of the restaurant and looked for Carl. I decided to stop off at the bathroom to relieve the six-pack, getting ready for another one. Coming back into the corridor I saw Jenny, "Hey little lady, can you get me a great table for three, my party has grown some?"
"No problem Mr. Decker, I'll have it ready in a minute. I'll come get you when it's set up."
"Thank you for your hospitality." Slipping a twenty-dollar bill into her tiny hand, causing a large grin to cover her face, her eyes and smile said "thank you a lot," I turned and walked back to the bar.
"Well, Ladies, our table will be ready in just a few minutes."

"That's wonderful. We ordered something special while you were gone. It is one of my favorite shots, called a Kamikaze. Will you join us for one, please?" Kaehla was bubbling over with enthusiasm as she slid a double whisky glass over in front of me.
"All right, on one condition though; you let me treat everyone to dinner tonight. Agreed?"
"It's a deal but on one of our conditions as well. You have to let us take you out dancing!," Moneeka jumping right into the conversation, added quickly.
"Gosh Moneeka I can't believe you said that! But would you Michael, please, it will be a blast, promise!" Kaehla had turned and placed her hand on top of mine, her warmth and softness so noticeable. It shouldn't be but it was, the train was calling "All aboard."
"Okay, we have a deal and I will shake on it. But can I trust you?"
"Of course you can, just look into these honest eyes and see!" She leaned plenty far enough forward and it wasn't just her eyes that were visible to mine.
"Contract signed, sealed and delivered! Here! Here!" The clinking of the glasses may have done just that, sealed the deal. I could hear the conductor calling out once again, "All aboard."

There are two and a half ounces of alcohol in a Kamikaze, since these were doubles, and we had thrown down the shot, five normal drinks had rocketed to our bloodstream in three seconds. Thank goodness it was time for dinner. Jenny was coming through the lounge and I needed some food, we all did.
"Mr. Decker, your table is ready. Please follow me to the dining room."
"Ladies, if you please!" Gesturing for them to follow Miss Jenny and I was following close.

As Moneeka and Kaehla got up and began to follow Jenny to the dining room, I quickly paid our tabs and caught up to them.

Carl's place was set up somewhat similar to the Montana's, with individual dining alcoves and four to five tables in each area. The furniture as well was very near the same style, efficient, sturdy and easily kept in top condition. The bottle of champagne that I had ordered was chilling in the silver ice bucket on the stand. Tattinger Gold Label Special Reserve 1958, a very good year and at three hundred dollars a bottle it should be.

Jenny held the chair for Kaehla and I held Moneeka's while she took her seat. Making an effort, a small one, to put some ice water on what was taking place. I had no business at all being here, but I was, and I wasn't leaving now. I would have dinner and then bow out gracefully later.

Several couples and individuals had turned to stare as we had walked back through the establishment and most all heads had turned when we entered our dining area. Both of the women were very attractive, stunning in their French/Polynesian refinement. The dancing, as a livelihood, demanded absolute perfect conditioning and tone, it was evident that they had not disappointed their choreographer. My own personal conditioning, at now 6'3" and 230 lbs and five percent body fat, had some curves and bulges of its own.
"Michael what kind of work do you do?" Moneeka asked, Kaehla suddenly listening attentively.
"I have a company named Sun Conglomerates, we are diversified into many things and areas of business."
"Sounds important, you must have worked hard to have such a big company." Moneeka continued with the affirmation.
"I don't remember saying anything about how large a firm it was!"

Wanting to get on to other topics, I gave her my raised eyebrows and asked about her dancing. Ten minutes later I felt like a fledgling student of Polynesian Cultural Arts, thankfully the diversion had worked. After ordering, we continued to talk about travel and some of the funnier sides to it. They both had done some extensive trips during the past few years, seeming to do quite a lot together.

Dinner came, the steak and lobster, MahiMahi and baked salmon were scrumptious. A bottle of Chardonnay Rose', made the palate and taste buds enjoy all the more. Dessert was offered but none of us could stand another smell of food, much less something more to consume it.
"I think about all the dessert I care for is the champagne."
"How about the two of you?"
"Sounds yummy, I love champagne, especially with strawberries!" There was a look of utter delight and savoring dreams in Kaehla's eyes, as well as something else. I heard the whistle of that train, one blast saying final call before leaving the station.

Signaling the waiter, Robert, he was soon on the way with a bowl of large red gourmet fruit, just what someone had wanted. She reached quickly to the bowl, took two and dropped one into each of our glasses. "After we are done with the champagne, you can eat mine and I'll eat yours!" As Kaehla flipped the words into the airwaves, I thought, "hmmm, too much of this is sounding too good," yet I smiled.

I smiled and chuckled, watching the fun she was having, Moneeka seemingly enjoying herself immensely. We, the group, had begun to elevate our volume, as others in the room made it evident with their looks. So excusing myself from the table, I went to use the bathroom and the phone. Needing a break to collect my thoughts and decide where the night was going from here. Knowing all too well that if I heard one more blast from that whistle on the train, the doors would close and there would be no turning off the tracks to where it would lead. The destination was already determined and decided, the ticket was in my hand welcoming me aboard. My choice was to turn and walk away, throwing the ticket to the ground, or getting it validated and enjoying the trip.

Leaving the restroom, I found the phone and gave the operator the number with the 505 area code, New Mexico.
"Hello!" Lisa's mother answered the telephone.
"Well hello to you as well, is Lisa there?" Praying for a yes to follow.
"Gosh, no she isn't Michael. Lisa took off with a bunch of her friends, they had finally talked her into going out dancing. You know how convincing that group can be!" Not what I wanted to hear, not at all.
"Tell her I called then and I will try again later."
"I'll tell her, but I will probably have to do that in the morning, I am sure that she will be late getting in."
"That's fine, talk to you later." All of the things that were flowing through my mind, one seemed to repeat itself more often than any other. What the hell, it's only going dancing! The convincing had already started. Seeing Carl at the front station I stopped and asked him to take care of a favor for me. There was no reason to take a chance in getting a DWI anyway.
"Ladies, ladies what is all the whispering about!" They were both buzzing like little bees as I approached the table.
"Oh just girl talk you know, kind of like we always have to go to the bathroom in pairs." Moneeka answered with Kaehla giggling in the background, the flushed look and color was very appealing.
"Yeah, why is it you can't go alone anyway?" Giving a false stern gaze with the teasing comment.
"It's a secret, one no woman will ever give out, ever. If someone did it would forever change the world."
"Sure Moneeka, sure. With that tidy bit of information, how about if we finish our glasses of champagne and let Carl have his table back."

Nodding in agreement they both picked up their stems and upended the holder until not a bubble remained. As our three glasses touched the table, Kaehla took the strawberry from hers and placed it against my lips.
"Here, we have some unfinished business. Nibble gently and savor the sweet juice, mmmmmmm! Now give me yours."

Lightly parting my lips, I bit into Kaehla's fruit and I did enjoy the sweet nectar. Responding by placing my glass in my hand and tipping it, I allowed the red delicacy to tumble slowly between my thumb and forefinger. As I grasped the bright fruit, she began to lower her mouth to my hand and the prize awaited, her fingers closed around my wrist, using both hands. With a gentle tug she pulled it to her lips, allowing them to part just wider than the berry, caressing the end of my finger with a moist brushing. The eye contact was fluid and fulfilling, that second whistle just blew, the doors were closing.
"Well if you two can stop killing those of us who are watching this erotic display, I'm ready to party!" Thank you Moneeka, thank you. We, all three began to laugh and break the tension, it had begun to cancel whatever airconditioning had possibly been there earlier.
"Ladies, your chariot awaits, believe me the party has begun."

The bar tab was $127.50, dinner came to $587.00, with the tip for both places, $875.00. It came in so fast, that making the speed of the money slow down was impossible. With the case of one of the best champagnes sitting in the "long car," a twenty-eight foot Golden Eagle stretch Lincoln, overall I had spent almost $3,400.00.

Of course we must not forget, the party had just started, several more lines had to be written to the story. All of which would drive the money machine even farther into insanity. Walking to the front lobby area, Carl made it a point to come and wish us well. It had been one hell of a night for him as well.
"Michael, I want to thank you and your guests for coming out tonight and giving us a chance to take care of you. I hope that you were pleased with the service and the food." Being very benevolent, he truly was a restaurateur, so much more than a regular owner or general manager. These people have a class, a certain savoirfaire that transcends above the crowd, it showed and was appreciated.
"I was not only pleased, but every aspect of the food, service, drink and atmosphere excelled expectation. From the greeting at the door to the paying of the tab, it is easy to see why you have so much return business. Please, certainly count on mine as well as many referrals."
"Thank you Michael, and coming from a man that knows the business. It's been a pleasure for me as well. All of you have a wonderful time."

Both of the ladies gave Carl a double hug and pecks on the cheek. He turned a slight shade of pink, but enjoyed the attention as well. Holding the door, I turned and said. "Ladies!" Kaehla and Moneeka floated through the opening to the lovely evening outside. The sky was so clear the stars looked extra close. A gentle breeze with that salt air purity smelled refreshing and a slight hint of honeysuckle added the spice. Two couples were admiring the car as we came out the entrance/exit passageway. Its long sleek black lines, trimmed in metallic gold stripes, highlighted and reflected the many exterior courtesy lamps. With the rear door open and some nice Kenny G playing, the plush leather seats and cashmere carpeting beckoned and welcomed you inside. Crystal flutes with the first bottle of Pierrie Jouet Rose poured, stood there in an elegant pose. The hand painted oils, which the artist had used to create the beautiful flowers, looked as if a bouquet set in the sterling silver ice bucket.

Kaehla turned and with a grin, having an intuitive feeling telling her something about the car had to do with us, said

"Ah, this particular vehicle wouldn't have anything to do with us would it?"

"Why don't you ask the driver and see young lady!"

"Excuse me sir! Is this car for me?"

"Yes ma'am, if you are with Mr. Decker it sure is." Paul, the driver, was personally recommended by Carl. He had been with the company for ten years, near forty, good shape and well trained in the arts.

"Michael, you are going to spoil us with all this pampering. This is something a woman could get used to." Kaehla said dreamily, peeking in the gorgeous vehicle. Moneeka right at her heels, nodded her approval as well.

"I certainly aim to please, and it made a lot more sense than having to drive. Don't you both agree?"

There was no quibbling in the least so we jumped in the back, myself in the middle of the two women. Picked up our glasses and with a toast, took the first libation in the limo. For the first half hour or so, we drank and laughed, I told several tales of things that had happened in the Montana Mining Company stores from time to time. Finding bras and panties during clean up, catching people having sex in various locations, under many circumstances. All of which is not only hilarious to see but to relate to others. One bottle finished, another well on its way, it was time to dance, move, and get some exercise.

"Well you two, I thought you were taking me dancing. Or have you backed out of your end of the agreement?"

"Paul, 4416 Pacific Beach Drive, over in the Mission district area, please. Do you know where it is?" Kaehla boomed the request.

"Of course, it's a great place to party and wonderful sound system as well. Fantastic D.J., Tommy B. is one of the best in southern California for sure."

I just knew that Paul probably knew where every single place in town was, both on and off the beaten path.

"Then let's hit the scene, I am ready to "Parrrrrrty!" Kaehla had her pump primed, Moneeka couldn't stop laughing and had been in the grin mode forever. I needed a breath of fresh air and man, needed to hit the head (bathroom, remember?), quick. Second bottle finished, third bottle opened before we got to the club. Each time Kaehla and I would stand up through the moonroof and fire the cork in the night sky. With each opening our bodies would come closer and there would be more contact, pressing against each other.

"Paul pull in that next gas station, rapidly!" My eyes were watering and a break was not going to wait, it was time to stop. The next station was only a block away, thankfully. I thought my eyes were watering before, oh what a relief. Both of the girls had done the same while I was inside. They still had not come out from their visit.

"Mr. Decker, you are going to have your hands full tonight. You should have heard those two when you first stepped out!"

"Paul, please, Michael is fine. Let's keep this informal tonight; there will be plenty of nights for the formality. And by the way, what was said?," curious about what had been overheard by my driver.

"The one in the tight dress thinks you hung the moon, Kaehla I think her name is. Her words were, and I quote, "This is going to be a night he will never forget!" Then they went on to say how handsome and charming and evidently rich and sexy, they are both infatuated beyond hope."

"Paul, whoa, whoa, this thing is getting way out of control. I am married to a wonderful little lady that just happens to be out of town for a few days. This whole arrangement fell into my lap totally by accident. I certainly have enjoyed myself and done absolutely zero to stop it, but an evening of fun is where it is going to end."

All the words were said, but I certainly was not positive that they came from any source of reality, because I was in fact having a good time. Third whistle just blew, conductor is waving the engineer to move the train on down the track, outside door is locked.

"Okay, Michael, whatever you say, you're the boss, but those are two hot numbers and the fire that is already burning, will not be quenched very easily at all." Paul was shaking his head and wiping his brow as the ladies rounded the corner. Oh God, I said to myself as I saw what was coming toward me. Kaehla had changed clothes, added to her makeup, and nearly took both Paul and my breath away.

The skirt, all ten inches of it, was a form fitting body wrap skirt, bright yellow. A tiny little halter-top, stylish & classy, but tiny was all there was. She had added some gold and diamonds here and there, which set everything off, drawing attention to all areas of her firm, smooth, bronze, freshly oiled skin and curves.

Moneeka had done her homework as well, this by adjusting the three zippers on the sides and front of her dress. Revealing an adding an allure of sensuality that I had not noticed before. I very well may be in trouble, as I looked at Paul and we both rolled our eyes.
"Damn ladies, you look absolutely breathtaking, both of you are beautiful. I knew that before, but now, oooooooh baby!"
"I'm glad you like what you see Michael, we are all yours for the evening." The little hip move of emphasis, with the toss of long black hair, made me say.
"Be still my heart." The train pulled out of the station, destination unknown.
"Senor Pablo, let this chariot fly!" Back in the same positions as before, the leather cool to the touch, thankfully, with the amount of long, bare skin wheels that were pressing against my thighs. Three full glasses poured and waiting for our delight, the third bottle was history before reaching the disco.

Great champagne has a way of making one feel absolutely superb, and at this point I was very possibly beyond that stage. Both Kaehla and Moneeka were there as well, but we were just shifting into high gear, far from stopping now.

As Paul glided the big Eagle to a halt outside the club, fifty pairs of eyes turned to gaze with envy at the impressive display. Over seventy-five people, maybe nearer a hundred were in line waiting to enter the popular place. A fifteen-dollar cover was no deterrent, nor the seven to ten dollar drinks. They had it and they would spend it any damn way they pleased. Leaning forward and moving to a closer seat by the driver's partition I spoke to Paul for instructions.
"Paul it seems to be a full house tonight, but I feel confident you can do something about that. We will need a private table setup, and near the dance floor, bottle of their best, if you please."

Handing him three hundred dollar bills to cover the smoothing he would have to do to make this happen. No hesitation at all, he was a professional, with the know how to handle this last minute type of requests. Turning toward the women at the rear of the extended limo, the amber mood lighting enhancing my view, a large smile came to my face. Reaching to the control panel I turned the tape player to some ZZ top and with the rocking going on, hit the switch for the moon roof. Pulling another bottle from the chilled case, I fired the projectile into the awaiting night. We certainly did not want to get thirsty while we waited. Sliding back towards the rear I began to pour. "Ladies shall we indulge?"

"Yes definitely!" Moneeka said, and Kaehla added, "But of course!"

"Michael if you make this evening any more special I am going to have to just fall in love with you, or something close to it!"

"Now, now Kaehla, I am just an old carpenter from Texas and I've been saving for almost two years to have this extravagant evening. I will have to go back and slave for another two years before it can ever be repeated. Besides with the way you look there are probably two thousand men in love, or maybe lust, with you!" Getting in a little teasing, but probably not as much as how many men would or could only dream of being with such a gorgeous creature.

"Nice try mister but no cigar, you are one hell of a man, in many ways. Any woman would be a fool not to see that. So there!"

"Well Goodness! Moneeka I think I saw a little dander rise, winking and grinning at them both, I liked the fire I saw, this lady definitely had some spunk.

"No dander, just fact, I am neither shy nor embarrassed to say that I think you are a HUNK! So there!" Her gaze never left mine for even a microsecond as she made the statement, she meant it, for sure, as they say out here in California.

"Thank you lady, I happen to think you are a mighty fine lady your own damn self. Bodacious, is the word we use in Texas, and you fit the term!"

Here comes Moneeka again, "God you two, this is worse than the strawberries!" We all burst out laughing and had another flute of champagne. As I looked out the side window Paul strolled up to the cab and got in.

"Michael, everything is all set, whenever you are ready."

"Let's go, we have had more than enough priming, how about you ladies?"

"Yes, that would be great."

All in agreement we waited for the door to be opened, I easily noticed that Paul was getting a hell of a view as he helped the two women from the car, also that several women were elbowing their dates or husbands, all of them staring at the beautiful array. I then stepped out of the car and joined my guests. Paul escorted us to the doorman, and then returned to stay with the limo.

"Mr. Decker, it is a pleasure serving you this evening, please step through here on the V.I.P. entrance."

As we were escorted inside, the club spread for over 7500 square feet of the very latest in lighting, sound and plush decor. It was certainly THE place to go, everyone was decked to the nines. The manger came to greet us immediately.

"Mr. Decker, ladies, we look forward to making your stay here at Castaways, a true pleasure. Absolutely anything you want or desire will be afforded you all." He was laying it on thick. "Please follow me to our V.I.P. section of the club."

He led us to a small elite area of the club, holding maybe forty to fifty people at the most. The club must have had a capacity of over seven hundred fifty on the main floor, at least. Furnishings several steps above the rest of the club, were apparent. A reserved card, embossed in Gold Leaf script, DECKER, sat on the table as we approached, matches with Decker on them as well.

"I hope this setting will be to your approval. Anything you may need, my name is Mario and it would be my pleasure to serve you."

"Thank you Mario, this will be fine." Mario and I held the chairs for the two ladies. Chilled Crystal Gold Ribbon Reserve sat on the table awaiting our savoring.

"Michael, I have a special request, you are probably going to think I am crazy. Anyway I want a double Kamikaze to start with!"

Waving at the waitress, they were delivered in what seemed like seconds. Yes, there were three of them, certainly didn't want to have Moneeka and I getting behind. I also sent instruction for the manager to have one of his staff go and see to it that Paul, our driver had whatever he wanted to eat or drink on my tab. He was doing a great job and I wanted to say thank you.

Another toast and the Kamikaze shooters, doubles, began to do their damage of intention. I had not had this much to drink in a long time.

"Michael, let's dance, I love this song!" Grabbing my hand as she got up. On the floor I went, no reluctance whatsoever. It was a great beat and as I had already decided, she was an incredible dancer. So good that I almost wanted to stop dancing myself and just watch her. So sensual, smooth and graceful and with rhythm never ever taught in a classroom. The true quality and dynamic shape she was in, fully came to life as she moved. Muscles cut and defined from years of dancing and working out professionally, as well as being blessed with a fabulous package to begin with.

I was far from the only admirer, and many of them were women as well. When a woman is truly exceptionally beautiful, women turn and look as well, many heads were looking her way. As the music ended, Moneeka came out and joined us for the next tune. We danced song after song for hours, stopping to keep the buzz well in flow with the progressing evening. The two of them seemed to be having a night for the record books. Finally I needed a rest and told them that I was not the professional dancer, no kidding, and went to sit a few out.

As I sat there, the music began and Kaehla and Moneeka began a dance that they had to have worked a routine with. It was kind of a combination of disco, rock & roll, and Polynesian, every step and move in perfect unison. It was beautiful, sensuous, sexy, sultry, physical, erotic, and expressionistic from their very souls, their heritage and background. A third of the way into the number, everyone else had stopped dancing and begun to watch the display. So evident was the professional quality, and the time it took to make it happen so precisely together, everyone appreciated it. The resulting applause showed the two of them so, but the joy in their faces while performing, was their true reward, they loved to dance.

"My, my, my, you take a man to dreamland, then send him on to nirvana. That was the most incredibly beautiful dance I have ever seen or witnessed. It is an understatement to say I am impressed."

With that statement came Kaehlas thank you for the compliment, her arms went around my neck, her lips to mine. Without any hesitation in any way, my arms went around her waist. Our bodies and lips touched in unison, the fire and the heat of the chemistry that had been brewing for hours began to ignite and flash sensations of pleasure pulsing through our bodies. Separating not by choice but by the necessity of our locale, embers glowing hot from our eyes and a sultry mist from our lips, I had failed in the temptation test. The train roared through the tunnel, gaining momentum, engines warm, power building, it was going to be a long ride for sure. Steam pressure storage tank, registering 475 on the 1000 point scale, red line at 825, I continued on.

"Shall we have another drink and try to cool down? Although if we ordered a five hundred pound block of ice, you two would melt it." Moneeka, it seemed, was in the mood for some attention and giving us a little of her frustration, she felt, was warranted.

"Moneeka, girlfriend, sounds to me like you are needing your man to be close. Either that or something else!" Kaehla gave a look, which I did not comprehend, but Moneeka did in totality. With an unspoken word they both stood.

"Michael, please excuse us for a moment, its ladies time!"

They went in the direction of the ladies room, it looked like from where we were seated. Mario, the manager, walked up to the table as he observed the two leaving,

"Mr. Decker, is everything fine for you sir?"

"Yes Mario, it couldn't be better, I don't think. Let me ask you a question. How often do Kaehla and Moneeka come here?"

"I see them usually three to four times a month. They are always by themselves and leave the same way after dancing for several hours. In fact you are the first person we have seen escorting them. That is in the two years that I have been running this club. Also, I might add, only as a compliment, that last dance was something that could be marketed, as sheer entertainment." With all the dancers that Mario sees in the night after night procession, and being in the business, I added this information to my files.

"Thank you, I take it the same, and I would like you to handle a special request for me."

"Certainly Mr. Decker, anything you want!" Eagerly he waited for the request.

"After Kaehla and Moneeka come back, I want to buy a round for the house, double Kamikaze's, so handle that for me!"

"No problem at all Mr. Decker, I will get the bartenders started now."

"That will be great and also have the D.J. do a fine toast to the ladies for the hot dance."

  Nodding as he left, I leaned back and took a deep breath. God what a night it had been. Although God had nothing to do with the insanity that was going on here, He would remind me of this fact later. Roughly two years later, to be exact.

"Excuse me, are we interrupting anything?" Kaehla whispered in my ear, her warm breath caressing my neck. A faint trace of mint and the Obsession perfume she wore drifting fragrantly to my senses.

"No, no, here please, sit down."

"You were certainly in deep thought. Any regrets?" She was searching deeper than the mere words were asking.

"None, in fact I was smiling about all the pleasure this evening has been. Especially the company!"

"I'm certainly glad to hear that!" Her look of false astonishment, then she continued, "Please excuse me for one more second, I have a special request for the D.J.!" Kaehla began walking towards the sound booth Moneeka leaned over to me and slipped her arm around mine. Her breast pressing a warmth against it in her movement.

"Michael, I have to say something to you. Kaehla and I have been friends for a long, long time. Almost fifteen years and I have never seen her so head over heels for someone. No matter how bold she may seem, her heart is very, very tender. Please do not break it, or try to

just use her. I am not implying anything or trying to, just please be careful with her feelings. You have been an absolute gentleman and more generous than anyone deserves, I mean extravagant to the max. And if I forget to say so later, thank you kind sir." She leaned closer and kissed me on the cheek, he eyes filled with the sincerity and thanks she had just conveyed. There was a lot more to these lovely ladies than first meets the eye, a whole lot more.
"Well goodness, isn't it just like another woman to try and steal her private hunk while she has her back turned." Kaehla stood there with her hands on her hips, a slight exaggeration to the right side. It was easy to tell for all concerned that no feelings had been trampled upon.
"Just you sit down here woman, and quit making a fuss." I said, standing to help her with her chair.
"Mr. Decker, your special order sir!" The waitress placed the drinks down and smiled sweetly. A look of wonder of what was going to happen on their faces, the two ladies that is. I just smiled and shrugged my shoulders, as I saw Mario nod to the D.J..
"Ladies and Gentlemen, I have a special announcement to make. In honor of the fabulous entertainment that was provided all of us by two very foxy ladies, Kaehla and Moneeka, I make a toast. Each and every one of you, have a complimentary Kamikaze, courtesy of Michael Decker, the gentleman as their escort. Thank you Mr. Decker from all of us. Raise your glasses! To the music that makes us groove, and the ladies in how they move. May they both provide those hidden pleasures, as we dig deep for buried treasures. Enjoy the spirits as you tip your glass, searching for the ultimate piece of ...! See how nasty you all are! Enjoy!"

The entire club shot the shooters and with the music rocking the airwaves everyone laughed and the party truly started now. The Harleys had all big kickstarted.
"Michael, Michael, what am I going to do with you? You keep doing such special and I must say, wild and crazy things. Is there no end?"
"Kaehla, I am fired up, having fun and ready to, as you said earlier, Parrrrrrty! In fact I just might have to show you a new dance step. One you have never, ever seen." Watching the expression on her face, as she waited as to what I was going to show her. Just at that moment, the music started and with it the shocking reality of what the hell I was doing.

Roberta Flack's, First Time Ever, Lisa and I, our song, began to play. The ultimate in duality; that black and white, angel and devil, began to stage their combat. Talk about a mood swing, this was it. I needed to get some air, now and alone.

"Ladies it is my turn to take a break." Both of them had seen the change, but only nodded and said nothing as I rose and left. I headed for the front door and the night air beyond.

"Mr. Decker, is everything all right?" Mario asked as I approached the entrance.

"Fine, I'm just going to get some fresh air for a minute."

Never breaking my stride I continued to the outside escape. Opening the door, I saw Paul and the limo parked to the right of the entrance.

"Michael, how is the club?"

"Club? Oh, it is fine I needed some fresh air is all."

Taking a little time for myself, I headed down the street and allowed the quiet of the night to filter my thoughts. I had consumed enough alcohol for six people, its effects causing my steps to not be as exact as earlier. I needed to talk to Lisa, and find out what was going on, maybe hearing her voice would make a difference.

Walking back to the car, I stepped in the back, waving Paul to stay where he was, I would get my own door. My heart pounding as I dialed the number, knowing that since it was almost one here, it was two there in New Mexico.

"Hello." Lisa's mother answered the phone sleepily.

"I am sorry for calling so late but I need to talk to Lisa."

"Michael she is not home. She called earlier and told me she would not be home till tomorrow. I'm sorry but that is all she said."

"Thank you, Good night." I said abruptly ending the call.

Fine and dandy, she wants to stay out all damn night, let the party truly begin. I blamed all of the undoing, which had been totally my choices, on Lisa not being home. It had nothing to do with her at all, only my weakness and diversions. Regardless, I was about to have my fun, NOW.

"Paul, fire this stallion up! Make a call as we are leaving to Mario and have him add another round for the house on my tab and inform him we will be back in ten minutes. Have him smooth my leaving the ladies so long, he can think of something."

"Yes sir, we are on our way"

While we were only a few minutes away from the small office I had rented, I went to the condo instead. I wanted to get some more cash. Down to only about three thousand now and I sure as hell did not want to run out now. It was about to be the biggest damn night the Castaways had ever seen. I was going to personally see to it.

"Just stop here at the driveway Paul and I'll be right back."

Running into the condo, I opened the small wall safe behind the picture of the "Old Gold Miner," a gift of commemoration from the guys of Montana Mining Company. Grabbing a healthy stack of hundreds, near fifteen thousand, I closed the safe and returned to the limo. Nine minutes from our departure, we rolled back to the front of the club. One o'clock and there was still a short line outside, maybe ten or twelve people. Mario was standing outside, waiting for my return.

After all he did not know me from Adam, I was a cash, no credit card patron, and my tab was near three thousand dollars. He knew Paul and the company he drove for, as well the personal recommendation from Carl. Still some apprehension remained, as could be expected. As Paul came around and opened my door, I slipped five hundred dollars in his hand.
"This is for the service tonight, we will have a long history together my friend. Getting rich and enjoying life."
"That is generous Michael and I appreciate it, really." It had been easy to see earlier in the evening that Paul took his job seriously. It was his livelihood, and rewarding this kind of professionalism was a pleasure.
"Mr. Decker, so glad to see your back." Mario excitedly expressed.
"Yes, I bet you are. Did you get everything covered for me inside?"
"Of course, Mr. Decker. There are two dozen, yellow roses on the table and another bottle, both compliments of the house, sir. I told them that you had to take care of some business, an emergency with the company. Even though I have no idea whatsoever what it is you do."
"Very good Mario, that will be fine, thank you."
"Goodness, pretty flowers and pretty ladies, what a combination. Did you miss me?" As I had walked up the two of them were deep within the throws of a conversation.
"Yes we missed you silly. I was getting cold and needed a hug!"
"With all these men around and you couldn't get a hug!"
"One of these days Michael, I am going to fix you a deal!"
"Oh Kaehla, you are not big enough to be threatening me."
"Just you wait and see, Mr. Texas Man!" Her eyes were making several additions to the statement with much more conclusive expressions.
"Well then come here and get one of those hugs." Our bodies molded together, almost immersing into one another. I bent down and gave her a kiss, tenderly on the cheek. Then leaned over and put a peck on Moneeka as well.
"I was wondering when I was going to get some of that sugar!" Her smile was once again infectious, the resulting chuckles evidence of that fact.
"Michael, while you were gone, Kaehla and I were talking and won-

dered if you would like to come over and continue the party at my house. We could have more personal time that way."

"Sounds great to me, I am up for anything."

Waving to my waitress, I asked for the tab. When she had finished totaling it her eyes widened. Almost with a shyness, she laid it on the table next to me. Total $2,948.00, with a 20% tip of six hundred it came to $3,548.00.

Counting out thirty-six hundred dollar bills from the stack in my pocket, she turned to get my change. She returned promptly with it in a leather bound folder.

"Thank you very much for the service, that is for you and all the bartenders and cocktail staff that helped you serve the rounds. Please make sure though, that you keep your share."

"But Mr. Decker there is over six hundred dollars in there."

"Yes, I am aware of that, so give twenty dollars to all the other waitresses, fifty to each of the bartenders, the rest is yours."

"Thank you very much Mr. Decker." She bowed and left the table a slight skip in her step. As I turned back towards the table, Kaehla sat there shaking her head, a pouting look of favor on her face.

"You truly love to share don't you, Mr. Decker? It shows all around you that the reason you give to everybody is not to impress them but to give part of the wealth someone has given you."

"Kaehla if you only knew." She didn't and never ever would know what I did for a living and where the wealth came from. The three of us left the V.I.P. section and went to the awaiting coach.

Needless to say, the night progressed on until the early hours of the morning and my first straying of the vows I had made to Lisa took place. The intimate details are not important, for all they would contain are facts of the betrayal itself. Where there is a first, of course there are others, many others. As the wealth continued to grow, the time Lisa and I spent together, was less and less. She never told me about her all night vigil, whether we had sinned in tandem. It didn't matter, I had.

Money, power, greed, control, and manipulation all of these were evident in the daily operations of the Sicilia-Falcon empire. There was no way to avoid the fallout from the infrastructure. It was a trend so strong that traits and habits of one would cycle themselves into touching and influencing many lives around them.

One day in the early fall, after some six months in the mercenary business, I went to New York to pick up some documents. An ordinary trip in many ways, but one in which I took the liberty of inspecting what I was bringing back to Mexico. Within the packages and two briefcases, were some thirty million dollars in negotiable Bearer Bonds and two Swiss bank passbooks. In one account was a balance of one hundred fifty-five million dollars, the other contained one hundred eleven million, in U.S. dollars not francs. Many of the trips I had made were to deliver money, as much as three million in just one shipment. The sheer bulk of the money, was a major problem in trying to move it undetected.

My jobs ranged from the far tip of South America to Canada, from the U.S. to Europe. It was a global business and one that touched the lives of millions of people. In a book titled, "The Underground Empire," author James Mills goes into serious detail as to the exploits and scope of its magnitude. The time I spent with Falcon continued to supply me with incredible wealth. All it ever served to do was drive Lisa and I farther and farther apart. So in sheer desperation I tried to make my last job a break from the organization. After watching the family work the business, I felt that I could set up a side deal and make enough profits that I would never have to work again. Liquidating everything I had acquired, all my cash on hand and every penny I could borrow, I made the deal of a lifetime.

Flying down to San Andreas, an island off the coast of Columbia, I arranged a buy to go down. Dennard had approached me several times to make a few side maneuvers. This one, he explained was hot because several of the people he had dealt with for over three years were going to get out of the business as well.

An area above Bogotá, Columbia called "Bluefields" was the purchase point. At near ten thousand a kilo, I had put together enough money to buy several million dollars worth when sold back in the U.S.. All aspects of the buy, the transportation, the delivery, went down like clockwork. I had made all the arrangements and followed up on every part of the journey. Afterwards, returning to the U.S., while all the money was being collected, product sold, I had begun trying to restore some of the relationship with Lisa.

We had actually been giving it an effort for three months now. Even to the point of her being pregnant with our first child. As fate would have it, the morning I was to go to Central America and pick up all the cash from the dope deal, Lisa became very ill. So much so that I took a huge chance and sent Dennard. Needless to say it resulted in a disaster, totally. He never came back to the U.S., and it was the last time I ever saw Brian Dennard. He stole all the money, leaving me almost totally broke, as I had taken literally my last dollar to make this buy the biggest deal of my life.

This life had been killing me for quite some time. Not only me but those around me. My justification of doing for Falcon what I had done for Uncle Sam, never really was totally swallowed and digested. I had finally realized that this manner of livelihood was going to be the death of me, and my marriage. Thus the only alternative I saw was to do what most thought could never be done, walk away form the organization.

I set up one last meeting with Falcon, knowing it was going to be a fiasco. I had made my mind up to leave, nothing and no one was going to stop me. I certainly didn't want it to escalate into violence, but this was it and if it took that, it did. I had called in each and every marker from every special forces buddy I had, and put them on standby. Letting them know what I was about to do and if in the event anything happened to me, to blow the hell out of Falcon and everyone near and far of his organization. It was a complete and total massacre.

January 10,1975, time to let the tiger loose, and I really was ready for whatever might take place. After having made all the necessary safety precautions, it was now time to finish this once and for all. I might in fact lose my life, but I would kill every bastard living in the near vicinity with my dying breath. The meeting took place in Falcon's house, around the same table as when I was offered the job.

He could tell from the phone call that something was up, something major. Thus the following scenario came to be.

"Albert, I came here today to do two things. Very simple and very direct. First I came to inform you that I am no longer working for you or anyone else in the mercenary business. I quit. Second, if the slightest wind of any action or rumors of such come about, I will see you and your entire organization blown to hell. I walked in and I'm walking out the same way."

The look in my eyes reinforced what I had said. His response was the following in very simple terms.

"No one and I repeat no one has ever left my employment. You want to walk away, walk away and take your chances. I say this not as a threat, just as a statement. But don't ever try and fuck me!"

"Let me reinform you of something Albert, I told you this the first time we talked and I am telling you again. When I walk out of here, I am doing so not as in taking some fucking chance. You want to play with the big boy's, I will send enough firepower into your family to blow each and every one of you to hell. So once again don't threaten me, or we will start settling this score as I speak. You are well aware of the contacts I have, they are the reason you wanted me to work here. The brotherhood there doesn't give a shit about your money and power. That kinship will paint this organization in red so fast it will amaze you, if necessary. I am leaving and the smartest thing you can do is absolutely nothing."

I rose and left the house in Chipultipec, never to return. A floater car followed me to make sure that no one else was around, some twenty other men watched the house and stood by for a signal that never had to be given. A feeling of regret had started many weeks before for ever leaving Montana Mining Company, so what if I had to step down a little in title. At least this type of chaos would not be part of my life.

Taking the last of my furniture, guns, clothing and a 1958 Chevy pickup that I had customized, also thankfully I had not hocked for dope money, Lisa and I along with our German Shepherd puppy Thor, headed for Albuquerque, New Mexico. It was a new place for a new start and a new life.

Lost in the last ten days were three exotic sports cars, the condo in Mission Bay, house in Rancho de Santa Fe which I had put three hundred thousand dollars down on for a cash thirty day pay off. With no refund, planning on taking the proceeds from the "big deal," this surprise to Lisa was a total bust. Everything put together, came to almost $2.6 million gone, it came fast and left even faster.

CHAPTER 5

trying for a normal life, introduction to the DEA

The trip to Albuquerque was long, hot, cramped and miserable. A trip which not only was uncomfortable physically, but the mental strain on both Lisa and me was possibly worse. There had been almost too much for the line to be walked, the truth began to leak out some months back, with it, bitter contempt and anger. This move would either mend or break our marriage; there was no room for anything other than restoration or certain death.

I had called ahead and arranged for a small apartment so that at the very least we would have a place to rest our heads and hang our clothes. This while I went out and found a job, something that would provide the income necessary to take care of my wife and soon to be child.

After arriving into the city that first afternoon, unpacked and exhausted, I went to find a phone while Lisa lay down to rest. I had decided, on the way out to New Mexico, that one quick way to raise some cash would be to sell all of the expensive guns that had been collected and confiscated over the past year. After placing an ad in the paper that afternoon, it took no time at all to sell these fine weapons. Within one week I had sold all but two of them, raising almost four thousand dollars. Many I sold way to cheap, but the cash to get started on was the most important thing.

Within two weeks Lisa and I had found a nice three bedroom house up in the northeast heights, moved in and started putting back together some semblance of a life. Employment had been fairly easy to obtain, European Health Spas on N.E. Menaul had an opening for a Salesman/ Trainer. Not only did I get the job, but also the commissions allowed me to work lots of hours and make good money very quickly. Clearing almost thirty-four hundred my first month, after working near eighty hours a week. What a change from two months previous to this and I had been making that a day. The reality of just how much money I had literally thrown away began to sink in.

How could someone be so nearsighted, so stupid, so wasteful as to not put away just a portion of the surplus for a rainy day. All I had put away was the rain, for if only ten percent of the money that was paid to me in the past year had been invested, it could have easily paid a dividend of thirty thousand dollars a year for the rest of my life. A mere ten percent, then the reality of what could have been returned if I had invested half was more than I could take. I had to forget the losses, for there was no way to get it back no matter how much I might think about it. Hard work and being careful were what had to be done, and now was the time to do it.

One of the other clubs in town, there were two in Albuquerque, had contacted the Regional office in Phoenix about the possibility of having a sales contest between the two stores. With a party being the spoils for the winner, I was going for the prize. A two thousand dollar bonus for the top salesperson who had sold the most number of contracts was another perk.

Within the two clubs this consisted of twenty-four sales people, ten men and fourteen women. No matter what I had to win this contest, Lisa and I needed a new vehicle to provide adequate space for the new addition that was about to arrive. Leaving the club that night after learning of the promotion I shared it with Lisa.

"Lisa they are going to have a big sales contest down at work."

"When?"

"It will start tomorrow and run for thirty days. The grand prize for the top salesperson is two thousand dollars. I thought we might use it to buy another car. What do you think?"

"Michael you haven't won it yet, isn't it a little premature to think about using the money until it is ours to use?"

"Lisa I understand that but I am going to win that damn contest. We need the money and I have the ability, just you wait and see. I will pick up the money and bring you home a new vehicle within the month." A cocky attitude yes, but I knew that I could do it.

"Okay, whatever you say, but let's not count our chickens before they hatch, agreed?"

"Agreed. How about if I give you one of my famous hot oil rubs tonight and make it so you get a good nights sleep?"

"Are you sure that you are not too tired? You have been at work for almost fourteen hours." Her eyes said yes please, but her kind thoughtful heart was always thinking of me, even if I didn't deserve it.

"Listen here young lady. I am a young strong virile man and I have more energy than I know what to do with. So you just go in there and get ready and I will get the oil and cream warm and be right in." Leaning forward and kissing her cheek I went to get ready and so did she. The look of satisfaction and relief already beginning to show and I had not even started to take away the muscle fatigue. She was getting so big so fast, the doctor had already said that it was going to be a large child. There were several nine and ten pound babies in my family, look out.

These times, and I tried to do this four or five times a week, were very healing to Lisa and I. The quiet, tender, caring, sensitive, sessions of parental intimacy allowed me to begin to restore some of the faith and dedication to our relationship that I had destroyed.

It was also a loving time, her body was changing so rapidly, and to me it was beautiful. As I massaged the oils and creams into Lisa's swollen belly I would sing and talk to the little one inside, making funny faces that would make us both laugh. Rubbing the sore, stiff areas of her lower back and feet and calves, allowing for a real relaxation to flow through Lisa's body and a good nights sleep to come. My patterns of sleep were still the same, three or four hours and I was ready to fly out the door to work.

That next month saw with it a change down at work, the manager was paying close attention to the amount of business I was bringing through the door. Not only that but the way I was working my customers for referrals and helping with their workouts and fitness programs.

Three weeks into the contest he called me into his office. Richard "Dick" Grebe, about five foot seven, short but built powerfully, having put his time in the gym for many years, raised his head as I walked in his office.
"Michael, please come in and shut the door." He stood and shook my hand as I entered. I was dressed as all the employees were, the white, short length, "doctors" jacket as we called them and black slacks.
"Good morning Dick!"
"Morning. Michael the reason I wanted you to come in this morning was to discuss some changes that are taking place here in the club. I need to have an assistant manager in this club that can sell and train the rest of the staff to sell as well. Also someone who can motivate and excite people, get them fired up to perform at their absolute best. I talked to the regional supervisor and told them of the choice I had made for this position. In so doing I am offering this position to you. It would carry with it an additional $1,000.00 a month bonus package, 10% more commission structure and full insurance with retirement. By the way the insurance goes into effect immediately, there's no waiting period. Since I know that Lisa is about to add to your family. What do you think?" The smile was beaming across the desk in anticipation.

"The promotion would be great, under one condition."
"What condition is that, Michael?" with a worried look on his face.
"That this promotion would not cause me to be disqualified for the sales contest. I want to win that contest and I have a good shot."
"It would in no way take you out of the running for the prize money. In fact that was one of the approval factors from the regional office, you are currently in the lead for the money." He said with a prideful expression, which was a compliment to me.
"Great, then you have yourself a new assistant manager. I appreciate the chance at management and you will not be disappointed."
"I truly believe that Michael, your dedication around here has been an encouragement to many already. Just keep up the good work."
"No problem whatsoever, thank you again."

No sooner had I left his office than one of the ladies from the juice bar came up and said congratulations, the word had been spread early, and then I saw why. Directly across from Dick Grebe's office was a new sign on the door, Michael Decker, Assistant Manger, I had my own office. The old Assistant didn't have an office, so this was an additional benefit. I walked in and tried out my new chair and phone.
"Hello." Lisa answered from the house.
"Well, Mrs. Decker, guess where I am calling you from?"
"And just where would that be, Mr. Decker?"
"From the new Assistant Manager's office, mine!"
"Michael! Really! You're not kidding!?"
"No I am not kidding and you had better sit down for this one. It includes a thousand dollar a month bonus, extra commissions and the best I saved for last. We get full insurance for our entire family with no waiting period. It will cover all of the hospital bills, follow-up visits and everything. Isn't it great!"
"Oh Michael it's wonderful. Thank you for working so hard and making this happen. I mean it, you have really done terrific, and not only at the office. I love you so much Michael." The words brought a feeling into my heart that I had not felt for over a year. An old joy and contentment and satisfaction of loving and providing for my family, just like the days at Montana Mining Company.
"Thank you baby, I appreciate what you said and I will continue to bust my butt and win that contest, you just wait and see!"
"I know you will Michael, hurry home tonight and we'll celebrate everything."
"You have got a date lover, take care and I'll see you then."

I was fired up and primed, encouraged by the events of the morning, but most of all by the words from Lisa. That tone, the love and warmth that had drifted away because of failures of my faith and honor was beginning to come back and be part of us. The customers had better watch out today and hold on to their cash, credit cards and checkbooks, because I was going to sell them, their friends and all of their families a membership today!

It must have been contagious to everyone because by the end of the day, our club had sold thirty-seven Gold Life's, and sixteen yearly memberships, a record for European Health Spas in this Region. A total of almost forty-five thousand dollars in one single day, Dick Grebe had a facebusting grin that night when he called in the daily totals and gave them the news. Accompanied I'm sure with some rubbing and gloating and future challenges to the other managers. He had asked for performance and had received exactly that, performance.

It had been a great day for me as well. Pushing my totals over the top once again allowed a little breathing room as well. The next closest salesperson was almost twelve thousand dollars behind on the leader board, it was a lady from Phoenix. Our local club had done a $100.00 cash bonus for the daily leader and I was going to buy some nice roses and a bottle of wine, since winning and getting a promotion in the same day was worth celebrating. Besides who I was going home to celebrate with, was the main reason anyway.

"Is there anyone here in this house?" Signaling my arrival as I came through the front door. "Hello, Lisa!"

"Wait just a minute, I'll be right there." Came her voice from the back of the house. There was something happening here, I could tell from her voice. My heart began to beat deeper and my breathing quickened as I awaited her debut.

Stepping on through the living room to the kitchen, I opened the refrigerator and set the bottle in the freezer to chill. Opening the cabinet over the stove I took down a vase and quickly put the flowers in an arrangement, turning to the other cabinet reached for two tulip glasses for the wine. It was a nice bottle of Zinfandel Rose,' which was one of Lisa's favorites. Looking out in the backyard I saw Thor doing his thing, chewing his big rawhide bone. He had grown so fast while we had been in Albuquerque. Obedience and protection training were part of his routine as well, I worked with him at least three and sometimes four times a week. Thor would top out somewhere near 100-110 pounds and a dog that size needs to have training for everyone's sake. The dog and family both benefit from this routine and regiment. Well it has been ten minutes, no Lisa, this must mean that I am supposed to go and try to find her. Yet if I am wrong then she will be upset, what to do. I decided to wait and give it a few more minutes. I am glad that I did, because two minutes later she came walking out.

Dressed in a beautiful long silk gown, white and flowing all the way to her ankles. Hair freshly washed and curled, makeup highlighted with the beautiful natural glow of carrying a new life inside. Lisa had so much natural beauty anyway, but tonight there was a charm and warmth, love shown from her eyes. I stood there staring and appreciating the loveliness that filled my eyes and my heart.

"Lisa you look absolutely gorgeous; I mean ravishing!" I had to swallow to get the entire sentence out. It was breath taking, to see her this way.

"Well Michael, I do declare that you were almost struck speechless!"

"Yes, my lady, your loveliness becomes you and is so alluring it causes a stirring in my heart and in my loins." Looking directly into her eyes with the words spoken from my heart.

"My, I think my man has grown a set of possible antlers during his absence today." Her coy smile and flippant tone teasing me in jest, but her heart was loving me as well.

"May I suggest a toast for the moment, the promotion and the winner of the hundred dollars sales bonus!" Holding up the hundred dollar bill and placing it in her hand.

"Thank you kind sir and I know just a place that can be used. This little one still needs a few things." She patted her tummy and gazed at me with her lovely eyes.

I poured the wine and toasted all the events of the day, allowing for the moment to warm us both and begin to wind down from the push of the day. I had broken the barrier today trying to win and stay on top. It was time to slow down and enjoy the specialness of the woman I was with and feel her closeness.

I kicked off my shoes and socks, took off my shirt, thankful I had showered at the Spa before coming home. Clean, relaxed and enjoying life, having now so much with so little. I had a lot to be thankful for, and I was. We talked and laughed, listened to some nice music, a little Carly Simon then later some Boz Skaggs. Touching, kissing and intimately loving one another. The tenderness, and slow easy progression of passion between two people that had so much chemistry, yet being gentle and taking so much care to be so delicate and soft, caused an eroticism all its own. Deliberately stopping at intervals to feel the sensations and allow them to be extended and intensified. The resulting satisfaction taking us both to a higher plane, the shudders and tremors, little gasps taking their time in ebbing from our bodies. It was truly an act of making love, the bonding was so special in the afterglow.

Later, much later I made some light snacks and nibble food. A glass and a half of wine was the total consumption for Lisa for the entire evening. She was making sure that the baby was not harmed in any way. Her regiment for food, vitamins and exercise would make the little one come out into this world, extremely healthy and large.

It was a wonderful time and the night seemed to fly by. A few winks and it was time to go back to the spa. Five o'clock in the morning was my leaving time since the spa opened at six. Getting all the lights and pumps and valves turned on. Chemicals checked in the three pools, as well as the eucalyptus in two steam baths. Also I put soap and shampoo in the shower areas for both men and women. The temperature was checked in the different areas for working out, along with the water for swimming and spa use. I liked to have all of it done early, with a minimum of fifteen minutes to spare.

Each day began early and continued until near ten o'clock in the evening. I split schedules of supervision with the Manager, Dick Grebe preferring the later shift. Productivity continued to be on the upswing, spirits and attitudes becoming more assertive and professional on the behalf of most of the staff. This next week would be the final drive to the finish of the Regional Sales Award, and the very much coveted two thousand dollar grand prize money.

Lisa was a jewel at home and being patient, she encouraged me and gave me the old slap on the buns, several mornings. Before I got out of bed that is, she was not inclined to get up with the chickens still asleep and most of the rest of mankind, as well. So it was up and off for me and sell my not so little buns off. Friday was the final day, they were cutting off results at three thirty. Then they would start the tabulations and totals for an announcement by conference multiline call at seven forty-five in the evening.

6:55 p.m., Friday, the big day had finally come to pass, and several sales people had been saving their ringer, last minute contracts for a Banzai finish. One of the top people from Denver, Colorado, the lady from Phoenix, Arizona and myself were in the upper quadrant of the running.Ced Dick came into my office and quizzed me how it was going.
"Michael, it is almost time for the announcement. How are you thinking that you did? Any bets?"
"It is going to be close Dick, but I think I have a damn good chance at bringing home the bacon. Carol Jamison from Phoenix is going to be the closest contender. She had a twelve person group contract come through this morning, for cash and it was one heck of a boost to her overall totals." Inside I still thought that I had made the grade!

"Regardless of the outcome you did one terrific job and your daily performance and work ethics inspired every single salesperson here."

Dick was being his managerial self and was forever stroking his staff. But the compliment was still sincere and the resulting overall totals of the club would give him a healthy bonus check, very healthy indeed.

"Thanks Dick, let's just see what takes place in the next few minutes."
"What would you think about putting the conference call on the P.A. system and letting everyone hear the results at the same time? After all most of the customers are excited about the contest as well."
"You're the boss Senor, you're the boss!" It really didn't make a difference to me, just give the damn totals.

That final half hour seemed like a day or more. So many were coming and saying basically the same thing. Pestering the heck out of me, I finally went back to the maintenance room and found a little peace and quiet. Not emerging until two minutes until countdown. As I was walking through the spa area back to the weights workout floor and lobby, the conference call began to come from the P.A. system.
"Dick Grebe this is Regional calling for the Sales Award final results, Tom Baker here." Everyone stopped and attentively listened.
"Tom we are standing by and waiting, I have the call being broadcast over the P.A. system as the entire club is a part of this including the customers." Grebe was still in there prospecting and smoozing.
"That is a great idea and I say good evening to each and every one of you, whether customer, visitor or salesperson involved in the contest itself. This particular event has generated more competition within the ranks, than any other contest I have seen since coming to the European Health Spa organization. It has produced results far exceeding any pre-event projections and for those facts and figures, a big thank you to all of you. This type of event brings out the best in all of us and allows for the dedicated individual with the great work ethics and determination to succeed." Damn this guy was going to give us some results and instead he is running for some kind of office and doing a promotion speech. Get to the results, already!
"It has come down to the wire for the grand prize winner and the title of Master Salesperson. In fact today's totals, as they were compiled, took many that were out of the running, into the thick of things. The winning totals a new record for contracts sold in this time period, ever in European's history. Now, for the final results of the contest. Third place with an overall total of $16,755.00, goes to Paul Grossman of Denver, Colorado, along with a cashiers check for $500.00. Congratu-

lations to you Paul. Second place goes to Billy Jo Cumberland from the Tucson, Arizona store with a total of $21,840.00, the $1000.00 is in the mail Ms. Cumberland."

They had not mentioned Carol Jamison yet and with the big group deal she had it is going to be close, damn close.

"Now for the announcement all of us have been waiting for. The winner overall, and a check for $2,000.00. First though I must say that this individual has done an outstanding job for their club. Also in achieving this position of first they, as I said earlier, have set a new record of sales excellence. Due to this fact that the Main Corporate offices have concurred and added an additional $1,000.00 to the prize money for a grand total of three thousand dollars. That grand total in sales came to $37,945.00 and the Master Salesperson award goes to Michael Decker of Albuquerque, New Mexico. Congratulations to you Mr. Decker."

Wow! I did it, I had won the contest and got a bonus as well! Three thousand dollars, added to the commissions for the month, I had made almost seventy-five hundred dollars. Handshakes and hugs and kisses all came as accolades for the acknowledgment of the accomplishment.

"Michael, one hell of a job. I want to throw something out to you. I know that you are looking for a vehicle right now and also that a four wheel drive interests you. My wife has been bugging me for months to sell our new Chevrolet Blazer. It is loaded and only has six thousand miles, if you are interested maybe we can make a deal.

"Dick do you mean the one I saw you driving last week. Hell, it's brand new."

"Yes I know but my wife wants a car to drive and I won't hear the end of it until I get her one. In fact I drove it tonight, why don't you drive it home and see how you like it!"

"I will take you up on that and I am going to leave now if you don't mind?" I was hoping to get out a little bit early and spend the extra time with Lisa.

"Michael you have earned some time off, in fact why don't we switch shifts tomorrow and you come in late."

He didn't have to tell me twice, grabbing the keys to the Blazer I headed home with the news and the new vehicle. It drove like a dream and with the heavy body would be safe for Lisa and the new baby. She was thrilled with the news and the Blazer. The treat of not going in until late was very nice for both of us, and the morning snuggles were one of my favorites. Something I had missed for the past few months while I was working all those hours.

The next two months flew by with all of the preparations for the baby and work taking a lot of commitment. I had made the deal on the new Blazer with Dick Grebe and he and I both had ended up with a new car. Lisa was absolutely gigantic, for the past two months I had massaged her almost every night and rubbed the vitamin E oil into the skin on her tummy. Natural childbirth classes had become part of our schedule as well. I only hoped that she would be able to have the baby, as big as the child seemed to be getting.

March 8,1975, early morning, the wee hours were just floating on and then there was a sound in the night. A sound that I was prepared for, but never hearing before, it was awesome. It came from a place in Lisa's voice box that no other source could have brought forth, other than a child about to enter the world.

"Woooo oooooooo OOOOOOOOOOOOOH!!!" It was a call, primeval in origin I think, a call to the Clan of the Cave Bear, signaling the spirit world. No it was Lisa telling me in a new tongue that the bambino was on its way. A bag had been packed and a fast call to the doctor and it was out the door to Presbyterian Hospital.

As expected there was no traffic, and as I had lifted Lisa in her flannel nightgown and Ski jacket into the car, a contraction had begun to attack. The "wha-wha-wha-wha" cadence of the breaths had started, I was trying to coach and drive, what a pair for an observer to see. Even at this early morning, awoken from the depth of sleep and nothing done for looks, Lisa looked beautiful to me. It was an event we had both been waiting for and now it was finally here. I think, that I drove a little faster than normal. I was already pulling into the emergency entrance of the hospital. Whoops!

Running around to the passenger door, I reached in and gently, sliding a hand and arm under Lisa at the knees and midback, I lowered her to the pavement. A nurse was waiting with a wheelchair. I quickly parked the Blazer and ran with the bag, to the entrance.

Dressed in my trusty old wranglers and a tshirt, tennies worn and comfortable, wind breaker from our time out in California, I was here for the marathon.

"Baby, are you okay?" I knelt down and touched Lisa on the thigh.
"Yes, he is fine and so am I."
"What do you mean he?" Raising my brow in question.
"I promise you that this baby is a he, too big and too powerful to be a girl." She was breathing deep and sighs were coming very regular.

Within just a few minutes the orderly was wheeling her to the fourth floor and a private room. The hallways and rooms were awake and buzzing even at this early hour. Babies weren't caring what the time is, just wanting to come out and say "Hello World." Moans and groans and coached breaths were coming from some of the rooms.

In jest, I had mentioned a marathon earlier, but this is what it turned out to be for real. Fifteen hours later we were not much farther along than when first arrived. Lisa had dilated to between seven and eight centimeters, but not near enough. An exam by the OB/GYN saw that the child needed at least eleven or twelve centimeters to make its exit through the tunnel of choice.

"Lisa, I know how much you wanted to have natural child birth, but it just isn't going to be possible. The baby is to large and you are not near large enough for it to pass. We will have to perform a cesarean section for the birth to take place." Warm, but direct with the facts.

"Oh, no, I will have a scar, please wait a while longer and I promise I will be big enough." Tears coming from her precious eyes and streaking down her face. I reached over and stroked her hair and softly touched her shoulder.

"Lisa it will not help honey; the baby is just to big."

The baby had come almost three weeks early, thankfully, because if he had been full term it would have been over ten pounds easily, maybe eleven. I leaned down and told Lisa it would be fine and to try and not worry. Holding her for a minute and then the nurse took her away for prepping and the surgery. It had been almost sixteen hours of labor.

So much came to pass through my thoughts as I sat there in the waiting room and passed the time. I was twenty-six years old and had already experienced more, in some areas, than most had in a lifetime. Right this very minute I felt much older than my years. Lying there near by, was the woman I loved more than life giving birth to a new life, an added responsibility for the two of us for many years to come. Where would I be in five years, ten, forecasting I made many scenarios come to the surface. Yet none would truly come to pass.

"Mr. Decker, you have a new baby boy in your family. And everything is working on the little guy, lots of fingers and toes. He is one of the strongest newborns I have ever seen."

"Really, really she had a boy?"

"Yes, a fine beautiful baby boy, you have a new son."

"Gosh, I can't believe it. When can I see him? Lisa too!"

" Lisa will be in recovery for some time yet, but your new son will be in the nursery in just a few minutes." With her statement she pointed in the direction of the nursery.

Turning and walking in that direction immediately I took long strides, almost running to the viewing window. There were so many babies of every description possible, many races and nationalities, in assorted colors. Some colors I had not noticed before, like bright hot pink and light to medium blue. As I stood there I realized that this was the first time I had ever been to a nursery window in my life.

The nurse seemed to take forever and a day to get my fine young son to his awaiting bed. First of course bringing him to the window for a thorough inspection. My request of her opening his blanket for a "full" look at all his equipment seemed to embarrass her. But I wanted to make sure he was "all" there. Smiling with satisfaction, pride and joy, I waved and talked to the little guy. Knowing in my heart what his name was going to be already. Christopher Robert Decker, named after, and for my friend and buddy Chris Roberts. It was to make us both proud and it was Lisa's choice as well. No doubt about it he was healthy, eight pounds ten ounces, a strapping young man. It almost killed me to watch them when the doctor circumcised him, but there was definitely no doubt as to the condition of his lungs afterwards. Young Christopher let out a haller that made the room jump.

Several hours later Lisa came out of recovery and they came to get me, for us to share in the news of our new son. She had a hard time with the surgery, for even with the c-section, Chris was one big kid for her little frame. I leaned over to her and kissed the perspiration from her cheek.

"Hello there, mother of a new baby boy. You did great and he is so perfect. I love you sweet lady and I want to say, thank you."
"Is he really pretty?" Her eyes were wide in anticipation.
"He is absolutely handsome and yes, pretty as well."
"I'm sorry I couldn't do the natural..."
"No, no, no, that is enough of that Lisa. You did wonderful and it was my fault not yours for his size. My family is the one with the oversized genes. I love you so much and we have a beautiful healthy boy, that is the main thing and that you are okay."

Just then they brought Christopher in the room and the look in Lisa's eyes and on her face is one I shall never forget for the rest of my life. A joy, love, pride, appreciation, bond, chemistry, belief, satisfaction, was there, all of this and more. There was a holy glow from the two of them. These two people had brought a level of love that I never knew existed, into my life. Shortly we would be back at home and beginning to live the family life I had dreamed of for a long, long, time.

I leaned across the bed and touched Lisa and Christopher. What an incredible feeling to physically be able to touch a tiny little person, that had been growing within the body of the that woman I loved. Seeing his fingers and hands as they grasped their first things in this world. Watching him react to sights and sounds, wiggle here and wiggle there, all an amazing feat. Yet when I saw my son nurse from the breast of his mother for the first time, this was the ultimate sight of newborn beauty.

Christopher's small perfectly formed mouth touched Lisa's flesh, with his pink cheek so smooth and soft nuzzling her supple breast. It was a fountain of life, nature's own complete nourishment. The warmth and radiant glow of love and devotion was descending from Lisa's eyes to her child. Sounds of my son as he enjoyed his first meal on God's earth, being fed from a woman that would give him the love, care, training and values, which would guide him through his life. Truly this was the most amazing, incredibly beautiful sight my eyes, had ever seen.
"Lisa, you and Christopher, make the most precious picture. I will treasure this photograph for the rest of my life."

As the tears of joy continued to flow, never ceasing from when they had first brought him in, she said, "I have been waiting for this moment all of my life. We did so good Michael; he is absolutely perfect in every way."

We hugged and kissed and slobbered all over Chris as he just laid there and enjoyed all of the new stuff going on around this great big room. After being in such a confining space for so long, he was glad to stretch, I was sure. This moment could have lasted forever and it would have ended too soon.

Two days later they allowed Lisa and the little man to come home. I had put a few extra things in his room, a football and other assorted necessities. I placed a dozen roses next to Lisa's side of the bed and headed off to the hospital. A new blanket, with a small teddy bear inside, with me for Christopher's first trip in the Blazer, I drove again pretty fast. The lot was near capacity, so I took the liberty to park in the doctor's area. Well my initials were M.D. after all, that was close enough for me. Hurrying inside I took the elevator to the fourth floor.
"Are you two ready to go home?"
"Well hello Daddy. Chris wave to your Pop!"

What a change in just twenty-four hours in the energy and color in Lisa, she looked great.
"I brought this along for my son to stay warm with. This young bear can be his buddy."

I kissed Lisa, gathered all the articles we had both brought and had delivered and proceeded downstairs. With Chris in my arms and Lisa in a wheelchair, such as was the policy for the hospital. At the door I put Christopher in Lisa's arms and went to bring the Blazer up to the entrance.

After helping Lisa in, I took our new son, to his new home and we began our family life once and for all. With all the excitement of the past few days there had been little full nights rest. This was the case especially for Lisa, so I gave her a break and watched Chris while she took a nap, very shortly after arriving at the house. Tomorrow was to be for me a normal work day, the five o'clock departure would come early. But this was going to be a night like none other in my life, and I was going to savor each and every minute. Sleep, this word was not in my vocabulary for tonight.

"Hey there little man, your Daddy loves you. Someday you will be just as big as me, maybe even your grandpa Decker. Even though you will probably never see him. He's not much for hanging around. But I'll be here and we will have lots of great times."

Christopher just lay there and did his little moving things and looked at me and now and then a tiny burp, gurgle or tiny toot would come from him. Within our first thirty minutes together I got to change our first poopy diaper. In completing this task I also was blessed by his little water pistol all across the front of my shirt.

"Now Christopher we must come to an understanding, this pee business needs to be in the diaper and not in Daddy's face. Deal?"

"ga ooo........." This was the overwhelming response I got from my first man to man talk between my son and me.

After I had mastered disposable diapers and cleaned up the mess, I think he and I tied on the mess. Dressed now in his new flannel, fuzzy, red and white pajamas, he and I walked to the back door to say hello to Thor.

"Christopher this is your puppy, Thor. He is going to be your best buddy one day and he will be lots of fun to play with. Thor this is Michael and Lisa's new baby son, Christopher. You had better be nice to him or daddy will beat your butt."

Of course the introduction was done through the screen door, but I was sure that they both got the jest of the conversation. Sure! I played him a little ZZ Top and Hank Williams, showed him a portion of television, then the final thing was his favorite I'm sure, I sang to him. With my voice, not really, but the experience of holding my son and knowing that part of me was in my arms, created some feelings so deep, so bonded that they will forever be scrolled in my heart.

The hours slipped by and then came time for feeding him, the little dude had an appetite like three children. He was going to be just like his dear old Dad, being one of the best at putting away groceries. At the hospital, because of some medication that the doctor had given Lisa to take, Christopher had to be put on formula. I know he was disappointed, after the one day, of scrumptious meals from Mom, and the container, my goodness. This was the only reason that I didn't have to wake Lisa for the feeding.

Late in the night as I lay there with my son at my side, my wife snuggled in behind my back with her leg and arm draped across my body, a very protective nature began to well up inside of me. Recalling the day that I had left Falcon, California and the life in the fast and dangerous lane I had been living. From Porsche and Ferrari to four wheel drive Chevy, from hundreds of thousands to mere hundreds, from 8,500 sq. ft. to 1,750 sq. ft. to live in. Today I would contact the Guad man and see just what was going on while I had been away. I knew down deep that if anything new and of a subject that needed my attention, Larry would have already gotten in contact with me. Now, more than ever, I wanted to maintain a watch and make absolute certain that all bases were covered and manned. No matter what it might take to make that situation stable and keep it under control.

Leaning across Christopher I saw the clock reading 4:30a.m., it was time to shower and have another successful day at work. Making the means to keep my family housed, clothed and fed, provided for. Soon dressed in my white jacket and black slacks, it was back to the bedroom to say goodbye to my family.
"Hey there pretty Momma, your hubby has to go make the bacon."
As Lisa stretched and a small yawn escaped her lips I kissed her gently on the cheek.
"Oh, Michael I can't believe that I slept so long. You have been up all night. Are you exhausted?"
"Are you kidding? With chasing Christopher around all night. He was running here and there and grabbing stuff from the refrigerator, my word woman what a dynamo we have brought into this world."
"Michael, what did you have for breakfast?" With a look of knowing, Lisa smiled at the rambling saga I had just laid down.
"Just love for breakfast, just love. I should say thank you as well, I meant to wake you but..."
"Michael Decker don't you even try to imply that you and I had sex and I didn't wake up. Shame on you, you know me better than to think that….." Now she was rambling as well.
"Joke sweet one, just a joke." A smile, another kiss to both of my family members, and it was out the door. My hotblooded Italian/ Spanish wife, was a classic in so many ways, gosh I loved her.

After getting the club opened and running I went to my office and dialed the West Coast. It was time to do some snooping of my own.

"Pablo's Publishing, where the new best seller, Antlers in the Treetops by Who Goosed the Moose is available."

"Guad man you need help my brother. You have finally gone off the entire planet."

"Well Mr. Pecker, oh yeah it starts with a "D" doesn't it. What's going on in River City?" I was going to have to pin his butt down to have a conversation this early in the day.

"We need to discuss what, if anything, is going on down south, Mexico way."

"Nothing to be concerning safety, but the word on the street, and I am talking from someone very, very close is as follows. Dennard and Falcon were hooked up together in taking your money. Dennard had gone to Falcon, told him about your deal and the money that was invested from Dennard's end was in reality from his boss. The whole thing was a setup to bust your ass financially. Sicilia-Falcon wanted you to be more dependent on him because he was getting worried that you might leave. He thought that you would come to him for a big loan and have to stay for some time to work it off.

As Guad man was talking, the rage of the betrayal began to burn down deep inside of me. These sorry bastards had stolen all the money that I had worked so hard to amass. Some day, someway I will get a chance to make this situation even, somehow.

"How long have you known about this brother?" Curious how long the pipeline had taken to leak.

"Within a few weeks of your departure. There has been no other word concerning you though. Without saying it, Decker man, I would be instantaneous in the event of any reprisal. Know this, if it was just you brother, I would say let's go make it even. You know what I mean by even?" His tone was one we had developed, one from many days and months under fire.

"Breaker four firebase, Guad man, Breaker four firebase. Northern sector of Arizona Territory, Operation Meade River. First Phoenix extraction, Col. Nyu." God it was rolling off my tongue like it was yesterday. There were no survivors, there were never meant to be any.

If Sicilia-Falcon made the slightest move, he would have none as well, no survivors. He along with Carlos Kyrikedes, Joan Beck, Brian Dennard, Roger Fry, and every other punk like Ruby Hernandez and Chu Cho, all would perish in the fire.

"Decker man it's still there, never to leave. I feel it sometimes so hot I want to explode. I gotta walk my man, Guad man out."

He was gone, the phone disconnected but in my gut I knew what had just happened. The fire at the core of his being was burning and the sights and the smells of burning flesh and little kids running down a dirt road with skin blown away and scorched. Dead bodies lying on the ground, floating in the rice paddies and waterways. It comes hurling back through the quadrants of the mind so real it is totally relived.

For some of the men who digested this life, tour after tour, it carved its initials, burned its stamp, tattooed the soul and heart, with a message so vile and sickening that it WOULD NOT GO AWAY. It had to be crammed, stuffed, hidden and camouflaged for the man to go out in public and live some semblance of a life. Maintaining a status quo on the outside while the inside was roaring to escape the cramped quarters, and express itself. Outlets for this release were found in bottles, needles, pills, and improvised methods of dealing with the demons hidden deep within. Where did the real answer lie? Who had the magic potion or wand to wipe it from their ravaged minds?

For some it never came and the release came only in death. Others still sit behind bars, the help never came and the release, while only partial, made for years of incarceration. Many men would try, thirty years later, to go back to the country, THE 'NAM, and let the inner voice beckon to the souls and spirits of the dead. Asking for them to take this one along in their journey, leaving a peace for the latter years, a wonderful, at long last, peace.

The ultimate answer would come from the only source powerful enough to cast out demons, rebuild lives, wash away fear, cleanse hearts, restore faith, give forgiveness and forgive sin of all kinds. For me, and many of my brothers and sisters, this would be a long time coming. Some of us, like me, had to be led, after first being knocked down and broken of the human will, many times over. More on this later.

Now, as the employees began to filter their early morning selves into the club, the switch had to be flipped to manual override.
"Bill, Georgia, good morning and a successful day to you both." Greeting the first two consultants to walk through the door, another day had begun.
"Good morning, Michael!" In almost rehearsed unison they replied.

The workday had started and with it the flow of people which would continue until near nine o'clock tonight. It would be another sixteen-hour day.

Such a diverse dichotomy of life passed through these portals each and every day. Businessmen, were getting ready for their day in the morning, or winding their day down at night. Some of each section, some that preferred both, each day. There were housewives trying to keep in shape, late morning and early afternoon were their times of entrance. Businesswomen, for the most part came early. Hard workouts of aerobics and multirepetition sets of weights were the most common. Body builders, the evenings when it was the most crowded, their egos needing the looks and stares of awe. Senior citizens came with varied schedules, as there were few to keep. Just enjoying the fellowship and the feeling of the exercise and especially the pools and spas and saunas, it was one big, for the most part, happy family.

Another unique group was the police officers, marshals, FBI, DEA and special agents of many different affiliations. This broad spectrum of men and women had a drum tuned to a different beat than most. The office most always followed them to the club. Talking of this arrest and that arrest, a bust here, a shooting, a murder, a trial, all aspects of their work consumed their existence. It was almost, as if they had to work, live and breathe law enforcement.

One of this group, Ben Marino, was different in many ways. He had a quiet side that most of the others didn't have. He was dedicated to his workout so regimented that there was never a missed day or skipped repetition. Dark black hair, mustache, five eleven, 235 lbs, muscular, a special task force drug agent with the New Mexico State Police, Ben knew the streets. He would be cordial when coming to do his workout, kept to himself for the most part while exercising, then would open up and hang to hear all the latest "hot news" from the other men and women.

Saturday nights, we closed the club at six rather than the Monday thru Friday nine p.m. Additionally the following morning, Sunday didn't unlock the doors until nine a.m. Allowing for all the employees to have a night off and a late morning the following day. For some time now the club would serve wine and beer for a small happy hour to many of the regulars who enjoyed staying a short while. Several of the members and the staff had developed long friendships in their patronage and employment of European Health Spa. This gave many a chance to socialize in a manner that during their normal workout would not be possible.

I would partake of a beer or glass of wine and then making sure all of the people who had stayed, were taken care of, roam. One or at the very most two drinks and out the door was the rule. But this particular Saturday night was different, very different indeed.

It had been now almost three months since Christopher was born, late May, 1975. Tonight, was a Saturday, and the final day for one of the staff, Lorrie Holingsworth. She was tall, with blonde hair, green eyes, attractive, from Nashville, Tennessee and an accent to go right along with it.

I closed the club about thirty minutes early that night, for some reason it was completely empty except for employees. A rainy day had kept many of the normal Saturday crowd away. The party included inviting some of the Lorrie's closer friends, and Ben Marino had been one of those people. With only the nightlights on, the spa and pool area was beautiful, with the bubbling water and floods casting patterns through the main pool. Large green leafed plants were hanging from the ceiling, and standing in huge pots were trees and special tropical plants of many descriptions. Music was coming from the intercom stereo, the drinks began to flow, a trace of eucalyptus in the air from the sauna, it was party time for all who had come for the festivities.
"Hey there, birthday girl, are we having fun yet?" I asked Lorrie as I came up to her, with several others. I took her hand and giving her a quick kiss on the cheek for the occasion.
"Yes, starting to, but I had a head start from home. These two came with two bottles of wine and "made" me drink with them."

Pointing to other girls about her age, twentytwo, all seemed to be into the party mode with a buzz noticeably in the air. Liquor flowing, music playing, by the 7:00 P.M. cut off, and most everyone was rolling. It was a unanimous decision for the group to go out dancing, and dancing they went, with all but one that stayed behind to help clean up the mess.

Ben Marino stayed as he felt like I did. It would be chaos in no time at all. Lorrie and her two friends already could barely walk, much less dance. Everyone else said yes they would come but chances were very good that less than half would in fact go.

We talked as we cleaned up the bulk of the mess, really not that much. The main clean up would be by the maintenance crew that came in each night and totally sparkled the club from top to bottom. There were several more sixpacks of cold beer so Ben and I sat and had a brew, enjoying the removal of the noise.

"That is going to be a hurting puppy tomorrow morning. Lorrie will be regretting the last two bottles she put away."
"Ben, tell me about it, and to think she is going to try and dance."

We both chuckled and had a laugh at someone else's expense. Finished the beer and popped another, and before we had hardly realized it had passed, an hour had slipped by. Also two sixpacks had vaporized before our eyes. There were still two to go so it was a mutual understanding that after the next two we would leave, sixpacks that is.

Conversations had now progressed from general topics and the club to some boasting of "big busts, shootouts and drug czars and kingpins. This was a subject that Ben Marino with his fifteen years in the field, had some knowledge of. One that I could also converse on, in a distant, "I heard" frame of reference.
"Hell, two weeks ago four of us busted a stash with over two thousand pounds in it. Yeah, it was grass but still was worth some large dollars." Ben was telling of one of the several "bust stories" of the night.
"Ben, I heard tell of a lumber yard down in Mexicali that could hold near a half million kilos of Marijuana."
"Halfmillion kilos, you are full of shit. No way to store and move those kind of quantities."
"That depends on if you own the oil company that moves it and the lumber yard that stores it. As well as the ranch that grows it."
"Those are just bullshit exaggerations from some burnt out druggie. It's like the cocaine traffic, we bust these guys all the time with five, ten maybe fifty and on a rare, very rare occasion one hundred kilos. The stories of the thousand kilo deals, even wild dreams in the ten thousand kilo stashes, no way, no how, man. It is too much quantity and would take a distribution network that is just not there."
"Guess it would depend on if you were a bird. A hawk or a falcon or something and could see into the minds and paperwork of the Customs agents, Border Patrol, and DEA plans. Then you would have all the necessary routes that were open and could be easily accessed."

Ben's face had completely changed. An inner knowing was formulating and the years of field work and exposure to the business, even though the beers had flowed, was clicking. He was memorizing words, facts and names. Even though given casual and "heard" from others.

A half an hour later I was headed home for the night. Ben Marino meanwhile, was squinting and leaving the window down in his cruiser, trying to make it back to the office. An hour later, the computer in operation was printing page after page about an organization. Worldwide distribution networks, offshore money laundering, payoffs reputed all the way to the Whitehouse. Possible drug shipments in ranges he could not even fathom from the limited exposure, his busts had given him. Jet planes, race boats, hitmen, private army, multiple homes and a villa in Europe, and exotic cars of every description.

Ben Marino sat there and read the files, page after page rolling by, something called Centac having something to do with the cataloged and compiled information. Not hundreds of thousands, not millions, but billions of dollars attached to this operation. My loose tongue had "really" not given any facts, just generalities. Digging words, like hawk, falcon, Mexicali, Morgan, Pemex, which had passed by in casual context and format. When pinpointed and directly quoted as source files, memory storage of the documentation resulted in a landslide of pertinent facts and contact personnel.

For me, that night had been a time of enjoying being home with Lisa and Christopher. A normal evening completely uneventful, a nice full nights rest, the end result. Not ever even dreaming that this search was being conducted and a special operations jet would be taking off within hours from Orange County Airport. Aboard would be two of the top investigators and agents for the Special Operations Task Force and Drug Enforcement Administration. Both men had the written authorization to do whatever necessary to obtain further information relating to the Sicilia-Falcon organized crime family. It was power, which came from the Whitehouse itself, and this meant all the way to the very top brass, there was no one higher than this where this authorization had come. Locking up the store the following night would be one closing I would never forget for as long as I should live.

Gosh what a beautiful day, clear skies, bright sunshine, one of the three hundred plus days that Albuquerque was famous for, each year. As I picked up the paper, the Albuquerque Journal, from the front yard, I looked up to the Sandia Crest. The Tramway cables glistening in the early morning light, made their track from the base in the foothills all the way to the summit. Looking up there reminded me that Doug Smith, formerly of Montana Mining Company, had built a restaurant in this location called High Finance. Another outlet down in the city proper, appropriately named Liquid Assets. Both of which had many similarities of operation and decor layout of the MMC days. Doug had enjoyed a great deal of success, and very deservedly so, as many months and years of dedicated sacrifice had proven.

Lisa and Christopher were up early that morning as usual, doing there normal routine. The growth in Chris that both Lisa and I had witnessed was phenomenal, his little body filling out and up rapidly. "You too jaybirds have a wonderful day. I have to take off now, so byebye sugars!" Waving at the young boy having a ball with some jello squares, tasting Lisa's sweet lips one more time before making my adios. It was the third goodbye kiss of the morning. I just couldn't get enough of a great thing!

Traffic so different at this time of morning, Dick had something he had to do today so had asked if I would switch with him. It was nice for a change, to alter the schedule. The workday proved to be steady but nothing to write home about. Yet had flown by at a seemingly rapid pace, before I knew it the closing hour had arrived.

All of the employees had left; I was finishing up the daily totals and the night deposit slips, when there was a buzz on the outside door.

"Who in the hell can that be?" I said to myself, rising and starting toward the front door. As I approached, I noticed that it was Ben Marino and two more men; somewhat hesitant, I unlocked the entry door.

"Michael, sorry to have to catch you so late but I need to talk for a minute." Ben stated very apprehensively.

"Why couldn't it have waited until tomorrow Ben, I am ready to go home?" Not moving a muscle until some answers were forthcoming.

"Because we wanted to talk tonight!" One of the other men answered for him sharply.

"Did you ever think that a phone call in advance might have helped set this up?" Waiting for his response before I asked them to leave.

"Decker I really don't care if you are inconvenienced; we are going to talk now!" This was the wrong answer and the wrong attitude.

"Let me tell you something, and I will be very clear. I don't know who the hell you are and really don't give a shit. But you can take your smart mouth and carry it right the hell out of my club, asshole." I was about three shakes, from kicking this guys butt up between his shoulders.

"Whoa, whoa, wait just a minute both of you." Ben quickly jumped in. "Coonces you're way out of line, way out. You have no damn right ordering anybody to do anything. This is my turf and it will stay that way. Understand?" Ben gave this guy a look that he might be the one to be kicking the butt. I relaxed a little but not much.

"Michael, this is Richard Gorman from the Drug Enforcement Administration; the rude guy is John Coonces from the Special Investigations Division of the Special Operations Task Force. They are here to ask you a few questions, and I promise you on my word, this won't take long at all. No more than fifteen minutes maximum." Coonces was busting a gut, wanting to continue his tough guy routine. I stood there just hoping he would say something else and I would kick his Special Task Force butt.

"You have something you ask me here and now? Make it quick or make it official; I really don't give a damn at the moment."

"Mr. Decker let me apologize for the start of this conversation, but please try and understand a fact that I know you are totally unaware of. But first, nice to have made your acquaintance." He put out his hand and from his eyes I could tell that he meant it. Responding I shook his hand.

"To continue. Myself along with two other field special agents, Pat Gregory and John Raftery, have been under strict surveillance of the Sicilia-Falcon organization for now almost three years. We have catalogued, identified and photographed each and every one of the people that have gone in and out of the house in Chapultipec. Somehow, someway, there is a very good chance that you were part of that operation, and very near the top. Yet in all the information we have, none of it correlates with you, your identity or anything about you. We came here tonight to ask for your cooperation. If given, you will be paid a substantial fee for whatever you can do in adding to what we already have." Silence, with each passing minute, louder, with each passing minute, the other agent turned redder and redder. A hand signal from Gorman had said, keep your mouth shut,

"I have no idea what you are talking about. Thus this talk as you put it is over. I am asking you to leave now, so that I can go home." Three sets of shrugged shoulders, no comment, they walked out. I went back to my office and sat down thinking, "what in the hell?"

Slowly from the subconscious to the conscious, the reflecting of the night before took place. Cells and memory chambers blurred and clogged by the alcohol began to clear with the catharsis processing, coming to life. In no way did I think the chat between Ben and me would come to this type of conclusion. In no way was their delving into my past, finished. If they were waiting in the parking lot it would not surprise me in the least. DEA, Special Task Force, christ this is all I need now.

My planned quiet evening at home was going to be far from that, another sleepless night in the making for sure. There was no sense at all, in me continuing to wait to leave. I secured the power and the lights, locked the front entrance, set the security system and walked toward the parking lot. As I turned the corner of the building, Dejavu! "Michael..." Instantly I transformed into a fighting stance and started to attack. Pulling back with a great effort, as I recognized Ben Marino. "Damn Michael, take it easy, you damn near got shot. Coones is right across the parking lot itching for an excuse."

"Fuck Coones, and any other bastard who might want some shit. You think you can just waltz in and disrupt any person's life that you might have some hairbrained idea about. Well let me clue you in, and this goes double for your punk ass." Pointing at the other side of the parking lot. "You have a problem with me, tough shit; you want to make it personal, tough shit again. I will make it so damn personal you won't know what the hell happened when the lights go out for good. Coones you can take your itch and shove it right up your ass. Or if you prefer we can settle this right now, it would be my pleasure truly, believe me it would." The fire raged, to a degree dangerously close to afterburner thrust.

"Look, let me apologize for this whole mess. This damn thing was handled from the beginning wrong and I take the full responsibility for the outcome. But I don't want any more of this to get out of hand either. Please just calm down and let me try and explain a few things. First, Coones has a hell of a chip on his shoulder, since a very close friend and colleague, of over twenty years, was killed by someone in the Sicilia-Falcon organization. It in no way justifies the attitude or disrespect, but that is a matter, which can be dealt with in other ways. Michael, I respect you as a man and as a professional at what you do here at the club. No matter whether you are some link in this investigation or not, there is a great deal more to you than what may exist on the surface. I got that from trying to obtain some of your military records."

I thought to myself quickly, you don't have near the pull some people do, and they don't even work for the government. He continued to try and lighten this situation.

"Please let this night just go on by and tomorrow I will call you and set up a meeting time and place. Which is what I should have done tonight. Also let me throw this out for you to be thinking about during the hours from now until we meet again. $100,000.00 cash and ten percent of whatever we can confiscate, in cash equivalent will be yours, if you decide to talk to us. That is if you might possibly be in some way attached, or affiliated with this organization in question. Again, please know that I am sorry about all the chaos."

Ben turned and started back across to the awaiting car. Both of the other two agents had already taken their seats and were waiting to leave. Pulling out of the parking lot, Gorman was the only one to keep my eye contact. He was very intelligent and shrewd as well, he seemed to be level headed and assertive, easily a leader.

Driving first to the bank to drop off the night deposit, I then turned north on Menual and headed for the house. What a night, I came very close to having a major incident take place. If it would have been Coones at the corner, I would be on the way to jail and he would be on the way to the hospital or worse.

Nearing Juan Tabo Avenue I turned right and headed west; a figure began to write itself in my brain. Ten percent of the two accounts in Switzerland, would be over twenty-five million dollars. With all of the rest of the property and vehicles, airplanes and boats, houses thrown in, it was one hell of a figure. But was it the truth, would they really give me that much money. It would be like the deal I had put together had paid off as planned, Lisa and Christopher would be set for life. Not only that, it would pay back Falcon for being part of the deal going sour and stealing my money. That fact alone was enough to break the stalemate of feelings and allow a small smile to cross my lips. There was so much to consider, so much indeed.

It was late when I got home and of course my young boy was snoozing, as well Lisa had been at it since the early morning. We were all ready for snoresville, but as I lay there next to Lisa, my brain would not shut off no matter what. There was too much stimuli activated, it would be hours, if at all, that sleep would come.
"Good night lady, I am sorry the meeting took so much extra time. Remember that I love you baby."
"Love you to Michael. Night!" We kissed good night and she snuggled in under my left arm. Laying on her right side, her left arm across my chest, left leg over my thigh and my shoulder her pillow for hours to come. Her body was soothing to my spirit, as our closeness was enjoyed by both of us. I listened for Christopher stirring in his room, he must be dreaming about something exciting. Thank God this day was over and did not have to be repeated. But what will tomorrow bring? Good question!

"Ngh...umm...ugh." Somebody was getting hungry, and his personal language, totally invented by his intelligent self, was being spoken.

Looking at the clock, I noticed that it was 2:18 a.m., sleep was still a ways off for me. My thoughts were still hashing the previous nights events, escapades and offer. Carefully slipping from the bed so as not to awaken Lisa, I went in and got Christopher. His little body was wiggling as he heard the door push open. Leaning over the crib I tickled and tossled him some before lifting his perfect frame to my arms and embracing him against my chest.
"Hey there guy, how's my little football star doing this morning? Are you hungry for some of that good milk?" This was one of my favorite times of the day. So quiet and just my son and me, no distractions or anything to interfere with our time together.

Taking the formula from the refrigerator, and a pan from the cabinet, I filled the pan with water and waited for it to warm. Chris and I continued to talk, man to man.
"Young man, your Dad has to make some big decisions later on today. It will be a change for us no matter what we do. Might even mean that all of us might have to go someplace new. What do you think,

Christopher? I see, well I tend to agree with you. We will let it ride until this afternoon and then make the final decision. You agree, then it is settled." He and I seemed to agree on most everything that was brought up between the two of us. Of course I heavily weighed his opinion and considered all his suggestions, what a son.

The milk was ready and so was Christopher, so taking the warmed bottle we strolled back down the hallway and into his room for the feeding. By the time he was done his eyes were closed and sleepy time had returned once again. I laid him down, changed him into a dry diaper, and let him go off to dreamland. One of the favorite places for little boys and girls, I was sure of that fact.

Trying to be very quiet and careful to not wake Lisa, I eased back into the bed. Gently my weight lowered to the mattress and once fully prone, slid back to the spot I had been before. As I reached with my left hand and grasped her left wrist, which was pressed against my thigh, I slowly lifted her arm and hand. Before the movement, which was to bring her hand and arm back to my chest, even got to my waist, the relaxed wrist I was moving, began to move on its own.

"You work all day and get up to feed our son at night, don't even dream of me not saying thank you and I love you." One of the most sensual, sultry voices ever known to mankind caressed my ears, as her hand caressed me as well. Rolling toward her our lips met, the fullness of her breasts brushing my chest, the passion instantly unleashing as my hand found her moist, and ready for her man. Soaring above and beyond where we lay, she pushed me to my back, taking us both to that ultimate ecstasy as she rode me into the night. Finally, exhausted, satisfied, and pleased beyond description, we both drifted to a far off sleep.

"I love you, for loving me." The last words that gasped from my mouth, my breaths still deep from making love, what a woman.

Early mornings light came just like that, early. The pink and gold streaks of the first rays of the sun were fanning a glow of the new day across the bed. My heart was calm, a smile still anointed my face, can't imagine why! Lisa felt so good next to me I wanted to stay for a late morning, but duty called. Heading for the shower and the start of this inaugural day, it would be one of those grab your boots, I was sure.

By nine that morning, Marino had already called and a twelve noon meeting had been arranged at the restaurant over in Coronado Shopping Center at Menual and Louisiana. One of the larger in the city, also a neutral position and one easily accessed and watched, if necessary. I had made the decision to not discuss this at all until after the second meeting. Nothing was solid enough to worry Lisa with any "possible" scenarios. Understandably the morning seemed to drag by as I was preoccupied with nothing else but what might lie ahead. Minutes were like hours themselves, and when 11:00 a.m. rolled around, I made my exit.

Carrying an extra set of clothes with me when I left home, I changed into Wranglers, western shirt with a deep blue color, Anaconda Boots and a windbreaker. The jacket was to conceal the .44 cal Magnum, which was going to accompany me in my shoulder holster. It was surely overkill, but whatever went down I wanted to have the firepower to shoot through a car if necessary. Some of the custom Black Rhino ammunition would do just that. Expensive but when and if the chips came down, no dollar amount mattered at all when a life was at stake.

From the club I drove west on Menual and continued all the way to San Pedro. It was one major cross street to far, on purpose, so that I could come back through the entire lot and park. Field glasses in hand, forty minutes early, I wanted to see just who and what was roving around the LZ. Might have well as been a Landing Zone, rather than a meeting place. Cautiously, I began to scan the entire general area, then came back and broke it down in quadrants and in much more detail scrutinized every leaf, twig and movement. Each and every vehicle that came within a five hundred yard radius was in my spectrum of view.

Six minutes after I had made my observation post, two unmarked vehicles came into the lot and proceeded to the restaurant location. Parking within fifty to seventy yards and deploying all their occupants. There four from the lead car and three from the other. The second had Ben Marino, Richard Gorman, and you know who. He was as nervous as a caged lion, understandably so. Coontz had a lot to learn, I don't give a damn how long he had been in law enforcement. Today would be no repeat of the previous night, or this group setting would get terminated very early.

Waiting until five minutes before noon, no other vehicles or sunglassed visitors arrived. Leaving my location, I walked through the outside entrance and came through the mall itself. One more look & see before I had committed myself inside the restaurant. Mall traffic was semiheavy, a little more than normal for this time of day. Shoppers were coming and going in any one of the two hundred stores. No problems encountered, it was time to start the show, all guns on the table, so to speak, except one!

Entering with a small group of four, I noticed two of the lead team sitting at the coffee bar. There was one single to my immediate left, and the last of the Mohicans back to the far right. Marino had chosen a table close to the window, he on the inside and the other two agents on the opposite side of the table. This positioning made me back to the entrance, and the window on one side and Marino on my right. Wrong, this was about to be changed, long before any chat took place.

"Gents, this arrangement needs to be altered somewhat as I want to sit there." Pointing to the seat next to Gorman, which meant Mr. Pleasant was going to have to move, just to kick things off with a smile. Incredibly, he jumped up and made the change without a hassle. In fact saying, "No problem whatsoever!" Someone, had reamed his butt about the altercation last night, it was obvious. I sat down, keeping my windbreaker on and twothirds zipped. It felt like I had a cannon under there, because that was exactly what it was. Nodding to the group as I took my seat. Marino started to break the ice, then was interrupted as follows. "Michael, we..."

"Please, Ben if I may, Mr. Decker I owe you an apology for the way I acted and talked to you last night. Even though this case has hit so close to home with the loss of my close friend, I had no reason to come after you. I am sorry." Maybe he wasn't such a bad guy after all, but I would refrain from a final judgment for some time. As Coontz finished he nodded to Marino.

"As I was saying Michael, this meeting is an integral part of what could develop between all of the parties gathered here this afternoon. The offer I talked about last night, stands as stated, with one addition, that being full and complete immunity to any portion of what you might want to divulge to us or the government. I have in my possession a letter from Terry Kissane, the United States Attorney heading this case. Briefly it states all of the things so far laid down." He was working the program, quite apparent to all seated at the table.

I nodded and continued to listen and remain silent. Amazing how loud that nonnoise can be, they had all expected a response. Gorman pitched his hat into the circle.

"Mr. Decker I have been involved with this case for many months now, in fact several years. As I had brought out last night you are somewhat of a mystery to the team that has put in the hours in Mexico and southern California. Through a very close friend and fellow U.S. Government agent, with another branch of the Justice Department, I have learned a few more facts concerning your work in the military. It is very hushed, meaning that someone has gone to a great deal of trouble to arrange what your files say and don't say. From a source in California I have been informed as to your ability in martial arts, as well as here at the University of New Mexico. Seems that you caused some major damage there to both property and persons during a fight."

There had been some homework done in the hours since last night, allowing for a picture to be at least partially painted. Silence continued to be my venue, my scope of vision noticing much more attention from the other four men in the room.
"From a file and talking to one of your instructors at the New Mexico Military Institute, your expertise with several types of weapons was ranked in the Master Expert category. Some of the highest scores recorded in marksmanship. All that remains is rather basic and simple, either you know something about this organization, or you were very close to the main cartel members. What is your answer?"
Silence once again, for near thirty seconds before I spoke.
"I have nothing to tell you about this organization, nor have I implied that I do. Whether or not your information is true or not, that is your business, my knowledge is mine. If there is anything that I might possess in the way of information, give me a number and I may give you a call. No promises, in any way am I stating any commitment to call, understand that pragmatically." For now that was it, the ball rolled back to their side of the table.
"That is agreeable, and in conjunction with that action I am going to leave you two envelopes. One contains a certified/notarized copy of the agreement outlined by the U.S. Attorney. The other is one thousand dollars, which is our way of saying thank you for the time you have spent last night and today. In the event you do want to talk further, before making a final deal, we will fly you out to San Diego and have you sit down with the U.S. Attorney and the other two agents on my team. That is all I have!" Gorman looked to Marino to close the meeting.
"Michael, I speak for all of us in saying thank you for taking your time and we hope to hear from you, if it's warranted." Case closed, I took the two envelopes and left the restaurant, never looking back.

There was nothing left now but to weigh all the positive and negative aspects of the offer. I felt that they, in fact, did not know who I was in the scope of La Familia de Falcon. From the very first time I had gone to the house in Chapultipec, a disguise had been utilized. Whether it was a mustache, beard, wig, hair color, clothing style, there are many ways to change the appearance of oneself. Especially with using a different vehicle each and every time I made that particular rendezvous. Additionally the fact that I had been in a commonly called "satellite" posture, greatly aided my identity.

This position was established within the first few weeks I had been in the organization. Meaning that if and when, any of the people, major players of the cartel, were in the company of Falcon, I circulated just out of immediate contact. Them not knowing who I was, nor my position in the hierarchy. In this way if any one of them had to be eliminated they would not know to be on edge with my presence.

Work was just that for the remainder of the afternoon. Writing two contracts, one for myself, a sale that I had been working on for now almost a week. It was a family membership, with six in the family, this made for a nice tidy contract amount. The other was a close for one of the other sales people. She had not been able to wrap the deal so I came into the presentation and finished selling the membership. This was one of the varied responsibilities of management in the club. My shift was over at 6:30p.m. and it only took a second to be out the door and on my way to the house.

Pulling into the driveway I put the Blazer in park, pushed on the emergency brake and took an extra deep breath. There was to be no more delay in discussing what was about to be laid out on the table. The cards had now been dealt, I had read the fine print of the letter from U.S. Attorney Terry Kissane while at the office. It contained exactly what they had presented at the meeting, it was decision time!

Lisa was in the kitchen cooking when I opened the door, no sign of my young son, mainly because none of his telltale noises were evident. Christopher just might be down for a nap, if so maybe Lisa and I could at least begin to talk.

"What's that smell, my woman is cooking up there in her kitchen?" With the question I walked up behind Lisa and encircled her waist with my arms, drawing her fine form up against me. Her bare feet, cutoff jeans and tshirt, with her dark bronze tan, the first stimulus to my senses, the touch of our bodies together was the second. Bending from the waist, I lowered my mouth and gave her a little love snuggle on the neck. Taking the sensitive neck muscle and nibbling gently.

"Michael! Quit that or I will spill the pan." She jumped with her exclamation. Squirming and fidgeting with the sensation it had given her, the tingling running up and down her cute self.

"Oh Baby, just a little nibble or two wouldn't hurt anything!" Watching for the smile to come on her face, and sure enough there it was.

"Michael John Decker!" Pointing the large serving spoon at me, and making a fawned defiant stance.

"Okay, okay, I give up, really I do." Bowing to her and then we both started to laugh with the silliness of the moment. Her neck had tasted so sweet, like it always did.

Lisa turned back to the meal that she was preparing. I meanwhile had slipped off my jacket and sat at the kitchen table. Admiring the view that was gracing my eyes with such pleasure and beauty to behold, I smiled inside and out.

"Lisa, is Christopher down for a nap?"

"No, my mother came by about thirty minutes ago and he went with her for a visit and will eat dinner with grandma. She was missing getting to spend some time with her grandson. Mom also wanted him to spend the night but I told her I wanted to talk to you first. I know how much you like to have your time with your son. So I said that we would give her a call later this evening." The night had been cleared for this discussion and I had not mentioned anything about it. Someone was opening the door, for now I didn't realize the answer, so accepting it as fate was my only alternative.

"Sounds like a deal to me, let's give your mother a call."

"Lisa after you hang up we need to sit and talk for a while!" A look came over her as she turned toward me and questioned silently.

"We will talk as soon as you are finished." Pointing to the phone as I finished speaking, the air had changed in the room, to a density of days gone by. Her intuition was tuned so close to me, being my soulmate, that whenever a subject of importance was at hand, she felt it in her precious heart. Lisa called her mother and was very brief with the message. She was ready to talk.

Click, the phone receiver closed the call as it went to the wall mounted stand. Lisa turned towards me and her eyes met mine as she slid the chair out and sat down. A deep breath held, waiting for me to break the silence with the news of the day.

"Lisa, I had a visit from some very important people in the area of law enforcement today. They had come here to talk with me about Mexico, Central and South America. All of them are agents with the Federal Government." Finally she exhaled, her eyes moist, her chin quivering just a trace. I reached out and took her hand, massaging it tenderly as I continued.

"Honey, everything is fine, please don't cry. Nothing bad happened, I promise. These agents want me to go undercover and help them in a largescale investigation. It would entail moving in the next few weeks or months and also would involve some travel. They need what I have in knowledge about some very major players operating a drug cartel in the three regions I just mentioned. In return for the help and my work, they would pay me one hundred thousand dollars cash, all my expenses, and ten percent of all the cash, property, planes, boats and narcotics that are confiscated. This sum could be in the tens of millions. During this time period, we, the three of us, would be moved to a safe area and given new identities. All communication with our friends and families would be only done through the U.S. Marshall's office in the location we are staying. This entire ordeal would take in the neighborhood of three to six months, or there about. I met with these men today at lunch and I have a letter from the U.S. Attorney stating all these facts and promises. Also they gave me one thousand dollars front money to pay for the time I had already spent with them. They had come by the club last night while I was closing up the spa. Until I had found out exactly what they had in mind and the full disclosure of facts, I did not want to bring it up to you, that is the only reason I didn't say anything last night."

Lisa's hand had gone from chilled and clammy to once again warm within the context of my explanation. She took one more deep breath and with it her reply.

"Are you in any kind of trouble with these men?" Straight to the heart was her style and manner.

"None that I know of."

"How dangerous would this be for you, or to us?"

"For you and Christopher none at all, there would be total security for you both, at all times. For me, I would be in the company of several federal agents and marshals at all times. All of what they need is in this brain of mine. I have facts, figures, locations and information, which can take this entire investigation all the way to completion. The money would set us up for life, forever and ever. I would be fine and once this was over, all key people would be gone forever."

We looked at one another for a long time. For me, reflecting on things in our past all the way back to the first time I had met Lisa. What joy she had brought into my life, and the failures I had brought on by my drinking and unfaithful behavior. Her being here now said so much to me about who and what she was. Lisa on the other hand was thinking about the here and now, at least that was what I felt.

"What happens next?" Calm, quiet and direct was her voice.

"Richard Gorman, one of the agents with the Drug Enforcement Administration said that they would take me out to California for an interview with the U.S. Attorney and the other two lead agents. A John Raftery and Pat Gregory, both of whom work with Gorman and have been assigned to this particular case for some time now. I don't know any of them but I know one of the New Mexico State Police Special Agents here. His name is Ben Marino, he is a member down at the club, and for some reason I feel that he is a straight up guy. Because of that fact I would insist that he accompany me on any and

all trips to California. My deciding to take this first step does in no way commit me to anything further down the road. How do you feel about taking this first step at least?"
"I don't know, I really don't know." Her sigh reinforced her words, rising to go to the stove, I concluded for now.
"Why don't we let this ride for the night, then tomorrow morning, after we have slept on it, and make a final decision. Agreed?" All I got was a shaking of her head, the wonderful evening that she had planned for just the two of us had been washed away. Rather than be light and full of close intimacy, the first night of being alone since Christopher was born, it was the antithesis. My fault entirely, for if I had never left Montana Mining Company, all of this would have never come to pass. I would never forgive myself for that fact.

The night was quiet, very quiet. A transparent shield had been placed in the house, for although physically seeing each other, it was as if I was home alone. One hour, then into two and now three, this icing of feeling had to change and it was going to be my doing. Come hell or highwater, I broke the shield of silence, which had engulfed our home.
"Lisa, we have to talk. Keeping this all bottled up inside is not healthy for either of us. Please tell me what you are thinking."

She had changed clothes and was dressed in a long terrycloth robe, sitting there in bed and pretending to read a magazine.
"I am thinking this needs to be over, I can't keep taking this up and down crap. First it was California and now it has followed us here to New Mexico. Why can't it just stop?" The level of frustration I was observing in Lisa said two pages and not two sentences. She was ready to unload and every right to do so was hers.
"Michael you work hard, from that is provided a good living for all of us. I know that you had big plans out in California, but it failed. Now there is a possibility that you can get it all back. But what happens if you do, is that going to make you happy? Will having so much money bring joy to our lives? When you were with Montana and now with the job at the club, we have more time together and we get by fine. No, I don't get to travel and do some of the things that I did, but so what? Tell me really what you are looking for in all this California junk?" I came from the doorway where I was standing and sat down on the edge of the bed. My right hand lying on Lisa's knee, I began my answer.
"Lisa, believe me that I want all of this over just as much as you do. When I say over, I never want to hear about Falcon ever again. In addition with that I want to have some peace, long lasting peace. If I go through with what the government wants me to do I can make his

organization die, complete and total collapse. In so doing, prevent anything else from rearing its head. This sudden appearance of the federal government means to me that I have an obligation to finish what I started. What I did in the war was exactly that, war, what this organization has done is bring war to the streets. I am not some selfrighteous bible thumper, out on a crusade. But the elimination of a group this size could have a marked impact on how much is brought into the states. Besides that the bastard stole from me and in so doing stole from my family. Getting even would not hurt my feelings either."
"Then what you need to do is call California and go check this whole thing out. Just please be careful, I don't want to lose you cowboy!" The final word told me, she supported me. That she had given her stamp of approval, a warmth returned to her eyes, as she continued.
"Would you come here and hold me?" I needed to hold her as much as she wanted me to. Responding to her request I lay down next to Lisa and drew her close against my chest. The rest of the night became what she had originally planned, thank God, for both of us.

Lisa drifted off to sleep about 11:30p.m. and I slipped out to the kitchen. Dialing the number given to me earlier by Gorman, I called to a patch phone and in minutes they had located him and put the call through. "Mr. Decker, thank you for calling, it's late!" Somewhat surprised to hear from me so soon.
"Let's forget the formalities Richard, and call me Michael. Here is the plan and how it will work. You make contact with all of your people and set them up for a meeting day after tomorrow. Make a flight reservation for both Ben Marino and myself. Each and every time we meet, if there is ever another session after tomorrow, Ben will accompany me. All accommodations will be where I decide, as I know where I will and won't stay. The U.S. Attorney will be there at this first meeting and that is that. You call Marino when all aspects of this trip is confirmed. Nothing and I repeat nothing will be said to anyone in my family or work situations. You deal square with me and I will do the same. If anyone tries anything in the slightest bit funky, you will have an immediate problem. That is no threat it is a promise. Do we have an understanding?" Direct was the only way this was ever going to fly.
"Clear Michael, and I can assure you that the beginning terms you have instructed will be facilitated fully. Marino will be back in touch with you tomorrow before noon. I will make all the arrangements personally, I give you my word." That was it and for some unknown reason I felt that this man's word meant something to him, unlike most. Now for some good rest next to the lady I love.

With the efficiency and effectiveness of a true professional, all arrangements were taken care of by 10:00a.m. the next morning. One call from Marino had been nothing more than a relay of the requests I had made the previous night. Nothing had been omitted or changed in any way. Marino came by the club and gave me my ticket, he offered to give me a ride to the airport, but I informed him that the airport would be the place to meet. The importance of this being handled as a business deal was paramount. There was nothing friendly about the task, which I was considering. If anything, this was a job interview, which could take me back into service with the government once again.

Later that evening, Lisa and I had a chance to talk about the next day's activities.

"I will be leaving here at 7:30 a.m. tomorrow morning Lisa. Then for this first trip anyway, I'll be back home tomorrow night. If and when another trip comes up I will probably stay overnight. But in no way will I be gone more than one night at a stretch, promise!"

"Do you want me to take you to the airport?"

"Honey that will be so early, with Christopher and everything, I will just catch a taxi and be done with it. Thank you though for offering." Taking her face in my hands I leaned down and kissed her full lips. Pulling back slowly and gazing into her eyes, the lights in the bedroom were reflecting off the highlights in her hair. It was so long and full, slightly curled and framing her face, its rich luster and body, was silky to the touch.

"So what all will go on tomorrow?" Lisa had not fully accepted all this but was trying her best, even though somewhat apprehensive.

"Basically it will be a meeting to outline in detail what they are interested in, specifics of my duties and a fine detail of the money, and how it will be distributed. All three of the special agents from the Drug Enforcement Administration, the U.S. Attorney and Special Task Force will be there as well. Ben Marino, the New Mexico State Police agent will be accompanying me."

"You promise that you will tell me absolutely everything when you get home? I mean every single word and sentence and leave nothing out, no matter what!" Her hands had gone to her hips and Lisa's little stance was held waiting for my answer.

"Well, I will tryyyyy to remember most of it." Grinning as I teased her a little. The knowing slap to the shoulder came without hesitation.

"Michael, don't even tease about something this serious. It is really important for me to know all phases of these talks, what is going on and how they are being handled." Her eyes told of her seriousness.

"Not only will I tell you everything I will bring back a copy of the taped interviews, because I want you to know everything as well. In addition to that I am going to leave you three contact numbers, one here in Albuquerque and two in California. One of the numbers in California is a patch locator number. Manned twenty-four hours a day and by the time I come home tomorrow, if this thing is all they say, I will have a code number for my personal identification."

"Thank you for taking the time to keep me informed. This is still kind of new and scary for me, you know?"

"I know baby, I know." Lisa came to me and encircled my waist and hugged me close, as I answered.

We had some together time with Christopher for the rest of the evening and then retired to our room for some other together time. The passion allowed for an outlet of many emotions, the indulgence being very physical almost to the point of athleticism, but necessary. Spent, late into the night, finally sleep took its course and allowed for a shallow rest to occur for me, awaiting the following day.

Dressed in casual slacks, boots, a linen shirt and light sports jacket, I met Ben Marino at the airport the following morning. The day had finally arrived for the beginning of a new era, deep inside the coveted secrecy of government intelligence. It had been many years now since I had taken access to this type of operational format. There was very little difference from the strategy rooms of the military and the agent headquarters, both run with the same basic "Rules of Conduct."

The flight over was one of casual conversation, this after Ben making a point once again to apologize for the first nights fiasco back in the city. I made it clear that it shouldn't be brought up again, it had been discarded by me in full.

As we disembarked the aircraft in San Diego, agent Richard Gorman stood at the ramp entrance to welcome Marino and me.

"Michael, Ben, welcome to San Diego. How was the flight?"

Shaking hands first with me then Marino, we began walking down the exit corridor.

"Flight was smooth and uneventful, how has the weather been?"

Ben was filling conversation, both of them were. By the time we walked out of the airport I knew about the weather, tide conditions and if the fish were biting. This arrival was quite different than the last time I had flown into San Diego, the caliber of guests greeting me had changed radically as well. For some strange reason I don't think the two groups could ever find a common denominator to agree upon.

Breaking out into the sunlight it showed exactly what I had

expected, another glorious bright day in southern California. Several cumulus and stratus clouds drifted lazily across the seascape, the salt twinge to the air quite prevalent and enjoyable. Two undercover cars parked directly in front of the curb, no doubt at all, who they were for! "Gentlemen here are our vehicles, let's load up and head downtown."

Even though these two vehicles did not meet the same criterion as most, they still, to me were easily recognizable. Both were of the confiscated fleet, ever growing with all the drug busts going on around the region. Where else would a government agent get a seven series BMW to drive, his escort being a Cadillac El Dorado, Presidential Package.

Arriving at an underground, secured parking area, there was no doubt that this was a headquarters building. FBI, DEA, ATF, U.S. Marshall, Border Patrol, the lot was full of staff and auxiliary vehicles of every description. Quickly we were whisked to the seventh floor and the introductions were about to begin.

The doors of the elevator began to open with the whine of the hydraulic pump as it built up the necessary pressure. Business of every description was to be beheld as I stepped in the midst of the organized pandemonium. Men, women, suits, slacks, undercover garb with some in elaborate hooker and biker attire, their shields looking out of place. Hooker with a badge just didn't fit, nor a biker. But they would certainly be hidden for their actual portrayals of choice.

Gorman navigated through the maze back to a large board/meeting room. Several men were inside waiting on our company to begin the first session. The agent had done everything so far just as he had promised, to the utmost detail.

"Michael Decker, I would like you to meet several people associated with the ongoing investigation. Terry Kissane, U.S. Attorney for this district, Pat Gregory and John Raftery from DEA, my partners, and this is Sally Portsmith, a liaison specialist attached to the DEA. These are the only people that will ever know any first hand information of who you are and any other pertinent facts concerning what you may pass on to us in this endeavor. No one outside of this room will ever know of any location where you and your family may be living. All knowledge of this meeting will be held in the strictest confidence. Every note and tape utilized will be in a sealed vault, secured by both the U.S. Attorney and the DEA." Greetings were exchanged by all parties. A dry marker board was at the far end of the conference room providing a stark contrast to the grained paneling and heavy oak shelves of the rest of the decor. Its white panel glistened from the light cast from the mirrored glass of the far wall. There was a single table, around which sat fourteen chairs, with a slide projector on the far end. A projection screen hung from the ceiling completing the total furnishing of the room.

"Thank you Richard. Mr. Decker the meeting this morning may be, for the government at least, one of the most integral parts of the Centac programs necessary links. If in fact you are the person, or have access to the person that is in close association with Alberto Sicilia Falcon. Having an inside top echelon executive of one of these families avails us to be privileged to the strategy and direct activities and planning. The offer of agent Gorman will be certified by me and my office. Each and every confiscation and acquisition will be logged and an ongoing record kept to facilitate accurate stats. At this point and time Mr. Decker, we don't know anything at all about you and any possible affiliation you may or may not have had or have with the organization in question. Agent Gorman has already indicated to you that we know, or let me say, have a general understanding of your training and abilities in several areas. These abilities can be put to our use and we are ready and willing to pay for this level of expertise. From here I have to swing the pendulum in your direction. If you have something, that you feel could be useful and are willing to take on this conquest, we await your comments." At five foot eight, clean cut and never done anything harder, in the area of real work, than pull up his trousers, Kissane laid the floor open to me.

"Before this gets any further involved for any one of us, I have to know what the government intends for my family and their safety and security." This was going to be dealt with first, my rules.

John Raftery decided to get into the foray. His California look, six foot one and maybe 175 pounds soaking wet with the blonde locks, levis and a Hawaii print shirt, he laid out the outline of events.

"All of this is directly coordinated by the U.S. Attorney's request but then controlled by the DEA and instituted by the U.S. Marshall's service. A contact deputy will be assigned directly to your family and provide you with a checklist of necessary, preflight requirements. I say it in that way because when the departure day arrives, it is a go and not be late procedure. Packing only the bare essentials, you and your family take whatever you can carry and head to a first checkpoint. From there, after calling a patch line, you will be given instructions on what route and destination to proceed towards. If necessary there will be another interim stop and directions once again instituted. When the final destination has been reached you will be in contact with the U.S. Marshall who will instruct you which hotel has been preselected for a safe house. This only as a temporary location while you look for suitable quarters. Once found, the shipper, who has already picked up your belongings and put them in storage, will deliver them to the final destination. Within seventy-two hours of arriving in the safe area you and your family will be provided all of the documentation necessary for your new identities. This is to include social security cards, drivers license, banking and anything else necessary. Once settled in, the DEA will contact the Marshall's and advise them of our contact times and schedules. All fees, fares, and tabs, will be completely paid for and picked up by the government and a monthly subsistence paid for you to live."

The oratory had concluded, with it a silence and uneasiness as static crackled through the electrified air. For me, the more they were uneasy, meant additional control of the meeting for myself.

Finally Ben Marino came to everyone of the Feds rescue, by breaking out of the roar.

"Mr. Kissane what are the guidelines of Mr. Decker's immunity, assuming he knows something and is willing to talk? What guarantees personally does he have that what you say today will be in effect, say a year or two from now." Give it to them Ben, head on and charging.

"As has been briefly eluded to, there would be complete and unequivocal immunity and this would be signed, sealed and certified by the Justice Department, in writing along with the other guarantees."

He looked like a little bandy rooster when he talked, kind of reminded me of one back on my Uncle Harris' place.

"I hear what you're saying, believe you mean it, but I personally have heard stories of total abandonment by the agencies when they are "finished" with all the testimony and need of information from some of their witnesses. The walk is not only in the physical sense, but in the financial as well." BOOM, BOOM, damn cannons were going off now. Marino had just thrown the napalm canister and the temperature was rising rapidly. People were shifting in their seats, tugging at their collars, coughing and uncomfortable to say the least.

"Marino," Gorman had the cajones to speak. "I am not sure what you may have or have not heard, but whatever guarantee has been duly promised by the government, will be upheld." An inaudible sigh of relief came from several of the remaining members.

Ben had stepped out in the faith of good investigating, by making the call to these agents in the first place. He and I had formed some degree of professional and personal friendship before this event took place. He was going to make sure that, within his ability everything was going to remain on the up and up.

Now it was time for me to say all that I was going to say today. Brief and to the point, no elaborate speeches or flowing stories, just short and simple statements.

"I think that I have heard all that I need to hear for this part of the session. I will let you know what I have decided within forty-eight hours. Until then I have absolutely nothing further to say." Cannon blast number three, after Marino had fired the first two salvos. Every one of these attorneys, field agents had expected that I would sing like a canary, at the least a few tidbits to tide them over until next time. If there was ever going to be a next time, as I had three necessary people on my list of decision makers, Lisa, Guad man, and of course myself.

They all sat there stone faced, and speechless, Marino had an ever so slight grin in utter amusement. When he said the following, I put the proverbial straw on the camel.

"Gorman if you will arrange a ride to the airport, Mr. Decker and I are ready to head back to New Mexico."

"Sure, certainly, I will have a car ready shortly!" Gregory shook his head in disgust and anger, with Gorman's answer. Raftery grinned with some silent thoughts, Kissane had lost control an hour ago, and was still on the bewildered mend.

Scarcely a goodbye or anything, just a "I'll be in touch," precluded Ben and I, being driven to the airport and stepping on the plane back to Albuquerque. For me, it concluded in a perfect setting, I certainly wouldn't have had it any other way.

Pulling out of the underground parking garage, with the vehicle holding only Gorman, Marino and myself, of course Gorman behind the wheel, a private chat ensued.

"Richard, one thing I have learned in my short time on this earth, is to go with my gut feelings when all the information is not so readily available. First off I would not trust Kissane to feed my dog, much less with my life. Second, Pat Gregory is a oneway, stuckup, ass, and I will never have anything to do with providing him anything. Raftery, on the other hand seems to be an okay guy and though somewhat lacking in formalities, probably a very dependable agent and someone that would cover your ass if need be. Coontz, you already know my thoughts there. As for yourself, you are cut from a different mold and your word is exactly that, your word. Thus any and all steps that are to be taken forward of this day will be handled, for the most part, through you. I want your personal guarantee and your choices to be known and instituted as to who the two Marshall's are, that are assigned to my family. The absolute best, there's no room for second fiddle there. I want men that can shoot with deadly accuracy and precision. This is not, as you have ascertained, my first time around the cargo net. The first slip, screwup in any way and I will close this book so fast you will never know it was ever open. You say you have been assigned to and have watched this organization for several years. If your observations were where they should have been, there would be no need of my services, but in fact you do need me. For now, all I am going to say is that there was no one, no other person closer to Sicilia-Falcon than I was. We will talk again, but for now this conversation never happened. Agreed?"

Two nodding heads concluded the statement, a look of wonder and inquisitive search on Gorman's face. After arriving at the airport, we all shook hands and said our goodbyes and Marino and I were gone, back to the Land of Enchantment, New Mexico. Gorman had slipped me another folder, envelope, containing ten hundreds, another thousand.

Locked in, completed, decided upon, agreed to, Lisa and I were about to depart on an adventure. One that would take us many places, and it was to take place within the next few weeks. I had flown back to California three times already, two more than the first, Ben Marino escorting me with each journey. No one, not one single person in either of our lives, not even close family knew that this disappearance was about to transpire.

Then suddenly by special courier an envelope with some very specialized instructions was delivered to the house one evening. It contained the contact numbers and codes for all of the preliminary patches to the main command center. No longer was Michael Decker alive, he was now called SR250010. Traveling to the nearest payphone, down at the 7-11 convenience store, I called the number, giving my code for identification.

"Baseline 147, how may I help you."

"This is SR250010, awaiting instructions." James Bond all the way.

"Proceed to checkpoint A, Phoenix, call coded number for further instructions. You have ten hours to next checkpoint." The receiver went dead, all references had been given, nothing further necessary.

Driving home, there was a slight race in my heartbeat, I knew that these next few months would be intense, but the pay would be substantial. Walking through the door, Lisa was pulling it open from the other side as I walked in. She had been waiting by the window, not too patiently at all.

"What happened? What did they say? When are we going? Is it tonight?"

"Lisa, honey slow down, you are firing questions like a machine gun. I'll tell you everything. We are to pack and leave in the next two hours, which means basically throw what is already packed in the Blazer and take off. Our first point is Phoenix and when we arrive I will call a contact number and then we will proceed to the next point."
"I am so nervous, excited, I can't stand it." This was a major understatement. She was definitely wired for sound.

We had prepacked all of the essentials in a small trailer during the evening for several nights, keeping the garage door down so as to raise no eyebrows of suspicion. Our clothes were already hung in suit bags and a rack was in the Blazer. Within forty-five minutes all was ready and stored neatly. Christopher's car seat was tied down with the seatbelt and secured, Lisa had put him down on a pallet so as to pack the crib as well. All loaded we put him in the car seat, loaded Thor in the back end and west bound we headed.
"Are you all right, lady?" I had noticed a tiny tear slip down her cheek.
"I will be fine. It is just going to take some getting used to. My family and friends, everyone that I know is here."
"I know that, but it will not be forever. I will work my absolute hardest to make this go quickly and get us back home. Okay?" It was not much in the way of consoling, but our decision had been a mutual one and her loneliness would finally change soon enough, I hoped.

Christopher and Thor slept almost all the way there, thankfully Lisa crashed as well. My thoughts were of the checkpoint and where might be our final destination. The Marshall's from Albuquerque had been pretty good with their following me, but there was no doubt that they were back there. They had left me just before reaching Gallup, and the Arizona men picked me up about 90 miles this side of Phoenix.

Gorman had promised all the security and had personally made many of the calls and arrangements. Phoenix was a rest stop, food, fuel and the instructions to continue on to northern California, capital itself, Sacramento was to be our new place of residence. Home for some period of time, but the exact length, was very indeterminate. The drive at least was somewhat scenic and was through some territory that Lisa had never seen. For me, it was a long, long, drive.

With prior instructions to proceed to the Ramada Inn West, just off the interstate, exit 48, true relief was experienced as that number came into view. Checking my rearview mirror, I noticed the unmarked vehicle that had appeared about seventy-five miles back was still in their same position.

"Hey all you sleepy heads, we are finally in Sacramento!" Moans and groans and a hearty, "Ruff" from the big dude in the back, signaled movement and life. Thor had begun to "breakwind" about fifteen minutes earlier, my eyes were watering and that was a long time to try and hold ones breath. Gasp, Gasp!

"Are we really here?" A barely awake form peered over my right side, the perfume a knowing smell.

"Well good morning loverly, how is my babycakes?" I loved her early morning smiles they fired up my day.

"Fine, but hungry and I really have to go, BAD!"

"Is my little tiger up and roaring yet?" I asked in anticipation of seeing Christopher's cute face soon.

"Nope, he is still sleeping. It took him a long time last night to get to sleep. He was so wound up with the trip and all."

Turning off the freeway, I made my way over into the right turn lane for the entrance into the hotel. It was time to begin looking for a spot which would allow for the Blazer and the trailer combination to be parked together. Luckily, I found a great place over under a big Cottonwood tree, some good bushes and a dirt area for Thor to take care of business, rapidly. Pulling to a halt, Lisa jumped out and headed for the lobby, I rolled the back window down and gave the hand signal to unload. He needed 4.8 seconds flat to find a good place.

Reaching for the glove box, I pulled the .44 caliber magnum out, checked the load and put it carefully in a small satchel with my personal papers and some of the documents, already in my possession. I looked at my sleeping son, his smile showing as his eyes saw who was making the noise in the front seat.

"Good morning young man. How's my little bubba this morning? Daddy loves you!" Christopher was ready to see his new place and get out of the car. What a long time in the car, had to be his thought.

Thor began his normal routine when I lifted Chris and brought him outside in my arms. Howooooooooo! Howooooooooo! Two long howls and then jumping up and down, Thor always got so excited with Christopher. They had already become best of friends and in no time would be howling together I was sure of it. Thor especially loved to see Christopher eating ice cream, his knowing that all the clean up was going to be his treat.

"Just look at all my men, jumping and howling, what will the neighbors say?" Grinning at the sight of the three of us goofing around. Christopher always loved it when I howled and jumped around just like his Thor. Seemed to me that I may have taught them to do this, this is no admission though, for sure.

"Lisa we are just happy, hungry and at least one of us is horny!"
"Michael Decker I can't believe you said that in front of your son!"
"Huh! My son is here because we both were horny, and still are!"

Reaching down and giving Lisa nice buns a tender pat and squeeze. Our smiles to one another showing we were thinking the same thing. To hurry up and get checked into our rooms, it was great to be healthy.

As we were standing there by the Blazer, another vehicle came up to the entrance. The bright sunshine of the early morning was a spotlight on the two occupants. The driver stayed seated, as the passenger left the vehicle and proceeded to the lobby area. Early forties, five ten, medium build, brown hair, short, easily government type, packing what looked like standard issue .38 cal. long barrel revolver from the body language and walk. Two minutestwenty seconds inside and returned to the car.

Shifting Christopher to Lisa and motioning for her to get behind the Blazer, I made a hand command to Thor for attention/alert status. Lisa walked slowly to the back tailgate. Thor instantly froze and stood by my side. His hair on the back of his neck, in the alert position as well. Thor not only responded instantly to my voice and hand commands, he had a chemistry response that was uncanny. Any one of the three of us, Lisa, Christopher and I, had only to change our mood and he came to the ready.

Medium tan in color, the LTD Ford came to a stop, in front of the Blazer. My hand was on the magnum as the satchel containing it was laid on top of the hood. So casual, the two men didn't realize that I was armed. This time the driver was the first to exit, a man in his late forties, possibly early fifties. He was six foot, slender build, large hands, sandy blonde hair, thin glasses with narrow rectangle lens. Looked to have been around the corner and up the block, so to speak. He seemed to be a veteran of many such meetings and experienced in how best to handle them.

He put his badge in his hand before leaving his vehicle, in so doing, it was not necessary to put his hand inside a coat or pocket which might make someone overly jumpy. He showed the badge clearly, not just a flash I.D., and then spoke.
"SR250010, welcome to Sacramento. My name is Deputy Mashall Warren Bearup. My partner is Deputy Marshall Bill Golden, and we are here to assist you and your families' transition into this program. Here are the keys to your rooms and everything is prepaid. Charge all expenses to the room, including gratuities. Sign the tickets with room number only, that has been prearranged. Take the rest of the day to get

settled, then tomorrow morning we will begin processing the necessary documentation.

Your rooms are the last ones on the bottom floor on the east side. A drive way allows you to park both the Blazer and the trailer. An unmarked unit will be positioned outside for the remainder of your stay here. On this piece of paper are several contact numbers. Do not go outside these premises without calling and asking for an escort. Your phones are directlinked, meaning that they will only dial these numbers. This is done in rotary and will cycle to the next number if no answer. The phones will not call any other numbers and this is for your safety and security.

In this envelope is five hundred dollars cash for any incidentals you might need while here at this temporary location. Additionally the dog can go inside your rooms, we got special permission and the rooms have a pass through partition, which will avail you some additional space. Relax as best you can and know that this place and you personally, are safe. Any questions?" Matter of fact, to the point, I liked the way Marshall Bearup had delivered the instructional speech. Military precision and efficiency, one of my favorites.

"No, no questions, thank you for the courtesy!" We shook hands and he left, time to go and get settled. I turned to look at Lisa and she smiled and came running. Thor looked at me for the release signal. His eyes had never left Bearups presence until now. Hand signal took him back to his normal, goodnatured self.

"Let's go and see what the rooms look like!" A sparkle back in her eyes, one I had not witnessed now for over a week.

"Let me have Christopher and you take Thor with you. Go ahead get some of that energy used up baby. We will bring the Blazer and trailer along in a few minutes." Like a flash she and Thor ran through the parking lot and on to the room location. Meanwhile I got into the Blazer, putting Chris on my lap, and drove over to the east side. I could tell from what Bearup had said that tomorrow would be a very busy day. I couldn't be sure who was more excited, Lisa with her smile or Thor with his antics as Christopher and I drove up to the rooms. Stepping from the vehicle, Lisa grabbed my neck and pulled me down for a kiss.

"Michael, it is so nice. Large rooms, a king size in one room and two doubles in the other. Even a kitchenette in the larger room, it's great!"

Unpacking only the barest of necessities for now, chaining Thor to the trailer hitch while we were gone, Lisa, Christopher and I went to the restaurant for some much needed nourishment. The food was above average for this type of establishment, and it was enjoyed, since it would be days before a suitable housing situation could be established.

After the meal, a walk around the grounds, which included feeding a few squirrels, we returned to give Thor a good run and brushing before retiring to the rooms. Christopher needed changing, which was my job, and Lisa put all of our things away in the dressers and closets. Thor meanwhile sniffing out every crook and cranny, exploring each new smell and odor was about to leave someone a present. He also had to stick his nose inside Christopher's crib. Thor and Chris had this little game they played, called grab and lick the noses. I guess it was a little of each for both of them to participate in while they romped around. The joy and happiness I saw there brought many memories of me and Chico when I was young. It seemed like such a long time ago. I was so old, right.

With everything squared away and in order, it was time for some "rest," well for some of the inhabitants. Lisa and I had some unfinished issues that needed close attention, very close attention. I seemed to have lost my voice and had to resort to using my hands for communication. Thor peeked in a couple of times to make sure that everyone was all right, something about the noises, strange as they were.

A nap followed, then lunch and the pool for the rest of the afternoon. For the evening meal we ordered a ton of food and took it out under a large shade tree, having a family picnic, of sorts. Thor enjoyed it immensely, along with all of us. Laughing, running and having fun, one would have thought we were just a regular family, with hardly a care in the world. Someday, maybe someday that would come to pass. For now, it was time to get a little rest and prepare for the first day of WC 1225, coded SR250010, another new number for my work and plan.

Because of Christopher and Thor and our personal belongings, Lisa and I decided that the hotel would be the easiest place to have the first meeting of the day. Introductions followed by the lay out of new identification samples, this included bank, personal and other assorted documents. John Raftery, in his outline of procedures, while I was in San Diego, had this process down to the dime.

Both of the Deputy Marshall's were efficient, courteous, and well versed in this type of dealing. Some temporary I.D.'s were given to both Lisa and I to use until the official ones arrived within the week. Now that the official part of the meeting was over, the real nittygritty came to the surface, the special rules and regulations.

"From this point forward," Marshall Bearup taking the lead, his voice and demeanor, along with the name reminded me of a marshal of the old west. "You will have the freedom to come and go anywhere within a one hundred mile radius. If the destination exceeds this distance, please contact the office for our notification. It will take some time to get used to these new names, be patient, and when talking, be aware of what you say. There is no reason to worry about anything else. I will be monitoring all aspects. On the first of each month I will bring your allotment to you in cash. Remember that it is for a month, although emergencies do come up and we understand that. If for any reason you need medical attention, we will get you in to see several of the specialists that are on our key payrolls.

This map will help you to find some of the more desired living locations in Sacramento. The ones that are circled are the best places. Additionally, this is a multiple listing of duplexes and homes that may or may not suit your tastes. I have included in the portfolio numerous points of interest and places to see.
"Bill, do you have anything to add to what I have covered?"
"No Bear I believe you covered all areas." Bill Golden didn't say much, but the manner in which he listened, told a lot about the man. I was glad to have him on the team.
"Then as a matter of conclusion, it will be maybe a week or so before your trips begin for southern California. So this vacation time will be precious to you both, believe me once the ball starts to roll, downhill it will race for some time, so enjoy it. Ma'am if there is ever a time when your husband is taken away on one of the trips and you need anything, this card has a twenty-four hour cellular number which is never away from my side." His eyes shone with a grandfatherly smile and it was easy to see the true concern and comforting warmth he was giving to Lisa. She and I both appreciated it. Lisa thanked him personally.
"Mr. Bearup, thank you very much and not only for me but for my husband and son as well. By the way, you may not have noticed but Thor approves of you both, as well." With his name came a wag of his tail, Lisa told him it was okay to approach and get a good whiff of both deputies. He approached both of them and when he turned to me I signaled him, "okay," his memory banks photographed all information.
"Thanks again to the two of you and we will be talking to you soon."
The door closed and with their leaving came a new line of questioning, from Lisa.
"When can we go and start looking for a house?"
"How about if we chain the trailer to that big tree, load Thor and Christopher and leave in fifteen minutes?" A smirk of approval was all that was necessary.

Walking out to the Blazer, I noticed how nice the weather was, clear, sunny, about 85 degrees, light breeze, definitely a good house hunting kind of day. It made for easy looking and pleasurable driving and sightseeing.

Within two days of looking a nice affordable duplex had been located. The furniture was delivered, and housekeeping set up. Life began to roll back into a routine of normalacy. Lisa, Christopher, Thor and myself became just ordinary citizens, living our lives and enjoying all that was available. But for me, all this peace was about to end, time was coming for me to begin my part of this ordeal.

Monday morning bright and early the phone rang to announce that I had an 11:00a.m. flight to Diego. Please pack light for two or three days, no weapons will be allowed. My ass, I said to myself, there was no way that I was traveling anywhere without some type of firearm. I just needed to take it long distance in a different manner of travel, which was easy to accomplish.

"Guad man, before you give me one of your originals, listen close! Make available in San Diego airport, first men's room, first stall, 9mm with two clips of Hipower ammo. Clear the room by 1330 hours."

"Peter's Wiggler's, catch the big ones here! See I got it in, any old way. I roger your twenty and will take care of the program. How are you doing up there in Canada? Isn't Montreal nice this time of year?"

"Just peachy Guad man, just peachy. How is the home front these days?"

"Tight, to damn tight, and I mean the lid is welded to the can for a soon big explosion. Will forty your twenty, GONE!" Something with Sicilia-Falcon was about to go down in a big way. I would follow up after getting to San Diego.

The "L" shape of a 9mm fits perfect around the back bowl stem of a commercial toilet like what is in almost one hundred percent of every airport facility. Using white, 2" plastic tape, it can be concealed to all but the knowing public, which would be someone looking for just such an item.

Raftery had come to pick me up as Gorman, Gregory and others were hot into something big at the office. They knew what, just didn't know exactly how the dope was coming across in such large quantities. After finding my present at the airport, I joined Raftery in the awaiting car out front. It would, at times, amaze me just how lackadaisical and nonchalant, some of these agents could be. Assuming since I had no checked baggage there would be no way to bring a weapon with me. One of the very reasons that a backup was going to accompany me where ever, my travels might take me. The vehicle for the day, or week, was a 500 SL Mercedes, some poor guy was sitting in jail and staring out the window knowing the Feds were enjoying all of his toys. As previously mentioned, the inventory of boats and exotic cars was literally endless. Thus allowing for some of the surveillance teams to change to a different mode of transportation so often, that possible identification by the "bad guys" was basically impossible. Raftery used his hand to signal where he was from inside the car, oh really, I said to myself.

"Raftery, how are things in Southern California?"

"Fine, just fine. We are going to be making somewhat of a quick trip downtown. There is something big going down and it needs our immediate attention. You are going to be a vital link in determining what the mode of transportation is!" From this basic of the explanation I already knew what they had, as well as what was missing. Of course formerly being on the inside, gave me the view from the other side.

"What kind of time period are you working with?" Raftery was hyper as hell, I could now just see the control room buzzing with calls and men and women running with their shirt sleeves rolled up, perspiration dripping from their brow, files and papers strewn here, there and yonder.

"From the inside tip it is going to be either tonight or early tomorrow morning. There is supposed to be near five tons of highgrade grass coming across at the Tijuana crossing. Ten thousand pounds is a tremendous amount of bulk cargo to come undetected. Must be on a big semi, but we can't figure out exactly the method. At this time and for the next three days, every big rig is being searched completely. If we can't physically see all the cargo, the entire load is being removed. It is causing a hell of a mess for traffic and just plain logistics." He was excited and the deep anticipation showed from his face. Nights of unrest, uneasiness and worry furrowed the small wrinkles of his forehead. The strain caused a puffiness around the underside of his eyes.

"I will show you how it is done as soon as we get to the office. It has been coming the same way now for almost seven years. Very ingenious, and so simple, it was never checked closely enough to discover. Your standard inspections have shown the vehicles to be just as they appeared. Yet, they were so different from what you observed. All of the large shipments of cocaine come in very similar fashion. Just a slightly different container mode."

He was transfixed on the road but I had his full and complete attention. A bulge in the veins of his neck showed his frustration with having to wait on the answer.

"You threw out that little bone of information just so that I could gnaw on it until we get to the office, didn't you?"

"Of course Raftery, hell, most of this will simply amaze you as to how it is being done. The federal government has been too tight assed for their own good. Maybe through this Centac they will finally allow you to go out and get dirty enough to find out all the secrets and idiosyncrasies of how these cartels work." The fifteenminute commute from the airport, down the waterfront, past the Star of India sailing ship, to the offices was almost over. Total elapsed time was just under six minutes. Parnelli had nothing on the John Raftery, man.

Same garage, same building, same weather, gorgeous, some things just never change, thank goodness. Zipping through the obstacle course of the lower lot, Raftery slid the Benz into handicapped parking next to the elevator. He was definitely in a hurry to get to the upper floor.

My earlier vision of the office condition was not too far from the reality of the situation. Raftery had radioed ahead from the entrance that we were on location. Gorman and Gregory were standing by as we exited the elevator.

"Sorry about the short notice, but some things are cooking and we need your full assistance and knowledge. By the way Michael, thank you for coming and welcome."

A greeting from Gorman and a grunt from Gregory, about what was expected with the fervor at its current level. Terry Kissane was down at the end of the room, waving frantically to the group.

"Seems there is an urgency in that wave!" I pointed behind the agents to the U.S. Attorney. All of the men turned and began in that direction. Gorman and Gregory both looked physically and from their wrinkled attire, like the two of them had not been home recently.

"That damn shipment had better not have left or we are in deep shit!," Gregory sighed heavily with the expressed condition of forlorn agony. He, as the other team members had put their heart and soul into this investigation for too long for a major break, like what was at hand, to slip away once again. Entering the boardroom, where the first discussion had taken place, the electricity was turned to maximum output.

A bank of phones had been installed, poster size prints of several areas I recognized from the many trips circling Falcon's operations in and around Tijuana, hung on the walls. Reams of paperwork and notes strewn across the top of the long table, coffee and water jugs here and there, cups at various locations around the room, most of them only sipped from once.

"Gentlemen we have a crisis, the informant called the patch phone and said that the shipment was leaving some warehouse and would be to the border checkpoint within the next 12-18 hours. He had no real specifics, only that message. The countdown to catch this shipment is slipping away from us. At present we know where it is coming through, but not in what or how."

Kissane was a gray/white color. He hadn't been out in the beautiful sunshine here for at least six months. Hell, all these guys needed a jaunt for a week or so. I knew every detail that they did not have. It was time for me to start delivering the goods.

"I am going to jump in here and need a few things before I do. Raftery I need that aerial map shot of the Tijuana border crossing. Gregory get me a highway map from Mexicali to the outer circle of Rosarita Beach. Kissane I need the full roster of guards on duty from U.S. Customs and their lane assignments, at the border. Next, give me a dry marker board and plenty of markers." The worker ants began to scurry around the room and the phone began to buzz. Within minutes all of the tools for the presentation were assembled, time for the lecture to begin.

"First the warehouse that you have been looking for in Tijuana, is not in Tijuana, the main warehouse is in Mexicali. You have been looking in the wrong city and the wrong place as well. Shipments moving through Juarez, Nogales, Laredo, Tijuana etc. have all been originating in Mexicali. A lumberyard there, Gonzales Ltd, fronts as just that, a lumberyard. But underneath in an underground storage area is one of the largest vaults ever assembled for marijuana storage. Easily room for nearly a million pounds of grass, one half million kilos more or less a few pounds. Seven to ten thousand pounds of marijuana a week goes in and out of this facility. The last time I was there, near two hundred thousand pounds were in storage. All of this is being transported aboard oil tanker trucks." A look of astonishment covered their faces already, Gregory shouted his disbelief.

"No way that much could be stockpiled and sure as hell they can't move it in a damn oil tanker. There is no where to put it, none." Looking confident that he had blown my statement, he leaned back in his chair.

"That is the very reason you have been missing this operation for so long. People like you with their smug knowledge of absolutely NOTHING. The tanker trucks that are used are custom built just for this type of transport. Gorman, give me one of those markers," Taking it I began to detail a drawing while continuing the explanation." All of the trailers have been built like this. These lines represent the outer wall of the actual stainless tank. From all exterior appearances, a normal unit, yet this is only the first skin. An inner panel constructing the actual dope container is hidden. This interim space is filled with water and oil mixed so that when a bang stick is tapped along the entire length of the tanker, a consistent sound is emitted. Telling the inspector that the entire tank is full. An upper and lower, observation storage has been constructed so that when the guard looks in from the top and sticks the dip pole down inside, it is full of oil. From the bottom, when the valve is turned, oil flows out. Once again the inspector or guard sees all indication of a regular tanker and waves him on through. The entire inside of this sixtyfoot tank however is empty of oil and full of high grade marijuana. They are filled by removing the upper dip tank, which when empty of the fifty gallons of fluid are unbolted and slipped out with the rubber sealing ring. Two men are placed down inside the inner sleeves and a large vacuum conveyor runs from the underground storage to the awaiting tanker, coming from the lumberyard to the Pemex storage facility next door. After filling them, the trucks are reassembled with the dip tanks reinstalled and off to the border they go for another successful crossing. This symbol of an arrow with a thunder bolt or lightning will be on the right forward section of the tanker, approximately two inches tall, a coded marker for all the trucks. All the rest of the tanker fleets are normal deliveries being made throughout the region."

Several heads were shaking in what was sinking in to their consciousness and understanding. The fax machine began to roll out the duty roster for the day at the border crossing inspection lanes. Taking the chart, which contained the aerial view of the two sections I had requested, I finished the presentation.

"This road coming out of the Mexicali area is the one used for the shipment. These lanes at the middle, not the end as would be assumed, are the "walk through " lanes. Over seventy percent of the trips are done through this same procedure, because of the lack of customs officials who can be bribed for the pass throughs. When a paid official is on duty, a small satchel will be left with him as the guard walks past the tractor pulling the trailer. If you will set up your observation for these two lanes and watch particularly for these three inspectors, this shipment will be yours. Later, when you are prepared to make a full raid of the Mexicali facility, I will show you how it can be done."

"Christ, no wonder we have not been able to get all the pieces put together for all this movement of product. How many thousands of pounds have come across, it makes me shudder to think of the quantities. Especially when you start to imagine the cocaine shipments as well."

Kissane was not believing that this quantity of narcotics had been flowing through his territory for so long, undetected. Gorman was in high gear now and a renewed energy came to his spirit.

"Guys, it is time to start this shake down at the border. I want three teams for this bust, one to cover the inbound of the first tanker. One ground unit to follow it on to the San Diego side, with a chopper at viewfinder range only, no close ups to spook anyone, to assist the ground team. The third team is going to be assisted by all of us and the border will be broken with their current arrangement of payoffs. Instead of payoffs, now it was going to be paybacks for this organization."

As Gorman finished his statement a confident air began to surround him, a knowing that finally all of his work and diligence was going to pay off. For me personally, it was an opportunity to pay back the people who had stolen all the wealth that I had accumulated. As the weeks and months passed by the agents and the agencies would continue to pick my brain and chronicle the times, events and circumstances. Wanting to know each and every detail to its fullest extent. Many stories and things that I related to them would be scoffed at and dismissed as impossibilities. Yet the more they dug and investigated, their validity would be observed, time and time again. The trips and the short notice of this first occasion were to become routine, not the exception.

With the long hours and the schedule, and a drink to relax, then another and another to follow for their effects became commonplace on the flights home. Also many nights back in Sacramento would be concluded with six to eight cocktails before bedtime. This formed a pattern, which never changed for some extended time to come.

Lisa and I had decided to buy a house after some four months in the duplex. Finding a nice sprawling ranch style onestory, 2,470 sq. feet, one third of an acre in the back yard for Christopher and Thor, what a gift this abode would be. It was an older neighborhood, thus the trees were very large and enhanced the landscaping and asthetics immensely. A lease option was the best way to purchase for us with the money coming in so slow. That big payoff was still several months away, so we had to be somewhat patient. It allowed for us to have the real space to relax and live more freely. It gave Lisa something to do with my long absences.

The bust in Mexicali, the big warehouse under the lumberyard, netted some seventy-five tons of marijuana. One hundred and fifty thousand pounds, about six times larger than any other stash ever discovered by any of the federal agencies, ever. Nearly fifteen million dollars worth, making my cut substantial, but this was only the beginning.

The three months became six and finally by the ninth month, I was beginning to think that this investigation was not going to end. Boats, planes, cash, drugs, all had been confiscated and seized by the millions of dollars in their value. Finally the accord with Mexico was approved, this was the stalemate which was causing certain aspects of the arrest procedures to be stalled. The President and the Attorney General themselves were key figures in the ongoing finalization. Their signatures were required for the documents and guarantees of prosecution. The entire Presidents' staff in Mexico City were on alert and had personally promised their support. Key men who had been undercover with the DEA, serving in the upper echelon of the Federal Police in Mexico had been hand picked and put on stand by. Falcon had so much power and so many connections everywhere that even the actual arrest of him, along with seven other major players was almost impossible. Had it not been for the continued presence and pressure put on the governments of both countries by men like Richard Gorman, this would have never come to its finalization and delivery.

Distance, long distance had brewed itself a thick curtain of separation between Lisa and me, by the ninth month. That strain of the phone ringing, sometimes in the middle of the night, yanking me from my life and family for as much as weeks at a time. The toll was severe, and many aspects of our home environment suffered. While we both just needed some air and some space to recoup the love and romance back into the relationship, I flat couldn't stop the machine that was now rolling at top speed.

"Michael, I have decided to go back to Albuquerque for a visit. My family and friends haven't seen me in what is now going on a year. When we left over nine months ago, this damn thing was to take some three to six months. You are gone all the time and I don't ever know when you may or may not be here and for how long. I can't take it any more, I need a break and a vacation for me and Christopher." Nothing she had said was anything but the truth, I understood her frustration.

"Lisa, I have been doing everything in my power to get this finished. But I don't have the control over all the people and things that are involved here. I wish you didn't have to go but I sure as hell understand why. I would like to leave as well, believe me you don't know how much!" She shook her head, her hands clasped together tightly.

"I know Michael, but I am going, tomorrow morning. I really don't give a shit if the Marshalls approve or not, I'm taking Christopher and going." There was no need in trying to persuade her of not leaving. She had stated something that was set in stone as far as her decision was concerned. As fate would have it, three o'clock in the morning and I got the call to come back to San Diego for more phases.

"See, they don't give a fuck what we are going through, they only care about that damn Falcon crap." Lisa was done with this deal all the way around. After the night we had experienced, the phone was the breaking point and all suppressed feelings came pouring, erupting out in the open.

"Fine, Lisa, enjoy your visit, have a real nice time." I would regret saying that last comment, more than anything I had ever said before. When the Marshall came to pick me up at five o'clock, she was packed and leaving at six, case closed.

My emergency trip was nothing more than signing documents under oath for the Attorney General of Mexico, along with three special prosecutors, they were picking up all of the special documentation, which had been prepared for the arrest to begin during the next four to six weeks. I would believe this when it happened, not until.

Sitting there with Richard Gorman and Terry Kissane I unloaded a bit of my grief and erupted on them for a short period.

"I want you two to know that this fucking investigation is killing my family and the relationship we once had. You gave me your word that this damned thing would be over long before now, and I still don't see any handwriting on the wall. If I didn't have so much invested already, I would tell you all to kiss my ass and leave. If this takes the toll that I am starting to be afraid it might, I will make every one of you pay dearly."

"Are you threatening me, Mr. Decker?" Kissane spoke up, his precious image was so damaged.

"Kissane, you can take it any way you want it, or you can stuff it up your ass for all I care. It is because of political bastards like you that this thing was not finished some months ago. You and all the pompous asses like you, with your damn protocol crap." I wished he was about a foot taller and one hundred pounds heavier and I would enjoy beating his ass.

"Well, I never..."

"Yes, that I do believe, you never did!" Cutting him off I got up and left the room for some air. Gorman got up with me and joined me out in the lobby.

"Michael, I want to apologize for what this must be doing to you and your family. I agree with what you said in there, there are times I would love to be able to say it just the way it felt, but I can't. Please try and hang in there for a while longer. I really believe that the arrests will begin within three to four weeks, maybe sooner." He was and had become a friend, one person in all the rat race who had never lied to me and had done what he said, and been a stand up individual.

I was glad to get on the plane that night and head back to Sacramento. The only semblance of a home that I had left in this world, empty though it was for a while.

Sitting there on the back patio, Thor retrieving the ball for the one hundred and seventy-eighth time, his tongue near the grass, but never thinking he might be tired, I thought of Lisa and Christopher. It had been less than twenty-four hours and I already missed them. It was different from when I would be away for the investigation. This was where we were supposed to be, together.

Several weeks earlier, in the hopes of starting something that might allow for Lisa and I to be able to do some activity together, I had joined a four-wheel drive club. Called the Sacramento Valley Varmits, they took monthly trips up into the high country and put their machines through the paces. Tomorrow was a trip up through the Rubicon trail, the old mining road over the top into Lake Tahoe. This had been a possible consideration for the daily activities.

Wednesday, Thursday, Friday, and now finally Saturday had come and still no call or word of any kind from Lisa. Meanwhile I had gone down to Capital Jeepers Supply, a four wheel drive parts store and inquired about working part time. Victor Borgman, the owner, had become an acquaintance from the purchases I had made over the past few months. He had said yes to the part time job and the diversion had helped immensely in passing the time while Lisa and Christopher were away.

By the evening I was going crazy from not talking to Lisa, so I broke down and gave her a call. Something was going on, inside my heart seemed to hardly beat, a strange dryness to my mouth, a darkness I couldn't explain, surrounded me.

"Hello." I had never heard Lisa sound like she did, the tone was so far from her normal one.

"Lisa, this is Michael. Why haven't you called and told me you were okay?"

"...I ...guess ...I ...ah ...have been ...too busy." Whoa, something was way wrong here, my spirit shuddered.

"What the hell is going on Lisa? What has happened? You are not being your normal self at all."

"I am just tired." A quivering in her voice, she was beginning to lose control.

"Oh, God, Lisa, no ...something has happened, hasn't it?" The silence lasted for a long time, then crying and sobbing, a familiar type of crying, the same kind I had heard when the phone call had been to Patti, my first wife, the night she had been left in Mexico. A million thoughts raced through my mind, what now.

"I …I went out to a party and …?" I knew then what had happened, without being told. She was my soul mate, I read her much too well for my spirit not to have read this story and scenario completely. What I was feeling inside was three things simultaneously: first, guilt – I had put her through too much; second, pain – for what she was feeling inside; third, disappointment – for the consequences of what had happened.

Lisa had gone to a party with a bunch of her friends, partying and drinking. Then at some point during the evening a few reefers/joints of marijuana had been passed around. All the frustration, and all the pent up emotion, with some smooth talk and consoling by a preying vulture. Defenses down by the alcohol and the dope, both taken far in excess of any control being possible, and the act was over, before it had even started.

I had been paid back without her even knowing it, my sins of the past came back to haunt me and grind the agony of the moment deep within my heart.

"Lisa, I love you, please just pack up and come home where you belong, please just get our son and come home. What happened was as much my fault, Lisa, you might not understand how I feel that way but I do. I just want you here and for this whole circumstance to finish itself."

"How can you say that after I have cheated on you?" The tears had finally calmed enough for her to talk.

"Lisa, the past is exactly that, the past. You can't change it, I can't change it either. We just have to go on, that's all. Just go on with our lives. All I know for sure is that I love you and always will, and that I miss you and Christopher terribly. Just come home." My heart was bumping in my throat as I awaited her reply.

"If you are sure that you want me home, I will be home tomorrow. My visit was not near what I thought it would be. A lot has changed in Albuquerque, a whole lot." That was all I needed to hear for now.

We said goodbye and, strangely enough I heard relief in Lisa's voice, immense relief. Now it was time for a drink, walking to the kitchen and taking the Jack Daniels from its perch in the cabinet. I proceeded to mix the whiskey with a little ice and a touch of water, the ice tea glass holding what I thought to be my relaxation for the voyage into sleep. Turning from the kitchen, opening the sliding glass door to the patio, I let Thor in to provide some company. The two of us strolled toward the master bedroom, Thor in a joyous mood he did not get to roam in the house except very rarely. Taking his favorite place at the foot of the bed, I hit the remote control and began to surf the channels.

Taking a long pull on my glass, the liquid soothing a dry throat, the liquor beginning to ease the tension and stress of the past day, I wondered what Lisa might be feeling right now. Wondering if my understanding was a comfort or was it strange behavior to her, my straying in the past giving me no right to get angry. This occurrence did in no way make the situation suddenly even. A balance of sin was impossible, an affair of any duration was still wrong. But who in the hell was I to preach, really now?

By the third glass of bourbon, the ice had now gone down to four cubes, the water stayed in the faucet. My analysis, which had now encompassed, for all practical purposes, the past five years of life, was in full production. I could almost justify every decision as one of sound and well thought planning, the rationalization of alcohol being all that was necessary to pat my drunk, self on the back. In the past hour I had consumed near twelve fingers of booze, since I have a size fifteen ring finger, it meant that two thirds of the quart had disappeared.

My thought patterns began to search in vain for some answers, there must be a way I can clean this situation up and give Lisa and myself a chance. A real chance at making it together, maybe, just maybe, starting over again was the answer. Get totally away from California, leaving the mistakes and the memories to die in their own misery. How can I talk the DEA and the Marshall's into moving us, they would never make all these preparations, this late in the program. Unless they didn't have a choice in the matter.

If some type of emergency situation were to occur, leaving them no other avenue to turn toward, a move would become imminent. A major violation of the protective nature which was in place here in this Sacramento location, a breech of the security, someone had sold out and told of where SR250010 was located. Paid handsomely for the information and then two men had come to kill the key informant and destroy the link of Alberto Sicilia-Falcon to the drug smuggling empire. Hired assassins, that were capable of planting a bomb on the exterior of the subject's house. With its detonation, and resulting explosion forcing fire and collapse of the main structure of the home, only one escape would be possible, the window. Strategically located outside the two bedroom windows with automatic weapons and shotguns, to silence the escaping occupant once and for all. Yet the one thing that they had not counted on, the dog, had foiled their plan.

Bursting out of the window came a chair to remove the glass, followed by one hundred ten pounds of raw unchained fury and rage. Trained to protect his master and defend this property, even with his life. The dedicated animal launched through the air and disabled one assailant, near tearing an arm from its socket, a near fatal wound to the neck as well. Screams of terror and fear coming from the soul making the second assailant turn and come to help. Explosions from the fire and materials bursting into flames causing the second hitman to not hear the thud of SR250010 hitting the ground, in a diving roll and springing to his feet. Disoriented from the explosion, initially stunned, no time to grab a weapon or even dress, Decker surveys the quarry at hand and realizes his only choice is to escape.

"THOR!!!" The roar is primieval, a command given from the soul of the hunter, now suddenly the prey being stalked. A situation so much the antithesis of his life, a knowing of his former victims spirits flashes through his thoughts. With the sound of a voice the assassin, coming to the aid of his comrade, turns and begins to raise the weapon. The barrel swinging slowly, yet the slow motion coming from the scene itself, not the reality of the speed whatsoever. Eyes locking on the target, message formulated in the brain, sent to the hands and awaiting finger on the trigger. Muscles and tendons begin to contract, life about to be ripped from my body as the projectiles tear the flesh stop the beating of this heart. Brain ebbing to a final ...! Wait, the picture begins to quickly redevelop!

"Ayeeeeeeeee! Nooooooooo!" Fangs clamping with 900 PSI on the calf muscle and with a ripping and twisting motion, tears and shreds the leg. The assailant falling in agony and pain, weapon dropped, a single shot fired aimlessly into the air. Thor, eyes gold with the rage of protection, had stimulated patterns of attack from his ancestors pouring through his veins. He breaks his assault for a fleeting instant, looking to his master for the signal to kill or release. Him willing and able to take life or be merciful, raw boned and muscled from the special diet he has had from birth, his heart and spirit bound into the same of his owner and friend. Blood coating the fringe of the black muzzle, glistening from the fangs that can take the lifeblood so swiftly.

The hand signal tells him to flee, like the wind and the lightning bolts flash into instant thunder of movement, his body leaping through the air. Leaving the bedraggled men writhing in their wounded state, slumped on the ground, people coming from their homes, up and down the block, lights illuminating and breaking the darkness, everyone was about to learn the true identity of their neighbor. Thor and his master, hearing the screech of tires, a powerful motor roaring its arrival went back into attack mode. The black sedan slamming into the curb and up on the front yard, sliding to a stop, the turf tearing from its grip of the earth slid to a stop.

Driver's door flies open, he grabs the first man and throws him into the back seat, his body loose, lifeless it seems. Whirling with the force of his large frame, he bends and with a gasp shoves the remaining participant across the front seat and climbs into the vehicle. With the rear wheels screaming for traction as they dig furrows and rut the ground, the car spins first to the sidewalk and vaults off the curb. No license plate to be copied is evident from the rear.

During this time the view of this activity has been from the neighbors across the street, for Thor and his master have slipped from view. The large hole in the seven foot tall picket fence, evidence of the speed and haste of their departure, the man and his faithful companion.

Working my way around the property, I slipped through the back yard and came to the Blazer from the shaded side, by the large Evergreen. First surveying the street in both directions, I opened the door and pulled the 9mm from the compartment under the console. Now let the bastards come back and I would empty the fifteen rounds of each clip, placing thirty projectiles within the center of each form. Ten apiece to carve their hearts from their chests, but return they never did. I grabbed a pair of tennis shoes and shorts from my workout bag in the vehicle, as I was still outfitted in the skivvies I had left the window in. "Thor, you are the best damn dog in the whole world. If it wasn't for you I would not be here now." Hugging his big neck and ruffling the coat on his back as I talked to him. He was one hell of a dog, proven and time tested. As I continued to praise him in front of the neighbors, coaching them on what they saw in their sleepy, barely conscious states. Within minutes while the Fire Department was enroute, their stories coincided and matched for all to hear, later when the authorities began to arrive.

I had built the scenario in my mind and played it out with the exacting precision of a staged play. Building the bomb, breaking the glass, breaking the hole in the fence, firing the shot, tearing up the lawn. The lawn had been easy, done with the Blazer and then washed clean. All the rest of the effects done within the imaginations of the excited neighbors, four had witnessed the men and the shot, and the attack of Thor. Many times in my work for Falcon and the government before, I had created events, which looked as if they had taken place. Some were for authentication, others for diversions and escape from countries deep within Central and South America.

The one thing that I had not counted on was the length of time the Fire Department would take with its response. Truly over one third of the structure had burned and our personal effects badly damaged, with no insurance in the least amount. All the paperwork had not cleared the title company and the insurance company would not pay on the claim. An hour later the authorities of every description were on the scene, scores of people with their badges and cameras. They were testing this and photographing that, interviewing the witnesses.

The results were as planned, within four days, moved to a temporary shelter first, Lisa, Christopher and I with my big dog Thor, had taken residence in Denver, Colorado. High in the Rocky Mountains, a place that neither of us had hung our hats before and the cold mountain air was invigorating and very alone, the distance between Lisa and I had widened.

Much earlier than we could have expected the arrests had started throughout Mexico and the United States, that same weekend. Over the next three weeks 287 people were in custody and all of the main players held on "no bail" sentences. In custody and there to remain for some time. With the arrests came the indictments, the trials began to be scheduled and dates set for my testimony. The evidence was staggering, mountains of photographs, documents on the multitudes of arrests and drug busts. Falcon was in a maximum security cell in Santa Maria prison, along with all of the coconspirators linked to his empire and operation. Things began to wrap up very quickly as deals were cut for the courts and sentencing. But only for the smaller players, the big guys had to face the music, which had specifically been arranged for their individual roles and offenses.

Meanwhile in the Mile High City, Lisa and I had finally purchased a nice little home. I had taken a job with a firm selling fire alarms and smoke protectors, Safety Products Inc., owned by Frank Luck, he had the regional distributorship for Vulcan Fire Alarms. These units were rated number one in the world for residential use, and the "in home" presentations made them easy to sell.

For now, waiting for the trips, which would be necessary to Detroit, I began to assimilate some semblance of a home life once again.

Safety Products Inc., south Evans Avenue, just off I-25, became a haven of sorts. Propelling me into the field of marketing, creative marketing, where a gift of gab, coupled with a top product and showing its importance to a homeowner, meant success. Not only to the company, but to the individual salesperson as well, if they were willing to work. Frank Luck, founder and president, accompanied by his two able young sons, Larry and Jim, have carved a large share of the market for their firm. Frank's wife Lucy, ran the office operation, thus the entire family came to work at the same address.

Here it was, May 1976, Frank had been in business for almost twenty years now, serving the men and women with high quality and good service. His reputation was one of integrity and excellence. Personally he was one of the finest marketing people in the nation. Zig Ziggler, W. Clement Stone, nobody had any more talent in working a client than Frank Luck. Three things he always stressed in his sales meetings: 1) Don't fix it if it ain't broke. 2) We are always smarter than I am. 3) If you promise someone the moon while in their home, be figuring how to assemble the ladder necessary to deliver it on the way back to the office. For either the moon or your moon was going to get delivered, one way or the other. He truly was a man of his word.

Within two weeks I had qualified for my basic pin of performance and began to add Diamonds, hitting the levels necessary for those qualification marks. Money began to come in on a regular basis, it being a full commission type of job. Eight hundred to a thousand a week was very realistic for someone that would dedicate themselves to the established program. My third week I won the top money contest and brought the cashier's check home to Lisa.
"Excuse me, Mrs. Decker, didn't you say something about wanting a new couch for your new living room in your new house?"
"Yes, Mr. Decker, I seem to recall that request coming forth in the recent past. Why do you ask?" She was playing right along with me.
"Because, I just happened to pick up an extra thousand dollars today and thought you might know where to spend it." Holding the check between my thumb and forefinger, I dangled it in front of her. With a cat quick snatch Lisa had taken possession of the morsel in her hand.
"Teach you to tease your wife," Looking down at the check and seeing the typed message, contest winner, she continued. "Well, you are back up to your old tricks, just not giving the other people a chance at the contest money. You always win those contests." She said it with a smart attitude but with a gleam in her eyes.

The past month had been a trying time for the two of us with all the fiasco of what had taken place, from every angle, the rebuilding had been a single brick at a time, at best. There were several major steps, rungs in the ladder of togetherness, that still had to be dealt with. "I gave them a chance, not a big one I must admit! Would you like to take our young son and go get a new couch?" Two hours and thirty minutes later I was carrying the new piece of furniture into the living room.

Nine hundred and thirty-four dollars and seventy-four cents, enough left for the pizza and beer and movie, the thousand dollars had vanished. Money seemed to do that with me on a very regular basis. This money though had brought some happiness and relief, a few hours of family together time, and that was all that was important, for now.

There would be many more contests in the future, I was sure of that, and we could save some then. Yet the "save" word was one that never seemed to register in my brain too often. That Saturday afternoon and evening and all day Sunday allowed us to smile, Christopher was now almost one and a half and he and I romped and played for hours on end.

Monday morning brought with it the phone call that both Lisa and I had been waiting for, now almost one full year had passed. All the turmoil and the unrest and the strife had surely taken its toll. Both of us had aged considerably, the young edges worn with the constant assault of the undercover witness chaos. Hanging up the telephone, I turned to Lisa, a knowing in her eyes already before I had begun to speak.

"Lady, that was the phone call from the U.S. Attorney. Things are to begin tomorrow morning around nine o'clock, in Detroit. My testimony should take about two to three days. I will be home no later than Friday night this is the final chapter. Once I leave Michigan, all that's left is to get paid, finally."

"You mean you will not have to do anything in any other of the trials? Nothing at all?" Lisa was holding her breath for my answer, her heart only able to accept one, no other.

"I mean the federal government can kiss my ass after the Detroit situation is over. I will file my request from the office while in Michigan, and when I come back to Denver it will be my final leg of any trip other than for the three of us. I swear my life and soul on that."

"Oh my God, can it really be finally almost over!"

Tears streaming down her face, the feeling, repressed for so long finally starting to journey out of this precious heart and person. This woman was the most loving and giving and wonderful person I had ever loved. I drew Lisa in my arms and held her for a long, long time. The sound and the feel of tiny arms around my leg broke the embrace, momentarily. Picking up Christopher, I continued to hold my family. Two hours later I was eastbound toward the "Motor City," three more days kept running it's taped message over and over in my brain.

"Welcome to Detroit!" Gorman met me as I stepped from the ramp. He, along with Raftery, Gregory, and all of the other witnesses and agents had accumulated here for the first of the big trials.

"Richard, I actually think you mean that, you are ready to see this damn thing wind itself up as well."

"That is one of the grandest understatements ever spoken. These past few years have been hard for any and all of the people surrounding and a part of this operation. You have been the master link, which has bound this long chain together. In so doing have closed all the escape routes and allowed for an almost air tight case. For that and the suffering your family has been put through, for those facts I both thank you and apologize." It was from his heart and straight to the point, like always.

"I appreciate that Richard, I really do. This next few days, will not possibly go too fast, I guarantee you that. Also, will there be any problem in my getting the money before I leave?" I looked him square in the eye.

"Peter Bensinger, Chief official for the DEA has already requested that you submit your request for payment directly to him for processing.

"That sounds official enough, but does not answer my question. I will have done my part, now it is time for you to do yours." Even more direct this time.

"Michael, as far as I know there will be no problem in you getting what you have coming to you. If you like, I will try and reach Washington when we get to the office. You can then ask the man himself, fair enough?"

"I would appreciate that." One hurdle out of the way, maybe.

This was the first time I had ever been to Detroit, it sprawled for miles and miles across the countryside. Lush green vegetation and trees lined the roadways. The large plants where the cars were made loomed for all eyes to behold along with all the major tire companies.

What Detroit had to offer in the way of sights did not make one bit of difference to me, the trial and its conclusion was my total focus. My one checked bag, from the baggage area was on the back seat of the car. Once in route I had leaned across the seat and pulled it to the front. I spoke to Richard before opening it.

"I want you to know that I will be armed the entire time that I am in Detroit. If something were being planned, it would transpire here. By the way the other car following us was noticed before we got out of the terminal area." Richard just smiled and continued to drive.

Taking my coat off, I slipped the shoulder holster on and snapped the big magnum inside. Six shots of pure thunder and lightning, custom packed, loaded and sent to me special from the Guad man himself. He had put a little extra punch in the powder with some of the new chemicals out on the market. The one time I had test fired the weapon, using these new loads, it kicked like a Missouri mule and blew flames eighteen inches from the end of the barrel. Designed and practiced for one sure shot in the sternum or spine, whichever way they might be coming or going. This game had long since been turned over to the "for keeps" stage.

The Federal Building in Detroit, San Diego, all of them were basically laid out the same. The underground parking lot a standard, downtown footage a premium anywhere, all had to be utilized.

As Gorman and I walked into the office, someone had been put in the wrong office at the wrong time. Talk about somebody jumping out of their skin. Barruetta came flying out of his chair. My presence in the room sent him rushing into the next office, he wanted no part of any common ground.
"Christ, who in the hell left him in here?" Gorman was about to chew some butt for real.
"I guess it was me, sir." The voice came from a new agent who was very recently assigned to the local office. He was about to be fully welcomed into the brotherhood by one of the top men around.

Gorman pointed to the office, and even through the door the smoke was rising and the sparks flying as he completed the new agent's training. For me it was amusing, and broke the tension associated with all the work and preparation, now it was time for the call to Washington. Using one of the phones on the desk I dialed the direct line, all of the numbers had been memorized months before.
"Drug Enforcement Administration, may I help you?" The operator answered in her usual cold style.
"Peter Bensinger, this is SR250010 calling."
"One moment, please." She began to transfer the call.
"Peter Bensinger's office, I am sorry the director is not in at the moment." His assistant answered quickly.
"Please tell him that SR250010 is in the house, and the door will not be opened until I receive a call from him." What I had just done was hang the trial for as long as necessary, until the director had confirmed the payment, part of dealing this final hand.

For the rest of the afternoon nothing took place, no interviews, final preparations, nothing. This was due to no call coming from the main man.
"Richard, I am ready to go on out to my hotel, seems that your boss doesn't want to fulfill his part of this deal. If you guys fuck me now, you won't like the result, no matter what you do to me afterwards."

Gorman shook his head, threw up his arms and said all he could for the moment. "Michael, I really don't know what to say, it is totally out of my hands in Washington. But I give you my word that I will do everything in my power to make all of this come to pass. Please know that and don't stop the trial, it would cause a tidal wave across the entire spectrum of this event and its success. What may be going on in Washington, I have no clue. I am asking you to consider all that has gone on here, and the length of time you have already given to see this thing finish." He was asking, not only as an agent but a friend. If it wouldn't have been for Gorman, and the fact that I had given Lisa my word that I would be home by Friday, I would have walked out the door and told them to forget it.

Instead I took the stand the next morning early and they drilled me nonstop for two solid days. Up one side and down the other, over and over the material, the facts, the events of the past two years were relived. My testimony burned all of the people, and with my flight back to Denver, came all unanimous verdicts, guilty. For me never a call or anything, not even a damn message. The standoff began, and the fight was only at the sparring stage, they had no idea what was next, and neither did I. But it was over, for the most part anyway, finally finished.

"Michael, I want to thank you for your commitment to see this ordeal to its completion. I owe you and your family a deep sincere thanks and gratitude for all of the time you have spent apart. If you don't mind I would like to call Lisa and thank her personally as well."

"Richard Gorman she would truly appreciate that very much. I will be talking to you soon, I promise." Leaving from the airport that afternoon, was leaving another world, maybe it was in fact all over. No more trauma and earth shaking events to live through, peace and maybe a little quiet. Was that even possible for "MY LIFE," time could only be the answer of that fact, only time.

Walking in the door of my house, I got the biggest hug ever received by man or beast. Lisa launched through the air as I passed through the door. She had received the phone call from Gorman along with the news. It had revived some of the old chemistry between us. The weekend that followed was a great one, a remarkable, fantastic one. WHEW!

My first week back at Safety Products, kept me very busy doing all of the presentation appointments, calling back referrals, signing contracts etc. Every spare minute, I was polishing the script of the product presentation, honed and sharp was what I wanted. Studying every piece I could get my hands on, concerning fire and home emergency information. The National Fire Protection Agency had countless manuals and publications, which were the latest in data compilation. All the facts and figures were important to provide the homeowner with the most up to date reports. Also when you, as a marketing representative, knew this in depth information, it availed a much more confidant presentation, which equated into more dollars. Clients purchased from knowledgeable salespeople, proven forever in the home, no matter the product.

At least daily, I was trying to get through to headquarters in Washington. The first week, there was no answer, then second and third, still nothing from the east. By the end of the first month and no type of response from anyone in the main office, I began to put pressure on Gorman, Kissane and anyone else who might answer the phone.
"Agent Gorman, may I help you?"
"Guess who Richard, this shit is getting old, real old, real fast. I need some answers as to what the hell is going on."
"Michael, I have no answers for you other than what I have been told, and that is not much. They say that the budget approval has not taken place, and as soon as it does, you will be paid." "That is nothing but a delay tactic and you know it. Honestly, I want you to level with me. Let's cut through all the bull and give it to me. You have always not beat around the bush, so let's not start now." My patience was almost gone.
"What I have told you is exactly what I have been told, positive about any other crap that might be going on would only be speculation. All of the help you gave was exactly what you had promised, if there is a problem, it's in the upper echelon of Justice, problem with what Kissane promised. The totals were just so much higher than he had anticipated and they may be balking at the numbers. Again, nothing for certain." He was leveling with me, as was normal.
"Okay, I hear you, but why the stiff from Bensinger, why no sort of communication? From here it seems to be that you used me and now that all of the events have concluded it's time to say bye and slam the door. This is exactly what we all went over back a year ago in San Diego, trying to avoid this exact scene."
"I know Michael, and if I could personally change or do something about all the delays, I would. But as you can be well aware, I'm sure. My hands are somewhat tied."

With that, I dropped it and the call was completed. But down inside it was burning a hole in my stomach. To cope with it my drinking had been on the rise. Lisa almost always went to bed before me and I had now gotten into the habit of drinking every night. It was the only way to fully relax, or so it seemed at the time.

June passed, then July and still no action at all from D.C., and then finally in August, a business opportunity came to me. Glenn Von-Dreele, a friend from the old days back at Del Norte High School and University of New Mexico, had moved to Denver. He and his wife Chip, were in the process of moving back to Albuquerque. Frank Luck, my boss was getting ready to expand into the New Mexico market. One thing led to another and "Boom," I cut a deal with Frank to take over the region. Glenn and I went in equal partners, six thousand each, to start a division of the fire alarm business called Vulcan International. The first office was to be in Albuquerque, then expand throughout the state. It was going to be a moneymaker, I was sure of it and couldn't wait to get there and get started. One of Mr. Luck's current managers was going to come down and help in opening the new store. The two of us had been top salespeople, trading back and forth as number one. So it was almost completely worked out and set to go. There was just one thing, my family.

All of the frustration I was feeling with the money situation, was taking its toll on Lisa and me, the wedge had driven farther and farther between us. Our levels of communication had almost totally disappeared entirely. She was beginning to believe that the money had been just some wild exaggeration of mine, and that the past fourteen months had been some crazy notion that I had cooked up. We were at each other's throats on a regular basis. This was countdown day, I had decided.

"Lisa, I am going to go to Albuquerque. This opportunity is one, which can provide a safe and secure level of income for the rest of our lives. If you want to stay here until I get settled and everything rolling, that is up to you. Although, I would like to have you come with me instead. I need to immerse myself into this, and quit thinking about all this shit with D.C. Truthfully I don't know that they are going to ever pay us, me or whatever. I am feeling like they are going to just screw me. Thus all the more reason to get this company working and get some real security for a change, rather than a pipe dream."

"Right now I am not going anywhere Michael. I am so sick of moving, I could spit. Off to California, Albuquerque, California, Denver, and three moves before that. Move is all that we have done since we were married. My moving days are on hold, I am not coming. You do what you need to do and I will do the same." Her temper was evident, and we were very near separation of the legal type.

The next morning I cut the final deal with Frank Luck, got Glenn's share of the deal and headed for the New Mexico State line.

Vulcan International was about to become a reality and I was going to bury myself in it.

What was going on, so to speak, back in Washington, was the same mendacious handling of my case, as with many others. The "rumors," as had been discussed by all of the original members present in San Diego, were nothing more than the direct facts. When Ben Marino, the New Mexico State Police agent, had confronted the men in the know, he and I both heard the same thing, "you won't get screwed." Once again the truth in the matter was that nearly everyone gets used, screwed and tattooed. Of all the hundreds of people that I had come in contact with over this past fifteen months, only two had been honest and backed up what they said. Ben Marino and Richard Gorman, they stood alone in the mire, which oozed from the mouths of politicians and Federal Agencies of many titles.

I had witnessed the payoffs, delivered the money, seen the power that greed could attain and control. From high up in the White House all the way down to the G-5 or G-7 series of employee. Corruption was rampant, evenwhere the corrupt, at times, were so oblivious to the fingers stretched out into their pockets. Forming their webs and nets, that when they began to be retracted for the "favors," it left the official so obligated he could not refuse the most serious request. How else did Sicilia-Falcon get a copy of my service record, case opened and case closed.

The using came from both directions, for too many years now the entire "system" had been run by those who had been dirty for so long they thought they were bullet proof. Watergate proved much of this; Halderman, Liddy, Colson, the list goes on and on. But the list of names is not the problem, it is the fire that goes unchecked, 'tis smoldering ash and soot covering the White House with a color not reminiscent of clean and pure and forthright. Just, the word means and stand for "morally or legally right." How long had it been since the "JUST" had gone out of the Justice Department? Ask and answer that question yourself.

Yes, I had a worthless piece of paper signed by a U.S. Attorney, it stated all the guarantees and promises of a department that kept very few promises. What had taken place within the context of the Centac investigations and resulting arrests was a one hundred percent conviction rate. It was the first time ever that the evidence and the overwhelming magnitude of physical proof had accomplished this feat. From the lowest pusher and street vendor all the way to Alberto Sicilia-Falcon himself, in prison and doing life, mandatory life. This had been a deal between the two countries, from the Capitals of both nations, that full prosecution would take place and the maximum sentence be given.

Santa Maria prison had built a new wing to house Falcon, and many upgrades were included for this particular addition. He was in prison but when you have access to the billions of dollars in cash, things still seem to have a way of equalizing themselves. How else would have Sicilia-Falcon received a copy of the blueprint, showing him the foundation and structural layout. Then hiring a professional engineer to design and facilitate the additional construction of a tunnel. One, in which had to be dug only at certain times of the day.

A house, purchased in a very strategic location to serve as the outer entrance, and one day soon would be an exit. Fresh unobstructed air to breathe, an escape route, with a team of commandos to take him to the awaiting plane where Falcon's private fleet was standing by, the cost, was somewhere between eight hundred thousand and a million dollars, mere change to a man like himself. Only by sheer chance and circumstance, was a phone call intercepted and the escape foiled at the very last stage. Falcon had already left the prison and was near the airstrip when he was apprehended. Again it was luck not anything else, that the police on duty that day were not on his payroll of some sort. Back in prison, Falcon was to finally begin to pay for the transgressions, in a sadistic and harsh way. Electrodes would be attached to his testicles and violent shocks given to try and make him disclose the location of hidden cash and reserves of drugs. These things were stashed in secret caches, throughout his vast domain and ruling area. Years would pass with this type of treatment, yet no inside tip would ever be divulged.

These facts, this information whirled through my brain, making me torn at what had taken place over the past year and a half. Cooperating with the government was the, well one of the, worst mistakes of my life. My course of action would have been much more productive to go and take back what had been stolen from me. Death itself would not have brought near the suffering and agony as this scene with the lies and deceit of the United States Government.

I had now managed to nearly lose the most precious people in my short life, my wife and son. Decisions made in the interest of money, power, and greed had evolved into a darkness, a shroud of cancer, which had eaten into the threads and fibers holding this family together. They were now weakened and very close to dismantling altogether. Alcohol became my true elixir, confidant, friend and companion. Through its false powers, I dove into the New Mexico market and Vulcan International began out in the N.E. section of Albuquerque, on Montgomery Blvd. Not far at all from where I had attended high school at Del Norte.

Dennis Pillar, the field manager from the home office in Denver, had proven to be an asset in the formulation and training of the first sales force to hit the city. With two of us riding and training behind the representatives, production accelerated immediately and with it the cash flow I had been counting on. That first fifteen day performance had generated almost fiftythree hundred in profits. By the end of the first month near thirteen thousand net for what looked like a growing and unstoppable business venture.

"Dennis, this has been one hell of a month, it is Saturday night, so why don't you let me treat you to dinner?" Having just finished balancing the books and seeing the figures I wanted to party.

"Hey, why not, I could sink my teeth into a big fat juicy steak. No problem at all. Where shall we dine?"

"No place other than Montana Mining Company, I seem to know a little about their food and service." Damn, was that ever an understatement.

"Think you might be able to get us a good table?" Laughing as he issued the challenge,

"Possible, just a chance!"

We agreed on seven thirty, meeting at the mine on Wyoming and Menaul, Gary Johnson, from the old Montana Mining Company days was the manager there and would it 'put on the dog' in taking care of us. The colloquialism coming from back when Vanstory, Hough, Johnson and I had been running together, a private tale between the four of us.

Ironically, Dennis' Lincoln pulled up simultaneously with my Blazer so "meeting" was not a problem. He was dressed casually with slacks and a light pullover cardigan, his dark hair and mustache trimmed and neat. Dennis Pillar, like all of the marketing professionals, myself included, liked to flash his success with the car, Rolex, diamonds and gold, so we entered ready to impress. Ego and self image was in no lack here in the least bit.

"Senor Decker, what in the hell are you doing here brother?" Gary grabbed my hand, from the shake came our usual hug and slap on the back.

"Well Gopher, we got hungry and drove all the way down from Denver!" Giving the caesura its full impact I continued. "No, actually Gary, I am in the process of moving back to the city, in fact my new business is up and doing quite well. Tonight is in fact, celebration of the great first month just completed. By the way this is my associate, Dennis Pillar."

"Dennis, nice to meet you and welcome to the Montana Mining Company. Any and everything you need in the way of great food and drinks is yours for the asking. I will also offer you, since you are in such ... good company, VIP specials." He had thrown in the hesitation on purpose, Gary's laugh and chuckle denoting our comradeship.
"Gary, I appreciate that, very much. I guess you and Michael go back a long ways."
"Back a spell, no war stories tonight, PLEASE!"
"All right, let's see a selection of that VIP service!" I grabbed Gary by the neck and pushed him toward the bar.

Seven cocktails, two bottles of wine, two snifters full of B&B, Brandy & Benedictine, two large rib eyes with lobster and the trimmings later we had taken all the VIP we could handle. The fellowship, friendship and the service were all extraordinaire. Gary had his best waitress and waiter laying it on the two of us all night. He was a hell of a guy, and this was a hell of an operation. It brought a sense of pride, as well a singe of longing for the memories of when Lisa and I had been a part of all this. So much water had flowed under the bridge of life since that day, two years ago, when I had left Montana Mining Company, the life stream was in its passing.
"Damn Decker, you just might be the best host I have ever had. I thank God that you did not order any dessert. There is no room anywhere for anything, believe that! I appreciate the hospitality, thank you."
"My pleasure, and now that I have introduced you to Gary, feel free to come again and I assure you that the food and the service will be exactly the same. We built our business on its consistency of quality, the best around. Tonight brought back many fine memories of this firms early development."
"I am thoroughly impressed and they will most definitely see my face again."

Feeling full, relaxed and relieved that the business had started off with such a burst of success, I headed for the apartment, and sleep.
"Hello!" Lisa answered the phone, awakened by the call.
"Hi there! I wanted to call and say I miss you, I do." I did, more than at times I was willing to admit.
"Why are you calling so late?" Not the response I had wanted, her tone was irritated.
"I called now because I just finished dinner with Dennis and wanted to tell you what I just told you and that the first month was a big success. I made thirteen thousand dollars my first month."
"Oh, that is nice you made all that money." Cold as ice, the chill factor was subzero at best.

"Lisa why the attitude? What is bothering you now?" This conversation was going nowhere but down the tubes.
"I am tired of all the shit accompanied with being married to you. There have been too many broken promises and…" I cut this crap off instantly.
"Let me tell you, miss know-it-all. This has not been any cakewalk for me either, least you forget. If you are so fucking tired of all the shit, as you call it, there are several alternatives which can become remedies." Suddenly the chill had reversed directions, she did not like it and I did not enjoy giving it, but my patience was worn out. There was no more available, the last ounce had been severed by the government. A silence followed for several minutes, finally, in the background, I could hear crying.
"I'm sorry Michael, this is so hard for me. Nothing seems to be going right and staying here in Denver probably was not the best idea for any of the three of us. Christopher misses his Daddy, a lot." She didn't say that she missed me but at least it was a start.
"Then put the house on the market and bring yourself and my son back to New Mexico. This is where we started and it can be where we start again. It is possible for us to still make this work, Lisa."

My arms were trying to reach with my heart and words, through the phone lines. Hopefully, she would hear what I was feeling with the stated plea.
"Do you think that this business will really continue to produce? That has been my hesitation in coming, as well, getting rid of the house. You can and have proven the market here in Denver, I just wasn't sure until now about Albuquerque. I will put the house up for sale next week, and begin the preparations of moving back, I promise." Her words, my sigh, both relief's to the thoughts and anticipation I was holding.
"Lisa, you will not regret it, I promise, we can make it here. How about coming down to Albuquerque for Labor Day weekend?"
"I would like to, but first let me see all that will be required for me to get the house on the market."

We agreed on the terms and the possible weekend, at the least a cordial goodbye, nothing romantic but civil. For me it gave a small degree of hope, I went to the liquor cabinet and had a nightcap for that last assurance of sleep. Down in the deep recesses of my brain, a voice asked once again, "are the storms finally over," I did not respond for the answer would have no true validity now.

Sleep finally came far into the night, a restless violent slumber that thrashed about in my dreams. What must this all mean? Later the next day I would reflect on this dream sequence and it would begin to seem like a predestination of events to come. The alcohol was beginning to take a toll at its pay booth, an amount that very soon would be nonpayable. No amount of money could redeem what was about to happen, a picture had been started many years before. With each passing month and eventual year, there was a course of destruction, which this lifestyle has invariably lead toward. No faith, no real truth, no righteousness, the snowball had increased its speed and size. There was no stopping the crescendo from exploding into the destiny my life, so far, had been leading to. The deciding factor had been going to California that first trip rather than wait on Montana Mining Company to recharge their expansion. During that time one of several things could have so easily taken place. A transfer to another national chain of restaurants or stores, with the track record I had, to become a field project manager. Many major corporations were constantly on the lookout, with the aid of a headhunter, to locate people with experience and many years of construction skills. Being young, energetic, strong, talented, all of the qualities they would like to have.

But the greed factor took the presiding lead in controlling any kind of rational thinking on my part. These last two years had only been a down payment on the turmoil and pain which I was about to commence. The countdown had begun. I just didn't know it quite yet!

One thing that was going to take place, I had already decided, was to start looking for a home. A real home, the apartment had long since grown to small and the sooner I had a beautiful home for Lisa and Chris to move down and fill, the quicker that would take place. This was only part of the problem though, my gut feeling said that something else was going on in Denver, I just didn't know what. Sooner or later the truth of the situation would come to the surface. For now, shopping for a nice, large, spacious home could occupy the few blank hours, other than work, for me. Decision made, I began to go through the yellow pages and single out real estate companyies, and watch for ads in the newspaper.

Earlier in the week an ad had caught my eye, to be honest a picture of an agent had pulled my attention to it. A beautiful blonde, working as an independent broker/agent, named Sherry Dunbar, her picture with a short synopsis of her talents and expertise. Seeing the ad had been a stimulus for the thought that had been tossed around for several days now.

Labor Day weekend came and went, Lisa and her escapades with the house were still continuing. Or so she had told me, I really don't know exactly what was keeping her so "busy." I had made the business my confidant, lover, friend and soul mate, resulting in some very long days and weeks. One hundred hours was a short week, my longest during the month of September was one hundred thirty-seven, it had become an obsession for me. The money was flowing in vast quantities. A new federal law requiring all homes to have a smoke detector was a lead in for every homeowner to have a full fire protection system.

We had fifteen full-time employees and ten part-time, Vulcan International was making its mark in the Albuquerque marketplace. Dennis Pillar had decided to stay and work with me for an additional sixty days. He did not want to leave the good money.

By the end of September I had put a down payment on a beautiful custom home and moved from the apartment. It was nice to leave the office and drive home to the large ranchstyle home and its 3,470 square feet of living space. I would light a fire in the massive flagstone fireplace, sitting there in front with my cocktail and dream of the future.

Sherry Dunbar, the real estate agent who had found me the house, was very attentive to every single upgrade or change I had asked for. In addition she would stop by the office and check to see how the work was coming, also to say hello. We had had lunch a few times and been to dinner once. Her company was appreciated and it was nice to have someone to talk with, in a nonbusiness setting. September 30, 1976 all of that began to change. This was the day she had suggested that I come by and have a home cooked meal, she insisted. I saw no harm in the invitation. I didn't want to see any other insinuation, yet inside I knew damn well what the invitation included, but I went anyway. If Lisa was going to hang around Denver, I did not have to be a hermit!

Leaving work early that Thursday night, a mere thirteenhour day, from five in the morning until six this evening, I went home to shower and to get ready. The long hot shower soothing to my body, had a real invigorating effect. Coupled with an extra close shave, some Eternity cologne, and I was ready for some nice threads to finish the production.

Choosing a pair of dark gray wool weave slacks, a soft brushed cotton shirt, long sleeve and a beautiful teal colored v-neck sweater, I had all but the feet covered. Here I chose my black Alligator Tony Lama boots, now the package was packed, wrapped and ready to deliver.

Clear and crisp was the night air, Albuquerque sitting at the base of the Rocky Mountains at 5,000 feet in altitude, the evenings by late September, brought with them a hint of winter. I had stopped on the way home and bought a small table arrangement of flowers and two nice bottles of Cabernet. As I pulled into Sherry's driveway I smiled, a home cooked meal after two months of restaurants sounded great.

The large brick home had been meticulously landscaped and groomed to Sherry's exact specifications and it was gorgeous. A carved set of doors with stained glass door light made for an impressive entry way. Knocking, as I hated doorbells, rapidly got a response from within the home.

"Good evening Ms. Dunbar, I do believe that these are for you." Handing her the flowers as I stepped in the door. The aroma of some type of marinade drifting through the air, it was very gourmet.

"Thank you, Sir, and welcome to my humble abode."

All of the inside, was even more perfect than the outside. Deep leather furniture, with all the Southwest style accents made for a warm and festive atmosphere. Her indian print dress cut perfectly to fit her petite figure, the turquoise jewelry gave Sherry an allure of mystery. She had stood on her tiptoes and given me a welcome peck on the cheek.

"Whatever you have cooking in that kitchen has me hungry already. It really smells marvelous!"

"Thank you, Michael, it is one of my favorites. I make a special herb and butter marinade and glazed the Cornish Game Hens which have been stuffed with a garlic, onion and spiced breadcrumb dressing." Her voice was soft, soothing and had the articulate quality of someone who had made their living making people understand exactly what they were buying. Her small hands talking with her mouth, the refined elegance of her short blonde hair and green eyes showing a warmth and beauty all their own. A subtle sensuality swirled in the aura that came with her movements.

"I brought some nice wine, would you like to have a glass or do you prefer a cocktail?"

"The wine would be fine, Michael, how about you?" Her eyes were bright and enthusiastic.

"That will be two, then. Where might I find an opener and two glasses?" Watching her walk away from me as she turned for the kitchen, I continued to observe the immaculate way that every room was decorated and kept so clean and orderly. Just what I liked, I was willing to bet that the entire house was exactly the same.

After the wine was opened and poured I handed her a glass and proposed a toast to the two of us. Given as we clinked the glasses together. "To you, dear lady, for the beautiful home you have found for me. To the meal you have fixed and the warmth that surrounds us. May this evening be special with its own chosen flair. And to your beauty and class of which both are so rare." With each word I saw her mood warm to the occasion, the conclusion brought with it an embrace.

"Michael, I do declare you make a woman's heart flutter so!" Her petite body, her arms extended around my waist, she pulled me close to thank me for the compliment.

"I will have to remember that fact!" Smiling with a broad grin.

"Huh, you know exactly what I mean and you certainly don't have to remember anything. I think all of this comes very natural for you." Sherry's words carried with them a teasing hint.

"Well, goodness! I declare there is a little fire down there in this pretty, petite body." Her five foot two and one hundred pound form so small next to me, but nice.

With that we laughed and carried on with the evening, having several glasses of wine before, during and after the scrumptious meal. Both bottles were empty and a nice snifter of Martell Brandy was to complete the setting. We had now moved to the living room and the large sofa. It was positioned in front of the fireplace and the fire, two large logs just added, crackled a tune and its warmth filled the air. I had taken a place near the right side of the large leather couch, the armrest supporting to my side and the fullness comfortable in the deep cushions. With a choice of two other matching chairs or the sofa next to me, Sherry took the last one for her nesting place. Her perfume was arousing as she walked past to sit, not at the far end but right next to me. My right arm rested on the back, upper portion and she snuggled close with a small shiver.

"Goodness, I got a chill suddenly." Looking up into my eyes with a face that shouldn't have looked so inviting. Instinctively I dropped my arm around her and pulled her even closer.

"Here, is that a little better?" Feeling her close, a warmth and certainly no chill.

"That is yummy!" She squirmed to be even closer.

Allowing the fire and the food and the brandy to settle in, we kept that position for a long time, too long for my troubled spirit. The safe time to exit was shortly after dinner. Her fragrance, soft warmth and her hand as it stroked my leg and thigh, had already gone on to the point of no return. My hands had not been still for some time now, caressing tenderly the arms, neck and face, they were ready for more, a lot more.

"Michael, you feel so good next to me. I want you even closer." Sherry turned toward me with her face, head tilted slightly back. I lowered my lips and savored her mouth in a passionate, moist kiss, my tongue probing deep and pulling the response I knew to be there. Lifting her with my strong arms, her hands clasping tightly around my upper arms as I lowered her to sit on my lap. Something, someone had put new fuel in the fire, it was now roaring and would not stop for many hours to come. In a reflection of days gone by at times in its intensity, then roaring back for another heated exchange until finally casting its occupants to eventual slumber in one another's arms. The ceremonial blanket that covered us, holding our spirits close. For I knew not the reason, but only the demise of the act itself, now there was no denying what had taken place or the resulting effect on my life, my marriage, my future. This was a destiny of events of which every move was a part, another cog of the gear, which was turning and causing the wheel to turn.

Early the next morning after some very rapid goodbyes, I left and retreated to my home and then to the office. Hoping that the busy work day would block the vision that I saw coming into view. A picture of a planned future falling in the black void of nothingness and wasted by the deceit and infidelity, which had so plagued my life. Whatever it was going to take to resurrect my life from the pits of hell I had placed it in, I welcomed. I thought.

"Dennis, I want to really push all of our people today and tomorrow. It being the first two days of the month I want October to be near thirty percent ahead of last month." Opening the day with a bang was my idea of selling.

"I think that those kinds of totals are within our grasp, maybe more if your big group deal flies tomorrow!" Dennis had many years of deep selling experience to rely on.

He was referring to a large project that I had put together, a group portfolio and presentation prospectus. It was for a new development up north of town called Cochita Lake. It was a retirement community, with all the perks that many of the active lifestyle senior citizens could enjoy. My system, which had been designed and built by U.S. Safety Engineering Corporation, was easily retrofitted and installed in an existing structure. It carried with it a lifetime warranty and its gold anodized finish was also very attractive.

I had put many hours into this possible sale and was competing with another national corporation, Vanguard. A much lower quality product, but very close in price, their bid was some eight thousand dollars less than mine. Yet, for these residents, I felt that the quality and designed high performance would not make the price the deciding factor. As well, my presentation had been on, I mean really on, fired up and believing in my product I had made them feel a fire and experience the safety and security from the Vulcan system.

"Judy Smith, this is Michael, do you have any messages for Lifeline International?" She was one of the answering services operators.

"Yes, two, sir. One from Jeremy Blackstone, it says that he would like to have someone at his home around 11:00 this morning. The second is from Cochita Lake, they asked for you to please call. That is all ,sir."

Dajevu, wouldn't you just know it, my heart pounded with the report. Quickly taking the portfolio from my briefcase, I turned to the number and began to dial.

"Cochita Lake, may I help you?" The operator said cheerily.

"Yes, please connect me to Paul Stevens, Lifeline International Calling." We had changed the name of the company the previous week, U.S. Safety did not want the Vulcan trademark used for any company name, which was no problem at all for us. With the new name had come a motto, "Protecting the Irreplaceable," everyone seemed to love it.

"Paul Stevens here, how may I help you Michael!" Mr. Stevens had a robust voice, today it carried a jovial note to it. He was the president of the Homeowners Association.

"Mr. Stevens, I am returning your call sir. How may I be of service to you?," anticipation flooded through my heart as I awaited his answer. This sale was for fifty-six systems, and the entire development of some two hundred fifty by its completion next year. This first segment would give me a fifteen thousand dollar profit margin. With another seventy-five thousand dollars income over the next year, together a $90,000.00 deal. Not bad for being in business less than two months.

"You may be of service by getting yourself up here and picking up our down payment check of thirty thousand dollars, and signing this contract while you are here. Congratulations!" WOW!

"Yes sir, I will be there within the hour, thank you very much." I had hit the first big one of my new company. It was a home run by any standards, in any bodies book.

"Pillar, get your butt in here!" I thundered his name.

"Christ! What the hell is going on?"

"I just got off the phone with Cochita Lake, they bought the whole deal!" His face was lighting up with the same excitement that I was feeling.

"Whew! That is absolutely awesome, amazing, whatever!"

"While I am up there finalizing the deal and picking up the check, call everyone in for an early sales meeting and let them know that we are going out for a company celebration tonight. Wives, girlfriends, husbands, boyfriends, whatever the case may be. Then call Gary and have him set a room up for us at Montana Mining."

With those instructions laid out I gathered all of the necessary documents and briefcase and headed for the Cochita Lake exit on the highway to Santa Fe. Tonight was going to be a blowout celebration.

The meeting with Mr. Stevens had gone exceptionally well, he told me about all the good things he had heard about the product. Also the parent firm of Safety Products up in Denver, and their twenty years in business had been a deciding source. Most of all the homeowners had bought the professional display and presentation. He emphasized that it was me and the service that they felt I would give, this was the final factor in making their choice. I was happy, and proud with a thirty thousand dollar check in my hand to prove it. Look out, Montana Mining Company, here comes Lifeline International to PARTY!

By the time the afternoon session and the early evening appointments had been completed, another seven contracts had been signed. It was a day to remember, for sure one I would never forget, October 1, 1976. We would bring in October 2, 1976 with a Bang! A big BANG at that!

Couples and some singles as well began drifting into the restaurant by 7:00 p.m., dinner was to be served at 8:00. I had already had two talls before leaving the house, a little priming of the pump.
"Dennis Pillar, we are knocking them dead in Albuquerque, my friend."
"It is truly incredible the way this thing has kicked off," he added, knowing all too well the work that goes into opening a new location.
"Tonight is a well deserved celebration, here's to our continued success." We toasted and enjoyed the moment at hand.

All but one of my employees had joined the group by 7:30, so it was time for the fireup round. Whatever their pleasure, it was a double pour for this round, with many to follow. This pattern of toasts and rounds continued through the happy hour, dinner and on into the after dinner, back in the lounge. By the finish of the dinner section, two thirds of the people and their respective dates had left the party. The buzz they were feeling had begun to hint on a roar. For Dennis and me, we were matching one for one and the count was growing at an alarming rate.
"Well Gary, you have once again done yourself and the Mine a fine service. I fully appreciate your great service and friendship, Bubba, I really do!" He had joined Dennis and me, for now all of our employ-

ees had long since gone from the scene. All of the people in the lounge were either employees or last minute customers, for now the clock had struck 1:30 a.m.

"Senor Miguel, I enjoy seeing you and tonight was no exception. Your money is always welcome here. The staff always enjoys serving you and your guests." He was forever the benevolent host.

"I think that I will have one more drink, and with me I would like to buy one for the house, the entire house." Hell, everyone might as well get tanked with me. There were four girls at a table next to the one where Dennis and I sat and they seemed to be feeling no pain as well. The waitress began to take everyone's order.

"I think I overheard your name is Michael, right?" A tall striking brunette leaned on the table and asked.

"Well, yes, you are absolutely correct and this is my friend Dennis," Pointing across the table where he sat.

"I just wanted to say thank you for the cocktails, hope you don't mind if we got Long Island Ice Tea?" Shrugging her shoulders with her words.

"Not at all, anything you might want, I am here to provide." My words were starting to run together, I would hold one eye closed and it would help, I was sure. Somewhere near one quart of alcohol had passed through this body and I was about to have my favorite, a Banzai Kami. A Long Island has four to five ounces of alcohol, a Banzai Kami has eight, where it gets its name is from the effect it has on the system. Never sipped but rather slammed down in one gulp.

A toast was given and not only me, but the entire staff and all of the patrons had decided on shots and each and everyone was finished by the end of the toast. Now it was reaching the magic hour of 2:00a.m., closing time controlled by a State Law.

"Michael," Dennis asked, "These ladies would like to know if we would like to take them for a ride. Seems it is Carol's twenty-first birthday and she had her heart set on going fourwheeling."

"I just happen to have a golden chariot parked right out in the parking lot. Ladies, it awaits your presence." I had about as much business driving as I had trying to pilot a rocket ship. But right now I would be willing to try anything. Thus Dennis and I, with the four girls in tow, headed for my Blazer. Three in the back and one on Dennis' lap and we were ready to motor.

"Where to ladies? Do you have a destination in mind?"

"There is supposed to be a party going on somewhere out in the foothills, let's try and find it." One from the back seat answered, other than the birthday girl, we knew absolutely none of their names.

"To the foothills it is, hold on tight."

CHAPTER 6

one night, one event, my life changed forever,
october 2, 1976

The big motor fired and we roared off towards the mountains. All the way out Wyoming Blvd. then cut up around the Albuquerque Academy. There were a bunch of big dams, which were fun to climb and it was on the way to the foothills. Up and down the dams, we went, when we arrived there, all of us were screaming and having a wild time. The final shots of booze were in full force and its effects were obvious. Coming up over the top of one of the dams, we saw a huge bonfire, and it was encircled by cars and people. It looked to be a party in the works.

"Hey, it's a party; let's go check it out," came the call from the back seat. Closing in on three o'clock in the morning, it had been a long day, now in fact it was October 2, 1976.

Pulling up to the location, it looked to be some twenty people, all Chicano, aged eighteen to twenty-five, couple of beer kegs and everyone seemed to be well lit. The smell of marijuana was evident, and drifting through my lowered window. If my vision had not been so blurred from all the drinks, I would have noticed several other things about this group.

A certain strange stillness was in the air, there was no wind, no sounds other than those which were man made. If the video recorder had been observing the past three hours, it would have noticed the kilo of cocaine being used in every form known to man. Also on print would be the used syringes and the needle marks on their prospective users along with the dilated pupils and the wild behavior from the empty Tequila and Whiskey fifths. Blood from the ceremonies of brotherhood, mixed and flowing within the groups veins and arteries. A common tattoo, worn for pride, for warnings to all that dared to counter their moves or wishes, this was no regular gathering. Weapons, knives, bats and chains ready to take a life or at least threaten it. The alcohol and drug use for me had not allowed for the actual count, seventeen men, not one solitary woman, until now.

The music was blaring as our group left the safety and confines of the Blazer. Flames flickered a dancing orange and red light, amplified the shadows and caused faces to change and images to appear. Thirty-four eyes, seventeen pairs engulfed the strangers who had broken their boundaries and challenged their turf. Only six people of the now twenty-three had any intention of fun, and this to, was about to change in a bolt of action and pain.

"Hey Dudes, what's happening." The tall brunette that had first come up to the table, at Montana, blurted out.

"Yeah, how's about something to drink?" chided in her friend at her side.

My inner voice, trained and honed with years of handling death, began to thunder a warning. Adrenalin pumping its effect to my heart and body, breath's were coming deep and full. I knew that this was a bad idea, to have stopped here. Even with the level of alcohol, my subconscious screamed out the words, "BE GONE FROM HERE!" With that came the scream of reality, one born in fear and primal escape.

"Nooooooooooo! Stop!" The birthday girl, was crying for her life. Five of the group had grabbed her from three sides and her blouse was already torn to shreds. Her hair in the hands of one of the attackers, she was thrown to the ground. Nine others formed a semicircle toward me to prevent any help from coming to the victim, the challenge sent memories of pain and death, Vietnam, and Glen Hancock all at the same time.

"YOU WILL DIE FOR THIS YOU BASTARDS!" A roar from my mouth was followed by a sound which had cultivated in my soul for twenty years. With it came the response I had waited for, to repay all the pain from the years of torture I had experienced as a child, this was my ultimate chance for revenge with no limits and death to the loser.

My hands went to my collar and shredded the clothing covering the upper torso. The back kick exploded from my left foot and sent the bones deep into the jaw of the first adversary, blood and teeth in a plume as he struck the ground. Twisting to the right, a high hand block shunted the ball bat away, a wrist lock and thrust from the shoulder snapped the arm and forced the elbow in a reverse ninety degrees. Grabbing the bat from the ground, two more went to the dirt quickly. Screams and cries from the other three girls in agony for their friend, they were fear gripped at their inability to help. Dennis was nowhere around, he had fled to the safety of the dark.

Two more of the gang running towards me screaming and totally wild with aggression, slobber coming from their jaws as they vented their fury. The body weight carrying forward with their run suddenly halted by the thrusting foot of a sidekick, full force to the sternum, taking the breath and very nearly the life from the first of the two. While the second lunged through the air and the hammer fist to the back of the skull sinking his face in the ground, the bat crushing ribs as it slammed full swing like an axe into the side of the victim.

I had now assessed that this was going for the count and it was time to even the numbers. The blood hyper pumping through my veins had somehow focused the polluted cells of my brain long enough to tell me to grab the weapon from under the seat of the Blazer. Attacking with a renewed burst I disabled one more attacker quickly, his leg turned right at the knee, not front or back but sideways as my foot drove deep, taking ball from socket and exploding the joint at the knee.

Launching myself to the Blazer, I grabbed the door and flinging it open, felt the cold steel of the .357 magnum come into my palm. Now the war was about to begin. They wanted to fight, fine let's fight.
"WHOOM! WHOOM! Now you motherfuckers had better get the hell out of here or you will all be dead." I was ready to kill every son-of-a-bitch here, NOW!

Thunder continued to roar wave after wave as the echoes of the explosion shattered the night. Flames shot three feet from the end of the weapon. From my hand it pointed death, certain death to the next movement. Silence, frozen in time, expressions of surprise and the sudden turn of events. Groans and cries of pain were muffled by the command, all save one.

A snap from just behind me, I whirled to my left, taking the pistol in a force capable of crushing a skull when it made contact. Whoosh! It just grazed the scalp of the stalking leader of the gang, a flash of chromed steel, glinted in the light of the fire as it drove deep into my left side. Grazing the kidney and severing the veins, five inches it thrust inside my body.
"Ayyyyyyyyyyy!" The scream broke the night once again. I whirled back to my right and carved a deep furrow into the face of my attacker, his fast hand danced once more and stabbed through the tissue and flesh severing the artery on my right. Pain and numbness, both shot through my body, and the animal that had been fueled within me, fully came to life. A rage, one nurtured for years, blinded all senses, there was no pain, only the man and the men before me. Blood spurting from my wounds, began to coat the ground, with it came a voice from within, from the grim reaper himself.
"This fucking night is over, NOW, it is over, the next movement will serve with it death, invited." WHOOM! My last warning shot, my

eyes the same color as my blood, red from the animal rage.
"Fuck you, gringo, I ain't scared of your blanks." His hand began to raise and point toward me, it was the one than had drawn my blood.

WHOOM! His head exploded from the force of the big magnum load, the projectile tearing through the front of his face between his eyes. The complete back of his skull exploded with a spray of life, coating everyone behind him with the dying words still coming from his mouth. He would never say another word, and they would never harm another person.

"Shit, let the girl go before more of us are killed!" The cry of anguish came and the group broke. Huddled together in a daze, their numbers now greatly reduced and their morale broken, the fight gone from their will and heart, the gang members wanted nothing else of the demon before them.

Quickly the other girls rushed to their friends' aid, only partially clothed, thankfully not raped, they took her into the Blazer and from the other side of the vehicle I heard Dennis.

"Michael get into the car, we have to get out of here." He ran around the front and helped me inside, slammed the door and rushed to drive us away from the scene of death and dismay.

"Oh God, Dennis, the blood is spraying back here. Michael is going to bleed to death." Where the artery had been severed, the blood was spurting over the seat as I leaned forward, landing on the girls in the back seat. With only partial consciousness I knew what to do and I put my finger in the hole, greatly stopping the bleeding. Meanwhile the Blazer was flying over the terrain on its way back to civilization.

"Dennis, you have to get us back to the restaurant to get our car. We can't be involved in this or we will get expelled from the University." This was their only concern it was very evident.

"Christ, Sherry, this guy took us where we wanted to go and risked his life to protect Carol. Got stabbed and is bleeding to death and you are worrying about fucking school." Well one of them cared anyway.

Dennis meanwhile was making a fast track to exactly that, their car. He dropped them off and then proceeded to drive, I thought to the hospital, but no, somewhere else, my house. During this time period I was drifting in and out of consciousness, the inside of the Blazer looked as if a cow had been slaughtered from all the blood. A whirling, different from when I was wounded in Vietnam, spun in many directions as the blood drained and flooded from my body.

"Come on, Michael, I am going to get you inside!" I thought that we had finally made it to the hospital, but the inside was so dark, so familiar. He laid me down on the floor next to the coffee table.

"I am going to get help Michael, I will be right back." With that Dennis walked out and drove himself back to his car and left me to die, what a friend.

The length of time I lay there, I do not know, but the pool of blood was enormous. Finally, through some unknown force, I raised my head, reached for the coffee table and something fell to the floor beside me. It was the phone. I had left it there as I left for the evening. A guardian angel hovered over me, my hand hit the on and the "0" button, I know not how or why.

"Operator, may I help you?" The voice brought a response from my lips.

"I am dying!"

"Excuse me, what did you say?" The voice had gone higher.

"Dying, I …bleeding …shot …Help …call Richard."

"Sir, I am going to call for help. Do not hang up."

"No ... call ... Richard...714-556-1239." From somewhere in my subconscious this came and for a reason still not known the operator dialed it and not the ambulance, thank God.

"Michael, this is Richard Gorman. What has happened?"

Rambling I told parts and pieces, then lost consciousness, a bright light began to flash on and off in my brain.

Many things happened after I lost consciousness that early morning of October 2, 1976. Things that I tell now, first of course I didn't die, but very close. I had lost over three pints of blood by the time I was rushed to the hospital in an ambulance.

Richard Gorman had saved my life, or maybe I should say he was a lifesaver. By making all the necessary emergency calls to police, medic and the hospital. I did not remember saying any of the following, but here is what Gorman relayed to me in the hospital, two days later. Yes, he cared enough to fly out to New Mexico and give me whatever help he could.

"Michael, don't try to talk, I will stay on the line and help will be there soon." He was calling on the cellular as I talked on the regular line.

"No have to …tell …you that Falcon …may have …been in on what happened …stabbed me …shot and …he's dea….I …killed."

"Michael it doesn't matter, later all of the facts will be known, please just keep your breath and your energy by being quiet."

BOOM!BOOM! and the front door came off the hinges and flew across the room.

Voices in the room talking, "Hello, hello, who is here?"

"This is Senior Agent Richard Gorman, to whom am I speaking?"

"Mr. Gorman this is Tom Percy, I am a medic and this individual is in bad shape. He has lost a tremendous amount of blood and needs to be emergency evacuated to the hospital. I have police backup and an investigation team on their way. I heard their radio messages on the way here. I will leave the phone line open if you like, but we must move this man immediately."

"I roger that Mr. Percy, the gentleman's name is Michael, and do not put any further information on the data card at the hospital until I personally call. That is a directive from the Department of Justice in Washington, D.C. Do you understand?" His command left no doubt for a no!

"Yes, sir, Mr. Gorman, sir, I fully understand and will make sure that it is carried out fully."

The medics moved me into the ambulance and off to the hospital I went. All of the normal police procedures continued for near some fourteen hours. Plus many people became involved assuring of a safe environment, for a few days until the government pulled the second of their disappearing acts.

Gorman flew in the next day, and was en route to the hospital when I came back to consciousness to find a Bernilillo County Sheriff's Deputy standing in my room.

"Why the hell are you here?" Yelling indignantly, the answer came promptly.

"I am here because you are under arrest for MURDER."

The words blew me back, almost to unconsciousness, I must have not heard what I thought he had said, correctly.

"What did you say? Murder, I am charged with murder. How in the hell do you get murder out of defending my life and the girls?" Even through the discomfort of the wounds I was beginning to come off the bed. Suddenly noticing that my left hand was cuffed to the bed.

"Take this fucking thing off before I tear it off!" The rage began to pour from my mouth.

"You had better just be still because your little smart ass is not going anywhere." The smug grin ground into my anger and amplified what I was feeling.

"You sorry son-of-a-bitch!" Wham! The water pitcher barely missed his face and crashed against the wall. Grabbing his radio he quickly exited the room as he called for assistance. What took place next was that they just left me there to boil out the steam. My display of anger had started the bleeding again, red blotches of blood began to soil the sheets.

For the next hour, then two, I tried to let the anger go away but it kept rising in my throat. So violently that it literally made me cough and gag.

Richard Gorman had meanwhile worked out a special arrangement with the Judge for a $100,000.00 bond. Signing for it with the guarantee of the Justice Department for the ten percent necessary in cash, it would be wired directly to the courts. He came to get me and gave me this and the rest of the news.

"Michael, you are to be released on bond within the hour. When you are you will no longer be on the program. SR250010/WC1225 will be deactivated and as far as the government is concerned you have been paid in full. It is a really crappy thing that they are doing but I have no control over D.C. and the main justice people at all. Basically they took you and all the help and sacrifice that you gave and screwed you in the end. From what I have been told and I have been searching this thing for now almost two weeks, an attorney could never touch justice in the least. Not even though you have all the documents signed by the U.S. Attorney. It is sad and I feel like a heel, but it is even worse because they have made me tell you. They did not even have enough balls to say it themselves."

I could never have suspected that the news I was about to get from Richard could make the situation I was in worse, but it had, immensely. "Richard, I can't believe you are saying this. It just can't be true. Not after all the things I have done for the government. Christ, I risked my life for those guys, ruined my marriage, gave up everything I had for this." Shaking my head in disbelief, I turned to the window.

"Michael, that isn't all." My heart sunk to the floor, I couldn't take any more of this kind of news, not now. "The guy that you killed last night, his name was Albert Montoya and he is related to U.S. Senator Joseph Montoya. Montoya has many friends in high places and he will try and bang it to you to try and make the murder charge stick. I have already talked to several of our people here and they say that Montoya is connected heavily with all sorts of city, county and state officials. Senator Montoya has been reputed to be involved in all types of illegal activities. For example the Don Bowles murder out in Arizona, he was a reporter and doing a story on a land deal that Montoya was tied to. It does not look good from any angle at all. I know these past forty-eight hours have been intense, to say the least, but you have got to keep it together. Do not, and I repeat, do not do anything stupid like you almost did with the water pitcher. These guys will revoke the bond and you will sit your rear in jail till the trial. That could be months and even years away from now."

Damn, I should have just let them kill me last night, what do I have to live for now? I never dreamed of all the other things that could and did take place over the next few weeks. Stories in the papers, newscasts on television, Montoya was flooding the city and state with garbage. Lies of how I drove up and shot this guy and drove off. I just must have been stabbed in a later incident, not at the time of the murder, murder my ass. No report, no interview ever with any of the four girls, Dennis Piller or anyone remotely connected with me.

Finally the coup de grace, leaks as to what I had done with the government and in the military. It destroyed me and my business as well, very quickly. I began to hit the bottle in magnitudes that should have finished off my body. Lisa and Christopher had finally moved back to town, we had seen each other a few times and there was little remaining between us, I thought in my blurred brain.

The lawyer I had hired gave me a trivial chance at best with the case so after three months of chaos, and some soul searching from outer space, I made a decision. From a newspaper article that I had read, it had told of the law that if a person had both a Federal and a State charge, the Federal charge took precedence. In other words one would have to do the Federal time first and be in their custody.

I was going to have to serve my time in the Santa Fe Penitentiary, a prison predominantly Chicano and where several of the "IN" people worked that were in close association with Montoya. Thus whatever sentence I received, would be a death sentence, once I reached the walls of the prison.

Driving to pick up my little boy Christopher that morning, January 4, 1977, I had a feeling of emptiness, and pain, almost of death. The previous month had seen the completion of my marriage to Lisa, a possible pending civil suit, for "wrongful death," made the immediacy of a divorce very necessary. To leave what little remained with Lisa and Christopher, all I had. After picking up my son we drove around a little before I went to drop him back off at home. It was my last moments with my son for a long, long time. Walking him to the front door, I knelt down and held his little face in my scarred hands. Tears streamed down my face, as I said my last goodbye, a wrenching of pain beyond words coursed through every cell of my body.
"Christopher, I love you more than anything or anybody on this earth. And I am about to have to leave for a long time. I want you to know that I am not leaving because of you, but for something I have done. Your mommy and I love you and she will keep you safe while I am away. I will miss you more than I want to live, but I have to go." I was dying inside, his eyes burned holes in my heart, his lips quivered a little and then he gave me something I will forever treasure, his love and

his heart. Christopher put his left hand on my face and his right on my shoulder and said, "I do wuff you too, Daddy and it will be okay!"

As the door closed behind him I turned away and went to the Blazer, my heart pounded, and my eyes were stinging from the tears. How could he have known what I needed to hear. Only God knows for sure.

I drove to the First National Bank, Heights Branch, pulled around to the side. It had snowed almost ten inches and the lot was almost vacant, of course the Blazer plowed right through the drifts. Leaving the motor running I walked to the front of the bank building. Snow whipped across the skin of my face, yet the cold could not be felt, the numbness had already taken over before I had even left the vehicle. I had a note asking for money in the front pocket of the jacket I was wearing.

Doorpull gripped in my hand, I pulled the large glass door open, the crisp wind announcing my arrival, its chill still walking with me, as the legs and feet carried this body to the teller's booth. The note was pushed between the thumb and forefinger and drifted through the air to its final resting place on the marble counter in a silent declaration. The teller's lips were moving but no sound reaching my ears as she greets me before reading the note.

Eyes wide with fear, breath suddenly held deep, hands trembling as they fumble the money into a bag, shaking so intense that her coworker turns. Instantly knowing far too well what is taking place, she ducks from view, activity in the back of the scene is blurred. My hand feels canvas and string as this body turns, looks straight at the camera and departs with the wind at its back. A Blazer drives away from the bank, snow leaving a trail for the followers to trace and to find. It is over, I am going away for a long, long, long, time, finally it is over.

A few hours later I am in the federal building, a holding cell, the FBI have the money and a plane is on the way to Albuquerque, New Mexico. Coming to pick up two U.S. Marshalls who have been ordered and instructed to bring me to Washington, D.C.

Once there, I was escorted through the underground, secret tunnel to the U.S. Senate, Special Investigations Division, subcommittee hearing on the relationship between organized crime and the government. Sen. Chiles, Sen. Jackson, Sen. Ervin, Sen. Nunn, Keith Adkinson, and many others too numerous to mention. These men wanted to know it all, from the early days in Vietnam, through the mercenary years with Falcon, and beyond.

They were promising to help me and do all those magical things that the government and politicians so earnestly speak and rarely do. "Your worries will be over in New Mexico if you agree to help us and bring us up to date on your knowledge of all this covert activity." Sen.

Jackson so stoically stated with his down home charm and manners.
"You will of course put that in writing, will you not Senator?" I said in a very caustic manner, knowing all to well of the "guarantees" and their true worth.
"Yes, we certainly will and I give you my personal word on that fact. It will be put in writing!" Senator Nunn spoke up with an eminent frown.

Consequently, once the bickering and the paddles were laid down, I began once again to lay my heart, life and soul to its barest existence. Allowing these leaders of our country to hear, first hand, just how dreadful the situation and the circumstances were. Whose hands were in the cookie jar of takes and bribes, how high up the ladder they needed to look. They were amazed at the level of infiltration organized crime had been able to achieve.

"If you count all aspects of "gifts" and people directly on Falcons payroll, bribes to selected officials, totals in the millions are very easily noted." Mouths agape, brows being rubbed and grimaces of inner pain and disbelief. Continuing with more," You gentlemen sit here in your leather chairs and fly all over the damn world to provide as many countries as possible with what you call aid. If you spent one year's "wasted funds" on fighting corruption and stopping the pipeline into this country from Mexico, Central and South America, rather than on some countries with names you couldn't spell, this problem would be over. Instead you do your damn spending frenzy of your individual selves, running into the hundreds of thousands of dollars. United States taxpayers shell out countless billions of dollars for your approval and allocations. If most of them could have an accounting of what is shit down the governmental toilet each day, most of you would not be elected next term. As a collective group you find desperate people like myself to stick their necks out for a "possible" ounce of help. Speaking of help I am going to relate one more scenario to this group and then you can all go to hell as far as I am concerned. I don't think I shall be so graphic as to tell you what you can do with your promised help and written guarantees, just sit on that one."

Shocked by my bluntness, they turned to one another and several comments were made with hands over their respective microphones. This had already been going on for three days and I was sick and tired of all of it.

Aside from the murmuring going on, was a show of support from both the stenographer and an aid, they were giving me looks of, "Tell the bastards what is really going on, give it to them," and this Bubba was about to unload some baggage. Let these bureaucrats chew on the next five minutes of story telling, I was ready for the final phase, no holds barred for this one.

"Roughly two years ago, a man by the name of James Morgan contacted Sicilia-Falcon and Carlos Kyrikedas about a proposal to build an arms manufacturing facility somewhere down in the Mexico, Central American direction. It was to provide ample arms for the use in drug trades, money and capital accumulation, and also to retrofit the militia unit that I had personally trained for Falcon. Falcon's Mexican partner, Gaston Santos, the son of the former General of the Army of Mexico, had major contacts throughout the entire region and felt that he could sell this weapon by the thousands.

The Morgan Assault Rifle was a 9mm clip fed automatic weapon with the firepower exceeding the AK-47, additionally outfitted with a balanced Gyro grenade launcher. It is capable of firing an RPG (Rifle Propelled Grenade) 1000 yards with zero degrees deflection, with an explosion capacity of a 105 howitzer, at detonation.

The setting was a small motel room down on the east side of Tijuana, present were all of the key players just mentioned, along with Morgan, two accomplices and myself. A very touchy meeting, because not one of the people present trusted the other in the least way. Guns were at their ever lovin' ready.

Morgan showed a film of the capabilities of the assault rifle, both with and without the grenade launcher. A squad of men would have the firepower of a company, a company would possess the power of a regiment. It was a hell of a firearm and all present knew it had the potential to make them powerful as well as rich, maybe richer is more correct.

No deal was cut here but one was finalized later and the manufacturing was set up in Portugal and the arms began to be shipped down to Central and South America. Weapons traded for cocaine, at unheralded profits, then shipped to the U.S. and the cash sent back for another circle. The cycle went on and on so efficiently that finally the CIA got involved and they began to make some of their "Black Money." This used for the covert action and the paid uprising which the Sandinista forces were supported by and with.

The ironic fact about the entire outlay of this successful venture was that the United States Government was given first option on the manufacturing of this weapon and they turned it down. Their collective opinions were that it would never get off the ground, it would fail.

Well it failed all right, to the tune of near half a billion dollars in the pockets of the key people who had the foresight and the connections to make it work. The CIA being a very integral link in the success process and a benefactor of the profits involved.

When one day you all finally get off your collective butts and start looking behind all the closed doors here in this big WHITE HOUSE, turn over a few cushions of paperwork and see what it really says, things may change. This perpetual wheel has rolled for so long in one direction that the resulting ruts have channeled your ways of thinking to believe that there is nothing serious here. If you still feel that way, its not because I have not told you something of worth.

I have paid the ultimate price for my "service" to my country, beyond death. I have lost my family to the rhetoric which was given to me about truth and honor. That the word of a U.S. Government official was, when in writing worth what was said, not what it was written on, at best. Yet the antithesis is the true reality of what takes place when you, yes I categorize the Senate and the Congress with the U.S. Attorney and all other departments, lie blatantly about the "guarantees" of help and remuneration. It just plain and simple does not happen as you say.

When I think of all the promises this governmental body has given to groups of men and women over the years and the misuse of human lives, money, materials and supplies, it sickens me. More than this when I think of the men and women who gave their lives in the service of a country that does not back up it words with action, it makes me sad.

I gave you all that I had for almost two years and risked my life so many times for a guarantee of millions of dollars. Which you collected, confiscated, took possession of and have laid claim to. My personal pay, so to speak, was less than one tenth of one percent of what was due and guaranteed and promised by you.

For that and many things, I will not take the time to mention or rehash, I say goodbye, so long and farewell. May somehow this statement sink into your brainwashed minds and cause some innovative responses. So that the next stupid bastard who sticks his neck out for "a cause" doesn't lose his life as well. I will never forgive the way you have raped and pillaged my life, family and friends.

I know where I am going after I leave here, you do as well, for you had and have no intention of doing one thing to prevent or lessen what has taken place. The illegalities, which have so predominantly shown themselves in my case, are nothing more than mirror images of the life you daily lead. Little glass chambers filled with the political bullshit, which has fostered the growth of inept service of which you are all guilty.

Wallow in the mire, I hope that you choke on the glutton ways that you exist. Know that somewhere in this country there will come a time when all the chaos which the United States has been neglecting, for now decades, will unleash itself and the landslide of parliamentary procedure will be reversed, forevermore."

I, shuffled from the room, still shackled like a wild animal. Yet the chains that bound my body did not chain my spirit, nor my heart, for it was a "Heart of Thunder." Its lightning would strike again, more powerful than ever before and reinforcements will have joined.

The road back to New Mexico was long and had but one course of repayment for the crime I was charged, MURDER. Part II of this autobiography, "Heart of Thunder," will chronicle the experience of what all took place from this day forward.

It's one hell of a story!

Follow me now toward the dawning of a new day, a new chapter and the beginning of a new me. This journey, through the hills and valleys of life, has brought forth the understanding that is required for eternal life! Though not fully manifested and anchored, yet, it is beginning to grow from the early seeds and continued watering from our Heavenly Father.

From a Heart of Thunder, now the saga continues into a new dawn, all the way to the Color of Grace! Turn the page and begin to see the Light and feel the Presence!

CHAPTER 7

to Prison and the White House

The United States Senate Subcommittee hearings in Washington D.C. had now been in session for eight weeks. Testimony from several agents and agencies would gain Department of Justice approval for funding to accelerate the Centac investigations. Agent Richard Gorman, DEA, would head the Southern California Division assisted by the other two men that had been part of the Sicilia-Falcon trials, Pat Gregory and John Raftery.

For the past six weeks, Michael John Decker had been sitting in a Federal Holding Facility in the Santa Fe County Jail. There awaiting sentencing for a murder charge from the State of New Mexico and a bank robbery for the Feds.

A holding cell originally designed for eight men had now swelled to nineteen, with no further remodeling. Built back in the mid fifties, never painted or upgraded in any way since the original, twenty-two years ago, it reeked of the countless thousands that had passed through its corridors. Odors of the bodies, their stench and unsanitary living permeated the area. The single cast iron toilet/sink combination, long since corroded and stained from decades of use and never cleaned, mold growing with its green, black and yellow tint was the only changed color. This relic, a centerpiece, was welded to the steel box shower and stood silently in the cell. A bedraggled old mattress cover, fart sack as they were referred to, hung from the top brace for privacy.

Occupied by men ranging in age from eighteen to fifty, all Chicano except for one angry, frustrated, mean as hell white man, a menagerie of lost souls. The charges ranging from DWI to drugs to murder and every combination in between, all were awaiting trial sentencing or a promise of freedom.

Chaco, twenty-six years of age, born-raised-cultured-indoctrinated with the street smarts and gang life of the barrios of Martinez

Town in Albuquerque, was the leader. The long knife scar across his chest was a testimony of the challenge he had made for the Patron, boss status he had won. Chaco ruled the cellblock. All the cash,drugs,contraband of any kind came through him or had his approval.

When the word had been funneled through the jail mail that a gringo who had killed one of their own was being transferred in, a greeting party was assembled.

Decker was meanwhile being shuffled from a lengthy stay at the D.C. jail in this nation's capital, where he had been testifying at the aforementioned Senate hearings. He was far more than just some normal citizen who had killed a fellow gang member. This man was born and bred in the finest karate schools available, seasoned in military schools, Vietnam and was a former hit man in one of the largest cartels in the world. Street, jungle and life tested and proven to be a literal machine when necessary, his family had just been ripped from his life and his heart. Add to this the fact that the United States government had not delivered several million dollars on their promise after he had risked his life to help break a huge drug empire. To say that Decker had an attitude was the understatement of the century. If these tough guys wanted to start a rumble, they picked just the right guy to accommodate their wishes. He would love to vent the pent up frustration and rage that had been brewing for two solid years.

Physically, Michael John Decker was a fine tuned machine. Six foot three, two hundred thirty pounds of raw fury with a body fat content of less than four percent, he absolutely knew how to wage war. Decker had worked hard all his life, trained even harder and fought hundreds of hand-to-hand matches, many for money and to date had not gone down. Decker's grandfather had told him long ago that it is not only the size of the dog in the fight, it is the size of the fight in the dog. Combine the two and you begin to understand how formidable the fact of having the big dog and the big heart could be.

It had turned cold outside that morning back in March 1977, the frost so heavy on the trees and ground that it looked as if the snow had fallen. The air inside the holding cell was very near the same temperature, not only from the weather, but from the reception which had been planned for the new arrival, me.

"Decker, you are going to like it here in Santa Fe, they enjoy white boys." Baca, jail guard and smart guy, his humor did nothing more than raise the temperature on the fire deep inside. A rattling of chains from the cuffs, leg irons and manacles, my hardware whenever they transported me, accompanied the choppy steps I had to take to enter the jail. No comments whatsoever from the two U.S. Marshals as they climbed back into the black sedan and headed back South to Albuquerque.

"So you are the notorious bad guy that killed Montoya. Pretty tough killing an unarmed dude, hey Decker, You will get yours, just you wait." No matter where I was or what I was doing, this jailer was going to ride my butt, well just maybe, if I was going to get mine, he would get his. I started to give Baca a piece of my mind but the results would have been solitary confinement in the hole. No phone calls, visits or daylight, I passed on the oratory, reluctantly.

Photographs, fingerprints, I.D. of every kind in every place I went they did the same redundant procedures. Tired from the long trip, all I wanted to do was get to my cell, I thought.

"Hey Vato, when the gringo gets to the cell wait till the guard locks the main door. When he turns to go into the third cell, Tomas will be waiting there. Then you three rush him from the back and take the motherfucker out." Instructions given, the participants awaited the new arrival.

The main door opened with a grinding of metal to metal, hinges not oiled or maintained in decades, the guard shoved me through the opening.

"Get your ass inside. This is going to be your new home." Baca not only pushed me, he was pushing my boundaries as well. A look was all that was necessary for him to understand that enough was enough. Guard he was, but his position did not include what was going on. My personal latitude of giving had been passed beyond acceptance. Then his final comment rang out, "You're going in the third cell, so have fun." His sarcasm made me sick.

As the cellblock slammed into the frame and the large brass key turned the lock with a snap of setting the drive bolt, I quickly began to survey the situation at hand. It was a time to view intently every set of eyes in the block, which were focused in my direction. One member of the group, seeming to be in charge, had a long scar across his chest. He motioned towards the third cell, a silent command and warning all the same. The issue blanket wrapped over my left arm from wrist to elbow, I stepped towards the cell. Something was about to go down and I knew it.

Listening to the rates of breathing, watching for veins flexing in necks and hands, muscle contractions as well, the scrutiny was automatic. There were three, at least, involved in whatever was going down. I turned to enter the cell and the assault began. The arm and hand flying towards my throat, shank formed from a sharpened spoon, driving towards the intended mark. The tagate bari knife hand block stopped the forward progress of the weapon, nukite' spear hand drove deep into the solar plexus and grasped the rib cage. A snap kick to the groin brought the head down and face forward so that my elbow strike shattered the nose and removed several teeth sending the assailant to the floor, screaming and bleeding.

Going immediately into "H form" fighting for multiple foes, the second man ran full speed into the spinning back kick. The heel driving solid into the sternum, a sharp crack followed by a suffocated cough came forth as the following reverse punch uncoiled the force exploding into the jaw and temple. Number three and four never saw the move that drove their faces into the steel bars leaving them motionless on the blood spattered floor. One more felt the urge to prove his machismo as the axe kick slammed into the side of his neck and skull, a forearm shunt bringing the final loss of consciousness.

"You bastards want a war, bring it on and I'll send your asses to the same place your cousin went, straight to Hell. Come on, chickenshits, let's have this out once and for all. You may take me in the end but I will have taken most of you out with me." Rage, sheer violent rage roared from my voice, eyes flashing and nostrils flared as the adrenaline coursed through my veins. Finally out of mere shock, one more threw himself my direction, my hand locking like a vice around the cords and muscles of his throat. Twenty years of constant work and exercise had made these huge hands strong enough to squeeze/crush bones. The tissue of the neck began to discolor, changing from flesh tone to red, black and blue. Fingers sinking deeper and deeper as the steel trap closed and life began to ebb, eyes bulging from the pressure and trauma, blood vessels rupturing. A shaking and trembling commenced across his body as life and motion began to leave.

"Okay, it is over, the fight is over, let him go before you kill him. Please let him go, that is my little brother." Chaco pleaded for his brother's life. I slowly eased my grip and with the easing of pressure, blood began to flow back into the brain, oxygen returning to the lungs to restore life. Chaco ran to help his kin, blue and black spots covering the neck, showing to all how close death had come.

"The next one of you that tries something will be your last to see this world or breathe this air. I have had all that I am going to take. No more from you, DO YOU UNDERSTAND!" Screaming at the top of my voice, the echo resounded down the corridor to the other cells.

"What the hell is going on in here?" Baca, Mr. Dumb Ass, said as he came to the rescue of his motley crew.

"Nada, nada, no importante, vamos!" Chaco had said that nothing was important and to leave. Surprise, surprise, somebody else on the take, payroll, goodness, it was everywhere. I turned back into the cell and sat on the bottom bunk. Rung out of all feelings, tired of fighting and yet so angry inside from all that had gone on these last few months. This situation was going to be a continuous assault for the remainder of the stay, however long it may be.

"Gringo, finito, no mas combate!" White boy there will be no more fighting. Chaco said it and for the rest of my stay it stopped. He fully realized that I was full of rage and would stop at nothing to answer a challenge. Just to make sure, I slept less than two hours a day "at most" and only after everyone else was down for the night. I had made the grade that afternoon and would hear the real story and the truth as to what had gone down October 2, 1976. Within an hour of the altercation another inmate was transferred into the cell. His older brother had been one of the men there in the foothills of Albuquerque that fateful night; confirmation to every detail was revealed and stamped with truth and authenticity.

Whoever was looking out for me was saving someone who had caused so much pain to so many, why bother? The next six weeks seemed to last forever, until the day arrived that the U.S. Marshals came to take me down to the court in Albuquerque for sentencing. As expected, there had been no more contact from the Senate or anyone else who had any pull in my case.

My attorney had cut some deals with the U.S. Attorney for a guilty plea on the bank charge. It was now categorized as a Bank Larceny and the sentence was a flat eight years. This sentence was to be served in the Federal Correctional Institution in Oxford, Wisconsin up near the Canadian border, brrrrrr! Cold country to say the least, sixty below zero was not uncommon in that region. This temperate zone was unlike any I had ever made residence in before in my life.

After getting my Federal time the State of New Mexico began to try and hedge their status in getting a conviction or guilty plea. They had heard of the Senate investigations and Senator Montoya was uneasy about the final outcome. Originally facing mandatory life with no possibility of parole, the case was reduced to forty years. The State came down from first to second degree murder, then three weeks after the Federal sentencing New Mexico took the charge to Voluntary Manslaughter. With this followed a bribe from the State of New Mexico, upon signing of their document professing my guilt, a sentence of 15 years would be given.

"What do you think about the offer?" My attorney calmly spoke of the DEAL!

"Just get the damn thing over and get me out of Santa Fe." I was more than tired of all the dealings and the lies which had surrounded all of the last two years. Yep, there was to be no parole but with the court influence from Montoya's friends even a chance of life was no chance at all. April 12, 1977 saw my departure of the Santa Fe facility with the Feds, on my way to the maximum security prison in the frozen tundra country of FCI Oxford.

    Wind whipped the late snow making small dancing clouds across the ground, ice shards like large diamonds glistened in the distance. Winters grip still encircled this territory so far north, Canada and the Great Lakes near enough to see their effects. A chill born far off where it never got to a point of warm, the effects visible on the large shield that showed from the side of the transport vehicle. Department of Justice, United States Marshal, and all their slogans and motto's, it was the Feds and nothing else. Traveling from the airport in Madison, the two Deputy's were delivering their prisoner to FCI Oxford, Wisconsin. There to spend the next fifteen years with the rest of the three thousand population, "just doin' time."

"Decker, this place will be just your cup of tea. If you are lucky you will have a cellblock with a few of the maximum lifers. They will cut your throat for a cake donut on Sunday morning, just before they walk on down to the chapel for services." A huge grin spread across the marshal's face. Thankfully Mr. Humor and Mr. Good news would be out of my face shortly.

    Rounding the final corner after some forty-five minutes driving, a large fenced in area loomed ahead. Gun towers every hundred yards, triple fences some twenty feet high with multiple rolls of razor wire, a roving automatic weapons armored vehicle cruising along, this was no country club. It had all the makings of a place where men stayed for a long, long time. The car pulled to the curb, very little of what was visible at first was anywhere in sight. It was almost if we had driven down into some sort of depression or hole. In fact we had dropped seventy feet below the main ground surface.

    Two large steel and glass doors with several panels on each side stood like silent guardians. My heart pounded and a parched feeling had spread down my throat. This was the last taste of fresh air that I would get to breathe for an extended period of time. There was no telling just how long that would be.

"Don't run now or I will have to shoot your ass." Fully chained and locked at every joint and body part, just which appendage did they think was going to run. It was just one last dig before they relinquished custody to the Bureau of Prisons. Hobbling to the doors, two men in prison guard uniforms stood ready to take control as we approached. Taking the paperwork from the deputies and marching me inside the mammoth doors took mere seconds. Whoop! The air shuddered with the closing of the inner chamber when the entrance locked shut.

"Let's get these chains off your legs. You will need your limbs to climb. Besides, you wouldn't have any complaints for the small freedom, right?" Thomas was the name on his I.D. tag and a little courtesy was sure not expected but greatly appreciated.

"Thank you, sir." A sigh came from my lips as I got the first flavoring of inside air.

What stretched out before me was the longest hallway I had ever seen, some five-hundred feet of glass-like floor. No doubt inmate polished to a mirrored sheen daily. This was the main tunnel corridor leading into the prison. Steps echoed and had uneven cadence as we progressed down the passageway. A vibrant shudder of sound marking the leaving of the world behind, entering of the foreign domain ahead, yet a knowing of what was to come. Visions of the death march at Huntsville Prison in Texas came across my mind, a silence and muffled sound blended to enhance the effect.

Dimly visible was the opening to a stairway and elevator, a choice of entrances that loomed in the forefront.

"Hell, Thomas, let's take the damn lift. I am tired of those darn stairs, anyway," Bradley said with a distinct displeasure.

"Okay, but if the Lieutenant catches us it was your idea."

Case closed, we took the elevator and ascended to the main prison. The ride much faster than a normal elevator, hundreds had preceded my journey, maybe thousands. Once on this level, population and people abounded. This was the beginning of the real nerves of the institution. Khaki uniforms were worn by all of the inmates that worked on this assignment.

"Get your ass in here and strip down buck naked. Throw everything in a pile. If you want to keep the clothing it will be shipped to the address you place on the green clipboard." As the chains came off so did the clothes with the deliverance of the command. Buck naked, it was to be the first of thousands of body and cavity searches. The routine was basic, cold, demanding and invasive.

"Hands up, palms forward."

"Stick your tongue out. Now lean forward and run your fingers through your hair. Lift your nuts. Turn around and lift your feet. Bend over and spread those cheeks." The big guard had a system and a manner that denoted years of experience, Woods was his name and probably where he was from.

"Get ready!" The large gloved hand dipped into the Vaseline jar and came finger pointing towards me.

As it prodded and pushed I never made a motion or sound, merely gritted my teeth and wondered what may be next. The same finger that had been stuck in my butt came out and pointed towards the shower with an intended message of, "take one." A towel and a short stack of my issued clothing, work boots and underwear sat on a small bench at the entrance of the shower stall. From the look on Woods' face I knew to make it quick, this was not going to be a time of relaxation.

"Now to the Admission and Orientation Unit, you will be there three to seven days then put in regular population."

"Any questions?"

Shaking my head, I was pushed into a cell and the sliding steel panel slammed shut. Six foot by seven was the total living area for the rest of the week. The doors opened twice a day to a corridor leading to a day room. A gathering arena for the twelve men going through the indoctrination processing, this thirty minute time period was utilized for information of the do's and don'ts. Both staff member and inmate cadre were the informers depending on the material to be covered. These sessions were nothing more than wasted time as my thoughts were revolving around Lisa and Christopher, two thousand miles away. I had screwed my life up to a point of no return over the past two years. Money, power, both were my downfall when coupled with drugs and drinking. I was addicted to both and the lifestyle they demanded. My son would be a grown man before I would ever see him again, Lisa, probably remarried.

At the end of the orientation period my assignment came for the A-1 unit, one that had to be volunteered for. I moved into the community cellblock, Askelapian being the name of this test program. Based on the principles of Eric Berne and other mental giants they used the Synanon Game. This was a high intensity confrontational device to break through to the core of emotional issues. There to begin rebuilding the man from the root of his being, day by day and week by week into a new man.

A doctoral staff working with former inmate graduates of the program as counselors after they had passed certain levels of performance evaluations, ran the program. The success was totally based on personal involvement and the records showed that when a man had completed the full session he would have a better chance of staying out of prison after release. Yeah, this is what the paperwork explained that first day. Reprogramming the mental tapes that had so much crap on them from years of physical and chemical abuse, this was a bunch of bullshit! I thought that this was to be a part of what I would do to pass the time. What I needed was far more than three thousand hours of concentrated counseling. My life had been far too violent, diverse and distorted even to think that mere mortal man and his circumstantial influence had the power to correct it.

April 30, 1977 a seminar was being held in the chapel auditorium. It was announced as a function by the Prison Fellowship organization. Some guy from Watergate had given his life to Jesus Christ and started the ministry and prison workshop. More than anything else it was a chance to get out of the cellblock for two consecutive nights and meet some free world people, so why not?

After being wounded in Vietnam on April 30, 1969 and my first meeting with Alberto Sicilia-Falcon taking place on April 30, 1974, what was the deal with April 30th? My mind was whirring with possibilities as to what might take place on this, another April 30th. I would have to go and find out for myself.

Nearly four hundred men turned out for the chance at getting out of their respective cellblocks. The room grew not only in number as the chairs began to fill, but the sounds grew. The noise, although increasing in volume, was far different from the continual roar of prison chatter. Many, in fact, most were speaking about what God and Jesus Christ had done in their lives and what peace they had found. Language and thought being shared from a source that I knew absolutely nothing about, my life was so distant from GOD! Suddenly the speakers broke the air with an announcement. "Men, take your seats and give me some quiet." It was the Chaplain asking for and remarkably getting results. A stillness came over the inmates, all of us, and quiet ushered itself into the room. There was a power to the silence, it was reverent in nature.

"Heavenly Father, I come to you now in request of your guidance, words and leadership for this time of worship and witness. Father God, I ask that each and every man here tonight hear not from one of us, rather from you Lord. May your Holy Spirit abound in this room and touch these souls and broken hearts with the tender loving Spirit of your Son, our Savior Jesus Christ. Be merciful and forgiving of these men, Father for they are your chosen warriors. Bless them with the understanding of what it means to follow you and take up the Cross for you daily. It is in the mighty Name of Jesus I pray, AMEN."

As the prayer ended many heads were still bowed and individual conversations continued with whomever they were murmuring to. I guess it was this man Jesus and God. People whom I had heard about twenty years before in Sunday school but had never truly known, yes, I knew about them but I did not know them, or what they could do.

George Soltau, a business executive from down in Texas spoke first. Then Paul Johnson, someone who had done time with Chuck Colson in prison was next. By the end of the first hour of testimony and worship, something was going on in my heart. A very strange peace and a breaking loose by the guiding of some unknown Hand allowed the pressure and strife of my situation to leave. Suddenly, a voice broke the silent meditation and like a wave, came flooding through the crowd.

"You there, third man from the right of the center walkway. God just told me to tell you to come and close this first night in prayer." On purpose I had sat as far to the rear as I could. After all there was no reason to be near the front. Now this man George Soltau is asking me to come up in front of all these men, and pray! As an elbow of encouragement came into my ribs from the man on my left, accompanied by a large smile, I stood to my feet and began the journey. I had no idea whatsoever as to what I was going to say, nor a hint of what to talk about during this "performance."

"I really don't know how to pray," Shaking my head as I leaned over and whispered into Mr. Soltau's ear. The response, a nudge and determined look from his eyes that said, just let God talk through you and only be the vessel for His Words. This took more guts, an entirely different kind, than anything I had ever done. It was so foreign and this strange feeling inside my body was doing something to my rotten soul that did not make sense. Well, I was up here and had to say something! I certainly did not want to lose face and be made the fool, the farthest thing from what actually was going to take place. I stepped to the microphone and opened my mouth and words began to flow.

What had begun to happen inside my body was a feeling, unknown and not recognizable to my heart/soul and physical makeup. Warm and glowing, shaking and trembling, I was intimidated but stood and allowed the flow to commence.

"God, I stand before you naked and alone, a man full of darkness and a man guilty of so much. Secrets which only you and I know about and the truth of which will never be told. Thankfully, you are here right now because I feel your presence. You are someone I do not know, this I admit. My brothers, Soltau and Johnson, spoke of the Holy Spirit and the Trinity and a new way of life. One that will prevent any one of us from coming back here once we have gone home. I ask you for this move of your power for me and every man in this room. Let the loneliness and the pain, the suffering of our families to leave with the washing of your Holiness. Make a heavenly love and a holy tenderness come forth to this room and bless these men with a righteous heart. Forgive me and my brothers, Lord and fill us with the River of Life so that we can walk in the ways of the Holy men that have served you. May the warrior spirit that so many of us have be channeled into fighting for the good. Kill the bad inside of us, of me God. Thank you for coming here tonight and allowing these men to come as well, guard them as they leave. Carry us to our next destination in life in a way that brings you honor and glory and praise. This is our prayer, AMEN!" Sweat dripped from my forehead and ran, no poured, down my back. Mr. Talk of the past, the smooth orator and habitual lying dog was as nervous as a small child. It must have had something to do with what Paul Johnson had said about coming to the Father.

As the group began to break up, men came to me and thanked me for the prayer. I didn't understand very much of the next few minutes, something inside of me kept burning a hole in my heart. Acknowledging the comments and talking as little as possible, I made my way to the door and back to my cell.

My knees hit the floor as the steel met steel in the locking of the vaultlike door. Elbows on the mattress and hands clasped together, I began to talk to my Father. He had kept me alive through so much, three decades of near death experiences and countless close calls with bullets, knives and weapons. My entire life had been covered by God's Hand and I did not have the intelligence or the vision to know what was taking place. I had avoided the issue of religion and definitely had no relationship. Remembering back when I came home from Vietnam and seeing the fish symbol with Jesus written in the middle, I thought it was just some hippie peace sign. Well, it was a sign of peace.

My body shuddered with the spasms of guilt as the sin and horrible acts committed were admitted and confessed before the throne. Crying out for forgiveness and restoration by the presence of the Holy Spirit, tears poured from my eyes. I choked with the amount of evil which had so indoctrinated my existence and ruled the way I lived. Hate and anger that had boiled and churned for so long were being

released and the energy needed to keep it alive, stopped.
"Where have you been all my life God? Why has this taken so long to happen?" As the words came from my lips the answer came to my heart like a rushing wind, so clear, so precise and simple.
"I have been here waiting my child. My arms open wide to encircle you and love you back to life. Your eyes were closed to the beauty which surrounded you. Now the scales have fallen from your eyes. Behold the newness in your heart and in your life. Beckon not into darkness for the Light of My Holy Spirit shines brilliant before you, your life has been illumined. Carry not fear, nor heavy burden, for I will take care of you my child. I am your Father, Lord, Savior and King forevermore. Do not turn from your saving grace and mercy." With the ending of God's Words came a vision before me that at first I did not think was real. A Bible was laying there on the bunk, opened to the fourth chapter of Philippians. How did this get here Lord? Did you place it here for me? The answer was not who or how, it was evident I was supposed to have His Word to find the comfort I needed.

Deep within the most remote confines of my heart, warmth and peace, that which passes all understanding, began to flow. My heart finally could feel. This peace was the one that Paul wrote so eloquently about in the fourth Chapter of Philippians, "Be anxious for nothing, but in everything, with thanksgiving let your requests be made known to God. And the peace of God that surpasses all understanding shall guard your heart and your mind in Christ Jesus." The verses from the open Word of God seemed to leap from the pages as my eyes and mind began to read and comprehend what was taking place.

The transformation was beginning in my life. All the details were unimportant to me. Only the results of the sudden freedom that had taken residence inside, this would be what made the difference. Sometime late that night or early morning I fell asleep after reading His Word for a long, long time. The early morning count bell seemed to ring after only a moments rest. The sunrise had brought forth a vision of the Son, God's Son rising and now this new son was rising as well. I had a new Father and a new life was being destined as a gift.

A sudden inspiration for knowledge came over me and I enrolled in the extension classes available from the University of Wisconsin. The next eighteen months flew by as the Word of God and the knowledge of university studies began to flood my brain. My prison job had grown from making twelve thousand pancakes a day in the chow hall to working in the records office. Programming in the therapy unit was coming to a close and I began to pray for a transfer to another institution which could offer more in the way of course work and further fellowship. Ask and you shall receive, yes God's Word does promise this and it came to pass very quickly.

Few inmates get a transfer at all and rarely this much of an accelerated schedule. God had answered my prayers and with every answered prayer comes a test of endurance. Two Marshals from the Minnesota office came to escort me to the new facility in Englewood, Colorado. It was to be a two day trip with no interruptions. The time spent at Oxford had allowed for growth and every ounce of what God had delivered to me was going to be tested.

"00488-124, well we have heard a few wild stories about you."
"Jim, he doesn't look like the mean dude I have been hearing about." Deputy to deputy they never change, except for the name.
"Sir, that is because I found a new way to live and the old person you heard about got left behind in Oxford. The new one is going on to Englewood." I tried to set them straight and begin an understanding in their hearts.
"What the hell, you having some kind of psycho change or something?" Here came the sick humor again.
"No Sir. I found a new life in Jesus Christ as my Lord and Savior and he is rebuilding the old nasty Michael into a new creature. He allows the old to pass away and the new to begin. It is called being Born Again into the Christian way of living." Now maybe he would get the picture.
"Well shit, if that don't beat all. This guy kills somebody and thinks......" The other deputy cut him short in mid-sentence.
"Knock off the talk. This man has a right to change and live and be whatever he wants to be. If you knew a little more about who and what God is and can be, you would still be married and would not have abandoned your children. So just be quiet! A man's religion and personal faith is between him and God." The deputy closed his lips in a pursed manner to signify for me to keep my mouth shut as well and shook his head. God certainly had messengers and servants everywhere. It was a mighty witness to my spirit to have this display before me as soon as I was leaving the prison gates.

Like the flight from Albuquerque, New Mexico to Oxford, Wisconsin so many months before, this was another chained up experience. The stares from people in the terminal and in the plane showed fear and intimidation. There was to be a brief stop over in Leavenworth, Kansas before continuing on to Englewood.

"You will be here in this holding cell until tomorrow morning and then we will finish the trip." This comment came as they removed the chains and cuffs and locked the door to the solitary confinement cell. Four by four, concrete walls, floors and ceiling, no light, no windows, no nothing, this was the complete accommodations. No bed, no sink or toilet, save for the six inch hole in the floor and bedding was one old Army blanket. It was not the RitzCarlton!

The insidious odor of urine and decaying excrement gorged my nostrils, the dampness musty with the mildewed cracks and crevasses. Once again the testing was being displayed and I must weather the storm of emotions. A faint clanging of steel meeting steel was the only random sound back in this old antiquated section of solitary confinement. Later I would find out that this section had been condemned for a long time, on purpose. One of the transport deputies' friends worked at this institution and as a favor repaid, I was locked up in this territory of "No man's land." They wanted to see just how tough I might be and whether they could get a reaction.

Twice a day the small, six by twelve inch flap at the bottom of the massive steel door would open. A tray of slop pushed inside and a tiny ray of light would stab the darkness. It was my only contact with anything living or breathing. Never a word was uttered no matter my request, just silence.

"Excuse me! Could you tell me what day it is?" It was like talking to a rock, the same response. Thus my alternative was to take the tray and make another mark on the floor of the cell, scratching another mark on my personal daily calendar. One day I would count these marks and see just how long this environmental journey had lasted.

Sixty-three days later the two deputies came to continue the transport. The excuses were lame and absolutely nothing but lies about misplaced paperwork and the like. God had kept me company. He had placed my safety in His heart and drawn me ever closer inside His Kingdom.

The Federal Correctional Institution at Englewood, Colorado was a breath of fresh air. Nestled near the foothills of the Rocky Mountains on the southwestern part of Denver, Colorado, the view from my new quarters was awesome. A huge lighted cross came to life each night up on the side of the mountain, it was a messenger from my Father. God was there, He was here and I am going to make it, another bestowed blessing from Him.

"Michael, from your reviews at FCI Oxford you seem to have done an outstanding job for the records office. I am going to look forward to having someone working that already knows the system." Mr. Reynolds was the Administrative Supervisor, short and scrawny with wiry red hair and a forehead that was ever enlarging with the oncoming inset of baldness. The stay in this work assignment would be very short lived, thankfully. Along with a tour in Food Service making the bread, pancakes and desserts which was nothing more than a den of thieves, this was one of the main supply areas for contraband. Yeast for making "hooch," the home brewed elixir which when added to fermented fruit made a powerfully intoxicating drink. Literally it was an order and delivery arena for most of the institution. With the daily food deliveries from the outside, connected inmates would have other items suddenly appear in the cartons and containers of perishables. Money and connections were funneled by notes and with additional deliveries and niceties returned to guards on the take. It was no different than what I had witnessed countless times with my association in the employment of Sicilia-Falcon. I made the transfer list to the Recreation Department and here I would find an anchor that brought about a more guarded atmosphere.

First on my major list of things to do was to find the church and get acquainted with the Chapel Services available here. The Senior Chaplain, Roy Tribe, had a strong Protestant program and the outside volunteers came in several days of the week. These were real street people, with real lives and jobs and families. The name on the brass plate that was attached to the office door before me signaled this was the place to be.
"Chaplain Tribe, I was just transferred in from FCI Oxford and I wanted to introduce myself and become familiar with your activities and programs. My Name is Michael Decker." I extended my hand as I stepped into the office and began the introduction.
"Nice to meet you Mr. Decker. Welcome to our institution." The lanky chaplain with the overgrown mustache began to fill me in on all of the details of what his program had to offer. It was a well organized and staffed program which availed every man the opportunity to be educated. The sheer numbers of outside volunteers was incredible. Their participation was almost daily with over fifty regulars and nearing a hundred counting the occasional man or woman that gave their time to this fellowship. Introduction was now complete, thus it was time to continue making the rounds of the institution.

Another top priority was to get registered for classes with Arapahoe College. After completing all of the available courses at Oxford, I was going to continue with my education goals. Once this was established, I I would turn on the steam and go full tilt into the college courses. This also availed me to get the funding of the G.I. Bill and begin to send support money back to Lisa and Christopher, my exwife and son.

I would soon find out the fact that Lisa had met and married another man. With news of the marriage came additionally information that they were expecting another child. It was a tough time for me because down deep in my heart a dream had remained of one day getting back together. Dream cancelled, there was no way I could have realistically expected her to wait on me for this extended period of time. My focus had to begin to realign and see the future with a different light. My heart would forever be attached, but my mind was strong and would prevail over the inner emptiness that drifted inside. Someday, yes someday, my relationship with my son Christopher would be restored.

Wally and Marge Westwood, Dale Morris, Bob Prangley, many of the volunteers like these precious people of the religious services department, gave of their time and heart unendingly. The bond that formed between us, was one founded on the Word of God and filled with the love of Jesus Christ. Their presence in my weekly life was part of becoming reattached to society and a normal way of living. Their presence brought warmth from the streets and a tie to the world beyond the walls so as to stay in contact with the rest of the world.

Wally Westwood had a gift for prayer and praying which would take one's heart right out of prison into a brief encounter with paradise. The eloquence and diction his voice displayed, so precise and beautiful, flowed into the descriptions of circumstances and events. His beckoning of the power of God made you know that He was real, present and alive in your heart. God was truly speaking through Him, no doubt.

Another April 30th was on the horizon and with it a group from Bear Valley Baptist Church was coming to the institution. Their choir was scheduled to perform a special presentation of "Bright New Wings" which included forty new volunteers. I had made a new friend in Russell Scharf. He was a mountain of a man standing 6'2" and making the scales turn to around 275. Strong as an ox and also gentle in spirit as he gave his all for Jesus Christ, Russell and I shared long talks on a regular basis.

"Brother Russ, are you going to the performance tonight?"

"Absolutely," the bear had spoken.

"There is just no telling what might take place, especially since it is the 30th day of April once again." I had shared all of my past with Big Russell and he knew that every major event in my life (many) had taken place on this date.

"I know. And I am going to make sure that you don't do anything

foolish like fall in love or something." His whiskers moving on the bushy beard framing that huge smile, eyes sparkling in the sunlight, my brother was always being his protective/kidding self.
"I will do my best to control myself, dude. I hear that the director of the choir, Sherwin Crumley has quite a program. I am looking forward to hearing the sounds and seeing the sights." Brother Russ nodded in agreement and off we went. This institution was so different than the maximum security regulations of FCI Oxford. Open movement most of the time and a relaxed atmosphere in comparison to the heaviness of the Wisconsin tundra camp.

Leaving the cellblock that night, the air cool and the sky crystal clear, the heavens were alive with the constellations and their stars. The Big Dipper and Orion were two of my favorites, their key stars like beacons in the distance. Russell and I walked the corridor leading to the chapel building. Reaching the main entrance, Chaplain Tribe was there greeting each man as they came to be blessed by the upcoming event. His black mustache and goatee looked false in contrast to his pearly, no sun at all skin tone. No doubt a little dye was used for removal of the gray or white!
"Well, here are two peas out of the same pod if I ever saw such. Welcome to you both. Michael, would you and Russell hand out the bulletins tonight?" His hand extended to both of us with the greeting, Chaplain Tribe had a large heart and it was full of the Father.
"Yes Sir! We would be glad to do that, where are they." Russell answered for the two of us. Chaplain Tribe pointed towards the two stacks on the deck in the entryway.

Within a half-hour the church was nearing capacity and the opening of the program was about to begin. Russell and I made our way to seats on the front row, making sure that we saw all of new faces, especially the female version. A pretty face was a rarity in this environment, believe that!

No sooner did I get to my seat did the vision of loveliness come into full view. Standing there in the middle of the choir ensemble, her blond hair and blue eyes were breathtaking, her charm unending. A sweetness and sheer radiance came forth as I gazed in amazement at the beauty before me. Brother Russell seeing the look on my face gave me a big elbow to the rib cage.
"Darn it Michael, take a breath and relax dude. You look like your going to have a heart attack."
"I think I already did." Yes, I was beaming, grinning, whatever. The music began to play and the director, Mr. Crumley, began to move his

hands in directing the singing.

The program commenced with three songs, testimonies of what God had done in some peoples' lives, and more music. With the completion of these numbers and the closing set, a time for fellowshipping was now the balance of the evening. Just the part that I was definitely looking forward to, meeting this young lady, I hoped. The old bird dog was sniffing the air and wagging his tail, there she was.

"Hello. My name is Michael and I wanted to personally thank you for taking your time to come and share with us. It was a blessing and you are absolutely beautiful." I made it very evident that she had touched my heart and her individual performance was outstanding. My hand came forward to hers with this overzealous greeting and the soft touch of her tiny hand melted my heart, completely. The past hour had been spent hearing the music and looking at her. What I was seeing in her eyes was a beauty far beyond any I had ever witnessed, for the presence of God was there.

"Thank you very much, it was our pleasure." Not only pretty but from Texas, no doubt whatsoever, and her words floated in the air.

"My name is Karen Cartrite." Whew, be still my heart!

"I am from Canyon, Texas just outside of Amarillo. What part are you from, Texas that is?" Her voice, her looks, I was enthralled by this lady as I began to find out who she was.

"Oh, I am from Sweetwater down near Snyder and out that way. You know, out of Lubbock southeast direction." Karen was speaking with her voice and her eyes and I liked it.

"I absolutely know just where that is. My grandfather and I hunted quail down that way and Sweetwater is where they have the big rattlesnake roundup."

"You got that right. More snakes each year and people as well." Her accent and drawl went right to the core of my being. Smile enchanting, personality warm and charm overwhelming, perfect in every way. Karen was nearing five foot four, about 115 pounds soaking wet, cute figure and firm muscle tone. I would find out that she stayed in shape training and working Saddle Bred horses for a large breeding farm.

My heart was going pitter patter from the beginning and within the fifteen minutes of conversation I had been as patient as possible, and courteous. It was time to step boldly to the plate and swing that bat.

"Would you be offended if I asked you to write me so that I could get to know you better?" It was like asking for that first date back in high school. My eyes were twinkling and a big smile spread across my face with the invitation. I awaited her reply.

"I, I will pray about whether God would have me do that. Let's leave this in God's Hands." Soft, tender and direct, with a air of strength in a way I had never seen nor heard. In the image and presence of Jesus Christ she had been polite and forthright. I liked her answer and my respect for who and what she was grew with her stand on His Will. Shaking hands once again was our final goodbye for the evening. Very quickly the entire group left the area and Russ and I helped with cleanup. I was floating around the chapel on a layer of air.

"Goodness, goodness, goodness, I warned you about this and look what has happened now." Big Russell punched me in the arm as he made the statement. Looking toward Chaplain Tribe he continued, "Well Chaplain, Michael won't be any good to anybody or for anything for weeks now. He may have to go to the doctor, look at those eyes all glassy and stuff."

Russell was rubbing the fact that he had witnessed the dreamy look that had come over me. All in good natured fun, but he was right, this young lady had taken my attention from the very start. Karen Cartrite was the first Christian woman I had ever met since coming to know Jesus Christ myself. That is other than the women that come to the weekly Bible studies.

For two weeks I waited somewhat impatiently for a letter, card, note or any form of correspondence. Nothing had arrived, it was time for some action on my behalf so that I could see some results. Karen was listed in one of the phone books in an area of Denver named Littleton. There it was, 6959 South Reed Court, Littleton, Colorado and my letter went on its way the very next morning. It was a Tuesday morning when I wrote that first letter, Saturday a reply came.

"Michael D., you got some mail!" Russell called from the corridor outside the cell door.

Like a flash I was out the cell door and heading for the guard station to retrieve the envelope. Even the sight of that pale blue envelope was enough to set my heart to the race mode. The eight seconds it took to get back to the cell was all that I could muster, envelope off and ready to read.

Karen wrote that she felt that if we were supposed to write one another that God would have to place it on my heart to commence this communication. She was somewhat old fashioned about this and her style was very appealing. The letter was newsy and she told me about her two children, Britt and Kristi, a son and daughter. Only three pages but it took me thirty minutes to read. That might have been because I had to go over every word five times to make sure that I had not missed anything. I may have memorized it, well not maybe, I had. Another letter and my first poem to her were out the door the next morning and that is how the relationship started. It was more of a courtship and the long process of getting to know one another had begun.

It was fantastic and my time in prison began to fly by. Before I knew it three months had passed and it was time for my first major request to Karen. This was to ask her if she would like to come for a visit, be put on my visiting list. She replied in her very next letter, YES! It would take nearly six weeks for all of the approval paperwork to take place and during this wait time, I began several more projects in the institution.

God's work within my heart had taken me from the darkness of hell to the light of His deliverance and salvation of my soul. His promise of forgiveness and a new life, to be born again, had revitalized and redirected my focus on life. So many areas of my existence were being changed, nurtured and developed into a new man. I felt this life of Christianity could never change. That all of the people of the free world that follow Jesus Christ were shielded from the normal stress and strain, pressures, and sin of the masses. Within the confines of this structured setting that the prison environment offered, those of us living with God as our Savior, isolated ourselves. From the drugs, the violence, the homosexuality and con games which run rampant throughout the penal system nationwide, we were safe in the Hands of God.

The college programming of Oxford and now Englewood had allowed me to complete three years of college in only two calendar years. With a grade point average of 3.73, based solely on the ample time for studying, I was shooting for a 4.0 this semester. The physical education department had now given me the freedom to begin running many of the program activities. Organized intramural leagues had been started in football, basketball, soccer, softball and the crowds of fans were nearing capacity attendance.

One of the guys I had become friends with, Jimmy Tidwell, had more raw talent as a sprinter than any athlete I had ever seen. His long legs and strong upper torso gave him the natural speed most men could not even dream to have, even through training. He had come to me and asked for help in improving his overall condition and especially his start out of the blocks.

"Jimmy, I am going to work your butt hard. You are going to think you are back on the farm working for your Dad."

"As long as I beat all those darn black guys, heck, those dudes run like crazy. When was the last time you saw a white boy win the sprints at the Olympics?" His smile beamed and the Texas drawl left no doubt of his origin.

"I must admit that only a couple of times have there been a speedy one, maybe the next one will be Jimmy Tidwell." Slapping him on the back with the comment, he just shrugged his shoulders.

After two months of rigorous workouts and constant repetitions of coming off that starting line, Jimmy was in rare form and going to lay it on the line. There was no doubt to me, nor no surprise when I was given the pleasure of watching the Physical Education Supervisor give him a blue ribbon for placing first in both of the sprint events. Betting on the sidelines was hot and heavy, and thankfully other than a few sore losers, no other pain or suffering occurred.

From Englewood, Jimmy Tidwell was headed on to the Texas Department of Criminal Justice after finishing his Federal time. His new home location would be Huntsville prison and then on to Ellis I where all the tough guys were sent, many doing long sentences and caring little about life. Jimmy had become interested in martial arts while watching me work out and do fighting forms called kata's. Thus Jimmy and I, were now teacher and student. Another man I had made the acquaintance of, Hang Hong Lu, one of the best Karate men I had ever had the pleasure of meeting, came and worked out with us. Henry, as we called him, had grown up in the back streets of Singapore, Malaysia. His uncle had begun instruction almost at birth into the finer techniques and mental/physical conditioning. He was a master in several disciplines and our times together gave me much joy and relaxation, as well as more experience and knowledge. Studying and practicing martial arts now was very different than before meeting God on a personal basis. The art of the exercise and the precision of the technique was my new focus, rather than sheer power, violence, and destructive force. Henry, Jimmy and I even got Big Russell down to the room, we call it a dojo, to work out and do a little light sparring. It was quite the site to see this huge bear of a man sparring with 135 pound Henry, his ability to maneuver Russell across the room. In a strange sort of way it was fellowship of a different nature. That is because every one of the workout sessions were begun and concluded in prayer, so to remain focused on the real Master.

God's Word began to manifest the truth of living in an even greater way the more I studied and fellowshipped with my brothers and the outside volunteers. I knew that each day spent in the presence of the Holy Spirit, was bringing forth death to the old Michael and reinforcing the new. It would be a long process though, for the depth of the dark roots of sin and violence were attached and woven into my heart and soul. Yes, there was the light of Jesus Christ, He was there. The daily regiment of prayer, reading, prayer and keeping a spiritual journal helped ward off the potential of falling back into old habits and actions. One major thing that was making me want the new life even more than before was Karen Cartrite. Especially today, June 8, 1978, because she was coming to the prison to visit Michael J. Decker, me!

The morning had come very early, as I was showered dressed and ready by 5:00a.m. and she would not get to the institution until 1:00p.m. After all, a man certainly would not want to be late on his first date. Visiting hours were from 1:00p.m. to 3:00p.m. on Saturday and Sunday here at the Englewood facility. With breaking rays of the morning sunrise cascading over the mighty Rocky Mountains, I knelt beside my bunk and began to talk to my Father God.

"Dear gracious Heavenly Father, I come before you in adoration and praise for all the miracles you have given me. It has brought about a new beginning in my life. Father, today is one of the most special because of the new lady, my new friend, that you have blessed me with. God, I ask for guidance and direction, even blessing on this visit today. Karen has known you her whole life, from a very small child, and I am a new child of the Kingdom. I ask for a sharing of the Spirit, a bonding of our love for you. Most of all Father God, I ask for your perfect Will to be bestowed upon this relationship. Wherever it is to go, let it only be in your leading. I praise you Father for the feeling of joy that wells up in my heart and the privilege it is to serve you my King. I thank you for the beauty I see in this young woman, not only outside but in her precious heart also. Guide both of us in this first step and allow a freedom to our communication so that no secrets will be hidden. Amen."

Breakfast and Chapel services consumed most of the morning hours, thankfully. The announcement over the loudspeaker would nearly knock me off my feet. "00488-124 proceed to the visiting control room." Yahoo, my heart yelled to every fiber of my being and off I went in the direction of the Captains office. A loud knock on the steel door would announce my arrival and stepping inside I stood at attention in reporting who I was.

"Decker, 00488-124, reporting for a visit Sir."

"Let me see, yes 00488-124 is on my list and it looks like this is your first one." The burly guard spoke with a voice like a bass instrument.

"Yes Sir! My family lives a long way off and so this meeting of a new friend is truly great, especially since she lives here in the Denver area." Beaming with both pride and pleasure, I awaited the go ahead to proceed through the corridor and into the waiting area.

"Well then you had better hurry up and get in there." The guard smiled from his heart when he motioned me towards the visiting room, this was very rare to see in this environment. Could it be that someone up there was keeping an Eye on this meeting from the very start?

The visiting room was already two-thirds full, maybe a hundred people, with every combination of race, creed, religion and family grouping imaginable in attendance. I began to look for a familiar face, finally my eyes came to rest and make contact with Karen Cartrite standing there, waving to me. Her blonde hair was soft, short, glowing, and she was wearing a blue dress with white flowers, accented by matching shoes and purse. Makeup so light and enhanced with a soft pink lipstick, it was doing nothing more than highlighting her natural beauty, what a picture. The eyes, be still my heart, silver, blue and radiating a shimmer of loveliness that captured my heart and near took my breath.

Approaching slowly, to enjoy every moment of that first time of closeness, I extended my hand and taking hers, drew her near for a light embrace. As we parted that first touch, her cheeks had a soft rose hue to their color, a flushed look and sparkle to Karen's eyes. What I beheld made my heart double beat and a deep breath was remaining in my lungs. Finally exhaling, we began to talk. She had left the kids with their aunt on purpose, for at least this first visit, to allow for a more intimate chat in getting to know one another.

"I can't begin to thank you enough for coming to see me. You look so pretty Karen, and the blue of your eyes and the dress, both so beautiful." I was serious, not meaning to make her uncomfortable, but express how I was touched.

"Michael, you are embarrassing me. But thank you for the compliments." She reached out and touched my hand as she spoke, the electricity seemingly almost sparked. It was the softest hand I had ever felt. So tiny and delicate with perfectly manicured nails and polish like the color of the lipstick, Karen took great pride and care in her appearance.

"I am just being honest Karen. From the first time that I saw you up there singing I have felt this way." If at all possible, my smile had widened and my right knee was definitely wiggling. Had I regressed back to high school, possibly, just possibly?

For the remainder of the visit she told me of her family and details of the children, all of the things that had taken place in her divorce. Abandonment was a closer description of the way her exhusband had run out on her and the kids. I shared parts and pieces of my life and

family not wanting to share anything too deep or intense yet, not on the first meeting. I didn't want to unload all of the drama until she first knew ME, the new Michael. Finally, the announcement came over the loudspeaker that the visiting time was ending.
"Gentlemen, you have three minutes to say your goodbyes, three minutes and then form a line to the left side of the room, visitors to the right wall."

We both looked at one another and just sat there, enjoying the company and warmth of one another's spirit and presence. Then standing up to say our final goodbyes and farewell greetings, I wondered if she would mind a small display of affection.
"Again lady I thank you so much for coming and I look forward to seeing you whenever you have the spare time in the future. Maybe one of these times you can bring the kids so that we can meet. It has truly been a wonderful time!"
"For me as well Michael, I look forward to seeing you again very soon. The kids will come one of these times too." She had said she was coming again and the excitement flowed, even bringing the kids. I was not the only one that had enjoyed the afternoon. I was taking a chance but being shy was not one of my traits, this was honest from the heart.
"Karen may I give you a tiny goodbye kiss." Her gaze and mine had never left since the beginning of the afternoon, now it parted momentarily as she dipped her face for an instant, then her reply.
"Certainly!" It was angels singing and came in such a soft, tender voice which had only the slightest hint of reservation in the agreement.

So gentle did I touch her shoulders with these large hands, merely brushing the fabric of her dress. Lowering my mouth and lips to hers, only a whisper of contact, lightly dancing flesh to flesh then floating apart, it was the dessert for the meal of the meeting. We both were glowing and felt the heat of the moment, but it was respectful and a manner in which she deserved and appreciated. What followed was a brief embrace, pulling her a little closer than our initial meeting, then giving our final words.
"Again thank you for coming and I will write you tonight."
"Thank you Michael. I enjoyed this time as well. Have a good week and God Bless you." With her words came one last contact before she walked from the room, stopping briefly to wave before turning through the exit doors.

A thousand wonderful feelings, sensations, thoughts, memories of the past two hours with Karen Cartrite flowed through my body, mind and spirit. She was all and even more than I had dreamed she would be. There was a vivacious energy and beautiful style to her spirit and personality. Every aspect of what I had heard, seen and felt made an impression on my heart, in fact, taken residence there.

Even the strip search and cavity probing could not dampen my spirit and the joy that was flowing through me. Walking back to the cellblock I noticed an extra bounce to my step. Pulling on the heavy brass handle of the security steel door, I stepped back into the inner chamber,

"I was afraid of this, my goodness. Bill, Samuel, come look at the face on this man. He has been afflicted, it seemingly is terminal." Big Russell was letting me have it for the way I had walked back into the unit with this look on my face. Before long at all Bill and Samuel, two brothers in Christ, were coming to give their assessment.

"Oh yes, there is no doubt about this case, Bill you had better go and get the medic, this man has been stricken. Goodness I only hope that it is not contagious in any way. Could you imagine the whole unit in this epidemic condition?"

"Okay, you guys, that is enough. I had a great visit and Karen Cartrite is a very special, beautiful lady. I do emphasize the term lady, she definitely is that!"

A few slaps on the back and hugs from my friends and brothers, for down deep they were pleased for their brother, sharing in my joy. Each member of this group, in our social and our prayer time, shared one another joys and sorrows. This allowed for the happiness to be twice as good and the sorrow to be half as bad. Groups of men like these, us, were similar to many others in the prison setting. Here was a brotherhood formed and fashioned on the rock of Christ, the need for camaraderie and the realization that we, together as one, could overcome. Bonded on the Word of God, forged in the fire and strengthened by the Sword, His Word delivered us from the influence of the general population and protected all who believed.

Many of the free world volunteers had shared with us in their testimonies that to try and walk through the jungle of life alone on the street was asking for disaster to strike. Only within the strength and fellowship of other believers was success in our walk with Jesus Christ, possible. God meant for us to fellowship and assist one another in the body of Christ, the church. There was no doubt of this reality to me after walking so long in the wilderness, alone. This new track was truly the roadway and the map of God's Word, His Will and direction for each of our lives.

That following evening, after such a special afternoon, brought with it a special kind of peace in my mind and heart. Not until today had even the possibility of ever loving another woman entered my mind. These past few years had been a concentrated effort between God and me. Our relationship was so much more important than anyone or anything else. With Karen's introduction, He was still number one in my life, but there was definitely a new addition to the picture.

As I began to write her a letter that night, a poem came to my heart, one of hundreds over the next few years: Sunshine was created when God created earth, and sunshine is always present at a new baby's birth. Sunshine colors the body with a bronze colored tone, it walks with you and warms the heart, even if on the beach and all alone. So take the sunshine and go down through your life, may it always give you happiness, and never sadness, sorrow or strife. Our letter exchange was a three to five time a week and the weekend visits became very regular. On Karen's fourth visit she brought along the children.

Kristi, eight years old, had never been held by a man, for her father had shunned her at birth. She was such a tiny little thing at only about forty pounds, delicate with the blondest hair and the bluest eyes, just like her mother. Within ten minutes of our first encounter she had come up to me and crawled into my lap and gone to sleep. Karen was so amazed that she was speechless and just watched the comforting of her little girl. Kristi was safe, secure, warm and at peace with her resting spot. My big arm encircled her tiny frame and I patted and stroked her small shoulder and arm. A true closeness of that same feeling when Christopher and I were together came over me. I could feel the tear welling up in my eye and cascading down my cheek.

When I looked up Karen was watching, her gaze loving, compassionate and tender. She rose silently from her chair, leaned across her child and kissed the tear from my face. Her hands squeezing my thick, muscled shoulders with thanks and appreciation, it was a showing of sincere gratitude.

"Michael, you have no idea how special that scene of you holding my daughter is to me. She has told me so often that her little heart yearned for just that, to be held by her Daddy. You have blessed Kristi's heart more than you know."

"Lady, she has blessed mine. I have not felt this way in a long time." Not realizing just how much until this very moment.

"I am glad that you are here too young man!" Turning to Karen's son Britt and acknowledging his presence as he had walked up and peaked over my shoulder at his sister sleeping. I gave him a hug with my free arm.

By the end of that first visit with the entire family, something very different had taken place between Karen and me. Not only the joy of being together and sharing, but a level of chemistry was sending sparks in many directions. We were touching one another when we talked, and that afternoon when the visit was over, our embrace was much closer and more intimate. At the end of the embrace, looking down into her eyes, we kissed, really kissed for the first time.

There was a sweet hunger for both of us, starting tender and gentle it blossomed into a deep, passionate exchange. Our tongues searching one another, lips savoring the flavor and the moist, vibrant contact, it left both of us breathless. It must have lasted longer than either of us realized. As we parted both of the children were giggling, Britt whispering in Kristi's ear.

"Hey there Dude, what kind of secret are you telling your sister?" I kidded Britt, pulling him to me and hugging him tight. We both loved the light roughhousing with one another.

"You guys have a great week and you two do well in school!"

"Michael, why don't you call me tonight, here is my number!" As Karen spoke and handed me the piece of paper with her number, she leaned up and gave me a kiss on the cheek. For both of these displays of affection I was very grateful and appreciative.

With school, work, writing and Chapel, my weeks seemingly flew by. Time was going faster than ever before. I was working on a novel, an autobiography and life story. It was a work of great importance in the final cleansing and admission of all that I had done and needed forgiveness for.

Inspired by God as part of the rebuilding process, this work was a daily chronicle of events that had impacted my life. It included growing up in violence, Vietnam and my time with Sicilia-Falcon as a hit man. A little over six hundred pages already and still so much more to confess before completing the project and sealing its contents, I thought! That night I made the first call to Karen and shared what I had been working on. It was a sharing time with no secrets. If she was going to love me then she had to know everything.

"Karen, I have been working on some writing. It is a story of all the things that I have done in my life. Would you like to read it so that you can know everything? Before you answer let me say that there will be many things that are very graphic and terrible. These are all things that happened before I knew God. It may not even sound like me, because it isn't the same man as lives today. I know that you will have a lot of questions and I will answer every single one of them." I took a deep breath after finishing the statement and awaiting her response.

"God has revealed to me already that there was a deep and dark portion of your past. I will read it and then it will be over with. You are the man that I know and Jesus has showed me that." Her voice calm, concerned and full of a knowing peace, she was ready (she thought) for the story to be presented.

Once again God had jumped out there on front street and began a work in her heart. He would always be so far ahead of me, thankfully. It was in the mail the next morning, being in the same city, only one day and it was delivered to Karen. I let three days go by before calling to hear what she thought and felt.

Karen Cartrite, her maiden name was Gent, had grown up in this world without ever being exposed to anything other than a very sheltered existence. Protected by God, and her parents and the church, the world view and circumstances of black sin had never crossed her life until now. The story told of violence and killing, weapons and drugs and many things that to date, this lady had never even hear of, much less experienced. I called to hear her reaction, somewhat with reservation as to what I might hear. I knew that the shock factor would be evident, at least in some way.

"Hello, Cartrite residence." Her voice hesitant, knowing that it might possibly be me.

"Well, good evening there Ms. Cartrite. How is everything and everyone?" I tried to be as casual as possible.

"Michael (gasp), I (sigh) have been waiting for your call."

"It is the story isn't it Karen?" A trembling and soft crying began at the other end of the line, I could hear sniffles and pain. My heart sank for the anguish she was experiencing.

"What can I do to help you Karen, I am so sorry for your discomfort. The story was meant only for you to know where I came from, never to cause all this anguish!" Her pain was my pain and I could feel her soul as it wept. She was silent in her misery for a long time. Finally, a word from where, in her heart, she felt about all the information, the story.

"I just had no idea it would be like this, this much. So much. It is about a person that I don't know and to think that this was you is so hard." Her trembling and tears were still coming through the phone, pain driving itself deep into my heart.

"Karen, I thought that God had told me to write the story, but maybe I was wrong. Maybe I mistook the message and the meaning from my quiet time with Him. Just throw it in the fireplace and burn the story for evermore, if that will stop your pain. I am sorry, believe me I am so sorry."

"I know Michael, I am sorry to that I cannot read and understand this without getting so emotional. Yet it is from a world that I know absolutely nothing about and it frightened me."

Before the end of the conversation the manuscript was roaring in the fireplace, a thousand hour typing endeavor, ended. This event would take some twenty-five years to mend, yet this story and chronicle would be written and told, because the world had a right to know, the truth.

Another month went by, then two and three, the closeness between Karen and me elevated with every passing day. A healing had taken place over my past, it was pushed aside and the feeling of joy that we gave one another, remained and flourished.

One night, while writing a letter, I had to lay the groundwork for the next visit. Here is how I closed the letter to Karen that night.
Dearest Karen,
These past few months have brought me into a realm of tender warmth and joy. All of this because of the special feeling I have for you and the children, Britt and Kristi. A very special bond has formed and a true closeness of our hearts. There is chemistry between the two of us as well, a passion which flows deep, a wanting for more. I am falling in love with you, very much in love with you. There is no other word for what I feel and this will not remain unspoken any longer. Your beauty, both of heart and body, and so many qualities and special area which make my heart beat like thunder, are at times overwhelming. Other than God, you have taken over all else that is important for my existence. I want you to be a part of my life forever, eternally joined and sealed before our Father. I pray that this is your feeling as well. I sealed the envelope and sent my proposal, my anticipated dream on to her hand and her heart.

One big mistake that had taken place was my sharing of my intention with "the guys."

"Michael, if you get that letter today, Samuel and Bill and I are going to make you wait until tomorrow to read it, even if we have to hold you down." Big Russell spoke in a jovial manner with his kidding nature.

"Russell Scharf, wild horses could not keep that letter from me, I promise. The first one that tries to take that letter will pay a dear, dear price in pain."

"See how you are! If you didn't know all that Oriental stuff I would do it just for the fun of it." With his size and strength he would be capable, but the IF was there. What I did not know was that the three of them had already worked a deal out with the guard on duty. He was in on the play, thus the conspiracy included someone that I had no power over whatsoever. That is if I ever wanted to see the letter or daylight.

Mail call that night went on and on, my name was called but the letter was not from Karen. Since I had no idea or warning of the fiasco that had been conjured up, my buddies and brothers were having a ball with the situation, including the guard.
"Well guys, this is all the mail for today. You can check back tomorrow and see if anything else comes through the mailroom. Oh, wait, there is ONE MORE letter down here in the bottom of the bag, it says…Michael Decker." By this time the three musketeers were rolling and having a good time. Meanwhile my heart was caught in my throat and I was near stuttering. The laughter was infectious so I joined in to break the tension of the moment, making the event even more dramatic.
"You dudes will pay for this, I promise, especially you Russell. I know that you were the ring leader in this covert action."
"Who? Me?" A look of total innocence crossing his burly whiskered face, he had enjoyed this charade immensely. For myself, I was on the way back to my cell and some privacy, very rapidly.

Karen's fragrance, her perfume which made me breathe so deep, coated the entire envelope and the letter within. My eyes closed as I raised the gift to my nostrils and inhaled, setting the stage for the reading and answer. Slowly opening the response, anticipating what it might contain, the words began to flow in an ebbing to my heart. I had sent my heart in the mail and was awaiting her heart in return. In fact, even the opening of the letter, the initial greeting, held with it a power and display that was spoken from Karen's very soul.
My Dearest Michael,
These past few months have been for me, well, they have been something of a surprise and true delight in many ways. You have given me joy, happiness and peace, as well given my children more than they had ever received from their own father. What I must tell you now is from my heart and I hope that you will receive it as such.
Only God could have brought all of what has taken place between us to this point. What was in your past, is there in your past, and there it will forever remain. Now about us (I took a long, deep breath), I must be honest and straight forward. All aspects of the prison setting bothered me a lot at first. In time though it has changed and I now see it as a refuge, sanctuary if you will. I see God at work there in your life and in the lives of many of the men. You have done something while you were/are in prison, and I do not mean only the college courses

and stuff, I mean in your heart and way of living. God has done something inside of you, a tremendous work. He has created a new man, Born Again in the Spirit of His Son and becoming a worker, one predestined for a mighty leader in Christ. God revealed to me this week, the exact time and day and event that the love I have for you began. It was when I saw you protectively holding my daughter and loving her in a way she had always dreamed of. From that day it has grown to where it is today, a deeper and more complete kind of love. Yes Michael, I love you very much, I loved you in the Lord first and now I love you in every way. I can hardly wait until this Sunday, to be with you once again.

Goodness! I leaned back against the concrete wall of the cell, holding the letter on my lap, letting the ring of Karen's words flow through to every part of me, almost an echo to my ears. So amazing what God had done with our two hearts, allowing them to become soulmates. Karen felt the same way that I did, the past had died to her and the future was all that mattered. So many more tests and obstacles lay before us, our relationship, but they would be overcome, together, with God.

For several months God had been opening doors in the judicial circles around the country. Many aspects of the circumstances surrounding my case were being brought before people of high authority, all of this action was totally unknown to me personally. Karen had a very close friend whose husband had been elected to the Supreme Court of the State of New Mexico. His central focus and assignment was dealing with organized crime and politically connected cases. At this very same time, my Uncle, Polk Brown, was elected to the State Senate and serving a term in the New Mexico capital of Santa Fe. God was working through areas and arenas that would go over and through the corrupt power circles. The illegal manipulations of the courts, false evidence and downright lying of the past was about to be overthrown, mightily.

The major part of this shakedown occurred with the death of Senator Joseph Montoya, his patriarch position now removed and the scurrying of the underlings was in haste. Many were running for their political lives and careers with the flood of truth being examined and the exposure of deceit which had run rampant for many, many years. District Attorney, Police, Investigators, there were countless removals from office and quick resignations to avoid prosecution. The United States Senate Subcommittee watch dogs had seen, witnessed, listened and confirmed all of the wrong doings which had been blatantly covering my case and many others. The vacancy rate of several positions was duly noted and brought relief to countless of the fellow workers that had stood strong through the storms of the past five years, and more.

Several new hearings had taken place and new evidence was filtering down to the people in the know. Great events were taking place in Colorado through the prison system as well. Things were happening that would bring dignitaries and leaders from around the nation and across the globe into the Denver area. Many of the Christian leaders worldwide had committed to attend an upcoming event.

This enormous celebration was the World Premiere of the Born Again movie which had been produced from the book by Brother Chuck Colson. Held at the Continental Theatre in Denver, Colorado, it was to be a gala celebration of the transformation in Mr. Colson's life. Following the premiere would be a party and special reception at the exclusive Cherry Creek Country Club. Over three thousand guests were invited and ten very special men would be ushers at this festive affair.

Each of these chosen men was a current Federal inmate, in custody for anything from fraud to murder. Men, the Lord had touched and brought into a new way of life, now serving Jesus Christ rather than man. God had given each of them a freedom to live and walk in the likeness of their new Father.

Only by God's choice would Michael Decker and Russell Scharf be two of these ten men chosen for this special affair. The organizing committee had rented each of us tuxedos and gone all out. My Karen and Russell's wife Sherry had been given special invitations to attend. Beautiful corsages had been purchased for the ladies and it was to be a night of memory making proportions.

It had taken a great deal of special paperwork and grinding through the red tape for this to take place. Institutions, wardens, guards, United States Marshall's, all were notified, certified and now occupied with the documents to make this become a reality. Not only that, but for the first time, all of us would be transported without the normal chaining and handcuffing which was direct protocol by normal regulations. This freedom and honor came directly from God as a gift, to savor the life He had promised. His awesome Hand had reached down and erased the bondages of man once again. God was working miracles in places where mortal man could not even fathom, resulting in awe and bewilderment for many of the officials on duty. What a witness to so many in such a special environment and setting.

Finally, the night of the big event, weather, absolutely perfect, of course God would not have had it any other way, right! The large, black, government van pulled to a stop in front of the FCI Englewood, its Governmental shield indicating the authority in brilliant gold. Chaplain Tribe, Russell and me, then proceeded from the doors and on to the awaiting vehicle.

"Men, this will be a night of memories and a special occasion which your lives will always remember, and recall to others. God will work in mighty ways tonight and you men are a big part of what will take place. You both have been leaders here at Englewood, and for that effort, this is a special reward from the Lord and the pastoral leadership, here. Michael, you and Russell have a calling on your lives of such immense magnitude. You two will lead many men into the Kingdom of warriors before God, so as to serve Him and bring Him glory. Strong men, men destined to fight the battle and defeat the wickedness and evil that runs rampant across this nation today. Tonight is the start of that very leadership, so I am saying, walk with pride for you are the representatives of incarcerated men and women across this land. People who have come to know Jesus Christ as their personal Savior and finding freedom even though they are behind bars, you both are their beacons tonight. A freedom that most of the free world, doesn't even know exists." Chaplain Tribe was one dedicated man of God and had endured so much hardship during his years as a prison Chaplain. He had worked far beyond the required hours of the Bureau of Prisons, this to make sure and complete every aspect of what God had called him to accomplish.

"Chaplain Tribe, and I speak for the two of us, we thank you for allowing us to be a part of this celebration and the added bonus and blessing of having Karen and Sherry being here. We appreciate everything you have done and the way in which you serve God."

As I finished, we all shook hands and had another word of prayer, asking for our Heavenly Father to guide every step of this gala affair. After arriving at the Continental Theatre, sitting right there on I-25 and Hampden Avenue, activities were in full swing with last minute preparations. Setting up and decorating, stocking supplies and readying themselves for two thousand in less than an hour. Karen and Sherry had come early, they had graciously offered to help with the programs while the men took people to their respective seats. The long, stylish cut, gown Karen had on was flowing and beautiful and she made it a showpiece of loveliness.

"Be still my heart, you look so gorgeous lady, I will try and not faint until later." Putting my hands over my heart and buckling at the knees, slightly, to over emphasize how wonderful she looked.

"Michael, thank you, thank you very much, handsome man of mine!"

Now my knees were really bending for sure, she had a way of saying the right thing in such a way that the accent put me away. What a lady, what a lady indeed, and she even loved me. Would the wonders never cease? Just kidding a little, Lord! God liked to have a "little" humor now and then, I was sure of it, otherwise it wouldn't feel so good to laugh.

People began arriving some thirty minutes earlier than the festivities actually were beginning. Some dressed in the latest fashions from around the world and others dressed just comfortable stylish. The job of seating all of these patrons was a joy in itself. What a dichotomy of the cross sections of people, all coming for one thing, from every walk of life.

Forty five minutes after that first couple graced the entrance, the auditorium had a packed house. Seating was preassigned, so I knew just where to go after finishing with my duties. Karen was already seated by the time I reached the area.
"Excuse me Miss, I got here late and was wondering if you would mind some company, that is if you are single! Pretty lady like yourself, probably got several knocking at your door." As I sat down she pinched me almost to the point of yelping, and I deserved every bit of it. She was blushing and I was giggling as quietly as I could. No matter what the situation, her company brought such inexplicable joy to my heart, a freedom in love which had to do with the blessing of God. For no other source could have made anything or anyone so perfect. I reached and took her delicate, yet strong, smallish hand in mine and awaited the opening prayer.

Chuck Colson opened the ceremony and after a word with God, began to give his testimony and relate several of the key facts and circumstances to which God had opened the door to his heart and the door for National Prison Fellowship.

It was a powerful talk and witness of how the Lord had woke him up in the middle of the night and gave the revelation of his destiny after prison. On just how he was to serve his Heavenly Father. Finally toward the end he made a very unique statement to all of the audience. "Ladies and gentlemen, I would like to now inform you of a very special group of people, attending this evenings function. They are ten men who, like myself, have been doing time in a Federal Prison. One difference though, they are still incarcerated and here tonight on a special furlough. These men serve God behind the walls of these institutions, in the cellblocks and through out the life of every day of prison living. Touching and leading others toward the power and majesty of the lord Jesus Christ. Somewhere between ten and twenty of you are now, this very minute, sitting next to one of these men. Look and see who they might be."

An elderly lady next to me leaned over and asked me, "What does and inmate look like?" I just shrugged my shoulders, for now, Karen squeezed my hand affectionately. Never letting go, I brought hers to my lips and kissed the back of her hand.
"Gentlemen, wherever you are now, please stand up."

We all began to rise from varied places throughout the seating area, gasps and bewilderment from the fact of how we looked and who was next to us, commenced. It was a glorious moment for God, a deep understanding came to these people that all of us, can fail and fall. Even those that know God can backslide and slip, falling from the grace and protection of Jesus. God took a gravest that night and over two hundred people gave or rededicated their lives to Jesus.

My love for God and for this wonderful woman was never greater that that night. My heart was overflowing, for many reasons.

The applause that followed was recognition and praise, for God and His wondrous works, as I sat down with the rest of my brothers, Karen turned to me.
"I love you Michael, and what Jesus is doing in your life. You and the rest of these men have made the Lord proud. He will have a special blessing for you." Her eyes glowing and her heart showing so clearly what she felt.
"He already has blessed me, with the lovely lady I am sitting next to!" I pointed to the elderly next to me, while with my gestures I teased her, she knew that I was really talking about her. Whether shallow or sincere depth, our love came in waves from the most remote regions of our hearts.

While the movie was good, a fine story, the fellowship before and the reception after was where the real celebration took place. Fielding questions and witnessing in the process, it was amazing how many of the guests knew so little about the correctional system and the men and women who are held there.

Karen and Sherry, as a wife and girlfriend of men currently incarcerated, were doing much of the same answer sessions. Both of the two ladies had a special gift of telling about Jesus while giving the requested information. Planting seeds of faith which would be watered by others and harvested on down through the individuals walk through life.

When the end came, for the affair to be concluded, all of those that had participated were full, the food, fellowship and spirit had given them all they needed. For me, all I wanted was a few moments with the lady I love. Taking the opportunity for exactly that, a few moments, I took Karen's hand and walked to a hallway, a little out of the mainstream of traffic.

Stopping, turning sharply, I brought my hand, our fingers still entwined, to the small of her back, pulling her close. Emotions stirred from many contacts, however fleeting, during the course of the night, kindled the simmering heat between us. Our bodies met, brushing one another as if stroking a canvas, preparing for the artistry to begin. Her eyes danced with the fluid passion we felt for one another, mine reflecting the swell of energy rising from within me. Raising the other hand to her neck, I swiftly, with a gentle tenderness placed my mouth over the sweetness of Karen's lips. Tasting her and meanwhile savoring the aroma, my nostrils pulling deep the perfume, hungrily we allowed a flicker of flame to dance between us. A searing fire, although we were allowed to only cavort fleetingly through its outermost rim, it instilled what lingered in intensity and pleasure.

Our bodies parted physically, yet the memory of the feeling would remain for many hours, even days. I loved God, but that did not keep me from having human wants, needs and desires. We were young; strong, healthy, and had been alone for a long, long time. God knew this and had all the control necessary to ensure our celibacy during this courting period, however difficult it might become for the two of us.

"Lady that I love, someday, somehow, somewhere, I will complete the cycle of loving we tasted here tonight. With God as my witness and the provider of the freedom to allow the opportunity, I will give you every fiber of my body, every ounce of my heart."

Both of my hands were on her shapely shoulders, hers on my hips, she responded to what I said.

"Man of my dreams, prayers and hopes for the future, I will await your calling and the arrival to our home. These lips, this body, my bed, will remain in chastity until that day, no matter how long that period of time may be. I shall love you forevermore. God had brought you to my side, only he can take you away. I love you with all my heart." The stirring inside of me had gone from shear passion, to added streams of love and affection. Karen Cartrite was, exactly what God had intended for my soulmate and companion, thankfully.

Leaving that night, as we were loaded back in the vehicle and on the way back to the prison, I felt closeness from God, different from all of the many touching moments that I shared with the Holy Spirit on a daily basis. Tonight had been a blessing in a very unique way. One that in the existence which had encompassed my life and lifestyle had never experienced in this manner. That being the passion realm, normally thought to be only a temptation, a new light had been cast, a new perspective shown. The Apostle Paul had written to the people of Corinth, "No temptation has over taken you but such as is common to man. With each temptation comes a way of escape also, so that you may be able to endure it."

Waiting was worth it, simple and straight forward were His Commandment, that honoring to one another would serve to further strengthen the foundation which we had now embarked on for so many months. Difficult, yes, impossible no, prison had taken on an additional perspective in the past eight hours. God was not finished in His teachings. I would remain here until He was, no matter how long a period of time that might be.

The more that I learned, it showed me how much remained to be gathered in the context of knowledge. A babe in the Lord, I would be for some time.

The days and weeks, with no time failures, kept occurring. Don't ever think that the walk with God, on an individual basis, suddenly makes all of life a utopia. If anything it makes it more difficult, but once again, worth it. All aspects of life become filled with richness, depth, diversity, challenge which avails the individual to experience life. Taken to levels of feeling and thought that would never be possible in any other format. Add to this the eternal nature to each facet, a knowing that the purity will continue forever, as long as you stay in fellowship with God.

This cannot be defined any more clearly than in the testing process we go through. Sin and darkness leaves a film within the confines of ones heart and soul. It takes fire to cleanse this residue that our unfaithful philandering has brought about.

I can attest to this, more than many, for my level of sin and wrongdoing amounted to catastrophic proportion. When darkness has resided inside of a heart for such a long time, harboring hate, discontent and ill feeling, many things must transpire.

Yes, full and complete forgiveness comes when we, as man, ask for it, through confessions to God. There is an immediate cleansing, restoration and deliverance from the evil. At the same time, there is also a period of growth, through teachings, scripture, prayer and devotion. This step, decision, moment is called "Born Again" for a reason. It is a transition of one's spirit which requires nurturing, knowledge and habits to be formulated to prevent the reintervention of old habits and failures. This change is very similar in circumstance to taking a blueprint and beginning to build a home. A strong foundation creates the base of which all the rest of the structure relies upon. The structural walls must be placed according to the specifications, if not, a weakness is introduced. This flaw, while not visible from the completed project, still remains. Day after day, months, years may even pass, but eventually the flaw, the weakness will be exposed. Causing massive damage and allowing for almost total destruction to occur.

This same process occurs within our spiritual lives as well. When we try to hurry, skip phases, not concentrate on each of the integral parts of God's plan, we miss. From daily prayer, fellowship, Bible reading, church, all must be attended to with regular diligence and devotion to detail.

The onslaught of sin and pressure from Satan, are likened to winds and storms. These are flung against the walls and roof, searching for that small weak spot. Looking for a point of entry which would allow for a festering wound to begin its rot into the purity that God would have us enjoy and experience. That one key part of your structure, which was so small and insignificant, left out, becomes just that point where Satan attacks. Unmercifully, he will throw wave after wave until a crack, then rip and finally a portion lets go and he invades the Holy Sanctuary.

Cause, once again, simple and basic, but so important to the full completion of one's walk in Jesus. This cause is that we leave out the one wall, do not dig the foundation deep as the blueprint requires. Our covering, the roof of our lives, this home, needs daily maintenance, not weekly, monthly and occasionally. Without it, degradation will most certainly occur, and the light will slowly dim. It, our spirit has to be fed to survive. All of the blueprints, their individual details and fine print of specifications are available in God's Word.

Your, my, mankind's only true source of salvation is in the book, His Book, the Bible. Within it is the blueprint, road map and all of the information, teaching and instructional sources a man or woman will ever need. Remember, do not leave out, overlook or dismiss the importance of any part of the growth steps necessary, when you are Born Again into the salvation of a life with Jesus Christ. God always does His part, we need only do ours.

CHAPTER 8

a new Love, a new Life, almost

One year had passed since that April day, a milestone event in many ways. Karen Cartrite was a part of my life, even more now that I had asked her to marry me. Yes, her acceptance was one of the happiest days in my life, made unique by being able to give her a ring. Saving for now almost six months, working every job possible in the prison and putting back some of my school money, the stewardship paid off. A mutual friend had been the "shopper" and availed me the opportunity, for which I was more than grateful.

During this same time period, men and women were working on my case in New Mexico. God had assembled some very talented, dedicated individuals. In conjunction with all of these proceedings, I had been compiling a portfolio. More than anything else it was a resume' which could be used for verification of all that I had completed over the past few years. This had every one of the superior work reports that had been done over the past two and a half years. Additionally, it contained all of the college transcripts, and the now 3.87 grade point average. After writing a cover letter to the State Board of Corrections, enclosing all of the items previously mentioned, I prayerfully left it in God's powerful hands.

Early morning hours, May 14, 1979, darkness still gripped the horizon, not even the faintest coloring of a new day. Not in the world, as is normally understood, was there anything special going on. The night, ever present in my cell, gave a quiet so foreign to what rides the day of excessive noise, one of the real hazards of prison. Tranquil silence, only two present, myself and the Holy Spirit, I lay there listening to my heart. A stirring had awakened me, one which was predestined to make this a marked day. It would be remembered for the rest of my life, and be a testimony to the will of God. Once again, the warm, flowing grace of peace enveloped my soul. I was talking to my friend, Father, Master and Savior.

"Most gracious Heavenly Father, I come now before you in supple awareness of your promised deliverance. I praise you for all the blessing you have so mercifully bestowed upon my life. The cleansing of my heart and the redirection of my thinking has made me whole again. Thank you Father for loving me so much, and giving me the gifts that will help me to become a leader of people for your glory. This feeling which you have showered me with here tonight is one so powerful, so protective and caring. I accept this blessing, and praise you and glorify you Father even while still awaiting the further understanding. Praise you Holy God, thank you Jesus. Amen." Tears flowing from my eyes, these tender moments with God had a healing, soothing presence almost indescribable in mortal words.

9:45 a.m. came to pass and the P. A. system had an announcement come across, "00488-124, 00488-124, come to the Warden's office immediately." Leaving my workstation quickly, I checked out with my boss, Mr. Harrison, "Sir, the Warden has just paged me to his office."

"I will see you when you get back, hurry on now." Mr. Harrison had a smile on his face and the phone had rung near ten minutes ago. My heart quickened, strides lengthened and the pace was rapid as I left for the front of the prison.

Knock, knock, I rapped firmly on the doorjamb announcing my arrival. The head of the prison motioned me inside, his main attention on the phone call in progress. As he hung up the phone, Warden Roberts pointed to the chair.

"Decker, I have called you in my office this morning for some very important news and information." Deep breath and holding, I awaited the next sentence anxiously. Praying for good news about whatever he was referring. "I have just got off the phone with the Director of Corrections from the State of New Mexico. I made that call after receiving a document from them concerning the case that has been listed on your record as a maximum hold, high security. That detaining order has been cancelled effective 0900 hours this morning and you have been released from custody by the State of New Mexico. He also informed me of the circumstances surrounding your case and wanted me to personally pass on for him his apologies for the judicial processes that occurred there. From me, Williams, I congratulate you on this news but more so for the superlative manner you have conducted yourself during your incarceration. You have accomplished a tremendous amount of personal improvement, and you should be proud. Good luck in the future."

"Thank you, sir; it was all the Lord's work, not mine." He didn't respond verbally, but that look in his eyes had a knowing to it.

As the door to the open yard was pushed clear of the jamb, sunshine touched my face. The warmth that was flowing through my body came from the real Son's shine of majesty and glory, Jesus Christ. God had set me free inside and now He was going to set me free outside.

Standing there, eyes closed, arms outstretched toward the heavens, I silently praised God and thanked Him for the grace and tender mercy.

By the time night meal was served, 5:00 p.m., most of the institution, both inmate and staff, had heard the news and who was responsible. This was a great witness to many of the fence linemen, not truly having something they could grab hold of. God used it mightily and bumped many over to His side in the process, praise Him.

Finally, six o'clock arrived so I could call Karen.
"Cartrite residence, Kristi speaking!" Her tiny little voice so precious.
"Hi, Honey, I love you and need to speak with your mother, please!" I almost forgot the "please."
"Mom, its Michael and it's important!" Very perceptive of an eight year old.
"What is so important in this handsome man's life?" I so needed to hear her voice, it kissed my heart.
"You need to sit down before I tell you."
"I'm sitting!" Her tone relayed the intensity she had heard from mine.
"This morning I got called from work to the Warden's office. (Deep breath.) He informed me that the State of New Mexico had cancelled the detainer and dropped their case against me. It is over, no more, it is completely gone. Now I can go for a parole hearing."

There was a long silence, then the explosion into the phone.
"MICHAEL! . . . Oh, I felt in my heart early this morning that something very special was going to be given to you and us today. Oh, thank you Father, praise you Lord . . ." She was just as excited as I had been and her joy of thanks went to the person responsible for the gift of this magnitude.
"How soon can you go before the Parole Commission?"
"July is the next board, only eight weeks away, two months."

It had been almost thirty one months since I had walked through the long tunnel at FCI Oxford, Wisconsin, what was a mere eight weeks! Soon, it was very soon indeed, thankfully, and I was ready.

Karen helped me immensely putting together a release plan, coordinating many of the letters and information that would be part of the material I wanted to submit to the Parole Board. July 24, 1979 was the official date and we had put the information package together, completed by the fifteenth. The last few days, of course, were the hardest to remain patient and submissive towards God's leading.

So much had changed in the course of my life. Inside I felt that nothing could ever move me in another direction. What had now been laid as a Christian foundation and teaching would certainly carry me on to great things. An assurance of peace swirled around my heart, yet the anticipation of the "board" was still enough to set the jitters loose.

Tuesday morning broke, sunrise at 5:44 a.m., with a shower and dressed and three letters written by the time the first rays had creased the darkness of the night with their gold streaks. Sleep had been something which had ended by 2:00 a.m., and even before was only in short spurts. Finally it was "late" enough to call Karen and have a word with her before the hearing.
"Hello!" She was wide awake as well, her tone excited.
"Good morning sweet lady of mine. How is the loveliest lady of the land?"
"Michael! I knew it was you, I have been awake for hours. You could have called earlier if you wanted."
"This is plenty early; I just wanted you to know that I love you and I will go into the meeting with us in mind. Maybe all of our waiting is close to completion. I am so ready for some alone time with you." Though needing the lessons that had been taught during my incarceration, I was ready for the rest of my freedom.
"Me too! I am longing for your arms to be around me for an entire day and night." Karen's voice brought a stirring inside of me, there was so much chemistry between us. My heart was pounding from the thought of unlimited time, snuggled close and lost within one another.
"It won't be long! I really think that this is almost over. Today will tell us all there is about when!" I held my breath as that last word came from my lips.
"I will be in constant prayer for you and this decision until I hear from you tonight. Please be careful and know that I love you so very much. You are my man, I am your woman. We will go to that meeting as soul mates even though I can't be there in person. You will feel my presence from my heart." She had such a way with words at just the right time. Karen's support was a great help and I knew that she was right, I would feel her closeness.
"Your phone will ring the second I have any news, even the slightest shred, I promise."

We signed off and I headed for the chow hall to pass a little more of the time remaining before the 9:00 a.m. hearing. Barely getting out of the door of my cell, I had two bodyguards there for an escort. Well, more like brothers, but it was a duel intention, I was sure of it.
"Michael, we didn't want you to be alone on this final morning so Samuel and I decided to come along for the trip. Rascal that you are, trying to slip out of the cellblock without coming to get the guys who have sat through every meal with you. For at least a year now, Sammy, I think we may need to take this here brother behind the barn. What do you think?" Russell's smile was flowing rich and warm as he kidded me to break the tension of the morning.
"Like I heard you say one time, Russell, we could do that if he didn't know all that Asian stuff." Sammy was going to give it to me as well, probably deserved it. I did and enjoyed every minute of the fellowship.
"Okay, you two, let's cut the lingo and go get some chow!"
    The three of us headed out for the breakfast, somewhere near a thousand others joined in the procession. That number, one thousand, was happening in another way as well. Today was the one thousandth morning for a meal behind bars, though not an anniversary, still a milestone. We were standing in the line within five minutes and Russell turned his large frame and stared directly toward me.
"Michael, this morning God gave me a word for you. Actually more than just one, He has shown me what a powerful calling there is on your life. God wants you to know that Satan has a great need for you as well. Your life, the old one, led many people, only the wrong direction. God wants you to know that it is going to be a fight, maybe to the death, either you or the dark side of your personality and thinking. He wants you to remember each and every step He has taught and shown you to follow. For without the entire format being completed, Satan will sneak in and destroy the grace God has so mercifully given.
"You must take the time and be careful to associate only with men who are strong and have followed the Lord for many years. They will be your mentors and also keep you accountable in walking a narrow path. When you have completed all that He has called you to accomplish, this within the framework of your personal strength, He will bestow the remainder of His will upon your life. Yet this will not transpire until you have successfully walked down His chosen road for you. There will be times that it will not seem worth it, as there will be another trip through the desert. While difficult, this is a necessary step needed to finish the fire necessary to forge the armor within your heart and mind.

"God wants you to be a warrior, an angel of war, disciple to the wicked and the black hearted. You are to witness to the men that most of His flock could not and would not feel safe to share the Holy Word. Doors will open for you to walk through, steel doors and enter your will, into the depths of near Hell! This will allow for the mighty hand and tender love of God to touch these ones which have never been shown His brand of freedom." Russell paused for a directing, the Holy Spirit alive in his heart and God's strength showing all around him. The three of us had long since passed through the line and were seated at a table way in the corner. My brother took a deep breath and allowed for the flow of the spirit to continue.

"When you go to the parole board, all minds and hearts will have been washed and only the truth will be allowed. Satan has already been bound from this arena. God will show His completion of the promise that He gave to you and to Karen. She has already seen the final results, her closeness with God has allowed for discernment and a knowing. Cling to her, Michael, she is a chosen woman of Jesus. This is a calling for the two of you, thus be careful, once again, to take every decision before the Father, allow for His directing. God bids you a mighty calling, watch constantly for the light, when darkness approaches, stop. Do not take even one step! You have come a long way, but have a long way to go." This was one of the most powerful and direct acknowledgments of a Word from God I had ever witnessed. My heart pounded, chills came through me as I looked at the Holy Spirit pouring forth from my brother's heart. When I looked at Samuel, it was easy to tell that he had the same feeling, no doubt where these words had come, no other place, only from God.

"Russell Scharf, you are not only my brother, you are a mighty man of God. Men like you and Samuel make it hard to be on the final leg of this prison experience. There will be such large shoes to fill the void, which will take place when I walk from that gate for the last time. The love I have in my heart for you guys is one that before I came to prison, was never experienced with anyone except my mother, sister and grandparents. You both mean the world to me and I will miss our fellowship together."

So much for eating, this morning was so full of God and the workings of the Holy Spirit that needing anything else was not even in the program. We were all breathing deep and tears running down our cheeks. What a sight for the rest of the men, three of the biggest guys here. Praise God for the witness it was to the others, the pride for all that He had done in our lives was immense. Thus filled and satisfied, the trip back to the cellblock was in progress. What a day and to think that tomorrow was the big day. It would take some real doing to top this last hour; thank you, Jesus.

After splitting up and retiring to our individual cells once again, many thoughts began to formulate. More than any other was how far I had come in the past few years. Equally as strong were Russell's words, that God was determined to see me through the completion of this walk. How careful I must stay to not falter and stumble from the narrow path. There was a certain uneasiness accompanying this line of thinking in comprehending that Satan and his onslaught was going to continue in force. The fight would be one of devotion and allegiance, not allowing that "one step" God had forewarned Russell about. His words had been prophetic, decidedly from God.

July 24, 1979, as long as I could keep breathing, it was at least feasible that I would make it through the day. Sleep had been something only slightly considered and if any, maybe a one hour nap had occurred somewhere during the last few hours. Russell and his words from the previous morning had replayed many times. I could quote them by now. A vision of the room had come to me repeatedly, although I had never physically seen the room before.

By the time 8:45 a.m. rolled around, I was more than ready to assault the building. This was a miracle and the moment would forever be etched in my brain and heart. If only I had learned these truths earlier in my life, I could have alleviated so much pain and suffering, for me and for so many other people, but then I would not be the man who was standing here today either. There was a reason, a very definite one, and some day soon, God would reveal it to me. Stopping at the entrance of the Administration building, I looked to the heavens and allowed for my heart to feel the warmth and the tenderness of the Holy Spirit. There was a peace, so soothing that no other source could have produced what I was experiencing. God was going to accompany me through every stage of this event. An escapade of sorts, with a precious outcome, it would never stop touching these men in the room upstairs. They would forever be blessed and there would be a special blessing given to each of them. Five minutes until my time with the board, I pulled the large door open and began the long stairs. "Okay, God, I lay this meeting at your feet. What comes will be from you, I trust this fact in the name of Jesus Christ.

As the words came from my lips, a rush of energy and anticipation followed. During the next thirty minutes, three men would decide the outcome of the performance factors, education and "rehabilitation," which had been completed over the past years. Down deep, I knew that all reports and records, as well as transcripts, revealed a tremendous amount of work and dedication. But more than anything else, I was standing on the feeling of control which I felt God had already established. There had been so much confirmation from Karen, Russell and also in my heart.

"Next man! 00488-124, step in now!" Boom! The command came from behind the door in the meeting room. This was it: no more waiting, no more wondering; time had come for the truth to be told. Questions, answers, no matter what I was going to see, all destiny had deemed for me was about to unfold. My khakis had a crease pressed sharp, hair cut short, shaved and polished; I was ready.

"Yes, sir!" I announced as I stepped through the door. The panel of men, somber faces painted on each one. A smell of freshly painted walls drifted through the air. One single Board member, a Case Manager and an official of the Administrative Staff, made up the group. God had already shown His presence, for the Case Manager was from my unit, the Administrative Staff was the director of records, for whom I had done some volunteer work with a great memorandum written in my central file.

No doubt who had control of the physical meeting here, the elderly gentleman sitting in the middle. His silver hair, weathered skin reflected a knowing in his eyes from decades of these meetings and hearings. His voice commanded attention and its deep baritone note crackled through the air, shattering the momentary silence.

"It says here that you have been incarcerated in two institutions since your confinement began back in 1977, is that correct?"

"Yes, sir, other than some sixty three days in USP Leavenworth, during transport." I added this because I wanted to see if the record was there in my file.

"Yes, I noticed that notation, seemed a bit irregular. Tried to test your mettle?" The look and the tone of his voice came across to me with an understanding. He had read and studied my file, after being around the system for over three decades, it was obvious to him what had gone on in Leavenworth. From the body language and look from my eyes I think we, only the two of us, had a mutual understanding of the truth.

"Your file is quite impressive, education, programs, counseling, and all the things that we look for in consideration of release. But I want you to tell me exactly what you have learned here that will prevent a replay of your offense, if set free!" My "mettle" as he would say, was being tested again, yet inside I knew it was my faith. God had made this forum available to me. It was the opportunity that I had been waiting for.

"Sir, more than anything else I have learned what makes the most difference in one's life, my life, is a knowledge and fellowship with Jesus Christ. God had come into my life and set me free, in a way which you and your panel do not have the power to facilitate. This freedom comes only with the power and love that a knowing of the Bible, God's Word, and a personal relationship with Him can give. No other format, no other situation, nothing else can compare with this glorious freedom. You have read my file I am sure, and all the facts relating to the charges both Federal and State of New Mexico are contained there. In those files are the sordid details which I will not go into or discuss, for they do not matter now. Whether you make the decision to set me outside the walls of this prison or not will not change the freedom that God has placed inside of my heart. Nothing and nobody can alter that precious gift. He alone is my master and it is in Him that I will serve, not the world, which was how I placed myself here some years ago. As long as my focus in on His will, God will protect and provide all of the things which will be necessary. I have learned a great deal while this period of incarceration has been unfolding; it has not been easy. Yet I want you all to know that I am glad that I came to prison and I am thankful as well. For within the confines of these institutions I have acquired a foundation which will provide me with the tools to be a success in life. I thank you for the opportunity to say a few things here this morning."

Silence followed for some time before anyone spoke, God had announced His presence by using my tongue and His spirit had filled the room. These men were feeling something so much more powerful than all but one realized, guess which one? As he began to speak, all of the panel turned to him and listened to the wisdom.

"Young man, I have read thousands of files during these past thirty years. In those files are the facts and secrets which tell those of us who govern these meetings to either set a man free or tell him no, stay here. It has been only in a rare case that the individual has learned or changed or been trained and counseled back to reality. But the largest factor is exactly what you stated here this morning, foundation. There is no other foundation but within the Holy Spirit.

"Yes, I have read your file and many of the facts and circumstances are overwhelming. You have been through more than many men three times your age. God has done some miraculous things in your life.

You have applied yourself in making prison a positive influence. The parole plan which has been put together is one of the best I have witnessed. You must remember that what you are about to embark on is a journey which will have many peaks and valleys. Only by your focus remaining on Jesus Christ will you be able to climb those mountains and enjoy those valleys without stumbling. Do not think for even an instant that it will be easy, it won't. Especially for you, there is such a vast depth to your past, darkness will lurk and await the slightest time in prison. I am going to do everything possible to get your paperwork processed as fast as possible. You deserve a break after all that we have put you through. Know that you have passed this first test with flying colors. Go now and may God go with you." His words carried forth and echoed in the room – I was free again. My heart raced, thoughts whirling, I stepped from the room after thanking the board, quickly. My smile said most of the thanks. Passing through the door I stopped there in the hallway, taking a much needed deep breath. It had been some time since I could last remember breathing. Whew!
"Thank you, Jesus; thank you, Father. Praise your Holy name."

He had done exactly what He had promised and today would be a part of my testimony to His grace. The walk back to the cellblock was more of a floating process. God had been so good to me; I owed Him so much. Heading for the phone, I made no other stop after entering my unit. A few deep breaths, just in case I stopped breathing again. I had to make a quick phone call!
"Hello, Michael!" Karen was out of breath as well, for after her answering the phone that way there was no breathing going on.
"Yes, baby, it's me."
"I knew it was you. I have been praying constantly and about five to ten minutes ago I felt a rush of the Holy Spirit in a wave so powerful it nearly swept me over." Just about the time the speech was being given.
"It is over, no more prison, God set me free. The paperwork will be processed and that usually takes from forty-five to sixty days minimum. But know that it is almost over. Besides that, I love you lady."
"Oh, Michael, I love you to so much. That means we will be together in the next six to eight weeks!" Karen's excitement was coming right through the phone lines.

We talked for some time but the knowing of prison being over was the main topic. God, as always filled His promise, kept His Word. Now it was time for me to keep mine to Him.

For the rest of that day and for the next two, there were many extended hours of prayer, fellowship and sharing between all of us. My brothers were happy and sad, and so was my heart. These next few weeks would be spent in close fellowship. At least that was our initial plan, but this was not His plan. God had made a promise and the balance of it was about to be parlayed into the winning ticket of my life, one that would be immediately redeemable, an instant winner.

Friday morning, July 27, 1979, God had made more than one visit while within the institution, so it seemed. The announcement came over the prison loudspeaker, one that had been broadcast not too many weeks before.

"00488-124, 00488-124, come to the Warden's office immediately." My heart jumped as the announcement boomed through the corridors of the prison. I had not the slightest hint of what this was to be about. Yet no grass grew under my feet, I assure you, as I ran to the Administration Building.

Stepping to the door I knocked loud to announce my presence. Once again the door was open and Warden Roberts waved me inside.
"Michael, this seems to be a pattern nowadays, take a seat." I quickly sat down, this breathing thing was getting difficult.
"I have paperwork here on my desk that states that I am to release you to the Parole Commission, effective at 9:00 a.m. this morning. You don't think that it will take you long to pack, do you?"
"No, sir, not at all." My smile was about to burst my face. It had only been sixty hours since the hearing, not sixty days.
"I have read your file, once again, and want you to know that after seeing what the Lord has done in your life over this period of incarceration, it has been a witness to me. I have been on the verge of a personal decision for some time now. God has used you and all the circumstances surrounding your case to bring me into His fold. Personally I want to congratulate you and wish you the very best for the future."
"Thank you, sir, and welcome to the family of God." What a day, there had been so many during this past few months. All of my functions, heart beat/breathing, were coming in spasms with the level of excitement rushing though me. It was time for another race to the phone. I knew there would be a squeal this time. Karen would not be able to restrain herself, me neither.
"Hello." Such a casual, relaxed tone flowed through the receiver.
"Well Ms. Cartrite, please hold on to something solid or sit down."
"What, what is it?" It had already started.
"I was wondering if you could possibly find the time to come to the prison here in about an hour. That is because I need a ride!" Here it comes! I pulled the phone a few inches from my ear in preparation.

Scream! "Oh! My goodness! Really! Now! Really! Michael, I can't believe it, goodness. I am leaving now, okay?"

She was out of control and justifiably so. We both were excited, not able to hold back in the least. Quickly I grabbed my things and said some rapid goodbyes, many tears flowed, believe me. Prison was about to fade away from my thinking. Walking through the quadrangle for the last time, I gazed at what had been part of my home, and life, for these last two years. "Goodbye," I said with a final wave of my hand, walking through the door.

Thirty years old, I should have been at least sixty to have experienced so much. War, marriage, divorce, children, prison, the list of things already within the memory banks, was staggering at times. How could so many events have transpired in such a short period of time? The answer, speed, for most of my life the fast lane was always chosen. Never taking the time to enjoy any one part for very long – that was about to change.

Two months had now passed with getting established. From the first ride with Karen in the car, to finding a place to live, it was all as if I had never done it before. There were some tense moments, as the adjustment unfurled into the everyday life of living. But for the most part, problems were never really observed. Of special note was the easy acceptance of Britt and Kristi; they both loved all the time we had together.

Finally, Karen and I made the decision to become as one. We were married in October, just before my birthday. It was a quiet, simple home ceremony with her pastor Frank Tillapaugh, his wife Mary, Sherwin Crumley and the kids. Sherwin of course was the minister of music that had brought the group to the prison when Karen and I had first met.

God directed, I followed, and within six months I had made several contacts with construction people from around the city. This by working as a foreman for Tim Sanford Homes, and quickly the opportunity to do it on my own came about.

Michael J. Decker Construction Inc. arose from the ashes, corporate charter established. Stock certificates issued, license, bonded and insured, I was ready for business. Ninety days later the business was so good and with contracts taking me through another full year, I bought my first new vehicle.

A three quarter ton F-250 Ford, metallic brown, four-wheel drive, it was beautiful. That logo and sign on the side set it off and I was enjoying life in every way. The first evening that I drove it home was a memorable one, Karen and the kids standing in the driveway awaiting my arrival. She had a surprise coming as well. Pulling up into the driveway at the end of the culdesac, I turned the big V-8 off, the special tuned exhaust giving a throaty rumble as I hit the accelerator one last note. There was still a little youngster in my personality.

"It is so big, my goodness, Michael, we will need a ladder!" Karen and the kids all had a big grin on their faces.

"Well, lady, big truck for big jobs, makes sense doesn't it?" She nodded with complete approval, Britt was overjoyed with the new arrival; he jumped right into the cab and grabbed the wheel.

"You want to take it for a spin around the block?"

"Yes sir, you bet!" He would have to, so I promised him that later he and I would go for a ride.

I reached down and picked Kristi up in my arms to let her get inside, for her the stereo was the favorite part – girls!

"Psst! Kristi I have a surprise for your Mom, tell Britt!" I whispered in Kristi's ear softly.

"And just what are you three up to? Come on let me hear it!" Karen, hands on her hips, was trying to hear the secrets being passed between us.

The three of us, laughing out loud, could not hold it in after seeing the look on her face. Karen did not like secrets she was not a part of. So I came around the door of the big Ford and put my hands on her hips. With a heave, I lifted her to the hood of the truck.

"Now, young lady, just what would you like to know?" Her beautiful eyes shining, the sunlight dancing off the blonde hair in a shimmering light, it made me think about several things which I couldn't discuss with the kids so close.

"What are you telling Britt and Kristi? If you are going to tell them, then they will have to share with me."

Standing there between her knees, I reached to her face and pulled her to me, my lips caressing hers before I spoke.

"For your information, this is what we were talking about!" Waving my hand a car suddenly pulled from the curb up the block and proceeded down to where we were. As the sleek Volvo Sports GT sedan pulled into the driveway, Karen's eyes widened and her lips parted. Pointing to her chest she exclaimed, "Mine?"

"Yes, my sweet and beautiful wife, yours, just because I love you so much and because I want you and the kids to be safe and extremely comfortable." The pearl silver glistened in the sunlight, she ran to the opening door. I had one of the sales people drive it home for me. He was more than happy to accommodate me after making a double sale.

While I was signing the papers and writing the check for the truck, the car had come up into the showroom. It had been a trade for a new Lincoln, with only 12,000 miles, barely broken in for a Volvo. Making a very low offer they cut me a deal and I signed the contract.

"It is so beautiful, Michael! Kids, come and see it!" They flew from the truck to the car and enjoyed all the fanfare of having two new vehicles in the family.

Once all the initial jubilation was over, Britt and I took the salesman back to the complex, taking a small jaunt of our own on the way home. He had a ball; so did I, as he sat on my lap and drove part of the way home. Meanwhile, as would be expected, Karen and Kristi were doing their girl thing on an excursion in the new Volvo. I was both proud and thankful for the blessing, the abundance God had so beautifully blessed me and my family. That month was the first time I was able to tithe to the church, one thousand dollars. It was a wonderful feeling, one I will never forget, to be part of the success chain. God to me to the church; I never realized how special it made you feel to be a part of a congregation. Bear Valley Baptist Church had welcomed me in with open arms, from the very first day. What a difference my life was today, it made me thankful God had made all of His promises come true. Each and every one of them had been brought into reality, larger than I had expected.

This great way of life, the fellowship, care groups, career, church, family, all was rolling along at a perfect speed. Each part was wonderful and the relationship with Karen was all and more of what I had dreamed and prayed. So for the next two years, we worked and skied, traveled, prospered, and enjoyed life. The tragedy, which was coming was not expected or planned for in any way. It revolved around one of my contracts, people from the church. People I thought were honest, forthright and not capable of wrongdoing, eventually attacked my livelihood.

The contract was for a major remodel of their house, near sixty thousand dollars. This was a project that involved some extensive demolition and updating of their entire home. Several upgrades had been added to the original contract. In blind faith I carried the paper on this job, paying out of my pocket for materials and labor, weekly. Finally, ten weeks into the job, nearing completion, I asked for a draw on the contract.

With all the add ons, I had run through all of my cash reserves, drawn most of my signature notes and was getting uneasy where we were heading. They were already four weeks late on the down payment, which was to have been paid upon delivery of material.

"Paul, I need to get some money from you today before I leave. I know that you are well aware of the situation you have put me in. Making me ask for a payment when I have bent over backward for you is not right. So I am asking to be paid up to date, which leaves you owing me fifty-three thousand dollars already. This does not include the extra eighteen thousand for the upgrades and addition, because with those, the tab is already at seventy-two thousand." He slowly lifted his eyes to mine, the air thickened instantly.

"Michael, I am sorry to inform you that I am not going to be able to pay you today." Statement, brief, then silence, I broke it quickly.

"What do you mean you can't pay me?" My heart was racing and an old boil, one I had not felt in many years began to pulse through my veins.

"I mean that my wife and I have overextended ourselves and we don't have the money to pay you. Not now and I really do not have any idea when that will, or might change. The loan as well as the bonus I was counting on did not come through." His attitude was almost nonchalant, the wrong one to be showing me after all the effort, money and sweat I had put into this project. This statement made me catch the fire inside.

"You mean to tell me that you have known about this situation for now two months and you allowed the job and my money to keep pouring into your home. This with no means nor intention of paying me?" The veins on my neck were swelling, the hair on the back of my neck was rising, and a tingling crept into my hands.

"I'm sorry, that's just the way it is." He shrugged his shoulders.

BAM! BOOM! I slammed my fist down on the countertop, he jumped at the sound and the anger exploding through my body.

"How in the hell could you do this to me? I can't believe that you could have the gall to rob me and my family. You have made a mistake trying to take advantage of me. I am someone who does not put up with this kind of thing, it wasn't that long ago that I would have beat your butt or taken your life for such a stunt. Know that; hear me close and carefully! I am going to pull off this job today. With me as I leave will be all of the material I can load on my truck. Tough if you don't like it, try to stop me and you will most assuredly regret it from a hospital bed." Shaking my head in disgust, I proceeded to the garage and began to load material on my truck. The second bomb of the day was on its way shortly.

As I was loading materials on my truck, three Jefferson County Sheriff cars pulled to the front of the house. A young deputy got out of his car and approached me, hand on his weapon, the memories of days gone by began to flash in my brain.

"Don't touch another thing in that garage!" He had spoken, but I continued working paying him no heed.

"I said don't touch another object." The deputy stepped close, too close.

"I will touch and continue to load any damn thing I bought and paid for. You don't like it, tough, because I have the receipts to show ownership." I stood there glaring at him and the other two officers approaching. Young, arrogant and thinking he was going to force me into doing something, he reached for my arm as I lifted another box into the truck.

"You touch me and I will crush that hand and break the arm." His weapon came from his holster instantly.

"Jones, put that weapon away before someone gets hurt here!" The voice thundered into the confines of the garage, coming from the duty sergeant of the watch.

"Let's all just calm down here for a minute, Mr. Decker. I am well aware of your military background and also aware of the fact that you are still on parole with the Feds. Let me inform you that we are not here to start anything, quite the opposite. My young deputy has a tendency to fly off the handle; later I will deal with him. Letting him know just how close he came to taking on someone he could not possibly control. But for now I want to inform you of the law here in Colorado. Once material is delivered to a job site, it becomes the property of the landlord of the premises. Right: hell, no, it isn't right, but it is the law. You will have to take this guy to court to get any kind of relief for payment.

"Also, please be aware that Colorado has a homestead law and very possible you will not see a penny until the property is sold. That once again is the law, like it or not. This situation happens much more than you would think."

"You are telling me that the seventy thousand dollars that I have tied up in this house may be here indefinitely? That there is nothing I can do about it legally?" The rage was growing by the minute.

"That is exactly what I am telling you. Also, you need to be aware that the owner is already in the process of filing a restraining order against you."

Slamming the tailgate to the truck, I announced, "Get that patrol car from out of the way of my truck, now!" Inside I almost wanted for the deputy to smart off again. My witness, spiritual side had vanished before my eyes. So far I had come, so far I had to go, now a surge of the old violence crept back inside of me. Foreign for so long, the pulsing inside of me made my hands shake, but not from fear. I pulled from the drive as the patrol car moved away.

This feeling was so intense that it made me shake with the anger boiling inside. How could these so called Christians steal from me? After all the hard work and bending over to make their "additions" to the original contract come true. The engine roared as I flew down the highway, Hampden Westbound towards the Wadsworth exit. As I sat there at the light, waiting for the turn signal, upon exiting the main freeway, many things ran through my mind.

How was I going to make the house payment, car payment, put food on the table after extending myself so far? Sure, I had a few thousand left, but I had to run my business and have operating money. The light had changed and I turned left and headed for the Littleton area, south on Wadsworth. Up ahead a large sign announced a welcome release, "Chili's," I sure could use a cold one right about now. It was the first time since being released from prison that I had even thought of having a drink without Karen around.

Happy hour was in full progress as I walked into the bar area, everyone dressed like they had just come from the office. My t-shirt and Wranglers, accompanied the work boots, but I wasn't there to fraternize, just have a beer. Walking straight to the bar I leaned against the rail, squeezing my hands together.
"Yes sir, may I serve you?" The bartender asked, placing a coaster down in front of me.
"Give me a Tecate, lime and salt back." Sounded like exactly what the doctor would have prescribed for my condition. He nodded and went for the brew. I took a scan around the room. Suits and dresses everywhere I looked; there were several places where all the construction guys hung out, this was not one of them. Most of the people there looked to be from twenty-five to forty-five, roughly half with wedding bands, but that certainly didn't signify anything anymore. This had become very evident in my travels around the city and dealing with so many customers. It was absolutely amazing how many times I was propositioned during the course of a week.
"Here you go, sir, will there be anything else?"
"Yes, I just ordered one beer!"
"Today is a special happy hour and it's two for the price of one." He grinned and waited for a tip. I pushed a dollar across the bar, reaching for the first bottle. Taking a lime wedge, I squeezed it into the bottle and pushed the rest into the mouth, watching it fizz as it slowly sank and then taking the salt shaker, coated the rim of the top. Tipping it to

my lips, the cold malt and barley mixture glided down my throat. An empty bottle came down with my hand, I was thirsty and the flavor was good. Repeating the process to the second bottle, I took my time to savor it.

Fifteen minutes and five beers later, I was beginning to relax from all the chaos of the afternoon. The music was getting louder and the crowd was responding, a voice inside me said that if I did not leave now, I might not. There was no doubt what was the right thing to do, yet a small struggle was still waging in my heart. A deep breath, one last drink and I walked to the exit and left.

Driving home was done at regular speed, I knew Karen and I were going to disagree entirely on the dispute with her friends from church. The alcohol aided the other voice inside of me, encouraging a stand of defiance and anger towards my customer. Turning the corner on South Reed Court, I could see the house at the end of the street. The kitchen light was on as the large bay window on the front gave a view of the great room inside. A large addition from the dining room out back had allowed for over one thousand square feet in this area, it was very well done, I had worked hard. Pulling up into the driveway, I noticed that none of the other lights were on in the house. This meant that the kids were probably not home, something was up. I stepped from the truck and walked through the garage into the side door of the house.

"I'm home, Karen. I am going to take a shower." Not waiting for a response I went directly to the bedroom, undressed and stepped into the shower. The warm water felt good as it soothed some of the tightness in my shoulders and neck. Through the shower door I noticed Karen enter the bathroom.

"Hi!" Her voice reserved; she had very apparently talked to her "friend" and heard their version.

"Hi back." A conversation was going to be strained at best. That was evident to both of us.

"I am very sorry for what happened today. Mary told me most of what happened when she got home from work. She said that Paul had not told her about the finances and didn't have any idea that you were not being paid. She apologizes, if that makes any difference." Karen was trying her best to be a peacemaker.

"Yeah, I will take her apology and go to the bank tomorrow and try to deposit it in my account. I certainly hope that you did not fall for that line. If Paul knew, she did as well and I am going to sue them for every penny they have." The heat began to rise once again as the afternoon replayed itself.

"Michael, we can't do that. God says that we are not to settle matters in court, but between each other ... I..." My words cut off what she was going to say.

"Well God says that you are not supposed to steal either but that is just exactly what they did, steal. There is no way I am going to turn my cheek or anything else for that matter for what was done." Turning the water off I stepped from the shower and began to dry off. She was crying, tears streaming down her face as she leaned back against the counter. I put my hands on her shoulders and pulled her to my chest.

"Karen, this is not something you need to worry about, I will take care of it." Sniffles continued as she answered.

"But, Michael, they are my friends. I have known them for almost fifteen years. In fact Mary was there when I had Britt and Kristi."

No answer, no reply from me, I continued to hold her and allowed the tears to subside. Several minutes later we walked on into the bedroom and she watched me getting dressed for dinner. Some old sweat pants and an old football jersey from the University of New Mexico were just the right combination for the mood I was in.

"Let's go eat dinner and we will talk later about this, okay?" Shaking her head in agreement we headed up the stairs of the bi-level home. The topic and subject was never discussed again that night, just left alone to simmer. All of the talking in the world would not change the situation and I was not going to stop living because of her "friends," they certainly were not mine. If I had not been on parole I would have been inclined to make a few phone calls of retribution, but this as well was best left undone. Late that night as the two of us lay in one another's arms, exhausted after an extended period of love making, Karen nestled up to my ear and whispered.

"Let's just take this to the Lord and leave it there, I will not bring it up again, please." Her spirit and heart were in exactly the right place and she was giving me the opportunity to do two things. Ask for forgiveness and ask for wisdom from God in His handling of the situation. Allowing for supreme intervention, exactly the way He had so majestically done while I was incarcerated.

"Okay, lover, let's take it to our Heavenly Father. By the way I am sorry for coming in tonight so short and not talking. I love you, Karen, and don't want anything to come between us. It just unnerved me to think about not being able to pay all the bills." She responded by snuggling closer and kissing me tenderly on the cheek.

"I know that, Michael, but God will not let us go without. He will provide for us as long as we stay within His will and His Word. God has provided for me always, even when I got down to nothing. His mercy comes from a Holy heart, unconditional love given without reserve, for all eternity. You have just had your first real taste of human failure, though a big one, from a fellow Christian. Allow God to work in their lives as well, the blessing will come in His timing, also the completed work in all of our hearts." One of the many reasons I loved this special, beautiful lady. We prayed and with forgiveness I received a much needed night's rest. Tomorrow would be a new day. Thankfully this one would not have to be repeated.

Morning did bring with it a new day, a cloud still remained but not near as stormy as yesterday. There was almost three weeks remaining in the job and a reworking of my schedule to facilitate the change was necessary. The tightness around my jaws still told me that things were not forgotten by any means. More than anything else, right now, I had to go out and hustle some fast cash. One of the remaining jobs on the books was a tear off and new roof not far from the house, thus it moved to the top of the list. A three day job and $2700.00 profit, it would require sixteen to eighteen hours a day to complete. No breaks and a ten minute lunch, humping it with every ounce of strength and stamina I was able to muster, the challenge encouraged me. It would be a great place to release some of the frustration and anger.

The drive home, three days later, certified check in my hand, brought with it a release of feelings. Bone tired, fingers cracked and bleeding, none of it mattered, my family was being provided for and that was the main fact. They were my responsibility and there was nothing that was going to stand in the way of me providing their livelihood.
"Excuse me, lady, would you mind putting this in the bank tomorrow morning for groceries and shopping?" I handed the check over to Karen as I walked into the house. The glow and smile were a welcome sight. She gave me peace in many ways. Another hurdle had been overcome and on we would trek to the next one.

This week had brought with it a change in habit for me. A beer or two on the way home was satisfying, so I kept a small six-pack cooler full in the truck. Never to be opened until after the workday had ended, just a little refreshment, for the moment.
The best laid plans of mice and men, this phrase would come to have valid meaning in my life very quickly. A voice from the past came across the phone waves one afternoon. Richard Gorman, Senior Special Agent from the Drug Enforcement Administration, called to say hello and ask if I was interested in an interview.

"Well, Richard, how the heck are you, stranger?" His voice a low baritone which was easily recognizable, I heard it many times in the past. Karen had passed me the phone and was standing there with a very puzzled look on her face. My hand signals were hindering rather than helping her dilemma of the person on the other end.

"Great, Michael! Just great! I am staying very busy as you might imagine. But the reason for my call is that I have been contacted by a well known author named James Mills. He is writing a book on the drug cartels and empires down in Central and South America, and their affiliation with government officials. Mr. Mills would like very much to interview you and utilize your story and comments in a book." Somewhat flattering to be wanted in this manner, a small check in my spirit as well.

"Have you checked out his authenticity, background and the like?"

"He writes for Doubleday Publishing. He has several novels out and a few have been made into movies. Some have been bestsellers. San Diego would probably be the best place to conduct them." My curiosity was aroused and I was intrigued by the possibility.

"How soon are you thinking this might come to pass?" Karen was sitting there about to pop, hearing only half of the conversation, she wanted to get in the know quickly.

"He is ready to take off from New York on short notice, so just whenever you might want to set it up."

"Give me your number, Richard, and I will call you back tomorrow morning." We signed off and I sat the phone number which was now written on a tablet on the nightstand. Waiting for Karen to say something before I relayed the context of my talk with Richard, I hesitated.

"Well?" Her shoulders and eyebrows lifting, not liking the silence, she waited.

"That was an agent, Richard Gorman, someone I used to work with. A man by the name of James Mills, an author, contacted him about the possibility of me flying to California and doing a series of interviews. Probably out to San Diego, of course being paid for my time there. Mr. Mills wants to use my story in a book about drug cartels and their interrelationship with governments."

"Would you even remotely consider that?" Her tone was one I rarely heard. A check in her spirit, as well as complete disapproval of the subject at hand, entirely.

"Why do you say that Karen?" Her answer had already come silently but I wanted to hear it verbalized.

"Because there is nothing glorifying to God about what happened back then. Yes, you came to know God as a result of the tragedy, for that I am thankful and so is God. But do you honestly think that this professional writer will put God to the forefront of the novel or the worldly dramas and acts of violence?"

"To be honest I have not considered it to that depth as of yet. A few thousand dollars bonus would be nice though. Don't you agree with that?" She was shaking her head even before I finished talking.

"No, Michael, I don't, and I think you will feel the same when you have had time to think and pray about it. At least I hope that is the case at hand, after you do. Although whatever you decide I will support, as I am supposed to before God, as your wife." That statement always was the one that got me. She had a way of saying it with body language and tone that hit like a ton of bricks.

For now the discussion was over, but I was considering it even as I walked from the room. Sounded pretty exciting and the trip would be nice. I had not gotten away for a long time, more than a weekend or so. Maybe it would be rewarding in more ways than one. Something to consider for sure!

Later that night I decided to go. Not waiting for a confirmation from God. The decision of giving the information and doing the interviews, would come back to haunt me many years later in a form that had with it, repercussions. Even from that day forward, the trip caused a division between Karen and me. One far greater than I realized at the time, she resented not only the fact that I went, but the way the trip came about.

All of the plans had to be postponed because of conflicting schedules. When it finally came time, Karen had a commitment at the church and I went anyway. This amplified the situation and made it even more of a rift between the two of us. While the trip itself was a success, James Mills got a very thorough interview, information containing more facts and documents than he had dreamed of obtaining, as I had an acute memory for detail. For me, I got the money and told the entire accounting of my life in the underworld and jungles of the world.

Three mistakes were made as a result of going to California, major ones. First, I had gone away on a trip that was not blessed nor confirmed by God. Second, I had crossed the boundary of the relationship with my wife. Karen had every right in the world to be upset and harbor ill feelings. Third, equally as important, Karen had mentioned in our first talk that if what I was going to say was not glorifying to God, it need not be said. All but a very few questions and the material I provided, had anything whatsoever to do with God.

The spiral of this event, added to several occurrences which she and I differed on, would begin to form a wall, a large one. With toll gates on each end, requiring "permission" to pass onward, it grew thicker by the day. That openness and close communication was void, it had left. For the final death blow to our relationship, a display of the power and violence of martial arts would be the delivering factor.

A call had come from the Rocky Mountain Council of the Professional Karate Association for a fighting, full contact championship. They would take the top black belt contenders and state champions to Mammoth Gardens, for a winner take all tournament. This covering all of the eight Rocky Mountain States, mostly instructors and master level enthusiasts.

"Michael, this is Kirby Baker, I am from the promotion staff of the upcoming Regional Finals. The PKA is sponsoring this event and it will be televised nationally on ESPN from the Mammoth Gardens Arena." He began the conversation as Kristi had handed me the phone.

"Yes, Kirby, I have seen several articles in the Denver Post and on T.V., how can I help you?"

"Well, I wanted to know if you would consider fighting in this tournament. I realize that you have not had a chance to formally train, but we are very interested in you competing."

"Kirby, I am curious about where you got my name?" Very curious as a matter of fact, and I would find out exactly who his source had been.

"Bob Adams is a personal friend of two of the promoters and he has passed on some pretty incredible stories. Down in San Diego with Bill Russell, Kurt Richards, Chuck Norris, even one special afternoon with the man himself, Bruce Lee, it must have been incredible. I personally have talked with a gentleman who witnessed the breaking demonstration and kata display at the prison in Englewood, Colorado. That person was my brother, Greg Baker, one of the men or inmates there."

Four months after I had gotten to Englewood there had been a talent contest. Several of the guys encouraged me to put on a show of martial arts skills and I had accepted the challenge. Breaking boards and concrete blocks and doing fighting forms (katas), with a final show of power breaking, well shattering a four hundred pound block of ice.

"Small world isn't it, Kirby?"

"Yes, that is one of the things I wanted to talk to you about. After what Greg shared with me and from the physical description, I called a friend of mine with the FBI. He is one of my fraternity brothers from college. All he would confirm was the fact that you had a great deal of training, both military and private. Also, that Vietnam and mercenary work were part of your history. I am bright enough to read between the lines and know that you would not like any publicity, background wise, and we would certainly uphold that. So what I am asking is would you consider honoring us, and this tournament, with your participation?"

No wonder why this guy was in marketing and promotion, he had a smooth approach.

"Kirby, leave me your number and I will get back to you within a couple of days. Is that fair enough?"

"That would be fine and if there are any other questions, please feel free to call. I will await your reply."

Hanging up the phone, a flood of memories of the last full contact fight I had participated in came back. So many fights, matches which were sanctioned, pit fights for money, brawls just for the fun of fighting. A question which came to me was whether I could fight the same way, now that I had changed my life? The fight and violence inside of me had been so deep for so long.

Other than the anger I had felt back when the job had gone sour, a few months back, no real anger had flowed through me since coming to know Jesus Christ, almost seven years before. Sitting there, thinking of the possibility, a spark flickered deep inside my soul. So infinitesimal, but it still flickered out as a reminder, maybe as a warning or messenger. My last fight had been the night of the killing, Albert Montoya in Albuquerque, New Mexico. Nine other men had gone into the hospital, three very badly injured. That night I had been fighting for my life, this contest would be only for a title. Yet to me an arena was still an arena, once the first blow had been delivered, what would it feel like?

After so many years of fighting for keeps, where it was win or die, had God changed that side of me? There was no other way to know other than get into the ring and see. Deciding to fight and compete for the title, I spent the rest of the afternoon waiting for Karen to come home from skiing, knowing that she would not like the idea in the least bit. Getting in shape was no problem, my work kept me that way. Stretching and practicing two to three times a week had been a part of my routine for years. Most of the technique and knowledge was way beyond the "automatic" stage anyway. The more I thought about it, the more energy it mustered inside.

It was a question that had to be answered, sooner or later, not only in my mind, but my heart. Eventually, allowing twenty years of training to resurface, it was inevitable. A sound from the garage told me

that Karen had made her return from a full day of skiing. Walking to the door by the den, I pushed it open to see her snapping the racks. Her new Rossignols had been a gift for Christmas, they along with all the trimmings, she was an avid skier. Twice a week minimum, this time of year, she and kids spent a great deal of time on the slopes.
"Hey there, how was the skiing?"
"It was wonderful! There was almost ten inches of fresh powder from the previous two nights. The back bowls were waist deep, the double blacks, freshly groomed and a challenge. It was a great day for sure." She was pleased, in a good mood. Glass of wine, dinner, hot shower, then, we would talk.

The evening had progressed as planned, smooth and relaxed, now for the subject at hand.
"Karen, I had a call today from one of the tournament directors for the upcoming Regional Championships. It is a full contact event; I have been invited to participate in their open, Masters black belt Division. There will be all of the champions from eight states vying for the titles in three weight divisions."
"When are they going to be having the tournament?" Karen was asking from a very reluctant tone to her voice. One I had heard before.
"It will be later this month and it is a modern rules event, meaning that gloves and footgear will be worn. No bare knuckles or anything of that nature."
"You mentioned this because you are thinking seriously about fighting." That knowing, furrow in her brow, coming with the statement as she awaited my answer, I replied.
"Yes, I would like to participate. It will be a strong field and also will be televised nationwide on ESPN."
"Huh!" End of the conversation, she stood up and walked from the room. Not a single bone in her body wanted me to go, much less fight. Once again, the differences in our background, way of growing up, was making a division between us.

At least an hour had gone by before I went down to the master bedroom. God showed me what I was supposed to be doing as I walked through the door. Karen was there, on her knees, an open Bible on the bed, praying for some answers. Instantly, the Holy Spirit, ever present, the guilt began to grow. It should have been the two of us down on our knees, as one, in one accord asking for God to provide the contented heart and confirmation of peace. I, the supposed leader of the family, had chosen to handle this in a worldly fashion, while Karen, meanwhile, had taken the situation to Jesus.

For the next three weeks, there was a struggle. It was an all out brawl going on in my heart. Up early every day to run and work like a wild person, my inner peace had departed. This due to lack of devotional time, something I had not missed in years. Four days before the fight, while tearing out a set of old windows on a job site, and accident took place. One of my men dropped the window, shattering the glass. As I reached to try and catch the frame, a large piece cut a long gash across the large first and second knuckles of my right hand. Of course, my power punching hand. Eleven stitches later and some swelling by the next morning, the possibility of fighting had been decided. At least it should have been.

Disregarding the final warning, so visible and evident to all concerned, I taped the wound as much as possible, pulled on my black tournament fighting Gi and went to compete anyway.

To make it into the final round, for the overall title and the championship, I would have to fight three preliminary fights. Winning the first two fights by knockout, the third by decision, by the end of the day my hand was a mess. All of the stitches had long since ripped through. Leaving a open wound, raw and ragged, gaping open and bleeding.

"Michael, your hand is in no condition to continue. I think we should enter a forfeit." The tournament trainer had given his opinion.

"No way! No how! I came this far and will continue. Just tape it back together as best as you can and I will go for the championship."

Karen was to be at ringside for the title match. I had called her and asked that she be there. She had agreed to come with one of her girl friends, making it clear the thought of watching two people beat on one another seemed wrong. Meanwhile, I was thinking about nothing else but the title shot. Karate was a true joy and the competition sent a surge of adrenaline through my veins, a feeling I had enjoyed for years. All of the questions I had been wondering about were now answered. Everything was still there, the power, strength, style, all of the skills which had been ingrained for so many years. Every single thing, except the most important, Jesus was not there. He was here in the building, I was not allowing the Holy Spirit to guide me; His knocking I could hear, yet I walked away.

During the second round of the fight, ESPN television cameras rolling, I could see that I had the fight won by points. Most of the crowd was roaring for a knockout, they wanted to see the gore and the blood. In between rounds I had looked over to where Karen was sitting and what I saw changed everything. The anguish, pain and most of all the Holy Spirit in her eyes, I was convicted. Her heart and mind was constantly, consistently, allowing the power of God to reign triumphant. A breaking began to take place, or I should say another breaking. This one came in a wave so powerful that the darkness, which I had allowed to reside for the past three weeks, vanished. God had control of the match.

My opponent could not respond for the bell and the title was awarded to me. Karen met me in the dressing room afterwards, as the trainer was taking the old dressing off my hand. The glove was full of blood, Karen had to turn away.

"Michael, I cannot believe you went into this match with a wound so serious. What were you thinking of?"

"I was thinking only about the title, nothing else, I am sorry to say. I was wrong to go ahead with this decision; once again, you were right." She was right, simply allowing her heart and actions to be guided by nothing other than the Will of God.

"I love you, Michael. Please try to hear God, He has been calling you, mightily, for a long time. There is so much He wants for your life, for our lives. But we have to respond to His call." She put her arms around my neck and hugged me lovingly. I truly could not believe that I had rebuked my God, He, the one who had granted me so much and opened the doors of prison. By early morning the next day, the full repercussion of my decision to fight would present itself, vividly.

Karen had risen early to get the kids off to the slopes. They went up with the Big Horn Ski Club, every weekend, skiing Saturday and Sunday for twenty consecutive weeks. They were great skiers and addicted. "Michael! Your hand!" Karen's exclamation startled me from my sleep. She was looking at the results of the fighting. During the night, infection had set in my hand. I had the beginnings of severe gangrene. It looked as if someone had hooked an air hose to my arm from the elbow to my hand.

"Oh my goodness, Karen, I have gangrene! I have seen this too many times in Vietnam. You had better call the doctor." She had him on the line within minutes, we had strict instructions to go straight to the emergency room.

Karen stayed next to my side for the entire ordeal, sure enough the surgeon later revealed that I had a solid case of gangrene and another few hours would have resulted in an amputation. Only by the grace of God and my wife did I still have an arm from the elbow down.

This struggle which had been going on inside me for almost a year, was enhanced by the occasional dependence on a drink, which had started at two drinks and now had gone to ten to get the same effect. Yet the base cause, the foundation of the problem, I, like so many others, was my lack of allegiance to Jesus Christ. No excuse, no justification, nothing, could make what I had done, and not done okay. Years later, I would look back on this time period and shake my head at the ignorance, almost sheer blindness I had to the life and relationship I was killing. Ever so slowly, independent of what I was before Karen, darkness crept silently into the house that God had built for me. This was due to not following the steps He had so beautifully laid before me.

Three years, eight months, fourteen days after I had been released from prison, Karen and I met in the Arapahoe County Court for a divorce.

The exact reason was an accumulation of wrongs. The largest being my walking a path which was not made, nor guided by the Holy Spirit. The divorce came from me; Karen was a beautiful, sensitive, wonderful wife – she is still one today for the lucky man that took my place in her life. So many memories remain of the talks Karen and I had enjoyed concerning growing old together. She had faith in God and her husband. I did not come through with the vows and promises I had given before our pastor and before God. This, a mistake, and the beginning of a backslide all the way to the worldly life.

CHAPTER 9

Streets, back to the back to *Prison!*

Nightclubs, drugs, big money, fast cars, drinking and partying, I ran to the streets. Not setting foot into a church for about five years.

A call from New York City, James Mills the author would start a spiral of change to my life.
"Hello!" Answering the phone one evening.
"Michael!" This is James Mills, I'm calling from New York City."
"Yes, James, I have not heard from you in a long time."
"It has been a busy time with working on the novels and raising a family. The reason I am calling is to ask if you could and would come to New York. Both the publisher and I would like to have you on the "Today Show" during the first week of June. Also, two articles are being done, as we speak, for Rolling Stone Magazine." He was laying all of his cards on the table in the first hand of play.
"You have been busy, James. It sounds like something I could work out with my boss. Let me check and I will be back to you in a couple of days. Will that work for you?"
"That will be fine, please let me know as soon as possible for scheduling."

As I hung up the phone, a rush of memories and thoughts began to flood my thoughts. Falcon, California, Lisa, Christopher, prison, all came flowing through my mind. So many dramatic events took place in such a short period of time. Now to relive many parts of it, both a thrill of the ride and the anticipation of what it would be like on a morning talk show with millions of people watching. That age old duality of opposing forces began to wrestle in my mind.

For the last four years, life in the fast lane had been taking its toll on my life, especially my health, spiritual that is. From 1981-1984, my old boss, Frank Luck, was once again in my life. His corporation, Safety Products Inc., still remained on Evans Ave. in Denver, it was home now of a Division called Sunland Solar. This was a part of a national chain of solar energy distributors, the manufacturing done in Phoenix, Arizona. I had joined them midway through the energy tax credit period. This enabled homeowners to receive a seventy percent tax refund for the installation of a solar system in their home. Sales were brisk and a tremendous amount of money was being made.

As I jumped on the bandwagon, it was a paradise for me. In home sales were easy for me, doing a two hour presentation and allowing them to purchase the finest equipment built in America. I thought it, felt it, then passed this conviction on to my customer. By the seventh month in the business I was awarded the coveted five diamond Sunland pin. Three months later the first six, seven and finally eight diamond, master salesman award was in my hand. Setting three national sales marks in a record length of time for most number of sales, highest dollar volume, and highest gross for both a month and a year, I was back in the big bucks.

Monetary success came in leaps and bounds, my highest commission, monthly totals, was almost $30,000.00. More than many people made in a year. None of the money bought me any lasting peace or happiness. I literally threw it away on wine, women and song, one night to the tune of $10,000.00 for a night of insanity, which I truly remember very little of. I had been working like a sled dog for three months and had won a regional contest. A new car and a cashier's check from the rewards of the success, but only the car remained the next morning when I awoke. A round for the bar, Bobbie MaGee's Conglomeration, Denver Colorado, one o'clock in the morning, for some unknown reason I ordered a bottle of Dom for every table in the house to have a toast with me. My success was the toasting item, my stupidity the only factor of relevance the next day. I had to call one of my friends to find out what had happened to the ten grand. What a laugh, later I would look back on this event, many other nights with the same type of behavior, shaking my head in utter disgust.

Over the five years I was in the employ of Sunland Solar, somewhere in the neighborhood of seven hundred thousand dollars was flushed down the sinful toilets of Denver, Dallas, L.A. and other stop over points. At the National Sales Championships, Awards Ceremony, in San Diego, California, I managed to leave all of the contest monies. After, once again, striving so hard and achieving national recognition for being the number one salesperson. The problem, too much booze, too little Jesus, none whatsoever, this was my foremost problem.

These last few pages may seem like a partial confession, they are, and to go into the actual details of the events, with all of their wild antics and deplorable acts, could do little else other than possibly glamorize and glorify the wrong thing. The message I want everyone to realize and understand is that there is only one true way to live life, if true life is to be attained. This is only possible with a continuing relationship, daily walk, with Jesus Christ.

There is nothing left at the end of the rainbow but an empty pot, I know because I have chased it. Once it was found, whether it was momentary stimulation or satisfaction, it left a void in its departure which I felt too many times. So often, the memories of Karen and the kids would be there, that knowing peace, special joy, while I sat in my big house and drove my Porsches and 500SLs. I promise you that there was not a moment within the confines of all the money, that one minute with God could compare. He showed me peace and joy and a high that the millions, the cars and the drugs could not. All of the world, with all of its material possessions could not either. For ten years of my life I ran with the so called jet set, big boys, mega rich, they could not hold a candle to the dimension of life which is only possible with a personal relationship with Jesus Christ.

He alone is the Way, the Truth and the Life. On the darkest day in the deepest confines of the maximum security cells in Leavenworth prison, I had found more freedom, peace and happiness than the worldly life had ever displayed or given. It is so amazing how the finite mind of man can rationalize and justify his shortcomings. These to the point of walking away from God after being delivered from the dark pits of hell and into the light, I speak of this fact because of fact, not fiction, facts and past history that I had so blatantly caused and committed.

Yes, I enjoyed the high roller life style, for the moment. If only I had kept my focus on God, His blessings would have been on the wealth. My tithe alone could have run many churches and fed thousands of starving people. God means for all of us to prosper; it is the manner in which we can handle this wealth that is visibly important. There are countless millions of monetarily wealthy Christians, they are a testimony to the way God intended for His money to be used. I, for one, did not and could not handle it, my heart and ways of thinking were still too weak. The foundation was there in my life, but the structure and continued maintenance of daily prayer and the Word, had left my routine.

For the failure, it was not long until I had lost everything. The spiral, spoken of earlier, was about to accelerate into a tornado. Let us now look at how the final motion of the storm took place.

NBC had made financial arrangements for a first class ticket to

New York, with a cash reimbursement of four thousand dollars to cover my personal expenses. Checking into the Hilton early, a full day under a different name for privacy, I lavished myself in luxury.

"Concierge's desk, may I help you, Mr. Summers?"

"Yes, please make arrangements for a limo to pick me up in one hour."

"Yes, sir. I will have the driver standing by in the lobby."

After a nice long leisurely shower and shave I began dressing in a nice gray pinstripe Brooks Brothers suit and a pale yellow Polo tight knit sweater. My Ostrich boots gleaming, their peanut brittle color a nice contract to the outfit and the matching Ostrich belt, set the ensemble to perfection. Slipping my diamond Presidential Rolex on, the money roll with the twenty dollar gold piece in my pocket, I was ready for the city.

Stepping from my room and walking toward the elevator, I had on Obsession for Men cologne, and New York had better be ready. The world I was trying to manufacture in my mind did not exist. The elevator arrived at the lobby floor, as the door opened the day began.

"Mr. Summers, your limo is ready and waiting, sir!" Such efficiency when they think a big tip is coming. Handing the Concierge a twenty, I followed the driver to the stretch Lincoln. Once inside, a first glass of champagne to start the ride off in style.

"Paul, let's take a short tour of the downtown and Central Park."

"Yes, sir, anything in particular that you would like to see?"

Shaking my head was my answer, as the driver was watching the rear view mirror. For the next hour and a half we toured the city and I enjoyed the flow of bubbly, it was relaxing and I felt like royalty. There had been tens of thousands spent on limousines over the past few years. Any time I felt like spoiling myself, I did. Finally tiring of the tour and feeling a slight bit of hunger, I asked Paul for a suggestion of restaurants.

"Paul, where is the best steak house in New York?"

"There are several sir, but Stark's is one of the finest."

"I will trust your judgment, let's try it." It was a twenty minute ride from where we had driven. Time for another glass of champagne before trying out a New York steak, I poured the glass full.

Several of the clientele were just arriving as the car pulled to the curb. Apparently Paul had called ahead because one of the staff was waiting for us out front. Paul quickly came around and opened the door.

"Mr. Summers, we welcome you to Stark's. You will enjoy our establishment. They are absolutely the best steaks in New York."

"We will see, you must know that I am from Texas, where the best steaks in the world come from."

"Mr. Summers, all of our beef comes from just outside Dallas. Black Angus Prime is all that we serve." The grin on his face was one of knowing that I would relate exactly to just the specifications he had so graciously delivered.

"Well then, I should feel at home. Paul, if you get hungry or thirsty, you just order whatever you might like. See to it that it is put on my bill." Giving orders and playing the role which I had portrayed for some time now, one would had thought I had unlimited wealth, at the speed I spent it.

The décor was very comfortably elegant, no doubt from the clientele that it was one of the "IN" places to dine. From the "no price" listed on the menu, it was a further indication of its exclusivity to the upper crust patron. Two bourbon and waters at the bar while they finished arranging the table and I was ready for the gourmet delight.

A bottle of Chateau Laffite Rothschild, 1964, to start the taste buds and the dinner was ordered and delivered, then served with the utmost in elegance and style. Allowing the bottle to breathe for several minutes to give that added body and aroma for the first taste and swirl. From the escargot to the Caesar's salad, to the Chateaubriand, the food was marvelous. Ordering a Brandy/Benedictine – B&B – I sat back and enjoyed the feeling of good food and good liquor.

For the last thirty minutes of my meal and after dinner drinks I had been noticing a group of five ladies nearby. From their accents they had to be from the Deep South. One in particular, a beautiful brunette, slim and shapely, and absolutely gorgeous, a couple of mutual looks and smiles had shown a mutual approval factor. There was no reason why I should be enjoying the money and city by myself. Signaling the waiter for a special order, he came quickly.

"Bring a bottle of Crystal to the ladies to my right."

"Yes, sir, it is done!" He answered and was off to deliver the premium champagne.

Upon its delivery and subsequent pour for a round of toasts, I strolled over for an introduction.

"Ladies, I must confess that I have been sitting there and enjoying the view for some time now. My way of thanking you for the beautiful scenery is a toast as a token of my gratitude. Down in Texas we do believe that a gentleman should pay for his pleasures. So if you will have a drink with me, in your honor, I would be most thankful." Smiles on every face, the flow of flowery words enjoyed, I was in my arena, with the gift of gab.

"We would be more than grateful to grant such a favor to you, sir."

"Please, let you just refer to me as Michael, my Dad is the only 'sir' in my family." It was the brunette who had spoken; with my words I reached for her hand. Taking it in mine, I bowed and kissed it lightly. "It is my pleasure to have formally met you, and your name, please?" "Katherine, Katherine Robertson from Florence, Alabama."

The remainder of the group introduced themselves and the evening was about to begin. Two more bottles of champagne, then it was time to head for the nightclubs. Of course I had to pay for the entire evening, including the dinner, drinks and entertainment. By the end of the night, after the festivities, it was five thirty in the morning. Wasted in more ways than one, the driver took everyone back to their respective hotels, including Katherine Robertson from Florence, Alabama.

Katherine was a buyer for a large department store chain. She dealt at the merchandise mart buying fashions and clothing for several stores. We had danced and partied and laughed and had a marvelous time. A final kiss before she exited the vehicle, I told her to watch the program. "Katherine, tomorrow morning, if you watch the TODAY show, I will be interviewed on the air. Rather than go into detail about all of my past, watch the show and I will call you at the hotel later." She shook her head in agreement, we kissed a sweet kiss and Paul escorted her to the awaiting doorman.

After returning to the hotel and paying for the limo, including a two hundred dollar tip for Paul, I retired for some much needed sleep. Waking near noon, I had a light lunch then traveled down to the studios of NBC for the initial talks and production procedural layout. It was here that I met James again and his agent, Betsy Nolan. She had her own agency in New York and had worked with James Mills for the entire work of the novel.

It was then that I was informed of their intentions to black out the screen to shadows for dramatic effect. The darkness was to instill an air of intrigue into the viewing audience. Watching the interview, with a real live "hit man" from the mafia and cartels of the drug lords, how much fun could it be? Sitting there and hearing all of the talk and discussion back and forth, it began to show me just how far I had walked away from God. The bickering and the language, all about greed and money and ratings, it sickened me, almost to the point of walking out. But I had been in the world too long by this time to leave the glory and prestige of being on a nationally shown television show.

One of the directors and agents with the show paid me the expense money. It almost covered the previous night's outing of forty three hundred dollars. Still playing the big man role, knowing it all, I saw the interview through to the end. Ratings wise, it had gone well, and the articles were published in Rolling Stone Magazine. I was infamous for a short time, for a period of some six months. Riding the crest of the storm to the very end, flying here, there and yonder, acting like it was my idea to put this entire package together.

Included in the travels was a trip to Florence, Alabama to see Katherine and she welcomed me into her community for the three days that I was there. We saw several of the others that had accompanied her to New York. She was lovely, a very gracious hostess and to this day, one of the loveliest ladies I have ever known. Now married to a Southern banker, she still resides in Florence and is probably still running the fashion center for the department stores. I will always think of her beauty, her heart was truly one made of the finest china and crystal, etched in the purest gold. A love I have in my heart will forever have her name on it. May God continue to bless and keep her safe and at peace, in her love and life.

There was a certain flair to the trip to Alabama, one that brought back memories of Grandee, my grandfather. Ironically enough, by the time I had returned back to Denver, life in the somewhat real world, a message from him that he was ill, brought with it an urgency to move back to Canyon, my birthplace. Canyon, Texas, meanwhile was not ready for the likes of one Michael J. Decker. Yes, if I had been walking in fellowship with God, there would have been no problems, but this was far from the reality of the truth at hand.

My past would come with me, my distant past. Falcon, DEA, Vietnam, all would be thrown into the West Texas winds, swirled about and cast as a net of sin over the Panhandle of Texas. Now it is time to take you back with me to Texas. You may want to put your boots on at this point.

Everyone at Sunland Solar/Safety Products was sad to see me leave the business. Some for personal reasons and many for financial, I had written millions of dollars of business during my career there. The CEO, Frank Luck had told me that in 1984 alone I had made him nearly a million, with my personally written contracts. During the four year period, I had never been out of the top five marketing executives in the corporation, nationwide. This was now history, as I drove the Benz down to the dealer and traded it in for a new Ford Bronco, four wheel drive. My grandfather had informed me that we could not go hunting in a Benz.

With the Bronco saddled, I headed for the Panhandle of Texas. Along with it, another chapter was coming to the light of my life. Driving the trip straight through, it took almost twelve hours. After living in Denver and having the mountains there for something to see, acres and acres of flat land was quite a change. Leaving a city of two million for a small town of ten thousand, when college was in session, was very different. Otherwise, when the college was out, closer to only six thousand, culture shock of the major variety, to say the least.

Most of that first year was spent with my grandfather, once he was feeling better. Hunting and fishing all over the country, it was very relaxing, in some ways, in others I was restless. No friends, no church, I started hitting the bars to find my friends, rather than to the place where some real friends and fellowship could have come about. It only took a few months for the handwriting to be evident of the final outcome of this life. Brushes with the law became a regular event, especially after the Chief Deputy of the local Sheriff's department discovered who I was and about my past. Of course, the book had a lot to do with this situation. It, along with my behavior was a road map for them to follow.

Within a year of starting the heavy drinking, out of fellowship, I ended up with a felony case in Randall County for insufficient funds checks. A wild night on the town for some three days in a limo had not only cost me a couple of thousand dollars, it also cost me three months in jail and a seven year sentence for probation. Alcohol was and is very much a drug, one which, although socially acceptable, ruins lives and kills souls as well as people. Guilty charged, guilty admitted, something had to change.

Trinity Fellowship Church, 5000 Hollywood Road, Amarillo, Texas, as I read the small ad in the newspaper, something touched my heart. So I took a chance the following Sunday, deciding to try something new in my life. Waking early that Sunday, I showered and dressed and was at the church forty-five minutes before the service was to begin. The main sanctuary was huge, with a seating capacity of near two thousand. Yet though it was so large, there was a peace to the expanse of the building. No doubt whatsoever, the Holy Spirit had been in residence here since its conception.

As the members began to filter through the five entrances, it took no time at all for the room to fill. From every walk of life they came, doctors, lawyers, carpenters, accountants, all for one purpose, to hear the Word of God. Once filled to overflowing, the music began and a song and chorus of thousands let the heavens know they were praising them. By far the most beautiful voices I personally had ever witnessed. Hands raised to the Lord Jesus Christ, organ, piano and instruments making it almost a concert performance. Eight songs and two solos later, my heart and soul were crying out to God for forgiveness.

Tears streaming down my face, God had laid His mighty hands on my filth and sin, holding me up and loving me. While totally undeserving, He still took me to His side.

Pastor Jimmy Evans stepped to the pulpit, I was about to understand the phenomenal growth in this church. Pastor Evans along with Pastor Tom Lane and many other men of God were the anointed pastorship of this thriving institution. It was one of God's true churches, where God's Word was spoken and lived.

The message was about temptation, in Corinthians, "no temptation has overtaken you but such as is common to man. With every temptation comes a way of escape also, so that you may be able to endure it." As Pastor Evans continued, his words had a simple elegance to them. He used personal examples that gave his words a realism. God's Word utilized for deeper and more thorough of an understanding. I sat there in sheer amazement of how all of the message seemed to speak directly to me. One hour and forty minutes later, as the final praise song was being sung, I could not understand for the life of me, why I had waited so long. Looking around the room, I saw Jesus everywhere I looked. Tears of joy and sorrow were wept in reverence to God Almighty. Somewhat embarrassed, yet empowered, I began to exit the sanctuary with the throng of people.

"Are you going to go to the Cornerstone Class today? Pastor Jerry Billington is speaking and it is a terrific group. We must have near two hundred in attendance." The two ladies in front of me, early to mid thirties were discussing a Sunday school class.

"What age group goes to the class?" The taller of the two, a brunette asked.

"For the most part it is from 30 to 50!"

Why not, I am already here and they seem to be friendly enough. My conversation was with myself as I followed the pair down the hallway. By the time I had reached the small chapel where the service and class was to be held, I had also found out that a fellowship meal was being served in the recreation area after class for the singles.

Pastor Jerry Billington's class was exciting and touching, he had a certain charisma that touched his class. He had a very personal interest in their well being and it showed in his love and care for the members. As I sat there observing, so much of what God intended for His people was being delivered by this man in service to his Abba Father. Pastor Jerry had sold out to Jesus Christ a long time ago. In years to come, through the suffering of his wife Ann, and her eventual passing, Jerry remained strong. But God, being the originator of love and devotion, would eventually take Pastor Billington on to another chapter. Replacing love with another soulmate and companion to share in the precious gifts of the Kingdom, this was the depth of the care of his Heavenly Father.

That day in his class continued with meeting and dating several women over the next few years. Brendia, Joy, Phyllis and many more, the unrest in my heart and life could not be healed with a relationship. It took a relationship and selling out to God for the fullness of His calling to come to life for me.

So many wrecks, so many disappointments, all caused by my lack of devotion to God, what would it take to bring me to a point of no return? With such mighty men of God around me, their faith around to see and gain counsel from, why was I still failing at life? Pastor Tom Lane took a very special interest in me, my life and fed me through his witness, counseling and mentor example. Pastor Tom, a senior pastor from Trinity Fellowship in Amarillo, Texas, brought me to a point of redemption and laid the groundwork for a plan of get well or get out of the church. This may seem strong, somewhat overboard, but when you're dealing with a person of my background, the kid gloves approach just plain does not work.

The final resolve was to ask me to leave the church because I was not being accountable to the leadership nor the basic laws of God Himself. This is where I took matters in my own hands and left the church, the city and the State of Texas, finally to embark on a journey that would lead me all the way to the throne of God's grace and mercy, eternally.

CHAPTER 10

off to the Virgin Islands, prison, and *finally* coming to know God!

Another chapter of my life begins with another journey, running from one situation and on to adventure, I thought. You see, the OTHER women of my relational socializing, like Joy, Phyllis and many others, were in many ways alike. I will not tell of the intimate secrets nor the failures, suffice to say that I had failed God and these ladies as well. Moments of glorious happiness, a decade of sadness and destruction, this included another stay in prison. Yes, an eight year sentence in the Texas Department of Criminal Justice. With the conclusion of my parole time and numerous other wrecks personally, financially and socially, I was ready for a new start.

St. Thomas, United States Virgin Islands was to be my destination and playground. Home to the Rich & Famous, money everywhere, alcohol/cocaine, women and no one knew me or my name, especially anything about my past. In twenty months I managed to offend and take advantage of near two dozen new friends, including taking their hard earned money and wrecking their lives. Spending every single penny I earned and additional funds I did not own, eventually would bring about my demise. One final trip to Manhattan, New York to visit another beauty, Laura Ropas, and break another heart, my days of freedom were coming to a halt, NOW!

The flight back from New York was a time of sobering after seven days of major partying. Doing the nightclub, restaurant, and jet-set circuit and pretending that I was incredibly rich, my heart was just not in it anymore. Stepping off the plane and making the short drive back up to Fortuna Mountain to the villa, the sun burning on my skin and the sin burning in my soul, there was an air of uncertainty that clouded my spirit. The Palm trees swaying in the tropical breeze, Mango, and other exotic plants, flowers and bushes lush in the early afternoon setting. Roaring waves crashing against the coral reef below, another crash was about to take place.

Stepping out of my old beach Jeep, one that was built, rebuilt and wired back together from countless trees, rocks and diversions over the edge of the highway, I headed for the front door. My mind drifting back to the collisions that were part of drunken trips home and only by the grace of God was I still alive and breathing. The last journey had taken place the night before my trip to New York I had awaken to find no vehicle out in the driveway, it had found a place to rest against a tree, a mere ten feet from a 200 foot drop over a cliff. This day, February 23rd, 1996 would be the beginning of the end.

Carrying my bags over my shoulder I made the final turn down the graveled pathway into the villa entrance. The white stucco finish gleaming in the Caribbean sunshine, red steel storm shutters contrasting the scene, what greeted my view was a picture out of a horror movie, mine. The safe was torn out of the inner wall, computer long gone and cash boxes from the vault closets open and empty! Utter amazement filled my mind as my eye's raced around the main room, the wasteland evident of a raid by both local and international authorities. One, fine linen sheet of paper with an official heading was the only foreign object, it read Federal Bureau of Investigation, United States of America! The FBI special agent that had written the note, in fact, was none other than someone that was a regular in many of the scuba diving trips I had made during the past few months.

The lies, cheating, deceit, misrepresentations, and most of down right evil had finally caught up and taken over my life.
"Oh! My God! What is going to happen now?" I was talking to the wall, the floor, or anything that possibly answer me back with a quick fix, none available. I had dug this hole and now I was going to have to dig my way out. I had several fake IDs and could fashion a Passport without too much difficulty, but this was not going to change the inevitable, not this time.

I certainly did not want to be seen driving the Jeep so I called for Ali's Taxi, one I had used on numerous occasions. Grabbing everything possible in a five minute fiasco of packing and toting to the curb, I awaited my ride. My heart was racing three hundred miles per hour, thoughts darting from one thing to another. As the taxi turned into the international airport, I knew that this would be my last chance to flee the island.
"One ticket for New York please, on the 4:05p.m. flight." The agent looked at my bewildered stare, checked my identification and began to issue the ticket and boarding pass.

"Any luggage to check?" Her smile so casual and her right foot going to the floor alarm which connected her to the United States Customs office at the turnstile gates. The picture taped to the back of the sales counter was there at every station, the FBI and Customs were not going to let me leave the island that easily.

"Here is your ticket and the luggage claim checks, Sir, please have a nice trip." This was going way to easy, or was it?

I grabbed the carry on and headed around the corner of the terminal towards the customs area. Once through this final checkpoint and I was FREE! One final deep breath, a smile and then my greeting to the agent on duty, his crisp white uniform starched and badge polished and gleaming.

"Heading out to New York for a visit, just to see some family members and sight see. Sure is a nice day isn't it?" The eye contact was there, but mine was direct and his was searching every single cell in my being. There was knowing and power to the agents gaze, his hand had already been played and he was about to sweep the table.

"Yes Sir, just one moment and I will have everything ready for your trip." Four additional agents from the FBI, guns drawn, came from behind and two in front. I was not going anywhere except to the official holding cell to await collection of my bags, luggage and prepare for a strip search. The trip was over, for me anyway. From a point deep within my soul, a voice was saying, it is over – it is over, no more running.

"DO NOT MOVE! Raise your hands slowly and DO NOT MOVE!" The agent's command was one that I had heard, many times in my career as a thug. I knew the drill and as the cold steel of the handcuffs locked around my wrists, my freedom vanished and to try and escape was not worth the effort, nor the risk.

"Mr. Decker, you are under arrest for money laundering and Intrastate Transportation of unregistered securities. Anything said by you will be used in a court of law. You have the right to an Attorney…" Yep. I knew all my rights under the Maranda ruling; the young agent acted if he had landed Al Capone rather than Michael John Decker.

"Just do your deal and let's get this over with. I am tired, hungover and sick of this crap!" I was tired and did not want to drag this scenario on down the road. Of course my comment was not going to change their protocol and procedure in the least. There was little use in trying to hurry up anything, as I was no longer a citizen with rights and freedom, I was chained and in custody of the United States Government once again. My only current right was the air I was breathing and the beating of my heart, yet even that was from God and He certainly didn't owe me for the way I had acted. He had seen my back, but I had never seen His. Jesus Christ still stood there with His nail scarred Hands and scarred brow, spear wound in His side, crying out for the lost soul, mine.

The black sedan whipped from the secured parking marked U.S. Justice, DEA, FBI, Customs parking only area, screeching to a halt. Another ride in the back of a police vehicle, hands cuffed, feet shackled and waist chains rattling, was about to commence.

"Get in the car, Mr. Decker, and do not do anything stupid!" My look spoke my opinion, words would have not done justice to the intimidation and glare that passed from my face to the agent who had given the order. His hand gripped around my elbow and helping was his intention, outwardly, but not in reality. I had placed myself in this situation, it was no one's fault other than my own. Finally facing the issues of my life that had continually caused me to backslide, falter and drift from the existence of my Abba Father, I remained silent and bowed before the authority.

Believe me when I try to describe that the conditions of the jail in St. Thomas were deplorable and reeked of the filth of many generations. Rats and mice, joined by legions of roaches and bugs, scurried and scampered, everywhere. Vomit and urine stained the walls, floors and steel bars rusted by decades, maybe centuries of overcrowded conditions and no maintenance or care. The interrogation room, the cellblock, packed with the murderers, drug dealers and offenders of the law, the stench of rotted food creased my nostrils as the facility became my new home. So many years around the jails and prisons of the world had prepared me for the next chapter or sequel to my ongoing odyssey which had chronicled my existence. No one to blame other than myself, I had made the dance and it was time to pay the fiddler.

"Do you want an attorney before we begin this interrogation?" Special Agent Gregg, my diving companion of days gone by asked me, bluntly. "No! You ask the questions and I will supply the information. I am tired of the cops and robbers; cat and mouse routine. I am guilty; you and I both know that, the records and computer logs from my house in Fortuna spell everything out. You have scanned and scrutinized every decimal and log sheet I am sure, talked to all of the victims, especially Bill McManus and Susan Rowe, my former friends and neighbors." It was the truth and I was not going to fight the inevitable any longer, or prolong the jail interment. I wanted to take a plea and get on to a spacious federal facility back in the states. Little did I know that, yes, I

WAS going to a federal facility, but not one like I had ever seen or experienced before.

I signed a paper, document, confession folder, which took nearly six hours of repeated questions and idiotic conversation. Found my new quarters, a cell built for two and housing ten, but it could have been worse, some had twelve. Sleep would never come from the noise and constant chaos, fights and disagreements rampant in the overcrowded filth.

Nine days later, after two or three hours rest, the rattling of chains down the corridor meant someone was about to be transported. Voices of the guards telling stories of the man they had read about and the life he had lived. Tales so unbelievable they could not possibly be true, no one man could have ever done all that. The guy in cellblock #4 was nothing more than a thief with a little style! An untruth and a truth in the two statements; for I had done all that and I was nothing more than a thief, a robber of peace and joy, alcoholic and addict, and most of all, a sinner. I had deserted my Father, my King, Counselor and Redeemer.

"Okay, James Bond, don't use any of your secret moves!" The big black guard, accompanied with his two cohorts thought he was a comedienne. WRONG!

"Yeah, Whitey, you may have fooled some of them, but we aren't fooled. We will kick your butt if you try anything with us." His words brought forth a surge of the old self. A raging lion roared inside, but a Hand closed the mouth of the animal, His Hand. Inside I heard a voice saying, "No more, no more."

Chained and hobbled, shuffling down the corridor and long stairway, I proceeded with my escort to the awaiting van. I thought maybe the journey was to the court or to the attorney, but neither of these was the intended location. It was midday, and the traffic so tourist infested from the seven cruise ships docked in the harbor that it flooded the streets and taxis. Shoppers, lookers, it was a scene born daily and the lifeblood of the islands. People from around the globe spending their money, most on plastic riches they really didn't own nor could afford. Yet some, a select few, there to buy seemingly the crown jewels to lavish their lives and console their desires, trying to find joy, peace and love where it not only did not exist, it couldn't be purchased for any price. I knew this for a fact, it was etched in my heart and written on my soul.

Rounding the Southern end of the thirteen mile long island, the private airstrip came into view as we left Veterans Drive, the main road. Each plane or aircraft in this area was official United States

Marshall's transports. They were used to shuttle prisoners around the islands of St. Thomas, St. John and St. Croix. Today they would be used to fly out of the Virgin Islands and on to the island of Puerto Rico. Another new residence, a stronghold in the midst of the jungle so to speak, this trip I would not soon forget.

"Decker, get out of the van and load up. We are going to take a little trip," stated Bill Hanover, U.S. Marshal for more than thirty years, on his final deployment and duty station. His command came with experience, respect given and respect would be returned.

"Yes Sir!" I knew that I could trust this man, his word was his bond and he had learned long ago that playing games with people was wrong, and very dangerous.

"We are taking you to Guaynabo, Puerto Rico to the Federal Correctional Center. You will await trial there, along with 1500 other men and women."

"Yes, Sir!" No further explanation was necessary, I had been down this road before and he knew that I knew what was in store for me.

The ride across the one hundred and fifty mile open expanse of the ocean was quick. The twin engine Turbo jet, a Beechcraft King Air knew how to cut through the air and clouds. No conversation, only indwelled silence and reflection came during the transportation of my body, my heart and my thoughts. That small voice deep inside was echoing and I could feel a knocking on my inner chamber. The door of my heart, so scarred and splintered, stained with the sins of life, stood momentarily strong and resistant. I was holding on to something, whatever it might be, as a last refuge and resolution of life itself.

"Mr. Decker you need to understand something, and I want you to listen. This facility is filled to its capacity with men that will take your life for a piece of bread. It is a United States lockup but it is run, in many ways, by the 2-7 and the Inyeta gangs of this region. I am very well aware of your past, I knew Golden and Bearup, the deputies that escorted you in days gone by, some twenty five years ago. You will be here for an extended stay as the court system in the Virgin Islands is over booked and understaffed." Simple, informative and directly to the point, this was his style. I liked it, appreciated it and knew that this part of my incarceration was going to be no cakewalk.

"Yes Sir! I fully understand and nothing is going to take my life, not here!" I made the statement and really do not know why. A churning down inside was burning a hole in my gut, itching to get out. I would know soon enough.

The ride to the institution was long, winding down street after street, turn after turn. The non-airconditioned van sweltering in the tropical sunshine, little draft through the narrow slit of open window. It was preparing me for the weather, the inside weather of this concrete and steel tower called Guaynabo.

Guards outside the facility lined the roadway to the massive steel doors and power gates of the institution. The van turned the final corner and made its way to the compound. From a hand signal to the security force guard, black fatigues and combat boots the uniform, a command through the hand held radio brought movement to the doors. Twenty-five high and nearing seventy five feet wide, the inner chamber/vault housed twenty vehicles of every description. A glassed in control module was the operation's central control unit. There was no movement anywhere that was done without their approval and command.

My heart began to race, eyes searching and registering every detail, the training and life script I had lived, flowed through my veins. The warrior in me began to reign and vibrate my soul, a feeling of battle began to whirl the power inside my heart. Thunder, yes the thunder rolled and lightning flashed for this arena, this prison would not be my demise. No mere mortal man was going to take my life, no gang, no guard, nobody. The thoughts and feelings played out their tunes, meanwhile the ten men of the welcoming party had surrounded the vehicle. Stories from the past, rumors of the violence, things I had done had followed me once again.

"So this is the bad guy, the former hit man of the Mafia!" Lt. Sanchez, leader of the team and smart mouth of the correction center was showing me his style and arrogance.

"Go take a break Sanchez. Let me be the first to tell you something your young ass has not had the opportunity to realize or learn. This man, if he decided to and had the reason and the chance, could break every bone in your body and then tear your heart out and cram it in your mouth before you took that last sweet breath." Deputy Hanover did not like men like Sanchez. He cut him off and cut him short, most of all embarrassed the dickens out of him in front of his men.

"Oh blow me Hanover. I could…!" The sentence ended with the cold stare from Hanover. His eyes and their thirty plus years of experience cancelled the rhetorical exchange. Sanchez, in his heart of hearts knew that the truth had been spoken and that any further comment was only going to worsen the situation.

"Take the prisoner to the holding/concentration area. Strip search him, lice powder and lock him up. We will see how tough this guy is." Sanchez spoke, the guards moved to facilitate the order and I knew this would not be a nice night.

Naked and sitting on the cold concrete floor, a six inch hole in the middle of the area for a toilet, this was everything in the cell. Law, man's law, states that the facility cannot lock an inmate down for more than 48 hours in these conditions. Wrong, this was man's jail and man would do anything he was told to do. Thirteen months and twenty six days later I would be released from this cell condition. But wait, what happened during this time of sanctuary, yes, this is what it became.

February 23rd, 1996, as I sat there in my new quarters, I began to replay the past forty seven years of my life. The cell, the supposed food ration and the overall darkness, near total, made the inner soul of a man speak. I heard voices of the past, felt pain and fleeting moments of satisfaction dispersed in between long periods of emptiness and lack of any conscience whatsoever. You see, the depravity of any sort of sensory stimulation is what gets to most people. But I was not most people and I had already lived through hell and everywhere in between.

Five months later, July 27th, 1996, I had a visitor to my cell. His hand touched my shoulder, His other Hand touched my heart, and the Holy Spirit began to carve the ugly sin and darkness from my heart & soul. Finally, my mother's forty-seven years of everyday interceding prayer was answered. I truly heard the exactness of God's voice once my voice had beckoned to Him.

"Oh my Father God I call out, I cry out to you. I beg for your mercy and deliverance from this hole in my life, my heart. I have failed you my Lord, I have turned from my King, and have blatantly sinned in your presence. I need you my Father, I ask for you to forgive my failure and my dishonoring of your Will. I declare this day to be eternally in your service for the rest of my life and beyond. Please Lord, let me have just one more chance to bring you honor and praise your Name." Every single fiber of my existence, my being was shaking and tears flooded my face and dripped to my chest and thighs. During the sobbing and retching that poured from my guts, His voice began to answer.

"My son, My chosen warrior, My child that has strayed from My flock, come to Me this day. I forgive you this day, this very day and accept you back into My Kingdom. Hear My voice and take heed to My command for this is your LAST CHANCE, at life. If you ever leave Me again, I will leave you FOREVER, ETERNALLY. There will be no more games, no more alcohol, no more drugs and no more lies. I love you My son, you are My child."

The resonation of God's voice resounded and echoed deep within my heart, bringing forth a fear. This was a feeling that I had never experienced, fear of anything or anyone. Not just fear but reverence that bowed my body and soul, prostrate and outstretched before His throne. My God had spoken to the filthy likes of me, Michael Decker, a sinner among sinners, life of shame and sadness. The washing of Jesus' Blood flooded over me in waves of forgiving rain, restoring peace and joy to a level and intensity that I did not know existed. Yes, I was naked before my Father and He had clothed me in His robe and fed my very soul to overflowing.

Daily, for the next eight months I spoke with God, everyday and all day. Asking questions and listening to what my heart and mind was receiving in the flood of Holy Spirit anointing. Songs came to my heart as a gift and I sang them to my Father with every ounce of my being. Sixteen of them in all, daily I gave Him my worship, my praise and my obedience. The guards probably thought I was crazy with all of the jabbering going on, who cared about what they thought?

What took place made for a total reformation, restoration and reincarnation of my very life, from the beginning of my existence, to this moment in time. The destiny of what God was calling me to do had implanted and burned its message in the core of my soul. He was my Father and had spoken directly to me, His son, child and now follower forever. There would be no faltering to this walk, nor stumbling back to addiction or sin. The drugs, alcohol and living in the world, this way had been crucified and buried, eternally. I was, would and will serve God forever and ever. Amen!

The months of waiting in the cell finally ended when God had received my full attention and restored my life, my mind and heart. Forty-seven years of chaos, totally changed in mere months by His Hand, His blessing. My new home was the open population cellblock where most of the leaders of the gangs resided. Along with my appearance into this network of sin and violence would come a test of what God had just completed in my life. He would allow this because through testing comes the furnace and the fire to purify one's soul and spirit, mine.

For many years the gangs had controlled everything, the cellblocks, the food distribution or lack there of. Who lived, who died, where the drugs came from and to whom they were given. Sex, drugs and money, controlling agents in themselves, the foundation of control and power in this facility, was about to meet the REAL BOSS once and for all. Over half of the men in this cellblock were facing fifty years or more, Federal sentences with no parole or probation. These individuals had grown up in the streets, on the streets and been seared with the evil doctrines of the enemy. Lust, greed, power, wealth and control, every aspect of what the world had to offer was imbedded in their hearts and way of life.

Now, after the period of indoctrination that I had just been through with God, holed up in that tiny concentration cell, this was a major suite to me. Only one problem was to follow, quickly, getting food. You see, the gang control had a scheme, you pay them money and then you get food. No money, no food, or at least nothing more than leftovers and the slop no body else wanted. This was not going to work for me and I was going to make a point of changing the current rules and regulations.

"Sgt. Peterson, if you will let me out of my cell during the food preparation time, I will make sure that everyone gets fed." He was the guard in charge and one of the ones the gang leaders had not bought. I was offering something he could not find anywhere else!

"Decker, do you really think you can make a difference?" His reply very skeptical and wary, but with an interested tone anyway.

 "Yes Sir! I can make a difference in ways that you don't have the authority to regulate." My smile and assured confidence bolstered the statement.

"O.K,, you get out twenty minutes early at chow time and I will watch you get your butt beat or killed." He was speaking from a point of not understanding the basic needs of one hungry white boy.

"Thank you sir, thank you."

The next meal came through later that morning. Normal protocol was four men, dividing the spoils and giving it out to only the ones they had been told to provide for. This had suddenly changed, completely. A rattling of the stainless steel food carts down the cellblock corridor signaled the beginning of the new way to serve.

"Listen up! Cells 10, 17, 49, 103 and 67, come out when your doors open to the kitchen serving area." The Sgt. had spoken and faces began to see who #67 was, for there was one extra being called out for service.

Rumbling and signaling began through out the cellblock. One of the workers made a quick dash to grab the spoils for his people. I cut him off and made it clear if he touched the food, in any way, I would not hesitate to bust his young face. Yes, I was now a full fledged Christian, and because of that I was not going to allow any more starving of God's people. The second man out decided he was going to be the bold and brave one.

"Understand me clearly and listen close to what I have to say. If you try and steal any food from this cart I will break every bone in your body." Statement made and action to follow, immediately.

"Up yours!" Carlino, one of the 2-7, was going for the carts and he never really thought that I would back up my promise.

Needless to say, I did and as he flew through the air out into the main corridor of cells, a roar erupted in the cellblock. Slamming on the steel doors, voices raging and threats coming in many forms and fashions, but I did not care about threats from man. To most it was as if I had signed a death warrant, to me it was nothing more than taking care of an immediate issue. God had made me a warrior, Uncle Sam had trained me, life had prepared me and what I was about to do would simplify the food issue once and for all.

"Listen up! There will be no more stealing of food and people going hungry any longer. That ended today. If you don't like it, I live in cell #67 and you can come pay me a visit. Today, everyone is going to get food, everyone." I was not going to back off. After all, my Father would send a legion of warrior angels if I called on Him. I believed it, it was fact and He was in charge, not that slimy Satan guy.

For the first time in this area of the institution, every man on every tier got the same amount, the same quality and the entire menu. No, it was not gourmet by any stretch of the imagination, but it was food. I had lost eighty-nine pounds during my tenure in the isolation unit and I was not going to lose any more. These men were dealing with a raw-boned hungry animal, one tested in the streets and jungles, and his Father had told him what to do. Me that is!

After that first feeding I was called out to the medical department for a physical. One of the procedures the Government uses to cover their selves after a long term of isolation so that someone doesn't croak on them. I was fine they said after the exam and then the guard took me back to the cell area.

From down the corridor leading into my tier I began to smell smoke, fire and knew immediately what was happening. As the guard turned the corner, leading me back to the cell in chains and handcuffs, the flames shooting out of my cell #67 signaled an emergency call. I stood there in both anger and disbelief as the emergency bells began to ring and the special tactics squad burst through the door. First things first, they hit the general release button that unlocked the entire cellblock and commanded everyone to move to the holding area. Second they brought the fire team in and extinguished the fire. Finally they turned me back to the corridor and began taking me back to solitary confinement. Before turning, I scanned the crowd to see the fear, the anticipation or anything in a pair of eyes.

"Why am I being moved when I did not do anything?" I asked the guard, somewhat in an irritated manner. Well, downright irritated is probably closer.

"It is for security reasons. You have been given a death threat. Code for this act is to move the inmate and keep him in solitary confinement until the investigation is concluded."

Shackled once again like some kind of wild animal I managed to do the chained-shuffle, back into solitary confinement. What was amazing to me was the freedom I was feeling. Yes, this was another test, but it was one that would not overthrow my peace that God has given as a gift. Besides that, the solitary cell was a suite in comparison to the former concentration cell.

The six days that I sat there reflecting on what had taken place, why and the eventual outcome, gave me ample opportunity to study the Word of my Father. During this time of study and reflection I penned the following poem concerning the event.

4th Floor MDC
The chains they may shackle me, Cuffs can lock my hands.
Isolation may serve your purpose now, in your knowing you make demands.
Yet beings, we are human now, God's creations will still remain.
With what you give, comes back to you, at times you must refrain.
For within an act of kindness, comes forth a smiling heart.
What you see and hear in anger, is often fear displayed in part.
Reflect a passage of olden lore, and walk in another man's shoes.
Have the courage to make a statement, bring to light for we must not lose.
To lose the common thread of need, of souls reaching for the peace.
For in solitude comes with it pain, looking, longing, for a soon release.
Back to freedom, back to breathe, much needed gasps of air.
Hear these words of beckoned woe, as if given in HAND CLASPED PRAYER.
5-20-97, Guaynabo, Puerto Rico

I wrote this poem and slipped it under the steel door of my cell so that all of the guards and officials could and would read it. Make a difference, I do not know, but it was written from my heart and from there, God had His hand on it. The days passed and within this, more time to study and more time to be in constant prayer. Nothing could rob me of the inner peace, or the consistent presence of the Holy Spirit. He gave me strength, warmth, consoling, and most of all He constantly was ministering to my heart and soul. It was like some eternal fountain of refreshment, cascading through my body and cleansing, soothing and bestowing grace and mercy.

"Decker, the Captain wants to have a word with you." Garza, the young guard, spoke curtly and with his voice came my presence to the cell door.

"Back up and put your hands through the security panel door." This was routine for this high security area. A man or woman would have to back up to the cell door, bend their knees and lower their hands clasped together through a small opening in the door. The guard would place the hand cuffs on and then, and only then would they open the door. We were all such violent people you know.

The Captain's office was very stark and military like. Steel desk and chair, filing cabinet metal and bare, whitewashed walls, no art work, only plaques and awards. He was exmilitary police and carried that attitude and demeanor everywhere he went. That is until today.

"Decker, I want you to tell me what this fire is all about. I don't want any crap or excuses. I want facts and facts only. Understand?" The white sidewall haircut amplified the creases in his brow and the wrinkles in his face.

"Sir, I know that it had something to do with my taking over the kitchen and getting food to ALL of the men in the cellblock. I was not going to let that situation continue." This questioning had an air of the Duty Officer's interrogation back in Boot Camp after the fight, many years before.

"Well, you are not in charge of the kitchen or responsible for getting food to anyone other than yourself. That is my job and I do not need your help." Matter of fact spoken and matter of fact replied towards.

"Then you are not being informed of the current situation in that cellblock because two thirds of the men there are not getting fed properly. I saw it and nothing was being done, thus I fixed it and will continue to stand up for the weak, help or no help. I do not mean to be disrespectful or arrogant, but the situation was to a serious scale." I had been praying about this situation during the past few days.

"Regardless of what you thought or felt, you will not be going back to that cellblock area. Federal rules and regulations state clearly that an inmate cannot return to an overt threat situation. So I will be moving you over to Dwing." The Captain had spoken his piece and it was time to let the Holy Spirit do His speaking and resolving.

"Captain, I need to tell you something that God has placed on my heart. He would have you send me back to the same unit. The threat you speak of is from man, not God. His Hand and His protection will accompany me back and keep me safe. More than anything else, this situation is a great opportunity to witness to hundreds of lost young men, hundreds and thousands. The entire facility knows of what happens. They will also know of the overall outcome. My walking back into that situation can change the situation and make that unit and the entire prison, different. You send me back in there and I guarantee you that I will not be harmed and God will restore order there like you have never before witnessed." I was speaking from my heart and that bold statement had come from my Father. He was in charge of my life and my safety, not me or the men or anyone else. I was His, totally and that would not be altered by some act of evil. Satan was a punk, is a punk and the Blood of Jesus was washing over this endeavor. Amen. "Decker, you are crazy. But something (I just wonder what the something is?) is telling me, somewhat against my better judgment to let you go back in that cesspool. Strange in a way, but for some reason I feel the need to let you try and prove this thing out. Guard, go pack up Decker and escort him back to his old block. Same cell, it is cleaned up and repainted." The smile on my face was thanks and the look on the young guard was one of utter amazement and wonder.

Quickly collecting my few meager belongings, I was rechained and proceeded to shuffle back to the cell area. Two floors down, the main cellblock door loomed ahead and its opening would be an opening for me to begin to change the format of prison to one of God, the first of many over the next few years.

"You are sick to want to come back here Decker, they are going to fry your butt and probably take your life. I have seen this situation before." He spoke of no faith and only from a worldly outlook, unknowing the power and majesty of God Almighty.

"No sir, it is not sick or crazy to want to come back here. It is an open forum to allow for the Holy Spirit, the presence of God to touch these men and begin to change their lives. He is the only answer, trust in that and stand by and watch Him totally change this dorm and these men."

Shaking his head, he reached the large brass key into the turnstile lock and moved the tumblers. The creaking of the steel to steel was a signal to all inside that someone, something was coming. "Get them Lord! Get them all in Jesus' Name." I was saying this to myself and knowing that He was going to make a mighty move. The door opened and I shuffled inside, standing still for the guard to remove all of the hardware. With each piece and the resulting clatter of steel to the concrete floor, more and more of the men came to their cell doors and peered out to see what the commotion was all about. One by one they saw it was me and began to pass on the word, the news. There was a very distinct fervor and buzz throughout the block, anticipation abounded.

Slowly taking my time to walk back down the long corridor, I turned towards all of the major players here. Making eye contact and to some a saluting wave of acknowledgment. This was not me walking, but the Holy Spirit walking in me and it was His power and awesome authority that was now in charge. I had placed my life in His Hands and trusted Him completely to overthrow the evil and restore peace and solitude. God promised, I believed and the rest was nothing more than circumstance.

The air was electrified, static crackled and popped with the vibrant display of change. Men who thought they had the power and authority were about to understand what real power and authority was all about. Many of these men had run gangs with membership in the hundreds, some in the thousands. Their word was life and death with the snapping of their fingers and an order. Unlimited wealth monetarily for some of them, millions stashed and controlled by their empires. My thought, just stand by and watch His Empire. One final turn to my cell and the chance to voice something from my heart, now was the time.

"Men, for those of you that speak English, understand what I am about to say. For those that don't, ask your neighbor or friend. I am back and whoever set my cell on fire you will pay for it. Eye has not seen the dynamic or intensity of fire. There will be a fire that will now come to this cellblock, it will burn the heart of a man and char his soul. The reigning fire of heaven is going to be sent down and overcome all that is not of God. I declare this in the Name of Jesus Christ of Nazareth and wash this cellblock in the Blood. I denounce you Satan and send you back to the fiery depths of Hell in Jesus' Name!" I spoke it with a fire in my voice and a power of awesome delivery. It came as a delivered blessing from God and on His authority I was standing. The resulting quiet was incredible. This cellblock had not been that quiet, ever.

During the next hour and a half, it gave the inmates, including myself the time to let this circumstance and its tributary flow of events to begin to be staged in hearts across the long expanse of concrete and steel. Many were still in a near shock state. Others thought that possibly a demon had possessed me. But it was no demon, it was a power far greater than any mere demon could obtain. The next serving of a meal would be the final breaking of the hold that darkness had on this area, once and for all.

I had made a special request that two more of the guys, my fellow brothers, would be allowed to help in serving the meals. Cam, a man waiting on another twenty or thirty years of sentence, and Carlos, a powerful drug dealer who I felt was looking to make a change in his heart and life. I went on gut instinct and the leading of the Holy Spirit on who to call upon. So often in my life, an instant decision was life or death, it had to be accurate. I trusted God to delivery superior intellect and discernment above reproach. This was going to be our arena and His overseeing and leadership, period.
"Carlos, I asked the guard to bring you out to assist me in making this craziness surrounding the food, end. I know that you are a leader in your own right and that your word means truth. Most of the men here know you and respect you. I am the new comer, and I am the gringo. I am also the man that God the Father in heaven has sent to change the infirmity that has been occurring here in this wing. You have an opportunity now to make a change in your life, turn from the old ways of drugs and prison and on to a new life. Earlier I overheard you speaking of your children and I ask you to think of their future." Mere words in certain respects but I had prayed long and hard for my mere words to be words anointed by the Holy Spirit when they were received. Seeds planted in tilled and fertile ground. Turning to Cam I continued with this staging of the forefront, so to speak. It was a saga of immense proportions with such diverse implications and the outcome so critical to and for the victory at hand.
"Cam, you are wise in the ways of the world and in the format of prison authority. Also you have a ton of street smarts. I am asking you to be a part of this so that you will no longer have to fight for everything here. You have been getting food with your strength, even though you are tired of getting it that way. I do not want for anyone to have to starve or get their selves hurt over food. We all have enough to worry with rather than to wonder if and when we will get something to eat." I awaited a response and it came in the form of a common agreement. Hands extended and a contract sealed as if by blood. Thank you Father, Praise you Lord. Amen
    It was now time for count, counting to make sure that no one had escaped. A process done in every jail and prison around the world, normally every four to six hours, the guards would lock everyone down in their cell and then, cell by cell, count heads. On this day, after my opening statement about fire, the count would contain a new event. After the counting had been done and all were awaiting the call from the control unit for a "clear count," meaning that the numbers were all adding up, a rattling of chains broke the silence.

Four additional guards suddenly entered the unit and moved to two of the cells. Doors were opened and the two men were quickly escorted out of the cellblock to never be seen or heard from, again. Later we would find out that they were the ones that started the fire in my cell and they had a fear of reprisal. Seems the Holy Spirit had lit a fire in their conscience, guilt the result and fear the deciding factor to leave the unit. This move of the presence of God was witness to all of the rest in a way that my violence could never have accomplished. It not only spoke to the men, it was confirmation to me that handling it God's way was the only way.

From that day forward, for the next three months, the attitude and the operation of the unit became a model of decorum and opened the door for GOD! Within three days after this happening, authorization came to begin a Bible study in the unit. The Word of God began to be spread, shared and be a part of men throughout the prison, not only in our wing. Our own revival, only by the grace and mercy of our Abba father, during that next ninety days, I would have the opportunity to witness and lead hundreds to the Lord. God was so good and He had done everything He had promised. It was not only the men, those incarcerated, this was infectious to the guards and upper administrators of the institution also, a witness of God's authority and majestic influence.

During this time I had been transported back to St. Thomas and received a sentence of thirty months with a three year probation period tacked on to the end of my sentence. I deserved it, every bit of it and would utilize the time to go further, deeper in the Word of God. Also I had the opportunity to begin studies through a correspondence course with Crossroads Bible Institute out of Grand Rapids, Michigan. The course work was great for it allowed me to focus in on how to make the Word of God applicable to everyday living and also to utilize the exactness of God's Word in understanding His Will for my life. Day by day I was strengthened and fortified by His wisdom, love and peaceful instruction. Yes, there were other small events that tested how far I had come with my Lord Jesus. This to me was a time in service to my King, His leading and calling being made more evident with each passing day.

With the rolling around of another month, September, it would be announced that I was going to be on the next chain. A chain was a movement of the inmate population on either bus, van, car or plane. Of course from Puerto Rico there was no other way to get to the mainland other than by plane. Orders had come in from the Bureau of Prisons that I was to be sent to the Federal Correctional Institution in

Beaumont, Texas. It was one of the new pod complex units that the Federal Government was building as full spread institutions. This comprised of a Camp, Low, Medium and High security prison sectors plus a Maximum Security unit. All of them located within a few hundred yards of one another. This allowed staffing and transfer of the guards and inmates to be utilized, one institution to another. An inmate could be moved up or down in classification and not have to be transported to another state or city, only across the field. One of the many cost savings in prison life today, sure!

Chain day was a scurrying of activity for it required a huge movement of people, normally 130-140 men and women. Additional guards moved into the act from both military and civilian police departments. Each clothed in all black fatigues, body armor vests and automatic weapons. Each person were chained individually and then chained together. There was absolutely no chance of running or escape, period. One by one herded into a bullpen like cattle as they were wrapped in their chains and hand and ankle cuffed. Once the entire group was processed, paperwork and personal items stored, the large transport buses began to arrive.

One by one marched, loaded and chained to their seats. Steel benches were welded to the floor of the transport vehicle. The bulletproof glass had steel bars covering it in an interlocking pattern. It was more of a tank than a mere bus. Flat black in color with no logo, insignia or markings of any kind on the outside, they were used for one thing and one thing only.

"Listen up! Make this move easy on yourselves and move quickly to the hallway. We will assist you in climbing the stairs to the bus. No talking at all. You talk and I will put you back and take someone else. Have a nice trip." The Sgt. was not funny and his sense of humor not appreciated by anyone. What he was calling help was nothing more than a guard pointing towards the steps and making everyone of us drag the chains on our own. Next time you think about what it was like, tie your hands and feet together. Place another rope around your waist and knees and tie all of the ropes together. Then, like some of us with violence on their record, tie a rope around your neck and extend it down to the one on your waist. Now walk up a set of stairs. Fun? Right? Then imagine the rope not to be ropes, rather heavy chains locked so tight that the circulation is cutting off. Let us go one step further and imagine this position and discomfort for 12-14 hours. Yes, the guards place you in the bull pens chained and ready to go for sometimes up to eight hours. Then with the bus ride and the plane, (yes, we are still chained in the plane and to the plane) the total becomes longer and larger. Do the crime, do the time and all the things that accompany a sentence to prison.

The transport experience lasted thirty-seven days with a lay over in Miami, Atlanta and Oklahoma, City. Two to four days in each one except Oklahoma, City, there for an extended stay. During that extended stay, it became a time of precious witness to a brother from the past, the far, very far distant past. His name was Chris Daskalos, and he had been one of my classmates at New Mexico Military Institute, back in the late sixties. This is how it came about, there being no doubt whatsoever that God's Hand was all over this meeting.

Oklahoma City, Oklahoma, not just a regular airport serves this great city. One additional full service terminal is located there, covertly, to provide passenger services. Airport number two serves the skies of a transport called Con Air. Yes, it wasn't only in a movie starring Nicholas Cage, it truly exists and has an enormous fleet of private aircraft. The aircraft come from confiscated planes that have been seized during drug raid operations. From the smaller variety, six to twelve passenger size like King Air's and Leer's to the 707, 727, BAC 111 and even a few 747's. Each one a former privately owned piece of property used to transport huge quantities of marijuana, cocaine and heroin from points all over the globe, as well as multi-million dollars bundles of cash, U.S. currency.

When they were confiscated, the United States Marshal's Service took them to begin transporting prisoners from points around this earth. Transcontinental, international, hundreds of flights every single day dancing from airport to airport. Yet when you, the innocent bystander saw them go by you did not realize it was Con Air in the friendly skies. Convicts by the thousands are transported this way and their main terminal, nationwide is Oklahoma City, Oklahoma. An aerial view shows it to be like any other commercial facility. A main terminal and multiple gate boarding and deplaning chutes exactly like the regular airport. Once inside, the true beast displays itself. Men and women move through the corridors chained and cuffed by the thousands as each flight loads and unloads. Hundreds of deputies there to herd the masses through the documentation, medical screening, clothing, feeding and cellblock housing units. Roughly three thousand men and women make this a temporary home for periods of time of a few days to many months. The United States Government allows the patrons or inmates, to accumulate one by one with similar destinations. Then, when the numbers are adequate for a full boarding, the jet airliner makes another move to that specific location. Thus the vast division in time spent for each incarcerated individual. Once they are in their general region by aircraft, the men and women are bused and transported the rest of the way by ground transportation, to their individual prison, correctional institution or camp. Con Air, alive and well in the United States and making a statement in the airline industry, their efficiency and occupancy among the top of their field.

My flight, with two layovers as previously mentioned in Miami and Atlanta, arrived late one Friday night, near midnight. The processing took near three hours, moving from location to location within the terminal. Tired, more like worn out, my group was finally moving out of their last registration point.

"Gentlemen, grab your clothing and supplies and follow Sgt. Jones." The young Lieutenant announced the command to march. Twenty-seven bedraggled men followed their leader down the long, glass floored corridor towards their housing area. Silently shuffling, some wondering who and what would be their welcoming committee. Never knowing the conditions, the environment or the occupants they may be thrown with, and the element of danger or bodily harm residing there. This was not the Holiday Inn nor was personal preference a part of the ordeal.

"Decker, Thomas, Storrs, Peterson, Sanchez, Pearson, you will be here in Pod A." Statement made and with it another guard appears with the opening of the huge vaultlike steel door. Ushered in like penguins, the hobbled leg irons rattling on the varnished concrete floor, directions and cell numbers began to be issued. Three additional guards began the removal of the cuffs and chains. Mine, were double locked and of the maximum security variety due to my criminal history, so it takes much longer to disassemble. Making me the last one to be free of the metal and sent to my cell.

"All right, Decker, it is your turn. Seems you are some kind of bad guy from the Virgin Islands, is that true?" The attitude sometimes went with the job and with it a chance to witness for me.

"No, sir. Only a man who made many mistakes in his life and has finally found Jesus Christ and true freedom." I smiled at the guard and waited his reply.

"Another one of those jail house converters, right?" His smirk and the tone of his voice dug deep.

"No, just another person who has finally seen the light and chooses to change his life, and through Christ that has happened. I realize where I came from and how I lived, but even in here that can begin to

change. Foremost in your heart does the realization come forth that Jesus Christ died for me and for you. He hung on a cross with two thieves and suffered for each of us. I, personally, owe Him my life and will serve Him forevermore. He loves me and He loves you too sir!" The presence of the Holy Spirit was talking to this man far more than my mere words were expressing. His demeanor changing and the look in his eyes moved from cold to warm.
"You are saying stuff I know, but I don't have time to read the Bible. I work all the time and am trying to raise four kids on my own. Heck, if I have ten minutes a day I'd be lucky, of free time." I could hear the pain and the anguish and the crying out inside this man's heart. He was lonely, tired and working in this environment only for the money and the benefits like insurance for his children.
"I promise you if you gave that ten minutes every day to Jesus Christ, He would bless you and allow a peace that surpasses all understanding to cover you and your family. His love is so much more than any love you have ever known. God's Hand on your life will make your life full of the richness of His grace, mercy and forgiveness." The quiet of the setting was allowing for additional time to plant a seed, water a seed or whatever the situation needed to provide.
"Decker, I need to get you processed. My supervisor is coming for count in ten minutes and I don't want to have a problem. Maybe we can talk again one night. I will be working this late shift for this quarter." He had been moved. Not by me, but by the presence of Christ, the Holy Spirit.
"Any time really, any time at all. Just knock on my cell. I do not sleep much anyway." He finished my paperwork and escorted me to cell 24.

Nearing four o'clock in the morning, the only sound in the cellblock was snoring and little else. The movement of the cell door stirred the bottom bunk occupant to partial alertness.
"Take the top bunk. Welcome to cell #24." My new celly, the name we call one another, greeted me with a chuckle.
"Yeah! Thanks, my name is Michael and I will meet you formally later today."
"Deal!" His reply came with it a deep breath and sigh, sensing that it was time to go back to sleep, and safe to do so. This was not always the case, especially in a transport or temporary holding tank like Oklahoma City.

The flat sheet steel bunk with the tiny 2" thick fiber mattress felt like a Beauty Rest from Simmons after the past seventy-two hours. A three hour nap would be all I needed to go on and be ready for my first full day in OKC. I jumped up on the bunk and pulled the old Army blanket over my bones, quietly reflecting the day and talking with my Father. Every day ended this way. Speaking with my Heavenly Father, letting Him know exactly how much I appreciated and cherished His presence in my life. I was laying my prayer requests before His throne, there at His feet. Listening in the quiet for His audible or inaudible voice, it was here that direction for the next day or event was given so that it could be instituted and savored. Sleep came and the sound of my heart beating reassured me of Him working there, thank you Father.

With the movement outside the cell door, alertness came rapidly. Even in the low light, the passing of the guard doing his official count brought about full attention. Taking time for the sharing with my Lord first, I arose and slid down to the cold concrete floor. My movement and rustling brought a greeting from the bunk below.
"Good morning! You don't sleep much do you?" My new friend was rubbing his eyes and stretching with the comment.
"No, I never was much of one to stay in the sack more than a few hours at most. That started pretty early in my life back at home and then at military school." At the mention of military school came a stare from the shadows of the bunk, a recollection quickly coming from old memories. Days gone by, years of drug and alcohol abuse clouding the clarity of thought, but a realism bursting through in overwhelming fashion.
"I know you! I know you from thirty years ago, I really do. You are Michael Decker aren't you? That is your name, isn't it?" This person was speaking words of knowing and it was shocking at OUR joint reaction. I stood there in total amazement as a familiar face stood up into the light.
"Chris, Chris Daskalos, what in the world are you doing here? Well, that is a dumb question. I haven't seen you since NMMI back in 1967." We shook hands and I gave him a big hug which nearly freaked him out of his socks. Men don't hug much in prison, for many reasons. But I did not care what most men did, this was one cool coincidence. Yeah, like it just happened that someone from thirty years before was in a holding cell with me in OKC.

For the next 12-14 hours, I shared, he shared and we recounted all of the water that had passed under the bridge over the past three decades. Our paths had nearly touched several times, common threads of the drug world and money laundering networks. Seems that Chris was doing time for possession of marijuana with intent to distribute, a charge he had picked up back east somewhere. He had been in for about four years and was being transferred down to the Big Springs

Federal Correctional Institution. I learned of his relationships and little girl, his sister's help in this time of incarceration, and a report on his parent's death. I shared all of my past, yes all of my past and it took forever. Chris wanted to know every single detail. Over the next two weeks that is exactly what happened.

I shared every single detail, especially my relationship with God and how my life was transformed along with the changing of my heart. Chris listened very intently. He was mesmerized by what he was hearing and who he was hearing it from. He had heard of my exploits and the life I had led for years. But to hear of this relationship with God and how He has changed my life from the inside out was powerful to him. God, the Hand of my Father was holding this young man's heart and leading him into the Kingdom. Seed by seed, watering by watering, the presence and majesty of the Holy Spirit came forth. My Lord and Savior Jesus Christ was standing by with each prayer I sent, in full intercession and relaying the message on to His Father, my Father. I could visibly see what was happening in Chris' heart, the tenderness in his eyes and the weeping of his spirit. It was time! It was his time to come home.

"Chris Daskalos, God is calling you into His Arms. I can see it, you can feel it and down deep in your heart of hearts, it is real."

"Yeah brother, something is making my insides tremble and my heart pound. I want what you got, I really do. My life has been nothing more than crap for so long. I want to be a new man and a real father to my little girl when I get home." He finished what he had to say and I nodded to him in acknowledgment of his hungry heart.

"My brother, I want you to repeat these words after me. God would have you confess all your sins and ask Him into your heart and life."

Chris answered," I know Michael and I am ready for a change, so ready."

"Dear Father in heaven…I admit that I need you…Please forgive my unbelief and the things I have done wrong. I believe that Jesus is the Son of God and that He paid for all my sins with His Blood on the Cross…I call on His Name to save me…I now receive His life….I believe Jesus is living in me…that I am forgiven…and now I am a Christian…Because of this free gift…of eternal life…I will go to be with Jesus when I die…Thank you Lord for saving me…Amen."

The angels began to rejoice in heaven for they had a new brother and God had another child in His family. Chris and I hugged once again and over the next few weeks shared the power of His Word and studied incessantly. What I saw was the life of a man changed, eternally. Nothing was going to bring this man back into darkness. He had chosen the new life, the new leading of his Father God. Early one Tuesday morning, totally unannounced, the cell door opened and the guard spoke.

"Daskalos, get your things. You are going out on the chain today. You have five minutes to collect and make the movement." The young guard left and Chris vaulted from the bunk.

"Well dude, I guess this is my time."

"Chris, you will do fine in Big Springs. Get to church and get hooked up with a Bible study group. Heck you will be out and home before you know it." I sat there on the upper bunk to give him room in gathering his personal things. Six by eight is not a lot of room for two guys, a bunk, toilet, sink and writing desk.

"I truly thank you for all that you shared. You will never know how much this time has meant to me. What I feel inside is something I never knew before even existed." His moist eyes said it all and I was thrilled. We prayed and he took off out of the cell, on to his new destination.

Later that morning, four hours to be exact, the cell door opened once again to the clanging of steel to steel and the rattling of heavy brass keys. My instant thought was that I was about to get a new celly, but God had another plan.

"Decker get your goods, you are catching the next chain." Well, well, it was just going to be a chain kind of day.

Three hours later I was on the Con Air heading towards Houston Hobby Airport with 157 other heavily chained and shackled men and women. Once on the ground the guards called names and separated groups by prison location. Shuttle buses came forward and one by one we marched into the prison delivery vehicles for our final destinations. Two hours later I saw the looming structures of Federal Correctional Institution Beaumont, Texas come into view. First one unit then another, this was to be my first experience inside a prison pod grouping.

The maximum security violent offenders got off first at the penitentiary, then the high security and finally the medium and the low. One by one these men would find themselves thrust into a new environment, many to find a change of heart, some to find no life at all. For me, it was the beginning of the end, for God had sealed my destiny and fate.

February 1998 saw me assigned to a new prison, a new cellblock and a new job as an instructor's assistant in the construction trades department. I was assisting two of the instructors with teaching men something about building this and that. It was a farce with the curriculum being general and the practical aspect of actually doing the construction was rarely done. The only bright point was when the

Associate Warden gave us permission to build the new baseball dug outs, from the ground up.

Chaplain Williams was in charge of the Religious Services department. He was a young, energetic pastor with a wealth of volunteers coming in to minister to the population. One thing you must understand is the vast coverage he was responsible for in the every widening scope of religions. Under the freedom of religion rules and regulations, every man had the right to worship any way he pleased. From the Indian Nations sweat lodge to the chanting of the Buddists and hundreds in between, Chaplain Williams was in charge. The results were his being pulled several directions and little time for one on one counseling. This was left to those of us that wanted to Shepard our brothers and share the love of Jesus Christ.

Steve Gregg, Scott Baker, Larry Brown, Ron Kimball, Joe Parker, Lowell Ames, Larry Maxwell, many names of men who would become a part of my daily life. Steve Gregg, Scott Baker and Ron Kimball would become part of my close circle of friends, comrades and brothers in Christ. Day by day, through fellowship, sharing and praying together, a bond built would be eternally formed and a kinship of hearts. From the Bible studies and fellowship, the food spreads we all contributed towards, the football challenges down on the field, the TV room escapades, each a part of making it in the prison environment and day to day living. Our group formed a Bible study back in 1998 to dig deeper into the Word of God and find greater calling in understanding His perfect Will for each of us.

My studies with Crossroads Bible Institute had continued on with courses now on the college level. The advanced curriculum allowed for me to have a private mentor for counsel, grading and intimate sharing. Bill was his name, eighty-four years young and so full of the Holy Spirit. Bill had been studying the Word for over eighty years and to say that he knew the Word was a vast understatement. He lived it, and his letters shared such vibrant depth in his counsel and reflections of practical application of taking God's Word to everyday life. The wealth of knowledge endless, the caring of heart immense and the individual attention, acute in detail and service, I was a fortunate student for sure.
"Michael, I have been noticing that you are not in any type of relationship right now." Steve Gregg was speaking as to my singular status. Well no kidding, like I have the opportunity to meet someone and get to know them from in here!
"Really, you have been noticing, huh?" A smile followed my statement, hands on my hips.

"Yep! I have a friend down in the Bryan Unit. Her roommate is a really fine lady and is not writing to anyone right now. She has been down for quite a while, I think like eight or nine years." Mister matchmaker was doing his best.
"And so, what are you trying to say?"
"Just thought you might want to write to Kelly, Kelly Stewart is her name." Steve was so proud of himself and his encouragement continued. "I am serious, how about it?" He was not going to give up on this issue.
"Okay, I guess it wouldn't hurt anything to write a letter or two." After all, I was a single man in prison and a little female company, even in letter form, would be nice. She might even turnout to be sweet, good hearted, pretty, a blessing and, most of all, a Christian.

Little did I know that this lady would turn out to be a fabulous woman with deep inner reflections and a commitment to God equal or even greater than what my heart had finally realized. Kelly had a spark, a sparkle that was contagious and in a matter of twenty or thirty letters during the next three months, my heart would be reeling. As we shared our love for God and our outlook on life and family and friends and everything, a kindred association began to form. Kindled by the fire within of the Holy Spirit, our likes were the same, our dislikes identical. Day by day this letter relationship was growing until one evening I began reading a one of her letters I had just received.

Most often I would wait to read my mail until after night meal. Putting on my headphones from my tiny transistor radio, I would walk around the outside compound of the cellblocks. With the noise of the prison momentarily drowned out, the music singing to my heart, I would begin reading the message. On this night, April 30th, 1998, as I read this most recent correspondence from Kelly Stewart, she spoke of a new song by Shania Twain called "From this Moment." As I read the words of the letter, exactly at the same moment, the song began to play on the radio. Yes, the very same song, exactly at the very moment that I read the message. My heart skipped several beats I am sure. Well, it felt like it at least.

"Lord, what are you trying to tell me? Is this a sign of sorts, from you?" Speaking to myself, and very possibly out loud also, I rolled the thoughts and feelings over in my spirit. I had not felt what I was feeling in a long, long time. Maybe never, because what I was feeling was deep inside, not just regular deep, but really DEEP!

Returning to the dorm that night I began to answer the letter, page by page and allowing my hand to translate from my mind and heart, to the pen. Nine pages later I wrote this passage.

Kelly Stewart, you have captured my heart and ministered to my soul, in a way only God could have guided. Your tender warmth I feel, even from the distance between us. Your words speaking of love, yes love and devotion without saying it directly. Tonight, while reading your letter and announcing one of your very favorite songs, that song began to play, From this Moment. It so moved me that I realized that I am falling in love with you. Listen to me Kelly Stewart, I love you, I really do. From this moment on, not the song title but the time at hand, I was immersed in an ongoing relationship which mounted and grew every single day.

"My goodness Ron! Come and look at this face, it is some sort of disease I am sure!" Steve Gregg sounded just like Russell Scharf from years gone by.

"Yes, it is terminal and may be contagious. Steve you had better notify authorities and call the hospital." Ron chided in with confidence and amplified expression.

"You two had better stop, NOW! I am doing nothing more than writing a letter." My attempt at removing the obvious was a vain tossing of the inevitable. Their immediate response signaled that fact.

"If THAT is nothing more than writing a letter, I am the president of the U.S.A."

"No, Steve, you are not." I was doomed from the very beginning of this conversation and it would not cease, the kidding, for several days.

Each passing day or two would bring another letter to me and see one going in the reverse direction. Kelly Stewart had taken claim to my heart and only rightly so. She had a calling on her life from God. There to serve in the Kingdom by going to the jails and prisons, speaking the truth of our Lord and bringing home a message of salvation to all that she met. Yes, it was an identical calling and mirrored the one given to me by our God Almighty. The unified vision brought forth a desire and fire for the presence of the Holy Spirit that nothing else could satisfy. Kelly and I shared scripture and messages regularly in each letter sent and received.

The days seemed to fly by and the elements of a solid foundation in Christ had been established for the Bible study group. This was a gathering of eight men who had a passion for the Word of God. Once shared, the bond that formed would be ongoing and would not cease to exist when one or the other of us was finally sent home, our time of sentence completed.

CHAPTER 11

Beyond the walls prison Ministry!

My time drew to an end in 1998, November 2nd to be exact. There was a sadness and void with my leaving. This was evident in my going, but also a definite joy for all of us to focus upon. With every man's departure it was a signaling to the spirit that their own time was drawing near.
"Brother Decker, we are going to miss you. I definitely am going to!" Steve Gregg announced his feelings to everyone near.
"Me too, Michael. I think you should stay around for a few more months," Scott Baker chided in with his jovial opinion. Larry Brown, Ron Kimball, Joe Clark and the others made their statements of farewell on this day and with that, I proceeded to the Control Office.

Bus ticket in hand and my meager personal belongings in a ditty bag, I caught the town shuttle into Beaumont, there to settle in a seat on the big Greyhound bus and focus in on the upcoming seventeen hour bus ride to Lubbock, Texas. I had been assigned to a halfway house there for the next three months, under the iron handed managing by Ms. Steele; she was the duly appointed manager and guided the everyday operation of all the residents, both male and female.

An immediate requirement was to find gainful employment and start paying the 25% surcharge of every paycheck to Ms. Steele. If a $300 dollar paycheck was given the worker, a $75.00 fee was assessed for living expenses and food costs back to the halfway house, weekly! The very first place I stopped – the first business, that is – my destiny was signed, sealed and delivered. The establishment was none other than Winnie's Car Wash. They had been in business for nearly thirty years.
"Excuse me, my name is Michael Decker and I am looking for a job. I need to work and I promise you I will give you everything I have in ability, strength and dedication. Additionally, I need to inform you that I was recently released from prison and reside currently in a halfway house." I

extended my hand to the owner and knew in my heart the job was mine. The peace from God had been delivered earlier in my quiet time of the day. Nothing, not one single aspect of my life was going to be undertaken without His Hand, His Will and His Authority being there.

"So you know how to work do you? We'll see if that is true very quickly. Come on back and let me show you the Winnie's Car Wash way to make a car sparkle." Fred Jones was about to launch me on a new career, temporarily that is.

Life in the car wash business is primarily conducted and completed by men and women who have very little drive and ambition, with only a few exceptions. Most have a past, jail/prison/drugs and alcohol, but need income and the work provides that. My particular situation was that I needed a job, needed money, and would work my buns off for anybody over the next three months with only a chance needed, for total dedication. Three weeks into this new endeavor I was offered a raise and promotion.

"Michael, you work like you have a fire built under you. I have talked it over with my wife and we would like to have you manage the business for us. This would give me some extra fishing time and my wife the freedom to do other things during the day." His raised eyebrows were the questioning part of his statement.

"More money and more responsibility, that is exactly what I need and I promise to do you a good job." Case closed as far as I was concerned, every penny was being saved for my final release date from the halfway house,, anyway. God was once again providing for me and the added responsibility allowed me to come in earlier and stay later, with time to accelerate in completing my tenure in the Lubbock area.

Weekends, since I was working and following all the rules and regulations of the halfway house, I was one of the fortunate few who were blessed with travel passes. Fridays, after finishing work and getting the paycheck cashed, I would bring in my payment to Ms. Steele and receive a forty-eight hour home pass. This was incredible because it allowed me to be completely free of the confines of the housing center. Additionally, it gave me the freedom to worship in church back in Amarillo, Texas. The greatest blessing came in finding that my mother had purchased an old summer cottage down in the Canyon Country Club, Canyon, Texas.

Only five hundred and sixty feet of living space with a long enclosed porch, it was a mansion to me. College students had lived in it for the past fifteen years and made their marks and left their signatures everywhere. There were wild colors on most of the walls, electric and phone wires hanging from the ceilings and stapled to the flat surfaces. While it was listed for a long time with a realtor, no one could see the possibilities it contained. I saw all the potential and spent countless hours remodeling, repairing and restoring. My first night there, all alone with the Holy Spirit, I praised God and thanked my Lord, countless hours on my knees. The precious tenderness of His love and anointing bathing me in the covenant warmth of His Kingdom and the power of the Blood, I treasured every moment.

Time at home was seemingly at the speed of light, the weekend flying by so rapidly and the hour to be back under the direction of the halfway house rules looming on the horizon. God had allowed me to meet one of my new neighbors, Kent Gable. Kent was a heavy hitter in the commercial real estate market, as well a multi-million acre land owner in both Texas and New Mexico. He had been attending the local cowboy churches for several years and his invitation to join him was very welcome.

"Michael, I am Kent Gable, your neighbor, and wondered if you would like to join me at Cowboy Church tonight?" His extended hand was more than enough for me to say an immediate, YES!

"Absolutely! I would enjoy going somewhere new." This adventure would launch me into the local Christian community and bring about a rapid deployment of requests to bring my testimony and preaching to churches throughout the Panhandle region.

Within six weeks of that first night in Cowboy Church with Pastor Ty Jones, I was on the circuit and this would never end. The calling to my heart, the calling to my life, which God had so definitely planted was manifesting by His Hand and guided by His Spirit. Each day, each night behind the pulpit, my energy and excitement about sharing the Word of God and bringing the lost, by God's power, into the Kingdom, elevated. Church after church, city after city, request after request came pouring in and the vision of ministry that God had shown me during the years in prison was displayed in reality. The destiny of what was to happen began to unfold, and with it a new way to live, in the powerful anointing of the Holy Spirit, the darkness of the past now forever, dead and buried.

The required three months in the halfway house came to a close and I was assigned to a new supervisor, Joe King. Mr. King was assigned as my parole or probation officer, a role he would carry for the next three years. Monthly visits in his office, weekly home visits and bimonthly visits to my work place, this would be the normal routine.

"Michael Decker! Seems you have quite an extensive criminal record over the past thirty years. I am sure that we won't have a problem during your probationary time, right?" His bearded face and profile leaning back in his chair as he placed the question, raised eyebrows waiting for a reply, he was expecting some lengthy dissertation.

"No, Sir! I am a man of God now," matter of fact, to the point and leaving no room of doubt with the tone of my voice, the subject dropped.

"Make sure you have your restitution payments with you the first Wednesday of each month. I also want you to begin alcohol counseling on a weekly basis with Gene Reynolds. He is excellent and a great counselor to deal with. I will be by the house to inspect everything tomorrow. By the way, you are going to have to wear an electronic monitoring device on your ankle for the next sixty days. Please take off your shoe and sock from your right foot." I had not been warned about this new turn of events – not that it really mattered, for I was free to serve God and some ankle device was not going to deter that in any way.

The device had a receiving and transmitting control unit that had to be plugged in and hooked to my home phone line. My perimeter of movement was 100 feet and if I strayed beyond that distance a signal activated with a warning beep. Three warning beeps and it then dialed an 800 number to say that I was out of bounds. Mr. King had preset the unit with time tables so that it automatically shut off at 7:00 a.m., when I went off to work and came on again at 6:00 p.m., this being my curfew hour. Another hurdle in the race of life that was tolerated and easily endured; the alternative was not a choice that was ever considered.

Removal of the equipment came and with it the freedom to move within a one hundred fifty mile area of my home. It was a gift, thereby opening the door to minister and speak throughout the Panhandle and begin to serve an ever widening audience for God. Each day brought a greater knowledge of His Kingdom and a further comprehension of exactly what God had called me to do. It seemed the increase of my knowledge through study of His Word each day coincided with the building and restoration and growth of my little abode, the scriptures containing the answers to life's questions and the roadmap to everyday living. For the first time in my existence I could not imagine trying to make it through a day without the majesty of knowing God. His Light, the presence of the Holy Spirit, made darkness disappear and made peace, mercy and grace abound. All glory be to the Father and to His Son, Jesus Christ, Amen!

From my heart I knew that there would never be a time that service to my Abba Father could ever cease, for His work and the salvation of the lost beckoned my spirit. This desire to serve and call in the harvest of souls grew and with it a distinct purpose and format formed. Beyond the Walls Prison Ministries came to life and was founded with all of the passion and fire that had smoldered inside me for so long. I knew that God would allow the violence and the dark misery of my past life to go behind the walls and touch men and women's lives. They, the incarcerated individuals, could not escape the message of truth and salvation any longer. Their excuse of "you don't know what it is like," and "it is different inside the prison," and, finally, "what makes you think you know what I feel?" – each phrase a cop out and a chance at providing truth to God's intended plan. When they heard that my prison number was 564488 from the Texas Department of Criminal Justice or 00488-124 from the Federal Prison System, they listened to what God had done for me. The real life examples of drugs, alcohol, violence and crime were spoken of in scenarios with which each man and woman could identify.

One by one, two by two, the numbers grew in accordance with the Will of God. He was having His way through the conversion of my life. The scriptures of Philippians, Romans, Proverbs, I Corinthians, II Peter, II Chronicles, Ephesians 6 and so many others were manifesting and bringing countless numbers into the Kingdom of God. The first year of the ministry's work brought about 310 salvations. With each success story came more requests to come into new churches and profess the mighty Word of God. The fire and desire ever growing and the outreach ever broadening, His Hand was on this ministry. The second year saw 3,596 salvations in the prisons and jails and countless others in what had become an ongoing television ministry.

God's Learning Channel, the programming for Prime Time Christian Broadcasting became an outlet and was a true gift from God. A man whom I had the pleasure of meeting, Brother Garre LaGrone, a very anointed man of God in the area of Praise & Worship, had asked that I accompany him on one of his tapings. Garre had toured with several nationally known Country & Western groups, Clint Black, Lorrie Morgan and others. God had given him a gift in music with a sensational, rich voice and words and melodies that told of the precious love of God. Almost to the top of the charts in the secular field but never quite getting the right break, God's calling to his life was the answer to his soaring achievement. Through the change in his heart, there came the amplification of God's purpose and anointing in Garre's music. Song after song was given as a gift, the Holy Spirit began to write through my brother, taking the melodies on his heart and turning them into powerful pieces of Praise and Worship. I will share more on Garre and other brothers, all mighty men of God.

As the months continued to pass, one by one, with them other feelings as a man, a human, began to grow and cause an overwhelming desire for a companion. The length of time between letters for Kelly and me had grown. Where before it was a three to five times a week correspondence, it had become a biweekly event with two to three letters a month being exchanged. She and I had spoken on the phone a few times but at $35-$40 per call, this was a major expenditure. The lack of physical contact, as I had never seen her other than pictures, was making the time factor ever more prevalent. Four years had passed since our initial contact and Kelly had another three years yet to serve. Additionally, she had just received word that a State of Oklahoma detainer had been filed. This meant that after her Federal prison time she would have to go back to Oklahoma and serve time in the women's facility. In my heart the love was the same as before, but reality of the situation and waiting another four or five years was proving to be somewhat overwhelming.

During this period of time, now the spring of 2000, my father Hank Decker had come back to the little town of Canyon, Texas. He, along with his nine malamute sled dogs and six of the Heinz variety, fifteen animals in all, the one ton van that he drove was likened to Noah's Ark with its overflowing of critter activity. Still rough in actions and in his vocabulary especially, my Dad was failing in his health and needed someone to care for him. My father, my job and my obligation, it was the opening of our relationship being healed and in many ways formed from the years, decades, of absence. He was eighty-five and I was now fifty-one, with the total time we had spent together maybe two of those fifty-plus years. I had been going to a wonderful little cowboy church over in Hereford, Texas, named Barn Church Dream Center under the direction of Senior Pastor Randy Bird. A wonderful and powerfully anointed man of God who had been instrumental in teaching me many of the fundamentals in ministry, preaching and serving the Kingdom of God. It was here in the Barn Church Dream Center that my father had seen and felt the presence of the Holy Spirit for the first time.

The nurturing and stirring of this loving warmth and conviction of his soul came by seeing, firsthand, all of the love and devotion of this congregation. Hank had visited the church on two occasions, then on a cold, misty morning in the old trailer he called home, his life forever changed. The diabetic sores on his lower legs needed constant attention and I as his son would come by the trailer. There first to greet the herd of canines before getting to the door, a barrage of barks and tail wagging accompanied by long wet tongues licking my hands as I told each one of the group hello. Inside, my father and I would start the day.

"Dad, better get those legs taken care of." His long, lanky frame normally asleep with the ball cap pulled down over his eyes and the television blaring.

"Well, hello there, Hoss, what's up?" Same conversation, every single morning, his low voice booming because of his lack of hearing, he felt he could overcome this by the echo he broadcast.

"How are you feeling today? Do you have an appetite this morning?" Hank would answer and I would proceed to wash his legs and feet, then two or three days a week we would go to a quaint little café named Coney Island and grab a bite of breakfast. It was in the fellowship of those minutes that his life and my life were joined and God's love covered and bathed us both.

This morning was different, because the urgency placed in my heart to share the gift of salvation by leading Hank into the presence of the Lord was intense. Earlier in the morning during my quiet time, God had spoken to me about my father. His voice was clear, to a prophetic calling and time table that was to be observed. My Abba Father had told me that I had three months, only three more, to spend with my earthly father. The exactness being to the minute with a further confirmation on this day February 11, 2000, coming at 2:10 p.m. that afternoon. The message repeated to my heart, "Michael, you have only three more months to love your father and be by his side."

Kneeling there on the old rug, coated with hair from the dogs, more like fur, a few kernels of dog food sprinkled around, I took the warm cloth and began to wash my father's feet. My position at his feet – yes, my Jesus was alive and speaking to my heart as I humbly looked up to my dad. The knowing of what was to follow brought about a surge of regret that it had taken so long for this moment. Yet at the very same instant, I was flooded by the emotional gifting from God that Hank Decker would not go to hell, he would find the Lord. I began to lead him to the throne of grace and mercy, Jesus Christ to be his link for salvation.

"Dad, I need you to listen very closely to what I have to say." His eyes immediately fell upon mine.

"Yes, son, what's that?" his gaze and demeanor were instantly readied by the Holy Spirit for what was to happen now.

"Dad it is time for you and me to pray together and for you to ask Jesus Christ in your heart and for God to forgive you for your sins." Our eyes bore the feeling of the same blood flowing through our veins and the touch of Jesus cascading any avenue of doubt on to the Book,

the Lamb's Book of Life where Hank Decker was about to be listed.
"Yep, it is time, Michael." A single tear began to trace across his cheek and a slight trembling came to his huge hands.
"Repeat these words of prayer as we ask for this blessing." As I spoke he began to say the words that would promise him eternal salvation.
"Father God, I ask you to forgive me for all of my sins. I confess all of them to you and beg for your forgiveness. My Jesus, I ask you to be my Lord and Savior forevermore. I will follow you; I will serve you; I will speak of you to everyone. May my life bring you honor and praise, from this day forward." A simple prayer placed before the throne of God and instant deliverance to both me and my dad.

The following Sunday at the morning service of Barn Church Dream Center, Hank Decker brought his tall body to attention and before the church, told of his salvation experience. It was a mighty witness to many, because of his age and many factors, and told of the power of God's love, His peace and His deliverance to the faithful of heart. To me, I was blessed beyond words by the loving grace and mercy of my Father God. The testimony as to the infinite detail of God's voice and Will came to the second, the very second on the clock, three months later.

During the end of April, 2000, Hank's health began to fail and it was necessary to place him in a constant care facility. Located in Canyon, Texas, where all of his old friends and college buddies could come by and visit, it became the final chapter of his life. The final visitor that windy West Texas afternoon was J. W. Malone, one of the men who had played basketball with Hank back in college. They had reminisced of days gone by and stories of great games and athletic endeavors accomplished. J.W. had said his final goodbye and then embraced my dad and me before leaving. The date, May 11, 2000, the time was 2:00 p.m., and I sat there with my father. My right hand on his chest, my left stroking his face and cheek, the labored breathing coming now in gasps and long intervals of time, we both knew what was about to take place.
"Dad, I love you so much and these last few months have meant so much to me. I am so proud to call you my father and I cherish this time we have had together." The tears began to fall from my eyes as I brought in his surprise: I knew one last visit from one of his favorite dogs, Buck, a crossbred mix of who knows what, but Hank's constant companion and friend, would truly mean a lot to him.
"Buck wanted to come say hello to you and give you a kiss." I raised the dog up so that he could see him. His hand curled around Buck's ears and a slight smile came to Hank's face. The wet tongue began to

lap the side of my dad's face, friend to friend, comrade to comrade. Slowly I began to lower the dog to the floor, the time was ebbing and with it the flow of life itself.

I began to talk with God and knew that the trip into the land of glory was close at hand. One last breath, a long sigh and the aura and presence of Jesus Christ filled the room. My father had gone home to his Father, to walk the streets of gold and see God, face to face. The peace that passes all understanding blessed the room and I looked at the watch on my wrist, ticking over from 2:10 to 2:11, to the second, the very second, exactly what God had spoken. The Will of God had been carried out and the result was not emptiness; there was no regret, only thanks and praise for the last few months together with my father.

Hank's death was spoken of during the Thursday night service at Cowboy Church. Praises lifted to the heavens and rejoicing by the body of Christ, it was testimony of eternal salvation and the truth of God's precious Word. For me personally, it was a launching into service and ministry with renewed energy and direction. My God had done what He said He would do, it was my turn to serve and bring honor and glory to Him, forevermore.

The covenant relationship that God had so mightily provided for me in the groups of men that I had fellowship with each week, made the loss of my father not a time of sadness. The International Fellowship of Christian Businessmen on Tuesday, Bill Gruehlkey's Barn fellowship out in Wildorado, Texas on Wednesday and the study group in the Divine Grind on Thursday morning, each a blessing and a source of strength. My life was full of fellowship with men who fought the good fight and served Jesus Christ as Lord, Savior and King.

Meanwhile, the ministry was growing by leaps and bounds. Doors opening literally everywhere to preach, minister and give service for God. The construction business that I used as my livelihood during the day was doing just that, providing an income source, but my heart was yearning for full time ministry. This yearning, this request, in God's perfect timing, would one day come to pass. There was so much to do in service for God and the visions, dreams and plans He placed in my mind, heart and body kept me soaring with little time to rest.

During one of my construction jobs, a remodel project for Cattlco Lonestar, down in Happy, Texas, my life began to change. It seemed that the years of loneliness were about to come to a close. This because of a certain young lady's comment, while I was working one afternoon, it was to be a start. She, Sherli Templeton, was speaking to one of her coworkers about her love for fresh cut wood.

"Emily, I just love the smell of freshly cut wood. It is so lovely!" I heard the voice from the hallway, but I never turned around to see a face or exactly who was speaking, I merely tossed a comment over my shoulder. "Well then, you ought to marry yourself a carpenter." Yes, the comment was thrown in the wind and it blew all the way to the lady and then back to me.

"Yeah, that would be a good idea." Sherli peeked around the corner and smiled. Well, more like beamed her approval of my statement. Her long brunette hair tossing as she whirled around the corner, the starched Rockies speaking.

By the end of the remodel I had asked her out to dinner and a few months later, after seeing her heart for Jesus and meeting her family, our relationship began to form. Sherli followed me from church to church in support of the ministry and calling to my life. She helped and shared her family, an older daughter Marty in college at West Texas A&M, another daughter Mikki who was a sophomore at Canyon High School, and a son Colten that was just entering the first grade. The more time we spent together, the more comfortable I became with sharing life together and not being alone. This time together also made my feelings for Kelly change, not leave, only change. What I was feeling was a freedom to go on with my life and not wait for another few years to begin a relationship. Both sadness and joy came with what was happening in my life, my heart.

On June 2, 2000, Sherli and I married and the sudden instant family meant a mountain of responsibility. Twenty-two years of being single and free to do whatever, whenever had disappeared and been replaced by a constant barrage of needs to be filled. A quick addition to my home had to be undertaken, more people needed more space. New bedrooms and bath, parking for more cars and room to roam, a new enclosed porch and also a deck, it all was completed in record time. My two dogs, Harley and Mariah, a pair of matched Drassar retrievers were thrilled at all of the new attention, especially with Colten to go exploring the fields and canyons; the three of them combed the terrain and built several forts and secret hideouts. Give this young man a hammer, some nails and a roll of duct tape, along with a piece of rope and there is no telling what might be invented or created. He was a joy to be around.

Time began to fly by with the business of married life and in just a little while my probation release date had come and gone. No more supervision, rules and regulations of what, when and where to put up with. With this freedom came authorization from the Texas Department of Criminal Justice to be a volunteer prison Chaplain, most definitely a

God thing with my criminal history and extensive record. He also had allowed me to complete my studies at the Crossroads Bible Institute and become an Ordained Pastor, now certified to perform in the field of my dreams. He, my God, was opening more of His Kingdom for me to operate within and with the added territory was also a larger view of what the ministry was called to perform and accomplish.

Beyond the Walls Prison Ministry had grown in scope and dimension, and God was making the doors of the jails and prisons open wide. The Kairos men's prison group had heard of my probation being terminated and they called regularly for me to be a part of their ongoing devotion and harvesting of souls. This in several of the areas prisons and lockup facilities, first only in Texas, then Oklahoma and New Mexico and other states, the requests continued to increase. One by one, state by state, the nation would beckon and inquire as to the availability of bringing a program, a revival, a seminar or a time of testimony. In days to come, other countries and nations of the world would ask for the services, preaching and evangelism gifts to be shared.

Pastor Lisa Scott would now come to join the ministries forces, her deep background in drugs and addiction was powerful in the jail ministries and deliverance. A new church, a new pastor would also be blessed into the life of the ministry and personally as well. The covering from Barn Church was moving into other realms of ministry and the logistics of being sixty miles away was also weighing on my heart. Senior Pastor Kyle Paris of God's Kingdom Church in Amarillo, Texas had reached out and offered his church and their body for support, prayer and covering of the ministry. His heart was felt and the move of the ministry came, and with it a peace and strength that God had made this union not only possible, but His Will. Another powerful Pastor/Evangelist, Lee Wayne Carthel, was a member at this great church and would add to the ministry format and depth of service. God's Kingdom Church was based on the fivefold ministry of God's Word, being preachers, teachers, apostles, prophets and evangelists. Each position was filled with chosen members of the body. Prophetic calling and ordination of the divine Word of God was manifested in several of this Body of Christ. Faye, Travis, Kim, Jennifer, Joe, so many gifted individuals in such a small congregation, I now mention only a few.

The destiny of service and ministry was unfolding for not only for Beyond the Walls and God's Kingdom Church. It was unfolding to the nation and the world as well. The wake up call sent to the world at large was given on September 11, 2001, with the ravaging of the twin towers and the destruction that was witnessed by every country, man, woman and child of this, His universe. God was not only speaking, He was heralding the return of His Son Jesus Christ and the prophetic deliverance of the end times through His Word. The truth of God's Word called to the masses to repent and come in one accord in worship, praise and honoring of the Kingdom of God.

To His service, to His calling, I am focused and I will do the work and ministry of my Abba Father forevermore. May you, who have read this story, this testimony, come into the completed call to your heart and no longer lean on your own understanding, but in all your ways acknowledge Him! Amen and Amen, Hallelujah to the King! I thank you for supporting the ministry by your purchase of this autobiography and the reading of my life story. May God get the glory, for it is all about Him and not about me! 'Bye for now!

Pastor Michael J. Decker

A special thank you to all of the wonderful people at Trafton Printing for their time, their help and their commitment to excellence in producing this book.
Amen!

Most of all, I thank my Heavenly Father, my Lord, Savior and King Jesus Christ and the presence of the Holy Spirit for manifesting in me and making my life change. I am forever indebted to my Master, my God, to serve every day of my life in bringing glory and honor to His Name, the Name above all Names.